SKUA!

A list of all Peter C. Smith's books is available at www.dive-bombers.co.uk

SKUA!

The Royal Navy's Dive-Bomber

by

PETER C. SMITH

Pen & Sword
AVIATION

First published in Great Britain in 2006 by
Pen & Sword Aviation
an imprint of
Pen & Sword Books Ltd
47 Church Street
Barnsley
South Yorkshire
S70 2AS

ISBN 1-84415-455-6

A CIP catalogue record for this book is
available from the British Library.

Typeset in 10/12 Times New Roman by
Concept, Huddersfield, West Yorkshire

Printed and bound in England by CPI UK

Pen & Sword Books Ltd incorporates the Imprints of Pen & Sword Aviation,
Pen & Sword Maritime, Pen & Sword Military, Wharncliffe Local History,
Pen & Sword Select, Pen & Sword Military Classics and Leo Cooper.

For a complete list of Pen & Sword titles please contact
PEN & SWORD BOOKS LIMITED
47 Church Street, Barnsley, South Yorkshire, S70 2AS, England
E-mail: enquiries@pen-and-sword.co.uk
Website: www.pen-and-sword.co.uk

'If Fleet aircraft are employed for the type of function *for which they were designed,* under careful planning and skilful leadership, they can achieve the results which have not been achieved by other aircraft when the prerequisites were lacking.'

Deputy Director, Naval Air Division, April 1940

To the memory of a Skua TAG –
Richard S. 'Dickie' Rolph, BEM

CONTENTS

TABLES AND DIAGRAMS

Tables

Diagrams

FOREWORD

I have wanted to write this book for half a century. I have been research-
ing and writing about dive-bombing and dive-bombers for most of that
time and have written the definitive histories of every aircraft of that type,
but not the Skua. It is not that this little aircraft did not interest me;
indeed, she has fascinated me for all that period. Why no book then? Well,
this is Britain, and in Britain we honour everyone and everything except
our own. So my various publishers down the decades would happily
publish the umpteenth book on the German Junkers Ju87 Stuka and the
American Douglas Dauntless, but not the British Skua. They took more
persuading for me to write the books on the Russian Petlyakov Pe-2
Peshka, the American North American A-34 Apache and Curtiss SB2C
Helldiver, the Japanese Aichi D3A1/2 Val and even the Vultee A31/A35
Vengeance, American-built, British and Australian flown – but not the
Skua. Even when the Fleet Air Arm Museum at Yeovilton dragged the
wreckage of a Skua from a Norwegian fiord and made a diorama of it, I
could not get a hearing for her.

Quite why the only British-built and British-operated dive-bomber
should be shunned when the others were favoured has always irked me.
So, down the years I spoke to veteran flyers, delved in untouched files and
asked questions. Much of what I discovered of the Skua story I used in
other, more general, books on dive-bombers, but I always knew that the
full story deserved to be told and needed to be told before it was too late
and all first-hand knowledge had faded.

That marvellous man, 'Dickie' Rolph, who for many years was a rock
and a guide in my Skua research, and to whom I confessed my frustration
at this lack of intelligence in the publishing fraternity, once advised me,
with the wisdom of age, 'Remember the story of Bruce and the spider . . .
don't give up'. Well Dickie, you are gone now, but I didn't give up, and
here, thanks to an enlightened editor, Peter Coles, and a fearless pub-
lisher, Henry Wilson of Pen & Sword, here at last is the full story of the
Royal Navy's only true dive-bomber and her achievements against the
odds.

Peter C. Smith
Riseley, Bedford, 2006

ACKNOWLEDGEMENTS

I would like to express my deep gratitude to all the many people who have helped me research the Skua in all her aspects over the course of fifty years.

Firstly to those who flew her: pilots, observers and TAGs. I have interviewed and corresponded with quite a number of these gallant, and modest, gentlemen. The majority have now, regretfully, 'crossed the bar', but it is hoped that their memories, both oral and written, conveyed personally to me and recorded within these pages, will be a small tribute to the enormous debt owed by the nation to their professionalism and self-sacrifice. So, thanks indeed to (in alphabetical order):

Mr R. V. Beckett
Mr W. H. C. Blake
Captain Eric M. Brown, Royal Navy
Colonel F. D. G. Bird, OBE, Royal Marines
Major V. B. G. Cheesman, DSO, MBE, DSC, Royal Marines
Captain R. Halliday, DSC, Royal Navy
Vice-Admiral Sir Donald Gibson
Mr A. E. T. Goble
Captain G. B. K. Griffiths, Royal Marines
Captain Tom W. Harrington, DSC, Royal Navy
Major L. A. Harris, OBE, DSC, Royal Marines
Lieutenant Commander Mike Horndern, Royal Navy
Mr Ronald G. Jordan, an armourer with No. 800 Squadron 1940
Major Alan M. Marsh, Royal Marines
Lieutenant Commander H. A. Monks, DSM, Royal Navy
Major R. T. Partridge, DSO, Royal Marines
Mr R. S. Rolph, BEM
Mr Ken Sims, DSM
Lieutenant Commander David Webb, Royal Navy
Mr Roy Stevens, armourer, RAF.

Also my thanks to the following very helpful people at the various repositories I visited and consulted:

Commander Graham Hobbs, RN, FAA Museum, Yeovilton, Somerset
Jerry R. Shore, Records, FAA Museum, Yeovilton, Somerset
Ms Debbie Stockford, FAA Museum, Yeovilton, Somerset
Mrs Catherine Rounsfell, Assistant Curator, Fleet Air Museum, Yeovilton, Somerset

Klas Gjølmesli, Norsk Luftfartmuseum, Bodø

Øyvind Lamo, Norsk Luftfartmuseum, Bodø

Birger Lansen, Curator Norsk Luftfartmuseum, Bodø (with thanks for their help and hospitality during my stay with them)

Mr Hugh Alexandria, The National Archives, Kew, London

Caroline Herbert, Churchill Archives Centre, Churchill College, Cambridge

Mr Thomas B. Smyth, Regimental Headquarters, The Black Watch, Perth.

And my deep gratitude to:

Jack Bryant, the former editor of *TAG* magazine, whose help and knowledge down the years has been inspirational.

John Dell, whose Web site on the Skua is outstanding in every respect.

Mr Simon Partridge, son of Richard, who has been kindness itself.

David Ostrowski for tracking down elusive documents.

Ray C. Sturtivant, ISO the doyen of researchers, who has patiently tolerated my questions for more years than I care to remember.

Tony Collinson, of Blackburns.

Jackie Hampson, for getting me to Bodø and back.

The Jennie Erwick Collection, Courtesy of Michael Hart who writes: 'My mother, Jennie Marie Erwick, without whom these pictures would not be possible, lived from 1931 to 1993. Born in Ketchikan, Alaska, she followed her mother, Johanna, to Bergen to care for her ageing grandparents in 1933. They were stuck in Norway when the war broke out and returned to the USA in 1945. These pictures she purchased and brought back with her at war's end'.

More information is available at http://www.militaryhistoryonline.com/wwii/photos/set5/default.aspx.

1

FORGING THE
FIRST-STRIKE WEAPON

The two-decade period 'between the wars' (1919–39) was difficult for the Royal Navy. Long accustomed to being by far and away the largest and most innovative navy in the world, this great institution had just ended a titanic war during which it had seen its most recent rival totally eliminated with the scuttling of the German High Seas Fleet at Scapa Flow. From 1919 to 1921 the old order seemed destined to continue as before, but within 12 months 300 years of proud and unique naval heritage and superiority was sacrificed to the pressure from the United States and thrown away by uncaring and uncomprehending politicians at the Washington Naval Conference. The Royal Navy was cut to the bone, forced to accept parity with the new navy of America and its old alliance with Japan, now the third-ranking naval power, was also cast adrift to pamper to the whims and prejudices of senators in Wisconsin! Shaken to the core, and with a hostile Treasury under Winston Churchill seeking even further cutbacks, the Royal Navy retrenched and fought to maintain even a shadowy semblance of its former might.

One of the many ways in which the Royal Navy had led the world in the first decade of the twentieth century, had been in the origination, development and application of the newly fledged air power at sea. The development of the aircraft carrier had been a British innovation, but loss of control of all the aircraft that operated from carriers was another retrograde step. The Royal Navy fought long and hard to regain control, but it took almost 20 years, and those two decades cost the Fleet Air Arm (FAA) dearly. From being a leading exponent of aircraft at sea in 1918, by 1939 the Royal Navy had fallen far behind the two principal navies, the United States and Japan[1], in this field, in both numbers of aircraft and in operating techniques.

Reconnaissance for the fleet had been the primary role envisaged for the aircraft carrier, followed by spotting for the battleship guns during the expected 'set-piece' battle. The development of the torpedo-bomber had proceeded apace during the final years of the First World War and plans had been made for a fleet of Sopwith Cuckoo aircraft to attack the reluctant German Fleet at its bases. The threat of aerial torpedo attack was always the principal threat that aircraft posed to the battleship during

the period under discussion, despite spectacular claims by the proponents
of high-level bombing. The slow progression of carrier-based torpedo-
bombers began to bring the threat of such attacks on the enemy fleet
closer to reality. At first, each carrier could only launch 'penny packets' of
such aircraft, such was the limited capacity of the carriers themselves, but
it was hoped these limitations could be overcome in time, when new ships
became available.

During the 1920s, despite the fact that most British politicians considered a war with the United States 'unthinkable', many American
politicians did not share that view, and among the United States Navy's
top brass there were many admirals eager to flex their newly found
muscles also. This led to some tension between the two western nations,
especially during naval limitation conferences. However, by the early
1930s, it was generally accepted that the most likely enemy the Royal
Navy would have to face in combat would be their former pupil, friend
and ally, Japan.

Britain's far-flung empire was extensive, but very vulnerable because of
that. With the main fleets maintained in home waters and the Mediterranean, the Indian Empire, including Burma and what was then Ceylon
(now known as Sri Lanka), as well as Malaya, Borneo and Hong Kong,
were left relatively undefended. Also at risk in that area were the
Commonwealth countries of Australia and New Zealand and their many
dependencies in the south Pacific.

Hong Kong was indefensible if war came with Japan, but Britain was
permitted to construct a new naval base at Singapore Island. This was far
enough from Japan to be classified as 'defensive' to guard the Indian
Ocean. However, it would, of course, serve as an advance base for the
'Main Fleet' to move to in readiness for war, should events dictate it.[2]
Over the years this concept, the movement of the Main Fleet to Singapore,
became a major war-game. However, it was all academic, for the base
itself became a political shuttlecock and progress towards its completion
dragged on and on. Until the base could be finished the fleet remained at
home, gradually shrinking in numbers. As the First Sea Lord, Earl Beatty,
once remarked, a naval base at Singapore, even if built, would merely be
'a sentry-box without a sentry'.

There was never much doubt in British naval circles that it was
Japanese aircraft carriers that would provide the main opponents for
British carrier aircraft, despite this being discounted as a late development
by many American historians.[3] Indeed, as early as July 1931 the Royal
Navy had begun operating its carriers in groups of two, three or more
during tactical exercises, at the urging of the Rear Admiral, Aircraft,
R. G. H. Henderson, with this view in mind.[4] Tactical School planning for
the Main Fleet to go out east in the event of war called for no fewer than
four aircraft carriers as part of that force. So the Royal Navy was far more

air-minded, within the parameters of possibility, than their many American critics have ever given them credit for.

Torpedo-bombers were vulnerable in their approach and it was expected that heavy losses would be suffered from both defending fighters and the enemy fleet's anti-aircraft guns. New formations (flight attacks) and tactics (sector formations), both of which involved a diving approach to the target in order to break through these defences, were also evolved from 1933. In July of that year the Royal Navy's Tactical Instructions stated quite clearly that the fleet's best defence against an opposing fleet's air attacks was '... offensive action against the enemy's air forces at the earliest possible moment'.[5] But what was needed was an aircraft that could achieve surprise, coupled with weight of ordnance, to launch a successful pre-emptive attack on the Japanese carriers, and this was not forthcoming with the small fleet fighter aircraft with their minimal bomb-carrying capacity. A fresh and radical approach was sought.

The dive-bomber concept revitalised

Although dive attacks had *always* been a feature of Fleet Air Arm procedures,[6] in 1931 a visit to the USA by Lieutenant Commander St John Printice, RN, gave a fresh impetus to its development in the Royal Navy.[7] Printice was impressed by the US Navy's revitalisation of the old concept in the form of the much-publicised 'Helldiver' approach of near-vertical attacks, mounted without warning against an enemy fleet, and against which the anti-aircraft weaponry of the day was unable to cope. Although Printice advocated a 'relatively steep' dive approach (about 70 degrees) rather than the American method (which the British dubbed Terminal Velocity or T/V), the potential of such a delivery of ordnance against such a lightly protected target as an enemy aircraft carrier was attractive. The torpedo was always going to be the preferred method of airborne attack against a heavily protected armour belt of contemporary battleships. However, against carriers, a precisely delivered bomb would knock the flight deck out and a carrier unable to operate her aircraft was merely a floating target with no war capability whatsoever.

Once the concept was explained and analysed, the Royal Navy was, on the whole, enthusiastic about the dive-bomber concept. One of the pilots who served with No. 800 Squadron, flying nine Hawker Nimrod and three Hawker Osprey aircraft aboard the carrier *Courageous* at this time, recounted how the Nimrod, '... was a great advance; it had no flaps, a fixed undercarriage, but some dubious brakes. Top speed was about 120 knots and it was very strong, capable of being dived vertically *ad infinitum*!'[8] Their role was defined as long-range air defence (outside the range of the Fleet's anti-aircraft [AA] guns), strike escort and dive-bombing.

It was recognised that the small bombs capable of being carried on the biplane fighters of the day were inadequate. What was needed, as both the United States and Japanese Navies were also to conclude about the same time, was a specialised delivery system capable of delivering at least a 500 lb payload.[9] However, unlike those two navies, which had retained complete control over their aircraft in every respect, the Royal Navy was hamstrung by the fact that a different service controlled the Fleet Air Arm, and had absolutely no interest in dive-bombing whatsoever. The RAF, following the heady predictions of the Italian prophet Douhert, Britain's Lord Trenchard and the publicity-seeking 'Billy' Mitchell in the United States and their ilk, of victory through air power alone and unaided, were firmly committed to the heavy bomber and the high-level mass attack. Against warship targets, this method was also considered by its advocates to be supreme (Mitchell once proclaimed to the press that it was easier to hit a moving ship and than a stationary target ship), but while the Admiralty had rejected that premise for their own aircraft as early as 1930, the RAF never did. Thus, while the Naval Staff were eager to adopt a specialised dive-bomber, and the Rear Admiral, Aircraft (RAA)[10] urged its introduction in November 1933, the Air Ministry remained uninterested[11] and thus delayed each Admiralty attempt to introduce such an aircraft.

There was another factor that tended to hamper the development of naval aircraft development and this was the much smaller numbers required compared with their land-based RAF equivalents. While the Treasury between 1918 and 1937 starved all the services of funds, the ratio between RAF and FAA orders always remained disadvantageous to Royal Navy requirements. Military aircraft manufacturers would welcome any contract in those lean years of course, but short production runs were always going to be more restrictive, and less cost-effective, than longer ones. There was a tendency to either adapt existing RAF aircraft to a makeshift maritime role, or for orders to be placed with specialised firms, which, by definition, meant that they were smaller and less geared to speedy mass-production methods. This remorseless logic led in turn, through no fault of these specialised manufacturers, to much-extended production runs, and so a cutting-edge design could, by the time it finally appeared with the fleet, be outdated by the pace of aircraft development. The Skua was to be a classic example of this seemingly unavoidable chain of consequences.

Moreover, Royal Navy aircraft suffered from yet a further handicap, even when funds were finally released for rearmament, competing for priority against the RAF counterparts in the rush to make up for two decades of neglect. Having run down the whole defence infrastructure to an all-time low ebb, pressing the cash switch could not automatically provide the designers, test pilots, plant and other essentials overnight. In the jostling for priority, the Fleet Air Arm was always to take a back seat in the allocation of scarce resources. This meant that with aircraft engines, as much as with any other resource, the best would be demanded for home defence fighter aircraft, while the Fleet Air Arm, which was not expected to have to face the most modern types of opposition anyway, would have to make do with what was left over. Again, the Skua was one of the first, but by no means the only, naval aircraft to suffer in this manner.

The debate begins

The need to replace both the delicate but under-armed Hawker Osprey and Nimrod biplanes as the fleet's principal interceptor was qualified by the need for the new aircraft to be fully strengthened and stressed for dive-bombing. The DNAD[12] had, in 1933, pointed out that: 'In general, sufficient evidence is available to indicate that dive bombing is likely to be far more effective than high level bombing against any target ....' He continued, 'So long as the FAA has no aircraft capable of really effective dive bombing attack with heavy bombs', then only the airborne torpedo remained in the Navy's armoury which would obtain results 'commensurate with the effort and probable losses'. However, 'the torpedo is not the most effective initial weapon of attack on enemy carriers, which will usually be our primary objective. At least in the first attack, which is designed to stop all flying operations, there is little doubt that dive bombing with SAP[13] bombs should form the main part of the attack.'

The Admiralty's requirements were based on the plain fact that the shipboard capacity for aircraft in the aircraft carriers it had in service in 1934, which had to meet both the defensive and offensive requirements of the fleet, were insufficient. What was wanted was an up-to-date aircraft that could not only provide the fleet with secure protection from air attack from enemy carriers, but which also had the capacity to mount a pre-emptive, or a retaliatory strike to gain air superiority. However, of the two duties the new aircraft was to fulfil, the *main* emphasis was put on the new aircraft's strike ability. Air Marshal Sir E. R. Ludlow-Hewitt, the Deputy Chief of the Air Staff, was crystal clear in what the Royal Navy had told him of the required priorities of these two conflicting duties. 'The first of these was dive bombing against hostile carriers, the second was the attack of enemy aircraft in the air.'[14]

Nothing could be clearer, which makes the subsequent recording of the subsequent history of this aircraft by historians since that time so inexplicable. Fixated by its inability totally to fulfil its fighter role against the first-class land-based opposition it was never designed to combat, historians have consistently relegated the Skua's specified main duty, that of a dive-bomber, to secondary consideration.

During the same meeting, Mr J. S. Buchanan, representing the Deputy Director Technical Development (DDTD), actually pointed out that the new aircraft would have a poor turn radius for a fighter aircraft, due to the fact that it was a two-plane machine (owing to the Royal Navy's navigational requirements) and to the high-wing loading necessary in its main role. He suggested that the RAF's proposed replacement for the Hawker Hart light bomber might be suitable, as it would have a top speed of 250 mph and also have limited capability for dive-bombing, but this RAF alternative was rejected as unsuitable.

To give the new aircraft better punch as a fighter, the Admiralty requested that four fixed frontal-guns be fitted, or, alternatively 'movable front guns'.[15] Mr Buchanan cast cold water on this request, stating that to find space for four guns would be difficult, and that there would be a weight penalty. Air Marshal Ludlow-Hewitt was scornful, and said that in his opinion, it was a waste of time providing an adequate gun armament if the aircraft lacked the performance to utilise it! He considered the performance of the new aircraft as the essential factor, both as a fighter and a dive-bomber. But, whereas he could see no difficulty in producing the latter, 'It is quite clear that in any one aircraft it was impossible to combine high qualities as a dive bomber with equally good qualities as a fighter'.[16]

Yet again, the Royal Navy representative stated that, if a choice had to be made, then the Admiralty would prefer the dive-bomber qualities of the new aircraft to take precedence to the fighter attributes. The RAF then warned them that, even so, the experimental model could not be expected prior to the middle of 1936, while the new aircraft was unlikely to enter service before 1938, and with that the Royal Navy had to be content.

In the end, the Committee summarised the decisions reached on the fleet's new Fighter Dive Bomber (FDB) as follows:

1. To recommend the issue of the specification of this new aircraft, with a view to adoption, if successful, in place of present fleet fighters.
2. To include in the specification a suitable description of the purpose and function of the aircraft.
3. To specify two front guns only.
4. To leave it to contractors whether it be a biplane or monoplane, in either case wing-folding must be as rapid as possible.
5. To have a landing speed of not more than 60 knots.
6. An overall length of not more than 36 feet, with 33 feet as ideal.
7. To leave the remainder of the specification as previously drawn up by the two staffs.

The specification issued

On 12 December 1934, Specification O.27/34 was duly issued for a replacement FDB to replace the existing Hawker Osprey aircraft in the fleet.

In the main, it followed the outline discussed already. The principal points were:

1. It was to be a single-engined ship-plane[17], either monoplane or biplane for the FAA to operate from carriers, and its role was defined as '(a) to disable the opposing FAA by dive bombing attacks on hostile carriers and other vessels, and to undertake such other dive bombing as may be required. (b) to engage hostile aircraft in the air'.
2. Dimensions to be a height of 14 feet 9 inches, a length of 33 feet, a wingspan of 46 feet, with wings folded this to be 16 feet only. The time given to fold the mainplanes to this dimension was 30 seconds.
3. Endurance, carrying a single 500 lb bomb, to be 3 hours, extended to 5 hours fully economical speed.

Alternative designs

The O.27/34 specification for a Fleet Fighter Dive Bomber had, at Mr Buchanan's insistence, been restricted to three firms only.[18] The most suitable firms to tender were considered to be Hawker and Fairey, with Armstrong, Blackburn, Bristol, Gloster, Vickers and Westland in the second most suitable grouping. Other commitments whittled both these lists down to just Blackburn, Hawker and Vickers, although Armstrong, which had already submitted similar proposals for a FDB fitted with the alternative Hyena engine as power plant, were permitted to have their design evaluated in the same tests. In the event, the short list included designs from just A. V. Roe and Vickers Development.

Following the issuing of the Air Ministry initial order for experimental prototypes in April 1935, the Blackburn design team, headed by Mr G. E. Petty, got to work on what they dubbed the 'D.B.1.'[19]

On 11 February 1936, Mr Pierson, of Vickers attended a meeting with the DTD in which he had to report that design work was at a standstill. This was because of difficulties with the RAE's (Royal Aircraft Establishment) spinning model. To overcome these difficulties, it had been found necessary to increase the fuselage length by at least 3 feet. The specification limit imposed was an overall length of 33 feet for this aircraft, due to hangar deck space restrictions. However, Vickers claimed that a later sheet seemed to indicate that 36 feet o.a. could be permitted for Fleet Air Arm shipborne aircraft. Vickers asked to be allowed to go to this, and the DTD agreed to talk to the DNAD about this. If granted, both the Blackburn and A. V. Roe designs would also be allowed this leeway.

The importance of 'not letting up' on this design was impressed on Mr Pierson. The DTD told him that he and his staff, 'had done their utmost' to try and improve Fleet Air Arm types. It was fully understood that the contractors faced difficulties due to the severe size limitations and folding wing requirements, which made them more difficult to design than RAF aircraft, but '. . . the difficulties should be tackled strongly and overcome'. The DTD requested '. . . the full co-operation of Vickers in proceeding with the design to the very best of their ability'.[20]

This exhortation was probably superfluous in the case of Vickers, because it was noted on 24 March 1936 that the decision had been made to order 150 fighter dive-bombers from Blackburn.[21] The order was actually placed in July (Contract 534298/36), with the first prototype still more than 6 months from her maiden flight, so urgent was the Admiralty's need for this aircraft.

NOTES

1. Of the other navies only France actually completed an aircraft carrier, and had plans to build two more. Both Germany and Italy later built aircraft carriers, but they were never commissioned into service.
2. See Captain Russell Grenfell, *Main Fleet to Singapore*, Faber & Faber, London, 1951 for the full story of this concept. Also Captain Stephen Roskill, *Naval Policy Between the Wars, 2 Vols*, Collins, London 1968 and 1976.
3. See for example, David C. Evans and Mark R. Peattie, *Kaigun: Strategy, Tactics, and Technology in the Imperial Japanese Navy 1887–1941*, Naval Institute Press, Annapolis, 1997.
4. Roskill, *Naval Policy Between the Wars, Vol 2. The period of reluctant re-armament, op cit.*
5. See Admiralty Handbook, *Aircraft Attack and Defence*, National Archives ADM 186/96.
6. For the origins of dive-bombing from 1918 onward, and the methods used by the Fleet Air Arm in the 1920s see, Peter C. Smith, *Dive Bomber!: An illustrated history*, Moorland Publishing, Ashbourne, 1982 and *Impact!: The dive bomber pilots speak*, William Kimber, London, 1982.
7. Admiral Sir Roger Backhouse, 7 May 1937, in National Archives ADM 116/4030.
8. Fact Sheet, *800 Naval Air Squadron – A History Nunquam Non Paratus 1933–1972*, Fleet Air Arm Museum Archives, RNAS Yeovilton, Somerset.
9. The US Navy was already aiming for its next series of dive-bombers to be capable of toting a 1,000 lb bomb, which some variants of the Curtiss SBC-3 biplane were capable of, and which both the Vought SB2U Vindicator, first flown in January 1935, and the Douglas SBD Dauntless monoplanes were capable of carrying as standard by 1940.
10. The post of RAA was introduced into the Royal Navy in 1931 and was later superseded by the post of VAA – Vice Admiral (Aircraft).
11. Geoffrey Till, *Air Power and the Royal Navy 1914–1945*, Jane's Publishing, London, 1979.
12. DNAD = Director, Naval Air Division.
13. SAP = Semi-Armour Piercing
14. Air Marshal Sir E. R. Ludlow-Hewitt, DCAS, during the *12th Meeting of the Advisory Committee on aircraft for Fleet Air Arm, held at the Air Ministry, 15th November 1934.* (Contained in National Archives AIR 2/607/359533/34).
15. This reference may possibly be a reference to a four-gun turret, as was later fitted (aft the pilot) in the Skua's sister aircraft, the Blackburn Roc, as well as the Boulton & Paul Defiant for the RAF.

16. Air Marshal Sir E. R. Ludlow-Hewitt, DCAS, during the *12th Meeting of the Advisory Committee on aircraft for Fleet Air Arm, held at the Air Ministry, 15th November 1934.* (Contained in National Archives AIR 2/607/359533/34.)

17. Originally, this was taken as being capable of working from the decks of aircraft carriers, fitted with a wheeled undercarriage as a dive-bomber or, when fitted with floats, to be capable of taking off from the sea, or of being launched from, or recovered by battleships or cruisers. In which case she was to be capable of shallow (or glide) bombing, plus reconnaissance duties. This involved complicated calculations involving strengthening to withstand catapult-launching requirements, which were 5,500 lb at 50 knots (later increased to 6,000 lb) the floats alone adding 250 lb weight. However, the DTD considered these two roles 'contradictory' and, after the Admiralty prioritised the dive-bomber requirement as far more urgent, the latter requirement was dropped. (See National Archives ADM1/10103.)

18. Mr Buchanan, DDTD to AMSR (Air Ministry Special Requirements), dated 13 December 1934.

19. D.B.1. = Dive Bomber Number 1. See A. J. Jackson, *Blackburn Aircraft since 1909*, Putnam, London, (Revised Edition) 1989.

20. Extract from 405230/35, Design Branch Specification B.1/35 11.2.36. (National Archives AVIA 46/144).

21. *Ibid.* 33rd EPM.

2

BUILDING THE CONCEPT

On 24 October 1936, Mr J. S. Buchanan, the Deputy Director, Technical Development, approved Specification 25/36 for the Blackburn O.27/34 Development Production part of the Contract Agreement.[1] A large number of Special Requirements (SR) were incorporated in addition to the existing prototype arrangements, the principal one being that the power plant was specified as the Perseus PRE3M engine. Table 1 lists the other SRs requested.

This document also specified exactly what the Air Ministry meant by 'Normal Load' (see Table 2). The Blackburn company was required to supply and fit these requests, together with all parts that ensured the specified items could be carried. It can be seen from these figures, just what the extra penalties were when designing aircraft for maritime use, over and above the more usual weights involved with conventional aircraft.

Moreover, the Normal Weight figure had also to include sufficient fuel to enable 3 hours flight time at the normal engine rpm at an altitude of 15,000 feet, plus additional fuel for 30 minutes' flight at full sea-level power and, on top of that, reserve oil for 2 hours more than the fuel endurance. This was specified as being not less than 164 gallons of fuel and 10 gallons of oil, respectively.

The structural strengths of the Skua under conditions of full load flying condition were also laid down. The loadings were as outlined in Table 3.

The first aircraft was to be presented by the company at the works for a final examination after Blackburn's own final inspection. The first aircraft also had to undergo the usual pre-acceptance flight-testing by the company's test pilot. This programme had to include general flight tests, diving tests, lateral stability tests, spinning tests and acrobatic tests to the various ADM standards. Each of the subsequent aircraft of the order had to undergo a 30 minute flight test in accordance with Air Ministry for AM838.

Checks on the weight and centre of gravity (CG) were to be submitted to the Technical Development Unit on the first, twenty-fifth and fiftieth aircraft of the order, and then every subsequent fiftieth aircraft. The final aircraft of the contract had to have an analysis form of the weights of its constituent parts submitted to RDA3, to measure any 'creep' during the construction run.

Table 1   Blackburn Skua – list of special requirements, 24 October 1936

Requirement	Detail
New Standard Flying Instrument Panel	Installed in the pilot's instrument board
Dual Control Conversion Set	First aircraft *only*, then to Special Order only. To include additional instruments for blind flying instruction, i.e. fore-and-aft level, turn indicator, compass
DR Master Compass	No provision for DR repeaters
Formation keeping lights	Including necessary wing wiring
Four Browning machine-guns in wings	Provision for 600 rounds of ammunition per gun
Two 4-inch parachute flares	In launching tubes with pilot release
Standard Bomb Loading Winch	Provision for use
Protective treatment for all metal parts	To ADM 323 and 324. *Alclad*[2] parts anodised 'to Seaplane Requirements'
Stainless steel parts	Wherever possible
Slinging point for normal aircraft salvage	Rear-top of fuselage
Detachable fin	For ease of maintenance
Provision for Target Towing Gear	First aircraft only. Conversion kits with stowage for three sleeve and/or flag targets
Inlet and outlet oil temperature thermometers	First aircraft only. Only inlet fitted thereafter
Blind flying hood	First aircraft only. Then to Special Order
RAE reflector floodlighting system	Instrument illumination
Fuel-tight joints	For each tank filler cap
Controllable warm air supply	Anti-freezing precaution with Pilot's Distant Reading thermometer
Aircraft brakes enhancement	To hold wheels locked on deck of an aircraft carrier with engine running full ground power
Speaking tubes	Possible requirement, dependent on Prototype tests
Engine intake air cleaner	Provision for ready attachment and dismantling
Fuel consumption measurements	First aircraft only
Provision for 250 lb LC bomb	
Locks for pilot's sliding coupé	

Table 2   Blackburn Skua – normal load list

Item(s)	Weight (lb)	Weight (kg)
Lewis gun and accessories	21.5	9.75
Six magazines for Lewis gun	54.0	24.49
Four Browning guns	80.0	36.28
2,400 rounds of ammunition for Browning guns	156.0	70.76
Sights for Browning guns	(2.0)	0.9
Bombs	250.0	113.4
Bombs carrier	12.0	5.44
Marine distress signals	10.5	4.76
Signal pistol and eight cartridges	6.5	2.94
Forced landing flares	26.5	12.02
Electrical equipment	1.0	0.45
Signalling lamp	4.5	2.04
Wireless power supply	33.0	14.97
Navigational equipment	33.5	15.19
Inflatable dinghy	25.0	11.34
First-aid equipment	3.0	1.36
Wireless equipment (T.1083 and R.1082)	71.0	32.2
Two crew (with parachutes)	400.0	181.44
Total	1,190.0	539.78

On 10 November 1936, it had been confirmed that 136 030/35s [Two-Seater Fleet Fighter – Roc] were already on order.[3] On the same date it was recorded that the original Skua order had been increased and that, '190 Skuas 027/34 [were] already on order with Blackburn'.

Blackburn of Brough

The Blackburn Aeroplane and Motor Company had been established in June 1914, by Robert Blackburn, the son of a Leeds lawn-mower manufacturer. Born in 1885, he had graduated with an honours degree in engineering and continued his study of the infant aviation industry in France. The young man, thus inspired, had designed and built a series of less than successful monoplanes and then started a flying school at Filey. During the First World War the manufacturing business in Leeds expanded with orders for over 100 military aircraft from both the Royal Naval Air Service and the Royal Flying Corps. Blackburn's came to specialise in seaplanes and built a special test facility on the banks of the Humber River at Brough, midway between Hull and Leeds.

Post-war orders for torpedo-bomber aircraft meant that the Blackburn facility continued to thrive, and a whole string of such aircraft, the Swift, the Dart, the Ripon, the Baffin, the Shark and the Botha, followed. Gradually, the main business was transferred from Leeds to Brough and

Table 3   Blackburn Skua – load factors

Condition	Load Factor
Throughout the structure with the centre of pressure in its most forward position, in normal flight	9.4
Wing structure with centre of pressure in rearmost position, horizontal flight, flaps down	6.0
Safety factor throughout structure in a dive, assumed terminal velocity of 450 mph, IAS (indicated airspeed)	2.0
Wing structure under 'down' gust of 25 fps at accelerated dive of 1.5 times maximum level speed	1.5
Throughout structure when diving, with flaps down at 70 degrees to horizontal (i) Steady glide	2.2
Do (ii) Under 'up' and 'down' gusts at 25 fps normal to flight path	1.5
Wing structure, with angle of incidence corresponding to inverted stall, centre of pressure at 0.35 chord	4.7
Throughout structure on launching by aircraft carrier accelerator, at accelerator speed of 56 knots	2.0+

an experienced team of designers and test pilots was built up to complement it. The Assistant Chief Designer from 1918 was G. E. Petty, FRAS, who worked under Major F. A. Bumpus, and it was he who took on the radical new project and challenge that was the O.27/34. He became the Chief Designer in 1937 and brought the project to its fruition.

As yet, no official name had been allocated, but Blackburn's had already given the new aircraft the in-house designation B-24. The Skuas were produced in three main batches, with sixty-nine aircraft produced under Works Orders 7371/1 to 69 inclusive. These were L2867 to L2935, of which all except L2867 to L2872, L2884, L2888 and L2892, were transferred over to the Admiralty on 24 May 1939, when the Fleet Air Arm became the Royal Naval Air Service. The second batch totalled twenty-one machines (L2936–L2956) under Works Orders 7375/1 to 21 inclusive, all of which became Admiralty property on 24 May. The penultimate batch, under Works Orders 7840/1 to 50 inclusively, comprised fifty aircraft (L2957–L3006) and were not transferred to the Admiralty until 7 October 1939. Finally, Works Orders 7842/1 to 50 saw the final batch of fifty machines, L3007–L3056, most of which were actually completed as target tugs. These were all delivered in 1939, save for L3056, which was delivered on 10 March 1940. They became Admiralty property on 7 October 1939. Design modifications and production line delays were severely to delay all these programmes.

The first prototype (K5178) took to the air, flown from Brough by Blackburn's Chief Test Pilot, Flight Lieutenant A. M. 'Dasher' Blake, on

9 February 1937. Painted 'Battleship Grey' but with an all-white main-plane, this aircraft, known as the 'short-nosed' machine, was put on display at the Hendon Air Show's 'New Types Park' as exhibition No. 8 on 26 June of the same year. On 28 June, 'Dasher' flew her at the SBAC Show at Hatfield, returning to Brough the following day. On 17 August the Air Ministry dubbed this aircraft Skua-I in a letter to the company. She had a tare weight of 57,222 lb, and a total armament loading of 1,069 lb, giving her an all-up weight of 7,807 lb.

The new aircraft was then transferred to the Aircraft and Armament Experimental Establishment (A&AEE) at Martlesham Heath, and between 20 October and 8 November 1937, underwent extensive handling trials totalling 11¼ hours. Overall, the impression was favourable, and the test pilots recorded that she climbed off from the runway at 70 mph with 30 degrees of flap, and the wheels were retracted within 35 seconds. The climb was made at 120 mph and once airborne it was said to be a relatively simple aircraft to handle, while landing was without problems. The machine was engaged in various trials at both Martlesham and RAE Farnborough throughout 1938, clocking up 127 hours of flying time.

On 30 January 1939, K5178 was flown to Gosport, where she was expended in ditching trials from the catapult ship *Pegasus* the following month.

The second prototype (K5179), built under Contract 769429/38, followed soon after, making her debut flight on 4 May 1938. She differed from the first machine by featuring an elongated nose, the extension being 2 feet 4 inches. This aircraft also featured the turned up wing tips. Both these aircraft were powered by the Bristol Mercury XII air-cooled radial engine, in a gilled cowling, and it was with this engine that trials were carried out with both machines. On 9 July the public got a glimpse of this aircraft at the Ipswich Aero Club, but on 13 August 1938 she was transferred to the RAE at Farnborough and subsequently was under test at Martlesham from 26 September of the same year, before arriving at Royal Naval Air Station Evanton on 18 October.

FDB or DBR?

Even while the prototypes were under development, the Admiralty had been reconsidering their policy with regard the type of dive-bomber they really wanted. This heart-searching had origins that went back to a memorandum on naval air policy in March 1936. Discussing the merits of various existing FAA aircraft to conduct dive-bombing, the DNAD, Captain C. M. Graham, RN, postulated:

1. If the Torpedo Spotter Reconnaissance (TSR) can 'Dive Bomb'.
2. If the TSR cannot 'Dive Bomb' but the 'Dive Bomber Reconnaissance' (DBR) (design under consideration), can.

3. If TSR cannot 'Dive Bomb' and 'DBR' is unsuccessful but the 'Fighter Dive Bomber' (FDB) (under construction before the DBR design is prepared) is not ready.

If, as seemed probable, the TSR could not 'Dive Bomb', then it would be necessary to consider a 'DBR' that could 'Dive Bomb' and also be able to carry out reconnaissance work, in preference to a FDB that could 'Dive Bomb', but also do some of the work of the existing two-seater fighters.

It was firmly reiterated that the Admiralty at this early date considered that among the main principles of policy for the Fleet Air Arm:

1. The primary duty of naval aircraft is the destruction of the enemy carrier.[4]
2. A fleet without carriers cannot with any hope of success, sustain major naval operations against a fleet with carriers.[5]

Thus it can be seen that the common view of the Royal Navy not understanding air power at sea in the 1930s is a false picture. Much thought had gone into the subject, but the limiting facts were, as always (i) a hostile Treasury refusing adequately to fund the Navy (ii) a hostile Air Ministry, responsible for the Fleet Air Arm, but having no interest in its development and (iii) International Treaties, entered into by politicians with no concept of naval armaments. Tonnage restrictions meant fewer, and smaller carriers, thus limiting the scope of advances, even those advances, like the adoption of the DBR, that were seen as desirable.

Further observations were received from various commanding officers around the world, who were invited to comment. The C-in-C of the America and West Indies Station, Vice-Admiral S. J. Meyrick, CB, RN, advised:

Experiments will, no doubt, settle the comparative efficiency of the Fighter Dive Bomber and the Dive Bomber Reconnaissance, but it would seem that on account of the structural requirements for an efficient Dive Bomber, the weight added would be too much for an efficient fighter.[6]

Prophetic words!

The C-in-C, Home Fleet, Admiral Sir Roger Backhouse, GCVO, KCB, CMG, RN, writing from his flagship, HMS *Nelson*, was equally realistic regarding the respective merits of dive-bombing over torpedo-bombing:

From what I have witnessed in the way of these attacks, I consider that dive-bombers are considerably more likely to effect surprise than are torpedo aircraft, and, as far as the present armament of our own ships is concerned, unlikely to be effectively engaged in time.[7]

He added that the merits of a combination of the two methods, would be the ideal scenario.

'A successful attack by dive-bombers just before or during an attack by torpedo bombers might have considerable results.'

Longitudinal instability

In March 1938, the RAE at Farnborough submitted a report, which revealed that the prototype Skua had been found longitudinally unstable at low gliding speeds.[8] This required further modifications.

This aircraft (K5178) had been delivered to the RAE in December 1937, in an attempt to improve longitudinal stability, and they tried various devices to rectify the fault. The problem manifested itself at low gliding speeds (about 80 knots ASI, with CG on aft limit) and the aircraft tended to stall itself, '... unless the stick was eased forward slightly the nose would rise and the stall be reached'. Also, if the speed was further reduced to 66–9 knots, 'the port wing suddenly drops [sometimes 50 to 60 degrees] and the nose also drops [fairly sharply]'. Worse, there was none of the usual warning vibration to alert the pilot this was about to occur. The report added: 'These defects seemed more serious since spinning tunnel tests showed a model of the aeroplane to be below the specified standard in recovery from stabilised spins'. Wind tunnel tests revealed that the stable slope of the pitching moment curve was considerably reduced above about 7 degree incidence.

Although lowering the flaps and undercarriage made the stall become less violent, the problem was serious mainly from the point of view of certain types of landings. While in a normal landing configuration it was immaterial, it was considered dangerous if the aircraft was held off too high or if the approach glide was rather slow.

The experimental solution to both the mild and the severe stall was to fit small spoilers near the wing root normal to the surface. In addition, since these appeared to produce their effect by causing a partial stall of the wing root, pointed fairings to make the wing section near the root 'sharp nosed' were fitted.

Flight-testing was carried out in December and January with weights of 7,200 lb and 7,800 lb, with the centre of gravity at the aft limit (35.8 inches aft of the leading edge at root, h 0.33). The opportunity was taken during these tests to also re-examine the Skua's stalling characteristics and associated airflow. Photographs were taken of the behaviour of wool tufts attached to the upper surface of the wing and to light posts erected upon it. Although the prototype was fitted with upturned wing tips, these were rejected as a contributory factory, and it was believed that, in normal flight, they 'probably improved the lateral stability'. Further examination revealed that the stall, although not vicious when approached slowly on a glide, could cause an involuntary spin in acrobatics, 'particularly with engine on'. Recovery from an established spin was 'expected to be impossible'. Because of this and the combination of other factors, it was recommended that certain modifications be incorporated:[9]

1. The various forms of root spoiler were considered 'of doubtful value', instead tail plane end-fins should be fitted.
2. Slots should be added to the Skua's wing tips, In order to improve lateral stability at the stall and prevent accidental spin.
3. Until all Skuas were so adapted, a tail parachute should be carried 'as an interim measure'.
4. Deliberate spinning on the Skua type should be universally and totally forbidden.

On 5 September 1938, Sir Ernest Lemon was writing to complain that Blackburn and Blackburn Denny were experiencing delays in the production of the Botha torpedo-bomber for the RAF. He claimed that this was because these two companies were jointly engaged in producing both the Botha and the Skua. However, although the original plan would have seen these designs coming into the programme at points reasonably separated in time, '. . . owing to technical difficulties with Skua, the present position is that the two programmes are trying to run concurrently. Moreover, the difficulties with the Skua are setting back the production of Blackburn design Roc aeroplane with Boulton Paul'.[10]

Meanwhile, Blackburn themselves were giving the Skua as much priority as they could. On the death of the Chief Test Pilot, Flight Lieutenant A. M. Blake, on 16 October 1937, during the Skua's critical gestation period, his former assistant, Flight Lieutenant H. Bailey, AMICE, AFRAeS had most ably taken his place. On 1 June 1938, with the Skua project fully underway, Bailey received welcome support with the arrival of Flight Lieutenant H. J. Wilson, CBE, AFC, and Flying Officer B. R. Rolfe.

By 28 August 1938, Wilson was piloting the first production aircraft, which became the Skua II, from Brough. This was L2867, and she and her sister, L2868, which followed her off the line, were both sent to Martlesham Heath. From September onward, both these machines underwent armament and performance testing at the hands of the A&AEE specialists. By 30 September 1938, with the Munich crisis at the forefront of defence thinking, it was estimated that the first Skua deliveries were expected in October and that the whole 190 ought to be delivered by 31 March 1940.[11]

The Munich crisis had finally brought home to the Government just how run-down our armed forces had become, and much concern was expressed at the lateness of many of the new rearmament programmes, the Skua being just one example of many. Capacity at Brough was limited and even though Blackburn had introduced combined assembly working, with the Skua's mainplanes being built at the company's Olympia factory in Leeds and transported to Brough for bolting on, they were forced to sub-contract some of the fuselage build to the General Aircraft Ltd located at Hanworth in an effort to catch up. Despite these efforts, although the Skua had original been expected to start entering service with the Royal Navy in 1937, only twelve aircraft (L2867 to L2878) had actually been delivered by the end of 1938, most of these being used for trials purposes.

Few of these first dozen aircraft had very long lives. L2867, after protracted tests at Martlesham from 14 September 1938 onward, was finally delivered to the fleet on 15 February 1940; L2868 arrived at Martlesham on 22 September 1938. The third aircraft from the original contract, L2869, was delivered to the FAA Pool at Lee-on-Solent on 14 October, and allocated to No. 800 Squadron. However, she was almost immediately written off in an accident at Worthy Down. She was then transferred to No. 4 Wing at RAF Henlow in Bedfordshire as an instructional airframe (1200M) as early as 16 December. The fourth production machine, L2870, was allocated to undertake full-load trials aboard the aircraft carrier *Courageous* in the Firth of Forth and flew to Leuchars on 2 November. However, on 16 December, while undertaking these trials, she was badly damaged aboard the carrier and written off. She was destined to join her sister at Henlow as instructional airframe 1201M, but this was aborted and she was instead transported to Worthy Down on 11 January 1939. She survived until 7 June 1940, when she was finally scrapped. The third of this ill-fated trio, L2871, joined the A&AEE at Martlesham on 14 November, and clocked up almost 20 hours flying time, before she had to make an emergency landing due to fuel starvation on 6 January 1939. She was declared a write-off and became another instructional airframe (1294M), this time at RAF Locking on 27 March.

Fated for a more extended career was L2872, which first flew on 17 November 1938 and was transferred to the RAE at Farnborough on 5 April 1939, for trial purposes. She remained there until 1 March 1940, when she returned to Brough and continued to be used as a test machine. Of the remaining six Skua-IIs completed in 1938, five, L2873, L2874, L2876, L2877 and L2878, joined No. 803 Squadron at Worthy Down from 6 December onwards. L2875 went to the Central Flying School at Upavon on 2 December, and later also joined No. 803 and then No. 800 Squadron. So the Fleet Air Arm had only received five Skuas by the end of the year. Such a slow rate was deemed 'unacceptable' and caused Blackburn's to be omitted from bidding for any new aircraft orders that year until the bottleneck had been sorted out.

At the third Liaison Meeting between DGRD and ACAS on 23 March 1939, conclusion 10 was that, '... neither the Admiralty nor the Air Staff

Table 4   Skua-II deliveries, 1939

Month	Total	Month	Total	Month	Total	Month	Total
January	9	April	23	July	26	October	16
February	15	May	23	August	14	November	5
March	15	June	17	September	11	December	3

would have any use for Skuas beyond the 190 already on order, but that the Admiralty wished the jigs and tools to be safeguarded until the Fulmar had proved itself as a type'. It was also added that: 'As the present Skua programme would dovetail with Botha production at Blackburns, it was agreed not to consider any further increase in the number of Skuas.'[12]

Fortunately, by 1939 the Skua-II was appearing in substantial numbers, peaking in July with twenty-six machines being completed.

On 1 September 1939, the day German troops entered Poland and while the British and French ultimatums were counting down, it was recorded that, as far as the fleet defence was concerned: 'The fighter position was not considered serious since the Skuas released from the RAF (*sic*) provided a good immediate reserve.'[13] At that time Blackburn's had delivered 154 Skua-IIs,[14] of which more than twenty had either been written off or were engaged in trials.[15]

NOTES

1. Air Ministry, Directorate of Technical Development, Confidential, Ref. No. 534615/36/RDAS (National Archives AVIA 46/144).
2. Alclad = Defined as a composite wrought product comprising an aluminium alloy core having one or both surfaces and a metallurgically bonded aluminium or aluminium alloy coating that is anodic to the core and thus electrochemically protects the core against corrosion.
3. Contained in National Archives AVIA 46/144.
4. Author's italics.
5. *Memorandum on Naval Air Policy, Vol. 1.* DNAD Naval Staff, dated 13 March 1936 (contained in National Archives ADM 116/4030).
6. Vice-Admiral S. J. Meyrick, CB, RN, *FAA Tactics and Equipment – Observations on Draft Memorandum*, dated 24 February 1937. (M05506/36 contained in National Archives ASM 116/4030.)
7. Admiral Sir Roger Backhouse, GCVO, KCB, CMG, RN, dated 7 May 1937. *Ibid.*
8. Report No. B.A. 1458, March, 1938, Royal Aircraft Establishment, Farnborough, R. H. Francis, MSc and G. E. Pringle, PhD, *Note on flight tests of the Blackburn Skua prototype* (AM Reference 409111/35/RDA2; RAE Reference BA/633/R/47; Item No. 12K/1/38. Contained in National Archives DSTR 23/6787; 3536 Src.945. DSTR 2116787.
9. Johnston and Smith; *Note on wind tunnel tests on the longitudinal stability of the Blackburn O.27/34 (Skua)*, RAE Report No. BA 1453 (3395), December 1937. Francis, *Safety devices for full scale spinning trials.* RAE. Report No. BA 1195 (1779) April 1935. Finn and Stephens, *Model spinning tests of the Blackburn O.27/34*, RAE Report BA 1306, June 1936.

10. EPM127 (38) contained in National Archives AVIA 46/144.

11. Dated 30 September 1938, contained in National Archives AVIA 46/144.

12. DGRD/ACAS *Liaison Meetings. 3rd Meeting. Conclusion 10, 23.3.39. Skua*, contained in National Archives AVIA 46/144.

13. EPM135 (39) contained in National Archives AVIA 46/144.

14. By way of comparison with this modest total, the equivalent dive-bomber products of rival nations' dive-bombers were: (a) Imperial Japanese Navy's Aichi D3A1 'Val' – 39 in 1939 (but with 55 by June 1940, 227 by July 1941 and 450 by September 1942); (b) United States Navy Douglas SBD Dauntless – almost 6,000 of these and their A2-4 counterparts were built by the end of the war.

15. The Skua was lucky to ever enter service at all. The Head of Air Material tried very hard to kill the project off in July 1938. In a Minute (M 04197/38) he claimed that, though not yet in service, was of poor quality as a fighter and that there were grave doubts as to whether it would be mechanically satisfactory, Blackburn's record in the latter case, being a poor one. He wanted the contract reduced from 190 aircraft to 88 only, releasing Blackburn's resources for 'more useful work'.However, by 3 March 1939, that tune had changed, mainly because,'experience with Skuas in 803 Squadron has been happier than was anticipated'. The Skuas had been fitted with a 'modified tail wheel oleo and arresting-hook damping device'. As a result, almost every landing had been 'consistently good'. Three experienced and four inexperienced pilots had been successfully trained in deck landing Skuas on *Courageous*. Wind speed over the deck has varied from 30–37 knots and weight of the aircraft was 7,400 lb for landings and 8,200 lb for take-offs (ADM1/9725).

3

THE SAGA OF THE
DIVE-BOMB SIGHT

The RAF's total opposition to dive-bombing had a malevolent effect on the Royal Navy's attempts to adopt the dive-bomber and make it an even more effective weapons system. The need for a fully automatic dive-bombing sight had long been apparent, and in Germany[1] and Sweden[2] development work proceeded apace in the 1930s. However, neither of the other two major navies that had developed aircraft carriers went down this route. The Americans certainly strove for such a dive-bomb sight and produced designs, but they found little favour with the pilots themselves who, on the whole, tended to prefer their own eye sighting.[3] The case of the Royal Navy was different, such a dive-bomb sight was thought highly necessary and desirable, but obfuscation on the part of the Air Ministry hampered them at every turn.

Lobbying by the Royal Navy eventually resulted in the establishment of the Dive-Bomb-Sight sub-committee of the Bombing Committee, which held its first meeting at the Air Ministry on Monday 11 May 1936.[4] Representing the Air Ministry were the Chairman, Air Commodore A. W. Tedder (DofT), Group Captain A. Gray, MC (T2), Squadron Leader C. N. H. Bilney (OR3) and Mr I. Bowen (RD Inst2); along with Air Commodore L. A. Pattinson, DSO, MC, DFC, of the Armament Group, Mr F. W. Meredith of the RAE and Flight Lieutenant G. G. Brockman, MBE (TW1) acting as Secretary. In the face of this ocean of light-blue prejudice, the Royal Navy's solitary representative was Commander G. M. B. Langley, OBE (NAD).

The Committee's terms of reference were modified, and were given as:

1. Ensuring that any dive-bomb sight development conformed to operational requirements, 'as far as they can be met'.
2. Testing of such sights under service conditions.
3. Suggesting tactics appropriate to any particular sight, 'which is found practicable'.
4. Suggesting appropriate methods of training.

The Royal Navy advanced their requirement, which was for a sight 'capable of use against a *moving target*[5], and it was necessary for this important point to be made clear from the outset'. However, AMRD proposed that just a simple sight for dive-bombing against a stationary target be produced. This would have a setting (for wind), with a pre-determined angle of dive, direction of dive (defined by wind direction) and height of bomb release (1,500 feet). The Air Ministry had their way and the rest of the discussion proceeded on the basis that the Royal Navy's requirement, 'could best be achieved by the preliminary development of a simple sight'. For the purpose of warfare at sea against high-speed targets (i.e. Japanese aircraft carriers) the whole basis of development was prac-tically useless from the start.

This was not the end of the setbacks for the Royal Navy, for it had been agreed previously that bomb release height be increased, '2,000 feet was more suitable than 1,500 feet'. Mr Meredith put forward the opinion that it might be possible to design a sight with both these heights as built-in options. The Committee decided that, should this prove impracticable, the height should be 2,000 feet.[6]

Some very naïve suggestions were made by the Air Ministry officials with regard to methods of ascertaining the wind direction prior to an attack. They put forward two methods by which they thought this could be done: (1) by smoke from the funnels of the ships to be attacked, and (2) by smoke caused by a preliminary attack with anti-personnel bombs or smoke generators! It took Commander Langley very little time to demolish both these nonsensical suggestions. In the first place he had to enlighten his RAF colleagues that modern warships actually made very little smoke from their funnels, even during sudden changes of speed, unless they made smoke deliberately as a screen.

With regard to the second point, even disregarding the obvious fact that any such 'preliminary' attack would eliminate one of the dive-bomber's greatest assets, surprise, Langley pointed out two other obvious facts. For a start, if the 'preliminary' bombing was to be of any value whatsoever, these small bombs would, themselves, have to be accurately placed, and if that was the case then so, also, could the main bombing attack itself! Also, it assumed that an enemy fleet would take no further avoiding action once the preliminary attack had been made, also rather an unlikely scenario.

Commander Langley had to point out that any enemy fleet would have first to be located and then shadowed continually so that the attacking force could be guided to the target. The shadowing aircraft themselves, if they survived the attentions of the enemy's defending fighters, could ascertain wind direction and speed over the target fleet and duly transmit this information as part of their continued monitoring of the situation. The dive-bomber force could then adapt its approach accordingly, and using an ordinary compass could define the line of advance of its target fleet. Commander Langley opined that, 'the pilot and the man in the back seat were quite capable of making these adjustments, which could be worked out and set as soon as the ships were sighted'.

In the face of such logic the agreement was that wind estimation using smoke was 'tactically impossible', and that the necessary adjustments for it would have to be computed 'by other methods'.

When it came to considering what type of current warplanes in Great Britain's inventory would be capable of delivering such dive-bombing attacks, an equal degree of unreality prevailed. While such proponents of the dive-bomber as the fledgling *Luftwaffe*, the Royal Navy, the Imperial Japanese Navy and United States Navy all thought of 70 degrees as the ideal angle of dive, the RAF stated that permissible diving angles could vary according to types and that 'Heavy bombers would be able to dive at angles up to 30 degrees'. This, of course, was not dive-bombing at all, but shallow glide-bombing, a very different (and far less accurate) type of bomb delivery. The types the RAF proposed to use were listed as the Blenheim, the Battle, the Wellesley and the Whitley, not one of them built with any dive-bombing capability. The Fleet Air Arm types were given as the Shark, the Swordfish and the 'Dive-Bomber-Reconnaissance Fighter Dive-Bomber'. Of these, the first two were Torpedo Spotter Reconnaissance (TSR) aircraft first and foremost, and biplanes to boot. Only the latter, the still on the drawing board Jack-of-all-Trades, Skua, had any real dive-bomber pretensions, even if they were lessened by commitments to all its other assigned tasks

Another divergence of opinion followed. It had been pointed out that during dive-bombing trials with the Hawker Hart light bomber (a biplane), the bomb's impact point, in a no-wind condition, was barely within the pilot's range of vision, and that, in an upwind attack, it would not be visible at all. This was 'a serious limitation', tactically, on the flexibility of any attack. The RAE had suggested the adoption of an integrating accelerometer to overcome this problem, but Mr Meredith announced another solution. This was a 'cheap and simple' gyroscope, which would be wired up to all the bomb releases. During the initial stage of the attacker's pull-out from the dive, this would automatically release the bomb. He claimed that as the bomb release would be directly effected concurrent with the pull-out, it would release the pilot from the task of synchronising both, and thus ensure a more accurate distribution of the weapons dropped.

The RAF members found this recommendation not to their taste. The cost of extra wiring was cited as one reason for not adopting it. Again, Commander Langley was in a minority of one when he stated that, in his opinion, the increased accuracy from the resulting better distribution would 'completely justify' this method. Moreover, he again had to state the obvious, which was that as Fleet Air Arm aircraft had no 'level bombing' mission or instrumentation whatsoever, their aircraft's internal wiring had already been reduced.

Tedder took another tack. He thought the introduction of any new method involving installation complications, was justified, or that weapon distribution would be that much improved. He cited photographic evidence of the spread of sticks of bombs from the Coast Defence Development Unit, perhaps forgetting that, in dive-bombing, it was a single bomb that actually hit the target that counted, rather than a 'stick', which merely straddled it. Accuracy, for accuracy's sake, seems to have been universally eradicated from the RAF's mindset during the 1930s and 1940s, their only vision being cities laid waste by 'area' attacks.

In the end, a typical compromise was reached, whereby although it was agreed that the hypothetical impact point (the 'a' line) would be within the pilot's vision, the impact point of the bomb (the 'b' line) often would not. There, some method of bomb release during the pull-out from the dive, as the 'b' line crossed the target, ought, ideally to be evolved, and if this could be done by a gyro release system so much the better. The sting was again in the tail, 'it was emphasised that the practical complications in regard to production and maintenance which might be involved ... must be borne in mind'.

Mr Meredith's next suggestion also received a rough ride! He proposed fitting a contacting altimeter, with a visual signal light to indicate when the correct bomb release height had been reached during a dive. He explained that the provision of a lamp (possible in a bead foresight) could be automatically triggered by such a device. This would mean that the pilot could concentrate on his attack and not have to take his eyes off the target. Mr Bowen was enthusiastic, suggesting that this device could be married with the gyroscopic device discussed earlier.

Again, the RAF representatives were luke-warm. If the device failed, any pilot that had come to rely on it would be at a loss; indeed, he might not even know when he had passed the correct release height. The Chairman also opposed it, but from the opposite point of view. 'A variation in height of 200 to 300 feet, did not really make very much difference to bombing accuracy.' Most dive-bomber pilots would have vehemently challenged that viewpoint, but, of course, Tedder had nobody with that knowledge and expertise to oppose him.

Once more the Royal Navy representative was the lone voice from the Services in favour, 'on several grounds', not least the opportunity to avoid barrage fire from the fleet. Tedder was adamant that 'too many complications should not be introduced'. With regard to anti-aircraft fire, 'in war risks would have to be, and would be, accepted. The presentation of such an attractive target as a warship would be a strong incentive to pilots to come lower'. The idea was thought to have some merit for training purposes and should be tried out, but its adoption was ruled out until it could be proven that it increased accuracy.

An RAE idea to set the contacting altimeter for sea-level barometric pressure, either by the pilot descending to sea level or timing the fall of a practice bomb, was ruled out for the same obvious reasons as earlier for wind direction estimation. The Committee then went on to consider whether a multi-directional sight should be given the go ahead.

Again, it was Meredith who thought that, to remove limitations in the direction of attack imposed by the sight as already discussed, a sight comprising two concentric rings with radial spokes, could be painted on the aircraft windscreen. He envisaged the pilot positioning the target so that the smoke line lay along a radius of these circles, and the wind strength could be estimated from the radial distance of the target from the centre. The pilot would need to have his head correctly positioned for this to work, and should have a bead foresight and a headrest to ensure he was correctly aligned.

Once more, it had to be pointed out that for this system to be effective it depended on smoke being visible from the ships under attack, and this had already been rejected as impracticable. How about the ensigns and flags of the ships being a good indication of wind direction instead of smoke? One wonders just what less scientific method the air lobby would come up with than this, which was more attuned to seventeenth century naval warfare than twentieth century air warfare! Yet, the majority were all for it. As it embodied the ring-sight principle, already well known to pilots, and overcame the single directional restriction, it offered greater flexibility. The only modification was that instead of painting the rings on the windshield, which might impair the efficiency of the reflector sight, thin metal rings could be utilised that could be swung into position when needed.

Commander Langley then stated that features that would totally meet Admiralty requirements in a dive-bomb sight would be an automatic or manual setting for angle of dive and/or height. These additional refinements were, however, 'deferred', but action on the other recommendations could 'proceed forthwith'. This latter point, at least, would mean progress at last. Unfortunately, despite the wording, it did not happen.

One step forward, two steps back

Some 6 months after the initial discussion, it appeared that some progress had been made. A second meeting of the sub-committee was convened on Wednesday 2 December 1936. On this occasion Tedder did not attend, delegating the Chairman's role to Group Captain Gray. New faces included Wing Commander J. C. M. Lowe of Bomber Command, and Squadron Leader C. W. Busk (Armament Group), MC and J. L. Wingate (RAE), while Mr J. W. Barnes was added to the RAE team.[7]

This group discussed the preliminary trial of the 'simple' bombsight, which Mr Meredith described as three sight-points or aiming aids:

1. A moveable foresight, situated 3 to 4 feet from the pilot. This was a ring, which could slide up and down allowing for wind in the direction of flight. It was moved by a Barber Watts remote control device.
2. Two further sights close to the pilot's optic. The first a ring, which defined the line upon which the aircraft was diving (the 'a' line). The closer of these two rings to the pilot was a bead, which defined the bomb impact point line, (the 'b' line).
3. A warning signal light. This lit up about 500 feet prior to a pre-set height. When the pre-set height was reached, this light went out.

Squadron Leader Wingate had flight-tested this sight in a Gloster Audax light bomber (a biplane), making several preliminary dives, but without actually dropping any bombs and without measuring the characteristics of the dive. During the day of the trial a high wind was encountered, higher than could be set on the sight. The test pilot therefore had no choice but to dive across wind from a height of 10,000 feet and about 245 mph, lining up on a straight section of railway track, his aircraft drifting sideways down the track. Furthermore, the sight as installed in the Audax could only be used downwind. If an upwind attack was made the pilot had to raise his head to such an extent that the 'b' line was no longer visible!

This made the preliminary trials practically useless and discussion then centred on the flight trials. The normal proving ground at Martlesham Heath had no suitable aircraft on hand and although No. 57 (Bomber) Squadron was offered instead, Air Commodore L. A. Pattinson thought that Eastleigh would be a better venue. There, the trials could be evaluated both technically and operationally. The question of accurate instrument measurement of the trial at that site was raised, but Mr Bowen said that Farnborough could loan two graticule (sic) sights to measure the angle of dive. Similarly, Air Commodore Pattinson raised doubts about accurately determining the wind, 'particularly when starting the initial dive at 10,000 feet and the second at 5,000 feet'. He considered that the pilots would find themselves relying on their own judgement instead of the sight. In the end, they decided that the RAE would oversee the fitting of the simple sight on one of the Eastchurch-based Hawker Harts of No. 25 Armament Group, and that trials would be conducted with both the mean wind during the dive and the wind at release height, and the results compared.

The Committee then came to discuss the multi-directional sight with gyro release. The RAF position was that this should be shelved until the simple sight results were analysed. Even worse news followed, Mr Meredith of the RAE revealing that due to 'pressure of work', this sight had been relegated to the 'C' Priority. Naturally, this blow was a hard knock to take for the Royal Navy. Commander Langley said that it was not his understanding of the last meeting 'that there was any question of this item going on Priority C'. On the contrary, he had been given the impression that the multi-directional sight plus gyro release 'would go on Priority A'. He went continued 'The Admiralty had said *for 7 years*[8] that the latter was the most urgent requirement for the FAA, as dive-bombing was of more importance to them than level bombing'.

Unperturbed, Mr Bowen replied that it had been agreed that a simple sight should be developed first, and this had been done. On the multi-directional sight, he added, 'they were averse to doing any constructional work upon it until the result of the trials of the simple sight were known'. The RAF representatives agreed with this, the Chairman adding, 'it seemed unlikely that a multi-directional sight would be justified'.

The lone Royal Navy voice fought on in the losing battle. 'The Admiralty's views', said Commander Langley, 'were that they were already satisfied that better results could and would be secured with a multi-directional sight, and therefore they would like it proceeded with'. He added that the simple sight imposed undesirable tactical restrictions, and that the Royal Navy flyers wanted to be able to dive from 8,000 to 4,000 feet and release there.

Mr Meredith replied that, due to 'limited staff and a very big programme' the question was how much could be done. He outlined a proposal for an Automatic Dive-Bomb Sight, evolved by himself and Mr Barnes, in which a gyroscope 'housed in some convenient place in the aircraft', would 'communicate its movement by electric repeater motors to the sight'. The target vessel's movements would also be automatically incorporated in the data. He admitted that in conditions of variable wind, 'there would always be residual error', but this would be less than with a pre-set vector sight. He suggested that if the Committee recommended its adoption, it could be placed in Category Priority B.

This new concept appealed to the Royal Navy, Commander Langley immediately stating that he was sure the Admiralty would welcome such a sight. But Mr Bowen immediately poured cold water on such enthusiasm, warning it would take at least 2 years to develop. Commander Langley considered yet a further 2 years' delay, on top of the existing 7 years' inaction, too big a price to pay, and asked that the multi-directional sight with gyro release 'be made up and tried out right away in the Fleet Air Arm rather than wait'. This was agreed to and there the matter rested for a further 9 months.

'Simple' dive-bomb sight trials

In September 1937, the RAE submitted a Departmental Note on the tests of the Dive-bomb Sight Experimental Type A.[9] The sight was initially tested at Eastchurch and subsequently tested again at Martlesham.[10] In the former case two pilots were selected from 'B' Squadron, one inexperienced in the art of dive-bombing, and one experienced. At Martlesham Heath both the pilots were experienced in this form of attack.

In fact, the 'trials' at RAF Eastchurch were farcical. In the first case it was revealed that the sight itself had been designed for a mean angle of dive of just 50 degrees. This might mean 'dive-bombing' as defined by the RAF, but to everyone else this was just steep glide-bombing. In fact, the pilots actually conducted the tests at 66 degrees, as deduced by the Ground Observation Sight on the range itself. Not surprisingly then, 'A considerable range of error' was expected!

Secondly, for most of the tests, the contacting altimeter was set to 1,900 feet instead of to 2,400 feet as laid down, because it was suspected that this instrument had a 500 feet error in it. However, 'this error probably did not exist and the mean height of release was 1,400 feet. As the angle of pull-out before the release of the bomb was calculated for a height of release of 2,000 feet, a further range error is to be expected ....'

The pilots, and especially the one inexperienced in dive-bombing, none-theless minimised the range errors because, as predicted, the pilots used their own judgement to correct observed errors. The experienced and inexperienced pilots had consistent range errors of +42 yards and −2 yards, and the probable values of the residual were 10 and 12 yards respectively. This was good for the individual pilot's natural reaction, but actually made the trials of the sight at RAF Eastchurch valueless.

At Martlesham Heath, achieved bombing accuracy was even more dismal than at Eastchurch, probably due to the fact that both pilots were experienced. One of these pilots obviously knew what true dive-bombing was, carrying out 'very steep dives' (averaging 78 degrees), but his bomb release height was 2,550 feet, while the second pilot made shallower dives that resulted in far less consistency. But, the results were the same as for Eastchurch, and were summarised as 'inadequate for the purpose of estimating the improvement of accuracy due to the use of the sight mainly because of the incorrect use of the sight'. It was therefore recommended that further tests should be carried out, preferably at Orfordness, with the universal dive bombsight now being developed.

It was freely admitted that, at Eastchurch, due to several faults with the data recording equipment used, 'the only useful data obtainable from the Ground Observation Sight are the mean angle of dive before pull-out, the height of release and the general shape of the path of the aircraft before pull-out'. At Martlesham Heath, only the first five exercises by each pilot were recorded, and the average range error for each exercise so recorded did not agree with the average range error measured by means of the quadrant sights.

The almost universal trend for the pilots to dive-bomb at angles steeper than the arbitrary 50 degrees imposed by RAF doctrine (which even refused to use the term 'dive-bombing' and referred only to 'losing height

Table 5 Trials of 'simple' dive-bomb sight at RAF Eastchurch and RAE Martlesham

No. of bombs	Mean wind speed 2,000–5,000 ft (mph)	Wind setting error (mph)	Mean dive angle relative to air axis (degrees) (from Ground Observation Sight)	Mean height of release (feet) (from Ground Observation Sight)	Range error (expected from 4, 5 and 6 yards)	Range error (actual yards)	Wind direction error (degrees)	Line error (yards)
E1 – Experienced – Eastchurch								
5	8	0	65	–	–	+39 +6	0	–36 +26
5	8	0	74	–	–	+47 +8	15	+2 +5
5	17	0	66	1,240	+62	+40 +15	30	–24 +5
5	20	+10	71	1,300	+58	+49 +12	0	–21 +16
5	20	–10	71	1,260	+80	+61 +8	0	+2 +16
5	8	+20	66	–	–	+28 +8	0	+6 +12
5	8	0	65	1,360	+64	+31 +10	0	–9 +16
E2 – Inexperienced – Eastchurch								
5	12	0	72	1,660*	+79	–1 +3	0	–31 +24
3	11	0	65	1,360*	+63	+10 +5	15	–11 +8
5	11	0	63	1,260	+59	+22 +9	30	+13 +5
5	11	–10	63	1,420*	+79	+7 +6	0	–13 +10
5	10	+10	63	1,560	+48	–19 +9	0	–5 +8
5	10	+15	63	1,500	+41	–23 +13	0	–5 +13
5	10	–15	62	1,340	+102	–7 +16	0	–2 +8
M1 – Experienced – Martlesham								
4	15	0	79	2,450	+120	+130	0	–3
4	15	–10	74	2,400	+124	+77	0	0
4	15	–15	79	2,800	+171	+116	0	–1
4	15	+10	83	2,700	+118	+105	0	–7
4	15	+20	76	2,500	+64	+70	0	–10
4	23	0	–	–	–	+116	15	+6
4	23	0	–	–	–	+110	30	+19
M2 – Experienced – Martlesham								
4	18	0	64	–	–	+58	0	–52
4	18	+10	60	2,000	+38	+50	0	–50
4	18	–10	60	1,900	+85	+53	0	–30
4	15	+20	47	1,600	–31	–100	0	–4
4	15	–15	50	1,700	+67	–93	0	+5
4	23	0	–	–	–	+19	15	+27
4	23	0	–	–	–	+26	30	+19

* Average of three observations only.

bombing') was explained away by Eastchurch. 'It was necessary to allow the target to pass under the plane for a judged period of time before turning into the dive.' In other words, the pilots were eye-sighting a natural dive-bombing approach instead of following the sight. There were also consistent line errors to the left, 11 yards by Eastchurch, and between

4 and 44 yards by the Martlesham Heath duo. This was recorded as being probably due to an error in the mounting of the sight on the aircraft.

The whole wasted effort was a good indication of how the RAF viewed dive-bombing in the 1930s. Recent internet discussions on the way that RAF control over Royal Navy aircraft held back British naval air power between the wars, featured American 'experts' proclaiming 'The Royal Navy got what [the aircraft] it wanted'.[11] Any study of the history of the Skua and dive-bombing generally via the actual documents of this period, quickly reveals just what a naïve and misinformed statement that is.

Further discussions

On Monday 18 October 1937, the third meeting of the Dive-Bomb-Sight sub-committee took place at the Air Ministry.[12] Air Commodore A. G. R. Garrod, OBE, MC, DFC, was present as Air Officer Commanding the RAF's Armaments Group, and this time Captain Langley had some support in the form of Commander R. M. Ellis, RN, of the Naval Armaments Division of the Admiralty. Mr Meredith dismissed the trials of the simple sight as being 'inadequate for a correct assessment of the value of the sight'. Shutting the stable door, Garrod thought it might be advisable for an RAE representative to attend any future trials, but Meredith stated that further tests of this simple sight, 'were not considered necessary'. It was the multi-directional sight, under development, that offered the chance of 'a large order of accuracy'.

The multi-directional sight linked to a gyroscopic mechanism would automatically release the bomb at the correct instant after the pilots had carried out the attack dive with the target vessel in his sight. The gyroscopic device was 'in an advanced state of construction, and would be ready shortly'. It was also revealed that Squadron Leader Wingate of the RAE, who liked the method, had practised the initial part of the operation, diving onto the target. The snag remained that, when bombing a moving vessel, the relative wind was a crucial factor and Wingate said that such judgement was proving difficult to work out. A repeater from the DR compass would help (but again, 'once the latter became available').

Any warship under dive-bombing attack could not be relied upon obligingly to steer a straight and steady course and Captain Langley had to remind his RAF hosts that, 'the possible alteration of the enemy's course would remain unaccounted for'. What was really required was a vector sight in which the enemy course could be adjusted for avoiding action. Mr Meredith reiterated that the fully Automatic Dive Sight, briefly discussed at the previous meeting, and strongly advocated by himself ('would cut out a tremendous amount of elaboration and would be much simpler to the operator'). It 'would prove the only really satisfactory solution'.

This ruffled the RAF's feathers and they quickly stomped on the idea. Mr Bowen asked whether they were justified in developing, 'at considerable trouble, a complicated sight for a type of bombing which might be obsolete in the very near future?' The RAF had decided, in their wisdom (a wisdom that was not shared by the *Luftwaffe*, the American and Japanese navies or the Soviet Air Force) that aircraft that could dive at angle of about 40 degrees would have 'disappeared' in about 2 years' time (1939).

Wing Commander Davis joined in enthusiastically. In his opinion, 'it was wrong to develop a special sight for dive-bombing only'. He stated that he had recently visited the Goerz works in Austria and that a modification of the High Level Bombing ('the normal method') sight would suffice.

Against these broadsides, Captain Langley repeated the Admiralty's viewpoint yet again. As far as the Fleet Air Arm was concerned, he stated, 'they did not look upon level bombing as the primary form of attack, and dive-bombing was considered as of first importance', even though the RAF was determined not to use it. In the fleet it was anticipated 'that dive-bombing, on similar lines to those practised at present would be a requirement for the Fleet Air Arm for at least 10 years, and that a dive-sight could be regarded as a definite requirement even if its development took 2 years'.

Langley also stated that, while '*ultra* high speed'[13] was not a requirement, and could be sacrificed, endurance could not. External bomb stowage was therefore acceptable, but they would not revert from pilot sighting to observer sighting as per the RAF's level technique as it had no relevance. While he agreed that Meredith's idea for a fully automatic sight was worth investigating, 'the vector type was necessary'. Under questioning, Langley revealed that bombing accuracy errors 'were unacceptably high'. These errors he gave as roughly 80 yards against a stationary target! 'The Admiralty would like to increase the height to 3,000 or 4,000 feet for bomb release, while at the same time considerably reducing the errors'.

However, there was no enthusiasm at all for this type of thinking on the RAF side; they were all fixated on enemy cities laid waste from end to end and winning the war unaided by things like armies and navies.[14] Precision hardly entered their equation; it was almost looked upon as a quaint relic of a bygone age. It was finally decided that only the multi-directional sight should be proceeded with, 'when the gyroscopic release was ready'. While it was strongly recommended that the sight should be tested on the type of aircraft upon which it was ultimately intended to use it, they instead agreed to conduct trials at Orfordness with a Fairey Swordfish TSR biplane, or, failing the RAF or Admiralty being able to supply one, a Hawker Hart! The RAF's D./Arm.D expressed the opinion that it would take several years even to find out whether the fully automatic sight was even feasible, but Langley reiterated that the multi-directional sight 'should not be regarded as by any means meeting the full requirements of the Admiralty' but, at best, would be but a 'temporary solution'. The Admiralty had, after all, already been requesting such a sight for 6 years now.

The RAF representative again returned to the attack. Even the 'Simple Sight' under trial was only intended to cater for dives of 50/80 degrees – 'virtually point-blank bombing'. Due to the diving limitations of new high-speed aircraft, bombing angles of 20 degrees would be the norm in future.[15] However, at the Admiralty the potential of the dive-bomber had long been recognised. Firstly in its inherent accuracy against ship targets, and particularly so against 'soft-skinned' warships, cruisers, destroyers and the like, but also, crucially, against their likeliest opponents (at the time of planning) the Japanese aircraft carriers with their unprotected wooden decks. Secondly, as a useful 'flak suppressor' against capital ships which, if they could not sink outright, they could cause so much damage to the ship's defences that it would both split defensive fire and increase the chances of a low-level torpedo-bomber attack doing the actual sinking. Such views were continually expressed at the highest level of the Royal Navy in the 1930s.[16] But it has to be remembered that, after a long, hard fight, the control of the Fleet Air Arm was only won back from the indifferent administration of the RAF in July 1937, becoming the Royal Naval Air Service.

Some 3 years later a Dive-bomber Sight was still not available to the Fleet Air Arm. On 10 October 1940, a report appeared from the RAE at South Farnborough comparing the methods then currently being employed to devastating effect by the *Luftwaffe*, with the still only 'proposed' British system.[17] They found, not surprisingly perhaps, that the German system was superior. This led to yet another meeting, on 14 December 1940, this time in Room 5002 of Thames House South, to further talk about the German system, which incorporated both automatic pull-out and automatic bomb release. It was proposed to hold trials to evaluate the German method '... in lieu of the system now in development at RAE, which is based on the gyroscope, with a view to its eventual adoption, if it should prove satisfactory, in any aircraft in which dive bombing will be an operational requirement'.[18] The actual wartime experiences of the German method in action in Poland, Norway, the Low Countries and France was, apparently, still not sufficient to convince the Air Marshals, although one Air Ministry official tardily conceded: 'The dive-bombing success obtained in Norway by the Stukas and Junkers has raised in the mind of the Air Staff the *suspicion that perhaps*[19] the pre-war policy of neglecting the dive bomber was not entirely sound.'[20] These weasel words could not disguise the fact that they were still reluctant to admit they had got it completely wrong, of course.[21]

As one historian was to record, 'Possibly because they had the same
priorities, the technical staff at the Air Ministry, and later at the M.A.P,
were in the Navy's opinion, sometimes neither as sympathetic to naval requirements nor as willing to solve particular problems as they might have
been'.[22] He also recorded how: 'The Air Staff were particularly defeatist
over those projects in which they had little or no departmental interest.
This was certainly the case in the prolonged controversy over the Navy's
dive-bomber requirement.'[23]

Admiral Sir Dudley Pound, soon to become the First Sea Lord, put
things more bluntly, stating, '... the navy only receive from the RAF in
the way of services that which the RAF is prepared to give. Symptomatic
of the latter was the failure of the RAF – which had no interest in dive
bombing – to produce a dive-bombing sight at the Admiralty's request in
the 6 years between 1932 and 1938'.

The Royal Navy's enthusiasm for dive-bombing met with disdain from
the Air Ministry, who, as Geoffrey Till correctly pointed out:

> ... were always politely unreceptive, preferring to pin their faith on
> high-level bombing. This made them sceptical and generally unhelp-
> ful about the production of necessary equipment. In the end, the
> Admiralty had to short-circuit the normal procedures by ordering the
> Blackburn Skua straight off the drawing board and, after the failure
> of its determined 6-year campaign to prise a good dive-bombing sight
> out of the Air Ministry, sending it to war without one.[24]

And so it was.

NOTES

1. See Royal Aircraft Establishment, Farnborough, *Dive Bombing as practiced by the
   German Air Force and a Comparison with proposed British system*, London, 1940.
2. See Wilkenson, Erik, *Dive Bombing: A Theoretical Study*, Norrkopings Tidningars
   Aktiebolag, Sweden, 1947.
3. For example, a former US Navy veteran SBD pilot, a veteran of the Battle of Midway no
   less, Rear-Admiral Paul A. Holmberg, recalled to the author on 5 June 1977, that: 'There
   were no automatic pull-out devices used operationally in the US Navy. I tested an
   experimental model installed in a Dauntless at the Test Center, Patuxent River in 1944. It
   worked all right as I recall, but since the aviators in the fleet were not interested in having
   them in their dive bombers they were not adopted for operational use.'
4. Air Ministry, *Minutes of the 1st Meeting of the Dive-Bomb-Sight sub-committee of the
   Bombing Committee, held at the Air Ministry on Monday, 11 May, 1936*. Secret. S 38156/
   AC 16602 contained in National Archives AIR 20/4155.
5. Emphasis in the original.
6. In passing, it is worthwhile noting that the foremost Japanese naval practitioner of the
   dive-bomber, Commander Takashige Egusa, after extensive trials at Kasanohara air
   base prior to the attack on Pearl Harbor, found that 1,500 feet was the best dive-bomb
   release height. As his units later achieved a dive-bombing hit ratio of 88 per cent against

British warships in the Indian Ocean, his opinion merits consideration compared with that of the Air Ministry. See Peter C. Smith, *Fist from the Sky*, Crecy, Manchester, 2006.

7. Air Ministry, *Minutes of the 2nd Meeting of the Dive-Bomb-Sight sub-committee of the Bombing Committee, held at the Air Ministry on Wednesday, December 2nd, 1936*. Secret. S 38156/AC 16602 contained in National Archives AIR 20/4155.

8. Author's italics.

9. RAE Farnborough, Secret, RAE Departmental Note No. H.240, *Note on the tests of the R.A.E. Dive Bombsight Experimental Type A*, Inst/S.953/29, September 1937 contained in National Archives AIR 20-4155. In addition, the sight itself was fully described in RAE Instruction Leaflet No. 214, and the method of testing (which involved the deliberate false setting of wind speed and execution of attacks at an angle to the wind in order to ascertain the importance of these errors) was suggested in RAE Instruction Leaflet No. 215.

10. See letter from Commanding Officer, 'B' Squadron, Eastchurch to the Chief Instructor, Eastchurch, dated 14 April 1937, and Martlesham Report No. M/Arm/503/1.

11. Mike Johnson, Fallon, Nevada – Post 1410 on *Military History Online*. 23 May 2005.

12. Air Ministry, *Minutes of the 3rd Meeting of the Dive-Bomb-Sight sub-committee of the Bombing Committee, held at the Air Ministry on Monday, December 18th, 1937*. Secret. S 38156/AC 16602 contained in National Archives AIR 20/4155.

13. Author's italics.

14. The tortuous path of the RAF in the dive-bomber story during the 1930s, including the abandonment of the Hawker Henley, the adoption of the term 'losing height bombing' and the commitment to the low-level method of attack with the Fairey Battle light bomber, is described in full depth in Peter C. Smith, *Dive Bomber! A Pictorial History*, Moorland Publishing, Ashbourne, 1982 and the same author's, *Impact!: The Dive Bomber Pilots Speak*, William Kimber, London, 1981.

15. It might be of interest to place again on record that this particular RAF argument was *totally* negated by wartime experience. The Soviet Petlyakov Pe-2 Peshka twin-engined dive-bomber was actually as fast in 1942 as the British Hawker Hurricane, a pure single-engined interceptor fighter! The US North American A-36 Apache, an adaptation of the well-known P-51 Mustang, was just as fast, and, fitted with dive brakes, performed perfectly. The Japanese Yokosuka D4Y Comet dive-bomber was one the fastest and most aerodynamically clean aircraft of the Pacific War and could outrun the Grumman F6F Hellcat fighter, and so on.

16. See for example, Admiral Sir Roger Backhouse, First Sea Lord, 7 May 1937 (National Archives ADM 115/4030).

17. RAE South Farnborough, *Report on dive bombing*, 10 October 1940. IIH/241/3/406, (contained in National Archives AIR 14/181). An Air Ministry report appeared 4 months later still *viz*: Air Ministry, *Notes on Dive Bombing and the German Ju.88 Bombing Aircraft*, IIH/241/3/406 (contained in National Archives AIR 14/181).

18. *Ibid.*

19. Author's Italics.

20. R. E. Willcock (Air Ministry) to DNAD, 5 May 1940 (National Archives PREM 3/171/6 and Captain R. M. Ellis MSS, CCC and minute to Staff discussions, 4 September 1939, ADM 116/3720).

21. Even the loss of thirty-five Fairey Battle bombers out of an attacking force of sixty-three, sent against the bridges across the River Meuse, failed to move them. One Battle unit, 218 Squadron on 14 May 1940, lost ten out of eleven aircraft despatched to halt the German advance, and all without one single hit being scored. Only Sholto Douglas ever hinted at any regret many years later, writing in his memoirs: 'I could not help feeling with the deepest regret that it would have been so much better if, some years earlier, we had developed a dive bomber along the lines of Ernst Udet's Stuka, instead of devoting

so much of our resources to the design, development and the production of those wretched Battles.' Marshal of the Royal Air Force Lord Douglas of Kirtleside, *Years of Command*, Collins, London, 1963.

22. Geoffrey Till, *Air Power and the Royal Navy 1914–1945*, Jane's Publishing, London, 1979.
23. *Ibid.*
24. *Ibid.*

4

THE SKUA IS HATCHED

The Skua I as she finally emerged, was described as 'a two-seater dive-bomber fighter'[1] (note the reversal of priorities from the original designation), suitable for operation as a ship plane or landplane.

Overall view

The Skua I was a single-engined, low-wing cantilever monoplane, of all-metal construction, powered by the Perseus XII engine. As a 'ship plane' she conformed to the requirements for deck operations and was strengthened for launch by catapult (from a cruiser) or accelerator (from a carrier). She was fitted with hydraulically operated arrester gear, but, because she had retractable landing gear with smaller wheels than the fixed undercarriage type biplanes hitherto used aboard carriers, problems were to be experienced with this. The mainplanes were arranged to fold back about inclined hinges aft of the rear main girders and to lie alongside the fuselage, with their leading edges uppermost. The Skua I was fitted with flotation in case of ditching at sea, with a series of watertight compartments integral to the fuselage and mainplanes' internal structure.

The two-man crew was seated in tandem inside a long, fully enclosed cabin. The front cockpit was accessed via a sliding section, and there was a hinged hood at the rear. The pilot's seat was adjustable vertically by means of a hand lever, and the rudder bar was also adjustable horizontally by use of screw gearing. The rear-seat configuration could be varied according to mission type, with either a fixed seat mounted on the aft end of the bomb recess structure, or an adjustable seat further aft for gunnery. To give head support during catapulting, a padded adjustable headrest was fitted in the front cockpit, while the person in the rear could utilise a hinged support bar fixed athwart the aft section. There was ducted hot air fed in from the oil cooler to heat the whole cockpit, another first for British naval aircraft.

The fuselage was of metal monocoque build, which comprised transverse frames, longitudinal stringers and shell plating secured by flush-rivets. The front structure, which extended from the fire-proof bulkhead to a joint just forward of the fin, was rendered watertight up to the coaming and had two closed watertight compartments, one located forward, beneath the front cockpit, the other positioned under the after cockpit. The whole rear structure was fully detachable, and included the empennage and fixed, adjustable, tail wheel. The Skua I had two main fuel tanks that were both located in the front portion of the rear cockpit, one on either side of the fuselage, with a smaller reserve tank mounted inside the forward watertight compartment itself. The oil tank was housed in the fuselage decking, immediately ahead of the front cockpit.

The wings were constructed in three units, a centre plane and two outer planes. The centre plane was bolted under the fuselage and was detachable, while the outer planes were secured by hinge and latch joints, with vertical latch pins that were operated by a rod, link and lever system, from a small gear box with a crank handle at the leading edge of the centre plane. The outer sections tapered in plan and thickness, and had hydraulically operated split-flaps let into troughs forward of the trailing edge between the ailerons and the folding joints. These 'Zapp' flaps had upper edges, which slid rearward as the main flaps lowered, their purpose being to give extra lift during take-off from carrier decks, and to steady the aircraft during a TV attack. The mainplanes were of stressed skin metal construction, with two main girders, flat plate ribs, transverse stringers and flush-riveted plating. Again, watertight compartments were located between the main girders, outboard of the gun mountings as far as the tip joints. The wing-tips were detachable to facilitate repair or replacement.

The two undercarriage units had oleo-pneumatic shock-absorber struts and retracted outwards into recesses in the outer planes between the main girders. These undercarriages were hydraulically operated and fitted with electrical and mechanical indicators. There was an audible warning signal, which operated at airspeeds in the range of 60 to 100 mph.

The engine was air-cooled and had an oil cooler mounted inside the cowling atop the engine mounting. The airscrew was a de Havilland D.H.5/8 three-bladed two-position, hydraulically operated, variable-pitch type. The engine fairing ring was equipped with cooling gills, which were cockpit-controlled.

All the controls to the control surfaces were internally arranged. The ailerons, elevators and rudder had inset hinge balancers, and were fabric-covered aft of the spar in order to aid mass balancing; the rudder also had a horn balance. The tail plane was fixed, fore-and-aft, trimming being effected by tables with irreversible cockpit control. Likewise, the rudder had controllable trim tabs and an automatic balance tab.

The Skua' s main payload was a single 500 lb bomb, which was carried in a recess in the fuselage and fused and released electrically. The Skua I was also fitted with two light-series carriers for practice bombs, fitted externally, one under each outer mainplane. The gun armament as completed, consisted of four fixed forward-firing Browning machine-guns mounted in the outer mainplanes, two to port and two to starboard so that they fired outside the airscrew diameter. These four machine-guns were pneumatically controlled by the pilot. Rear defence was limited to a single Mk IIIE Lewis gun mounted on a pillar-type flexible mounting in the rear cockpit.

The electrical installation, powered by a 500 watt engine-driven generator, serviced the usual lighting, a landing lamp in the leading edge of the port mainplane, landing flares, formation-keeping lamps, undercarriage indicators and warning lamps, etc. The Skua I's radio equipment included alternative types of transmitters and receivers, with both fixed and trailing aerials.

Special maritime and ancillary equipment needs were catered for by the inclusion of an inflatable dinghy and distress signals, which were both housed in the after decking astern of the rear cockpit. Equipment included a signal pistol and cartridges in a box in the front cockpit, fire extinguishers, oxygen apparatus and provision for target-towing gear.

Let us examine each of these in more detail to give a closer view of just how revolutionary the Skua was for its day.

Fuselage

In the Skua I the fuselage itself was constructed of three sections, a tubular engine mounting, the main fuselage and the detachable rear section, which was secured to the main structure with four bolts. The contour of the shell plating was swept upward to form an enclosed cabin.

The tubular engine mounting was a tube-braced, two-bay structure. The forward end carried the mounting ring and the rearmost tubes were bolted to the attachment fittings on the fuselage bulkhead. The tube socket joints at the intermediate truss and the lower attachments to the fuselage, were effected by split bushes through which were passed taper bolts. Part of the engine ring was detachable, which enabled the engine to be installed or removed without detaching the carburettor. Access footsteps were clamped to the lower end of the tubes on both the port and starboard sides of the engine mounting.

The main structure was built of Alclad plates, frames, stringers and special sections, flush-riveted together. The two watertight compartments were formed by the shell plating under the front and rear of the cockpit. A vent pipe connected the two compartments, and another vent pipe ran to the foot of the fin. The forward underside of the fuselage was shaped to the contour of the upper surface of the centre plane, which, when bolted in place, formed the bottom of the forward watertight compartment. The reserve fuel tank was mounted in that space, and its filler neck was carried through a watertight joint in the cockpit floor up to the top decking.

The front cockpit extended from the fireproof bulkhead to bulkhead D, and the rear cockpit from D to bulkhead H. The main fuel tanks were installed in the forward end of the rear cockpit, and access to the filler caps was via doors in the fuselage shell. The wireless, oxygen gear, Lewis gun and other equipment were located aft of these tanks. When the Lewis gun was shipped, it fitted into a well in the top decking. From bulkhead D to frame F, a recess ran below the fuselage, which formed the bomb stowage space and the cockpit floor. Supports were fitted for catapulting, with the forward spools built into the centre plane, and the rear spools were carried on a transverse tube just ahead of bulkhead H. The sliding cabin panels incorporated an automatic wind deflector on either side, which prevented the slipstream entering the cockpit when the panels were opened. Access to the front cockpit was via the sliding hood, and the rear cockpit via a hinged hood. Support frames were fixed to bulkhead D and frame E, which extended up to the cabin roof and stiffened the superstructure to give rollover crew protection.

The rearmost watertight compartment ran from bulkhead H to the end of the main structure, and up to the cockpit coaming line, maintaining the elliptical shape of the fuselage by way of decking, which contained the collapsible dinghy and its accompanying carbon-dioxide inflation cylinder. The control cables for the empennage ran through two watertight tunnels that ran the whole length of this rearmost compartment, while the arrester gear struts were accommodated in two troughs built into the bottom plating. For inspection purposes, there was a large door underneath the fuselage, a hand hole in the decking and another in the port side for the watertight space. Small inspection doors also ran along the tunnels and also enabled replacement of the control cables.

The detachable rear structure was of similar build to the main structure, and contained the tail wheel and tail unit. The four securing bolts were accessed via small inspection doors, while frames M and N were drilled to take the fin attachment bolts. The top decking aft of frame P was cut away to take the tail plane, which was bolted to frames P and R. This portion carried the control shafts for the rudder elevators and the trimming gear, with inspection and lubrication access doors. The tail wheel was emplaced in a fairing riveted to the underside, and the lines were maintained by a detachable fairing on the tail plane.

Alighting gear

The undercarriage was divided into two units, which could be retracted outward into recesses in the outer mainplanes between the main girders. They were hydraulically operated, and fitted with mechanical and electrical indicators. Both units had Vickers oleo-pneumatic shock-absorber struts fitted with a stub axle. The Dunlop wheels were equipped with intermediate pressure tyres and pneumatic brakes. The fixed tail wheel had a simple Dowty coil spring shock-absorber strut with oil damp-ing; the castoring motion was self-centring.

In general, the hydraulically operated undercarriage consisted of two separate units, each comprising an oleo-pneumatic shock-absorber strut, a rear stay tube and a telescopic side stay strut; the inner member of the latter locked the unit in the down position when engaged by the latch pin. The upper end of the oleo strut hinged about a bolt carried between the rear of the centre plane front girder and the box end rib. A collar, with lugs for the attachment of the telescopic and rear struts, was keyed and secured to the oleo strut cylinder. The stub axels for the landing wheels were machined forgings bolted onto the ends of the oleo strut rams.

The undercarriage retraction was activated by six hydraulic jacks, which were incorporated in the undercarriage retractor gear and were automatically controlled by restrictor valves to operate at appropriate stages during the retracting cycle. Two main jacks were used actually to raise and lower the undercarriage units, with two smaller jacks operating the telescopic strut latch pins, and a further small jack in each wheel recess for actuating the stowage catch. The main jacks were opposed to each other, having their cylinder ends anchored to a compression tube mounted behind the front girder of the centre plane, the rams being connected through universal blocks to levers bolted to the lugs at the top joints of the oleo struts. When the rams were fully extended, the undercarriage units were in the 'Down' position.

Normally, an engine-driven pump operated the retracting gear, although, when the engine was not running, or in the event of a failure of this system, a hand pump provided a back-up. This hand pump was mounted on the starboard side of the cockpit, and was brought into operation by moving the selector valve lever, mounted on the port side of the cockpit, to the appropriate position. Locking devices were provided to secure the undercarriage units, along with an electrical indicator to confirm the locking operation was fully completed.

When the undercarriage was retracted, the stirrup extensions on the wheel axles engaged with the stowage catch gear in the wheel recesses in the mainplanes. In this position, push switches were operated and each illuminated an amber lamp on the undercarriage indicator, which was located on the pilot's instrument panel.

Moving the selector valve to 'Undercarriage Down' the stowage catches were automatically released by their hydraulic jacks and the units swung downward, the inner members of the telescopic struts travelling upward to the latch pin joints. When the undercarriage units were fully extended, the hole in the socket of each inner member was coincident with the latch pin guide bushes, and the latch pins were inserted by their hydraulic jacks, which thereby secured the inner tube, preventing any further movement. When fully inserted, each latch pin operated a switch, which illuminated a green lamp on the undercarriage warning indicator. The intermediate positions of the undercarriage were not, however, indicated.

Should there be a total main system failure, an emergency fluid line could be activated to lower the undercarriage. This was done via the emergency selector valve mounted on the starboard side of the cockpit and the hand pump. However, this combination could not be used to raise the undercarriage.

Again, both an audible indicator and electrically and mechanically operated visual indicators were incorporated into the system. An undercarriage-warning indicator was mounted on the pilot's instrument panel in the cockpit. This comprised a master switch, two amber lamps, two green lamps and a single red lamp. The latter lit up only when the Skua's undercarriage was retracted and the airspeed of the aircraft approached that of the normal landing manoeuvre. The red lamp was controlled by the airspeed, the tube from the pressure head of the airspeed indicator being connected to a pressure chamber in which the air pressure operated an electrical relay regulated to cut-in at any airspeed between 60 and 100 mph. The relay closed the circuit and the red lamp was illuminated. A push switch on the control, which was mounted on the starboard side of the cockpit floor, was provided to test the system on the ground before flight.

Two mechanical indicators were fixed to port and starboard of the aircraft. Each had a finger, which protruded above the top surfaces of the wing, and were visible from the cockpit. They were attached to the centre-plane end ribs and were connected by a rod to the top of the rear-stay struts of the undercarriage units. Their movements followed that of the unit to which they were connected, but these indicators did not indicate that the units were locked.

The electrical visual warning relay, already described, also activated an audible warning, sounding an electronic buzzer mounted in the cockpit close to the pilot's ear. The test switch also operated this buzzer.

Finally, the latch pin gear in the centre plane was provided with spring-loaded plungers. When these latch pins were withdrawn, the top sockets of the telescopic struts left their seatings; the plungers, following the action of the springs, followed them into the jaws of the outer tube sockets, thus blanking off the latch pin apertures. This, in turn, prevented the latch pins from obstructing free entry of the telescopic struts into the jaws when the undercarriage units were being lowered to the 'Down' position.

The tail-wheel unit shock-absorber strut consisted of an outer tube, inside which slid an inner tube carrying the wheel fork and axle. The crown-fork fitting was secured to the sliding tube by the pins, which were riveted over. Fixed to the outer tube by means of a bush, were the end cap and the centre tube, to which was attached the centring cone, which in turn was locked by a grub-screw. Screwed into the centre tube was a spring cage in which was fitted a spring-and-ball valve. A self-centring bush was attached to the inner sliding tube by means of grub-screws. This bush also formed the reservoir for the oil, which provided the dampening medium. Inside the bush two piston rings were fitted to prevent oil leakage. The rings were positioned by a spacer and could be tightened by means of a gland nut. On the centre tube was fitted a gland washer, which acted as a piston in the bush. A spring, which took all the compression loads of the unit, was fitted between the centring cone and the crown fork fitting. A friction band was fitted in a housing on the lower end of the outer tube, and when adjusted the band tended to grip the sliding inner member, thus preventing side-to-side oscillation of the wheel when the Skua was taxiing.

During the aircraft's flight the tail-wheel unit was held in the extended position by a spring, and was self-centred by a pair of cones, which ensured the wheel was always aligned fore-and-aft. Once the tail wheel came in contact with a surface and the unit was partially compressed, the cones came out of engagement, leaving the wheel free to caster through any number of turns. The damping action was provided by the oil in the reservoir that was formed by the bush and the piston rings. On landing, the inner tube slid up the outer tube, compressing a spring. As the centre tube was fixed, the bush moved freely.

The tail unit

In its day, the tail unit was unorthodox in that the fin and rudder were situated forward of the tail plane and elevators. Both the fin and tail plane were unbraced cantilevers of stressed-skin metal construction. The rudder and elevators were of metal construction with fabric covering. Trimming tabs, operable by the pilot, were fitted to the elevators and rudder, and a automatic balance tab was also fitted to the rudder. All the control surfaces were hinged in ball bearings.

The tail plane itself was a two-spar, non-adjustable structure, constructed of girder-type spars with formers stationed at intervals, being braced by transverse Z-section stringers. Hollow rivets secured the plating to the formers and stringers. The outer elevator hinges, which were of similar construction to the rudder upper hinge, were built into the structure near the tips and the inner hinges were attached to a cross shaft located on the rear end of the tail plane. A detachable fairing, secured to the rear of the fuselage and to the tail plane, was provided to complete the aerofoil section of the tail plane.

The elevators were fabric-covered, as was the custom at that time, and were girder-type spar structures braced with Alclad formers and Alclad leading edges. These were interconnected by means of the elevator cross shaft to which they were attached by special studs on a flanged fitting at the inboard end of the elevator control tube. These studs picked up holes in the flanged dockets of the elevator cross shaft and ensured correct alignment. A lever on the cross shaft was connected by a tube to the elevator mass-balance arm, which was located in the rear end of the fuselage.

Trimming tabs were fitted to the elevators and operated by an irreversible system of levers, which could be controlled from the cockpit. The trimming tabs were constructed of spruce formers spaced at intervals on a metal tube, with plywood and fabric-covering overall. Rigging of the trimming tabs could be effected by adjustment of the external control rod, which was accessible between the detachable tail plane faring and the elevators.

The fin, which could be detached from the fuselage, was of metal stressed skin construction, consisting of an Alclad sternpost, a sternpost bracing strut, flanged formers and flanged leading edge formers. Both the sternpost and the sternpost bracing strut had flanges of angle strip riveted onto them. Hollow rivets secured the skin to the frame. The top rudder hinge fitting was secured by bolts to the upper sternpost fairing.

The rudder was of similar construction to the elevators. Balance was effected by a horn balance, a balance tab and inset hinges. The rudder was hinged about two points to the rear finpost. An automatic balance tab and a trimming tab were inset at the trailing edge, the trimming tab being operated by an irreversible system of levers, which could be controlled from the cockpit.

The mainplanes

On the Skua I the mainplanes consisted of two metal-covered outer planes arranged to fold backward from the metal-covered centre plane. The outer planes tapered in plan and thickness and the swept-up tips were detachable. A hydraulically operated flap was fitted to each outer plane, which also contained a watertight compartment and the mountings for the guns. Provision was made for fitting slats. The ailerons were of metal construction and fabric-covered.

The centre plane was bolted on the underside of the fuselage and its centre portion, aft of the rear spar, was cut away to continue the formation of the bomb compartment in the fuselage. The girder ends carried fitting for the outer plane latch pins.

The centre planes were constructed around two main box girders, which were built up of Alclad plate webs reinforced by vertical stiffeners and flanges of extruded angle, riveted on. Two rider plates of extruded metal riveted to the angles completed the assembly of each girder. Fitted inside the lower flange of the rear girder was a tension member, which consisted of a flat duralumin bar that lay between the webs and extended the length of the girder; the ends were attached to the lower latch-pin fittings, and, after the metal covering was fitted, the member was secured by pierced rivets to the rider place and skin. The girders were braced by ribs assembled in three separate sections, these being (a) the leading edge, (b) an inter-girder and (c) a trailing edge portion, the ribs being secured to the girder webs by angle plates and rivets. The rib edges were flanged to suit the contour of the plane, and slotted to take the Z-section stringers, the rib being reinforced on both sides along the base line of the slots by angle stiffeners. The plating was riveted to the rib flanges and stringers.

An offset girder was built into the structure at each end of the rear main girder and supported the outer plane hinges; the ends of both main girders had fittings for the latch pins. The latch-pin gear was assembled on each end rib and was mechanically operated by a screw jack and crank-handle installed in the centre-plane leading edge. The cells of the structure provided accommodation for various accessories and pipelines, access to these being gained through inspection doors. All external surfaces were flush-riveted, either by solid or pierced rivets.

The outer mainplane had two main girders of similar construction to those of the centre plane, save that each had three members. Two members of unequal length formed a box girder at the root end, while the third member formed an extension of the box girder. The depth of the girder web tapered continuously from root to tip.

The general construction of the outer plane was similar to that of the centre plane, having ribs and longitudinal stringers. The leading edge, inter-girder and trailing edge portions of the three ribs that carried the flap runners were braced together by eyebolts that accommodated the under-carriage wheel, and troughs in the underside plating formed housings for the flaps and undercarriage struts when retracted. The outer section of the plane contained a watertight compartment formed by the two girders, ribs 8 and 12 and the skin plating. This compartment was fitted with a vent pipe, which was connected to the fuselage vent system. The mainplane tip was provided with a grip for handling purposes and was detachable simply by removing a series of set-screws.

The two ribs at the ends of the aileron gap supported the aileron end bearings; an extension fitting from a rib supported the intermediate bearing. The metal leading edge was cut away between the gun apertures and at the tip, and was replaced by flush-fitting moulded windows for the landing navigation lamps. A stay tube for securing the folded mainplane was stowed in a recess at the trailing edge. Inspection doors were provided for access to the various installations along the wing.

The ailerons were of normal construction for the period, with a single girder-type spar, reinforced by a metal leading edge and ribs pressed from Alclad sheet. The whole was fabric-covered. The hinges were inset and each comprised a self-aligning ball bearing carried in a housing on the outer mainplane, a trunnion fitted in the inner race of the ball bearing, and a clamping socket, which was screwed into a fitting attached to the aileron rib. These sockets fitted over the trunnions and, when screwed fully in, clamped the inner races of the ball bearings. The two outer hinges had one clamping socket, and the centre hinge had two sockets; they were secured in position by split pins, which passed through the socket and fitting. The aileron was connected to the control system by a link plate attached to the leading edge by a sliding bolt, which was secured by a locking plate and a set screw.

The flaps were hydraulically operated and were fitted to each outer mainplane, forward of the trailing edge, and extended from the aileron to the plane root. The flap was a shallow aerofoil of all-metal construction, which, when retracted into the trough, was flush with the plating on the lower surface of the mainplane.

There was a pair of tubular links from the mainplane that suspended the flaps forward of their longitudinal centre line, the leading edges being attached to two carriages apiece, which travelled in runners. The inner carriage of each of these was attached to the jack ram, whose motion was transferred by cables to the outer carriage. An electrical flap position indicator was provided and consisted of a rheostat, connected to the port inner flap link, and an indicator, calibrated in degrees and mounted on the port side of the cockpit below the instrument panel.

To lower the flaps, a lever marked 'F' on the main selector valve box had to be moved to the 'Down' position. Then as soon as the indicator denoted that the flap had reached the desired attitude, the lever had to be returned to the neutral position. The lever would automatically return itself to neutral whenever the flaps were completely down. Similarly, when moved to the 'Up' setting, it would be returned to neutral when the flaps became completely retracted. A balance cable ensured that the individual flap movements were synchronised. In the event of failure of the engine-driven pump, the flaps could also be operated by a hand-lever pump through the main system, and the selector lever operated in the normal manner.

Each of the folding outer planes of the wing were secured to the centre plane by four latch pins, two at each girder, the folding hinge being located abaft the rear girder. Each pin had a crosshead and was connected through a series of levers and links to the screw jack, in which was incorporated a clutch, adjusted to slip at 30 lb, the force required fully to insert the latch pins. A crank handle on the underside of the leading edge operated this jack. An extractor was provided for use in the event of the jack failing to withdraw the pins due to damage to some part of the mechanism.

The method used to fold an outer mainplane, was as follows. The handling rope (BFL 92) was engaged in the hand-hole at the tip and manned by three persons, or, should the hook not be available, a rope sling could be substituted. A fourth handler was required to operate the screw jack. To withdraw the latch pins, the crank handle was turned clockwise. It was essential that the tip had to be supported by the folding crew whilst the latch pins were being withdrawn and that the footstep on the port side of the fuselage had to be in the 'Stowed' position. When the pins were completely withdrawn, the plane could be pulled carefully backwards until it reached the top of its travel, after which point it had firmly to be checked. The fourth handler had to stand by ready to guide the plane stay tube into the socket in the fuselage, turning the head a quarter of a turn once inserted, in order to lock it. The tailplane could not be used as a platform for removing the handling ropes. After folding the planes, the ropes had to remain engaged in each hand-hole until the planes were re-spread and then, and only then, could the ropes be readily detached. To spread the plane, the operations had to be carried out in the reverse order, with the tip supported whilst the latch pins were being inserted. The clutch in the screw jack would slip when the pins were fully inserted.

Should there be damage to the mechanism, which resulted in the latch pins being unable to be withdrawn, an extractor (BGL 85) had to be used to extract each pin individually. This extractor, which had a left-hand thread, had to be screwed into the latch pin and, when fully screwed, was rotated further to shear the aluminium locking pin and to detach the latch pin from the crosshead. The pin could then be withdrawn by using a small mallet on the underside of the tommy bar.

The flying controls

The control surfaces were operated by a system of cables in the then conventional manner. The control column had a knuckle joint, which enabled the upper portion to be moved laterally for aileron control. Near its lower end the column provided an attachment for a tubular member, which was coupled to a lever on the inboard end of the elevator cross shaft. A double-ended lever on the outboard end of the cross shaft provided connection for the elevator cables, which were led rearward to the tail unit. The rudder bar was adjustable and the rudder cables were connected to a lever on the lower end of the rudder bar spindle. Controls were fitted for the rudder and elevator trimming tabs, together with mechanical position indicators.

The control column base was supported in ball bearings, and the knuckle joint enabled the upper portion to move laterally for aileron control. From the foot of the upper portion two chains were led down the column and round chain sprockets, and connected by tie rods and inter-mediate levers to a three-armed lever, which was mounted on the forward wall of the bomb compartment.

A hinge block was secured to the lower portion of the column for the attachment of the tube that connected the column to the elevator cross shaft, the port end of which carried the double-ended lever for the attachment of the elevator control cables.

For aileron control, the chains on the column were connected by tie rods to two levers, which, in turn, were coupled by further tie rods to the horizontal members of a three-armed lever. Cables from the vertical member of this lever were led over pulleys down the centre line of each outer plane hinge and into the leading edges of the ailerons. A balance cable connected both ailerons. A stop, which limited the aileron movement, was incorporated in the knuckle joint on the control column. The aileron movement was 3 inches each way, measured at the trailing edge.

For the elevator control, the control column was connected to the inboard end of the elevator cross shaft by means of a tube that passed beneath the pilot's seat. At the outboard end of the cross shaft was a double-ended lever, from which the control cables were taken and led down the port side of the fuselage and over pulleys to a lever on the intermediate portion of the elevator spar. Fibre guards protected these whenever the cables were led through frames and bulkheads. A second lever on the spar was connected by a link tube to the mass balance arm installed in the fuselage. The elevator movement was 23 degrees up and 17 degrees down and was limited by two collars on the control column connecting tube.

The elevator trim tabs were operated by a hand wheel mounted on the port side of the cockpit. The hand wheel, the larger of two, was connected by a short chain to a sprocket on the port end of a cross shaft. From a sprocket and chain on the opposite end of the shaft, cables were led down the starboard side of the fuselage to terminate at a chain and sprocket. This sprocket formed a nut for the operating screw, which was coupled to a short countershaft; links from this shaft were connected to rocking levers, which in turn were connected to levers on the trimming tab spindles.

The indicator in the cockpit consisted of a short pointer, which slid in a slotted guide tube, and a calibrated scale. The pointer was secured to a push-pull cable, which was operated on the rack and pinion principle through gearing on the end of the cross shaft. The movement of the trimming tab, which was 25 degrees each way, was limited by an aluminium block clamped on the cable. This block travelled with the cable and bore alternately against frame G and bulkhead H.

The rudder control had an adjustable rudder bar and the pedals, which were pivoted on the ends, had parallel motion. The rudder bar was hinged on a centre pivot and a star wheel rotated a screw that had right and left-hand threads, which passed into trunnions, supported by offset lugs on each half of the rudder bar. The action of rotating the star wheel caused the outer extremities of the rudder bar to travel forward or backward as required.

Two pairs of cables were attached to a lever on the rudder bar spindle. Each pair was taken over pulleys on the port and starboard sides of the cockpit and led down the sides of the fuselage to a lever on the rudder post, which extended downward into the fuselage rear end. Again, fibre guards were fitted where the cables passed through frames and bulkheads. The range of movement of the rudder was 28 degrees each way and was limited by the lever slot in the rudder bar pedestal.

The rudder trimming tab control system was similar to that of the elevator tab control. It was operated by the smaller of the two hand-wheels mounted on the port side of the cockpit, and by cables connected to the screw-adjusting gear in the fuselage rear end. The screw was connected to a short, vertically mounted countershaft, which, in turn, was coupled through links and a rocking lever to the tab spindle.

A tab position indicator, identical to that for the elevator tab control, was mounted in a horizontal position on the lower instrument panel and operated by a cable and gearing on the end of the cross shaft. The movement of the tab, which was 25¼ degrees to starboard and 45 degrees to port, was limited by an aluminium block clamped on the cable. This block was located behind the starboard fuel tank, and travelled with the cable and bore alternately on frames D and E.

The rudder balance tab, which was adjusted when the aeroplane was on the ground, was connected by an adjustable tube to a fitting on the rudder hinge. The angle of the tab, relative to the centre line of the aircraft, remained approximately constant through all angular movements of the rudder.

Dual control conversion set

This was introduced for training purposes. It was a complete set of controls that could be installed in the rear cockpit. The assembly was mounted on a floor structure of channel-section members bolted to bulk-head E and frame G. The arrangement of the dual flying controls was similar to that of the normal controls. The lower portion of the control column was connected by two tubes through the medium of an inter-mediate lever to the elevator control countershaft in the front cockpit. The upper portion of the control column was connected by cables, which were led over pulleys on bulkhead D to the aileron control levers. The rudder bar and pedestal were similar to the normal units. The rudder bar was connected by a tube to a quadrant assembled on the port side of the con-version set, the quadrant being connected by two short lengths of cable to links provided.

The instrument panel in the rear cockpit carried the following:

1. Compass, Type P6
2. Fore-and-aft level, Type B
3. Airspeed indicator
4. Altimeter, Mark XIII D
5. Turn-and-bank indicator, Mark IA, Type D
6. Ignition switch
7. Deviation card holder
8. Dimmer switch, Type A
9. Cockpit lamp, Mark II
10. Clock, Mark II

Compressed air systems

The Skua used compressed air systems to operate the wheel brakes and the gun-firing mechanism. The principal components of the installations were the engine-driven BTH/AV-A compressor, in which a relief valve was incorporated, an air reservoir, an oil reservoir and oil trap, an air filter, a pressure-reducing valve and an air pressure gauge. A charging union at the bottom of the fireproof bulkhead was connected through a non-return valve to the main system, and enabled the air reservoir to be charged from an external source.

For the Dunlop Pneumatic Wheel Brake system, with which the Skua I was equipped, the air supply pipe from the engine-driven compressor was connected by way of the oil reservoir and oil trap to the inboard end of the air reservoir mounted on the engine-mounting lower tubes. From a union on the outboard end of the air reservoir, the supply was taken through an air filter to a T-piece, from which pipe lines were taken, respectively, to the pressure gauge in the cockpit and the pressure-reducing valve mounted on the fireproof bulkhead. The reducing valve received air at a pressure of $300 \, lb/in^2$ and reduced the supply pressure to $200 \, lb/in^2$. From the reducing valve, the supply was taken to a second T-piece on the port side of the pilot's cockpit, and this T-piece was connected by pipe lines to the wheel brake system and the gun-firing system, respectively. The brake control lever, attached to the upper end of the control column, was connected to the relay valve mounted on the floor of the cockpit. For parking purposes the lever could be locked in the braking position by a catch.[2] The relay valve was linked to the rudder bar via a short tube.

The gunnery systems

The four forward-firing Browning machine-guns could not be fired individually. The fire control was a single-press button mounted on the upper end of the control column. From the second T-piece, mentioned above, the pressure supply was taken to the button and back to a T-piece in the bomb recess, thence pipes were led to the port and starboard pair of guns in the mainplanes. Flexible pipes were used for the connections on the control column.

The gun-firing button in the Skua I consisted of a valve that was opened by pushing the button. The valve body was screwed into the sub-assembly of the unit and packing formed an airtight joint between the inlet and outlet air pipes. A light spring normally held the valve against its seat and prevented air flowing from the inlet to the outlet pipe. When the push button was depressed against the force of the spring, a pin pressed against the stem of the valve and opened it; the escape of air past the push button was prevented by contact of the seat with a cover and by a lead ring. The button was locked in the 'Safe' position by leaf springs. By turning the knurled head through a quarter of a turn, it could be moved to the 'Fire' position. The button head was locked in position with a bolt and spring washer in the hole.

The fixed Browning automatic forward-firing guns were mounted in pairs in each outer mainplane. They were fired through blast tubes that were passed through the front girder and secured at their front ends to the leading edge of the mainplane, the rear ends being clipped to the gun barrels. The rear support of each gun mounting was adjustable for align-ment and elevation of the gun. Two screws, with star wheels, were pro-vided for this purpose and were locked by their check-nuts after the gun had been correctly sighted. The front gun support could be adjusted for height prior to the gun being placed in position, by fitting shims under the fork seating. The guns were aligned so that their lines of fire were parallel with the ground line and converged at a point 300 to 400 yards ahead of the Skua, when the chord line of the mainplane was at zero incidence.

The Lewis gun was carried on a special mounting and was free to swivel about the top of the mounting arm, which in turn could be moved laterally on a quadrant. Notches were cut in the quadrant to enable the arm to be locked in any desired position by a spring-loaded plunger, which was controlled by a lever and Bowden cable. Compensating gear in the form of a chain and two chain sprockets were incorporated so that the axis of the swivel attachment for the gun, relative to the centre line of the air-craft, remained constant irrespective of its position on the quadrant. A footstep was provided on each side of the cockpit for use when the gun was being operated. When not in use, the Lewis was stowed in a well in the fuselage decking and secured by a catch. The brutal, if unacceptable fact, was that the Lewis gun was a First World War 'left-over' weapon, and was for all intents and purposes, a useless defensive weapon against modern fighter aircraft. It was a disgrace that it was ever contemplated for use and was a good illustration of how low Britain's defences had fallen since 1918.

The Browning magazines each had a capacity for 600 rounds of 0.303 inch (7.62 mm) belted ammunition, and were mounted side-by-side between each pair of guns, the forward magazine feeding the inboard gun and the rear magazine the outboard gun. For loading purposes, a sliding panel was provided on top of each magazine, which could be removed through a door in the underside of the mainplane.

The ammunition was fed to the gun via a feed chute, which linked the magazine to the feed block. The empty cartridges were discharged through a chute fitted beneath the breech casing of each gun, whilst a chute on the inboard side of the inner gun and on the outboard side of the outer gun, discharged the cartridge links through the underside of the mainplane. The Lewis gun ammunition was carried in six magazines, each holding ninety-seven rounds and stowed on the magazine pegs fitted on the port side of the gun station.

To load the Browning, the safety catch of both the firing button on the control column and the gun itself had to first be set to the 'Safe' position; the gun cover was then raised, ammunition passed through the feed chute and the first round entered into the feed block over the belt-holding pawl. The cover was then lowered and the loading handle operated until the first round was ejected through the empty case chute, the cocking stud remaining at the rear of its slide. It was stressed that when feeding the gun from the port side (looking forward) that the double loop of the first link should be fed into the breech. When the gun was fed from the right-hand side, the single loop had to be entered first and the magazine charged accordingly. The gun was then ready to fire when the safety catches were set to the 'Fire' position.

Gun camera provision

Provision was made for the installation of a pneumatically operated cine-camera gun (Type G22B) for practice or training purposes, together with a press switch mounted on the spade grip of the control column, which permitted the camera operation to be independent of the guns. The switch was connected by wiring and a plug to the camera control panel, the plug being marked green. When it was required to operate the camera only, the green socket was plugged in the camera control panel; when the camera and the guns were required to be operated simultaneously, the red socket was plugged in. There was a label fitted on the camera control panel with full instructions. A stowage socket was also provided for the socket, connecting the exposure and footage indicator when the latter was removed from the aircraft.

Bomb gear

The most important armament carried by the Skua was, of course, its single 500 lb bomb. The 500 lb bomb carrier was fitted to a beam attached to the roof of the bomb compartment and could be loaded with a 500 lb SAP weapon. The light series carriers mounted under each wing could be loaded with either four 30 lb bombs, with 11 lb practice bombs or with flares. As with all dive-bombers in the late 1930s, in order to guarantee that the 500 lb bomb cleared the airscrew when released in a steep dive, a bomb ejector arm was fitted. This ejector arm was of tubular construction, with two main longitudinal members, the forward ends of which rotated about a fulcrum attached to the underside of the centre plane front girder. The rear ends of the longitudinal members carried adjustable trunnion caps, which engaged with the trunnions on the bomb. The travel of the ejector arm was limited by rubber buffers on the fulcrum, and compression springs on a central telescopic tube returned the arm to the 'Up' position after the bomb was released. The ejector arm was retained in the 'Up' position by spring-loaded latch pins, which engaged with latch brackets attached to the forward end of the bomb trunk. Provision was made for the use of bomb hoisting gear, which was not carried in the Skua during flight. A panel was provided to close the aperture in the fairing when a bomb was not carried.

The bomb was loaded into the carrier by means of the hoist, doors being provided in the fairing for the hoisting cables. When the bomb was engaged with and held by the claw of the bomb carrier, the ejector arm was raised into position and the trunnion caps on the end adjusted to engage the trunnions on the bomb. The adjusting screw had to be locked by its locknuts after the adjustment had been made. When the ejector arm was raised into position, care had to be taken to set the latch pins correctly, both pins being pulled out so that the stop engaged with the inboard face of the stop plate. On release of the bomb from the carrier, its weight carried the ejector arm downwards, the bomb automatically leaving the open jaws of the trunnion caps. The bomb fusing and release controls were electronically operated from the cockpit.

Smoke floats

On each side of the bomb compartment were two smaller compartments, which housed smoke floats, in-line fore-and-aft, and let into the under-surface of the centre plane. The upper portion of the main compartment was closed by the detachable fairing as mentioned above, the bomb being carried below this fairing. The smaller compartments had hinged doors, which were opened by the weight of the floats when they were released; springs on the hinges returned the doors to the closed positions.

*: The original 'short-nosed' prototype
th her distinctive colour scheme, with
nding gear fully down. From the second
ototype onward, the nose was lengthened
2 feet 4³/₄ inches. The wing-tip slots,
own here locked, were dropped from the
oduction batches due to stalling problems.
e Aeroplane)

ntre: The first prototype, K5178, banks
*r*ay from the camera during her maiden
*g*ht. (*Author's collection*)

The first prototype Skua-1, as finished early in 1937, with Mercury engine,
before being painted up for the Hendon Air Display promotion. (*Author's Collection*)

The first prototype, K5178, with the Mercury engine cowling removed. The RAF wanted this power plant for its own aircraft, forcing the Skua to adopt the Pegasus engine as the only alternative.
(*Author's collection*)

The unique wing-foldi[ng] method utilised [by] Blackburn's for the Sk[ua] demonstrated here on [the] first prototype, K5178. T[his] method had been first us[ed] on the same compan[y's] Airedale ten years earli[er]. (*Oyvind Lar*[sen])

4. The first prototype, K5178, was completed with the Mercury engine as her maiden flight on 9 February 1937, painted in a unique colour scheme of overall 'Battleship Grey' fuselage, with white wing surfaces and mainplane.
(*RAF Museum, Hendon, London*)

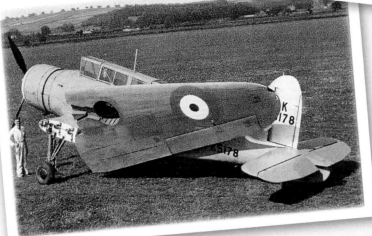

The first production Skua, L2867, in a steady climb. She was completed in 1937 and immediately flown to the A & AEE at Martlesham Heath on 14 of that month for intensive trials. These revealed several shortcomings, not the least a tendancy to spin, which caused many headaches before it was 'cured', including the fitting of a special 'lash-up', a spin parachute. (*MOI via Author's Collection*)

The production line at Brough really got into its stride in 1939. Here a batch of freshly minted Skuas is given a final shine for the benefit of the cameras. (*The Aeroplane*)

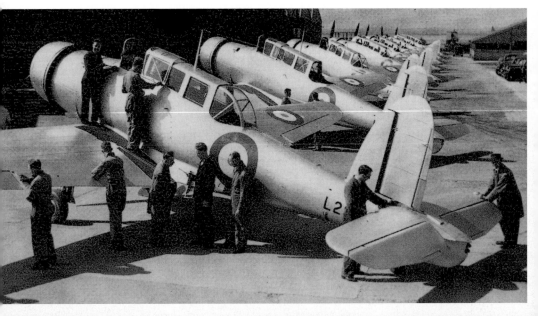

Line-up of the very last production batch of nine Skuas outside the Brough factory, May 1939. L2953 is in the foreground. These aircraft were delivered to No. 10 Maintenance Unit, RAF, on 22 May and transferred to the Admiralty two days later. (*Imperial War Museum, London*)

L2887 of No. 803 Squadron, coded A7F, seen here in her pre-war colour scheme. She totes a single practice bomb on her port outboard light carrier.
(*Ray C. Sturtivent*)

Skua L2873 at Brough. She was delivered to No. 803 Squadron at Worthy Down on 2 January 1939. (*Author's collection*)

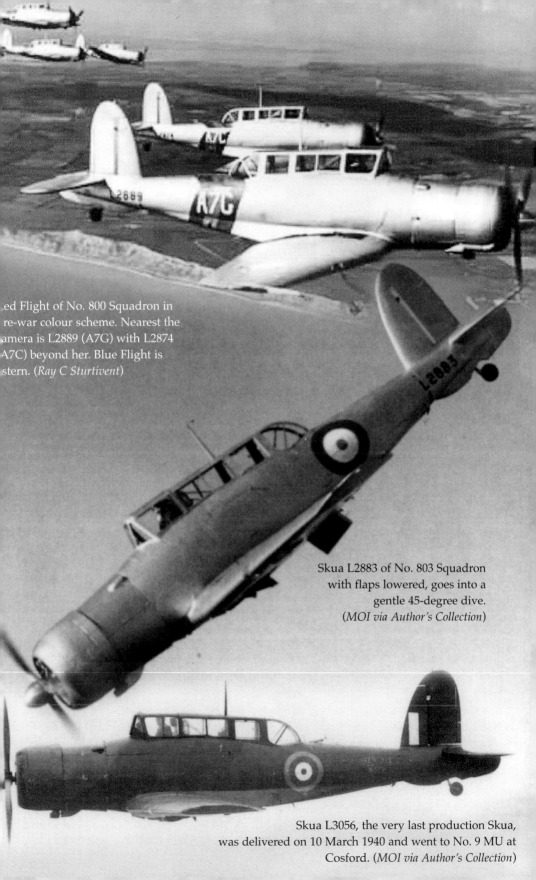

...ed Flight of No. 800 Squadron in
...re-war colour scheme. Nearest the
...amera is L2889 (A7G) with L2874
...A7C) beyond her. Blue Flight is
...stern. (*Ray C Sturtivent*)

Skua L2883 of No. 803 Squadron
with flaps lowered, goes into a
gentle 45-degree dive.
(*MOI via Author's Collection*)

Skua L3056, the very last production Skua,
was delivered on 10 March 1940 and went to No. 9 MU at
Cosford. (*MOI via Author's Collection*)

The Skua pilot's domain. Above the ring stick is the ring-and-bead electronic sight, which the pilots used in lieu of the automatic dive-bombing sight the Royal Navy had requested but failed to obtain. On the main panel the dials are for the airspeed indicator, artificial horizon, clime rate indicator, altimeter, turn and bank indicator and gyro compass. To the port side the panel houses the undercarriage position indicator, clock, magneto switches, starter push button and panel lamp dimmers switches; that on the startboard side houses the rev counter, boost pressure gauge, cylinder head temperature gauge and oil temperature gauges, and cowl flap level. The lower port side panel houses the elevator and rudder trim indicators, flap position indicator and hydraulic pressure gauge. The lower starboard side panel contains the auxiliary tank, port and starboard tank fuel gauge and f primer pump. (*Oyvind Lamo*)

Looking forward from the rear cabin toward the pilot's cabin along the long cockpit. The two main fuel tanks made for uneasy company between the two aircrew! (*Oyvind Lamo*)

Along the starboard side of the cockpit the pilot had various controls, among them those controlling the navigation lights, release of smoke floats, initiating the spin parachute, with the map box in the cockpit floor. (*Oyvind Lamo*).

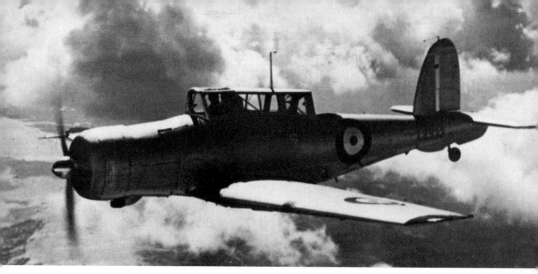

L2933 of No. 800 Squadron. Seen over Portsmouth Harbour in early 1939.

(*MOI via Author's Collection*)

First 'confirmed' kill. The Dornier Do18 floatplane brought down by attacks from the Skuas of Lieutenant B. S. McEwan and Petty Officer B. M. 'Horse' Seymour and Lieutenant C. L. G. Evans and Lieutenant W. A. Robertson, on 26 September 1939. No. 803 Squadron operating from *Ark Royal*. (*MOI via John Dell*)

Another view of the Dornier Do18 brough down by the Skuas of No. 803 Squadron on 26 September 1939. The destroyer *Somali*, part of *Ark Royal*'s escort, is seen closing her to rescue the crew. Claims of an earlier kill being made by RAF Battles had not been fully confirmed when this aircraft was destroyed, and only later, with French eyewitness statements, was the Skua claim disputed. (*MOI via John Dell*)

Bombing-up a Skua aboard a carrier early in the war. With a mixed team of both Royal Navy and RAF personnel utilising the special bomb-trolley. The swing bomb-crutch designed to throw the bomb clear of the aircraft propeller during a dive attack can clearly be seen.

(Courtesy Fleet Air Arm Museum, Yeovilton)

Even with her wings fully folded the Skua was an nice fit for some of the lifts of the fleet aircraft carriers. Here an aircraft of No. 803 Squadron is seen being struck down.

(Courtesy Fleet Air Arm Museum, Yeovilton)

The old aircraft carrier *Argus* was used as a training carrier in the sheltered waters of the western Mediterranean during 1939/40. Here Captain A. E. Marsh, R. M. (centre) is seen with LAC Brooks, R. (to Marsh's left) at Bordeaux with French officers, while ferrying a Skua out to Toulon for training duties. (*Courtesy Fleet Air Arm Museum, Yeovilton*)

A nice view of a Skua with hook fully extended and flaps down, making her final approach to land aboard the carrier *Furious*. (*Author's collection*)

Skua L2933, 'K' with No. 800 Squadron from 18 April 1939, here seen flown by Lieutenant K. V. V. Spurway. (*Ray C. Sturtivent*)

A rather murcky photo, which nonetheless illustrates the camouflage pattern adopted by land-based Skuas in 1940. (*Ray C. Sturtivent*)

A flurry of activity as ground crew rush to attend to a just-arrived Skua, which has taken a wire nicely to full stretch aboard the *Furious*. The guns would have to be unloaded by the armourers before the aircraft was struck down on the lifts to the hangar deck, where the riggers would secure her in position and the engineers would check her power plant. (*Author's collection*).

Hunting the *Admiral Graf Spee*. Patrolling the South Atlantic 1940. A Skua leaves the *Ark Royal*'s port accelerator. In the background the battlecruiser HMS *Renown* refuels the destroyer *Hero*. A second 'H' class destroyer patrols in the background. (*Author's collection*)

No. 800 Squadron aboard HMS *Ark Royal* at Freetown, Sierra Leone, in January 1940.

(*Courtesy of the late R.S. Rolph, BEM*)

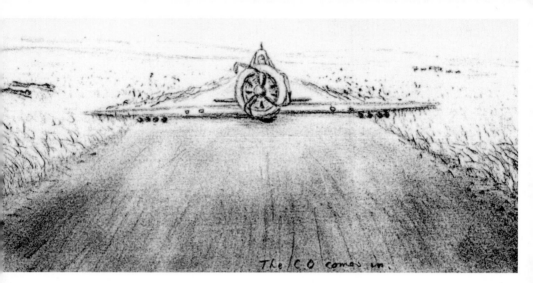

he CO comes in!' Black and white sketch by one of the squadron armourers showing an emergency wheels-up' landing back at Hatston by the Commanding Officer of No. 800 Squadron, Lieutenant ommander G. N. Torry, during the early days of 1940. (*R. S. Rolph, BEM*)

Some landings are better than others! Here a Skua comes to an unfortunate termination aboard the carrier *Furious*.
(*MOI via Author's Collection*)

The defining attack of the Skua's career, the sinking of the German light cruiser *Königsberg* at Bergen in April 1940. It is perfectly captured in the well known painting by C. E. Turner. (*Fleet Air Arm Museum, Yeovilton*)

'Bombing-up' the Skua. The bombs were brought up from the bomb rooms and loaded on the carrier decks in Royal Navy practice. The ground team (still a mix of RN and RAF personnel) manoeuvred the bomb trolley with a 550-lb SAP in place, on the flight deck of a carrier to lead it onto the bomb cradle of Skua '6H'. (*Author's collection*)

Sequence of photos taken of the *Königsberg* 'being put out of action' by Skua bombs at Bergen on 10 April 1940. (*The Jennie Erwick Collection, courtesy of Michael Hart via John Dell*)

The *Königsberg* just after the Skua attack, with large fuel fires burning aft and the ship starting to list.
(*The Jennie Erwick Collection, courtesy of Michael Hart via John Dell*)

The *Königsberg* burning and keeling over to port at Bergen. (*The Jennie Erwick Collection, courtesy of Michael Hart via John Dell*)

The *Königsberg's* final plunge. (*The Jennie Erwick Collection, courtesy of Michael Hart via John Dell*)

The wreckage of the *Königsberg's* Arado floatplane alongside on the dock. (*The Jennie Erwick Collection, courtesy of Michael Hart via John Dell*)

A Skua takes off from the flight deck of HMS *Glorious* into the dawn sky. Operations from *Glorious* off Norway were successful, but finally curtailed by her captain's insistence on only having one type of aircraft aboard his ship, the Gladiator, to simplify handling and stowage. (*MOI via Author's collection*)

Skua down in Norway, with the engine separated from the fuselage and the cockpit gutted by fire by her aircrew. (*Via John Dell*)

Another Skua wreck in the Norwegian snow. (*Oyvind Lamo*)

Electrical equipment

In general, the electrical equipment provided the lighting and bomb-release functions. The power supply derived from a 12 volt, 500 watt engine-driven generator that charged a 12 volt 25 ampere-per-hour accumulator.

The navigation, formation, flying and identification lamps comprised the following:

1. Port and starboard navigation lamps, installed in the leading edges of the mainplane tips and the tail lamp in the fuselage and fairing. These were controlled by a switch in the pilot's cockpit.
2. Formation flying lamps installed in the trailing edges of the mainplane tips and in the rear end fairing. The light intensity of these lamps was controlled by a rheostat.
3. Upward and downward Identification lamps were fitted with a circuit that allowed independent or simultaneous use, via the Morse key or, alternatively, emitted a steady illumination from either or both lamps.
4. A Type G landing lamp was installed in the leading edge of the port mainplane. This was a spring-loaded unit and had cockpit-control deflection.
5. Cockpit lighting for the instruments was provided with lamps with dimmer switches to both front and rear cockpits, with an explosive-proof lamp fitted above the chart board.
6. Inspection lamp and lead, stowed on the starboard side of the bomb recess in the rear cockpit, with several plug-in sockets distributed around at 'suitable locations'.

Signalling lamp and pistol

An Aldis signalling lamp was stowed on the starboard side of the bomb recess in the rear cockpit. The signalling pistol was mounted on the floor of the front cockpit and fired through a tube that passed through the watertight compartment to the lower surface of the centre plane. This pistol was held in position by a pair of clips bolted to the floor. A second signal pistol and holster were provided in the rear cockpit.

Marine gear and ancillary equipment

Determined to burden its first monoplane with every conceivable device to add yet more weight and reduce whatever fighter potential it might posses, the Admiralty loaded the following items, some vital for carrier operations, some perhaps not, onto the already overtaxed Skua before sending her into combat.

The arrester gear arrangement comprised three units, the tailhook, the stowage catch and control, and the damping system. The tailhook was mounted at the apex of two V-struts, the opposite ends of which were supported in bearings attached to frame H. The whole unit was free to swing in the vertical plane, and was detachable for maintenance or replacement purposes. The stowage latch was installed in a recess of the watertight compartment, and was connected by cables to the release control rod in the cockpit. To lower the arrester hook, the control rod was depressed to withdraw the latch bar and the hook swung downward. The pilot was unable to raise the hook from the cockpit and once down, it remained down!

An electric indicator, consisting of a green lamp, was mounted on the cockpit coaming adjacent to the control lever. A plunger switch, in contact with a cam on the arrester gear bearing tube, switched on the lamp when the hook went down, and extinguished it immediately the hook was moved from that position.

A collapsible dinghy and a cylinder containing carbon dioxide for its inflation were installed in a locker on the starboard side of the fuselage above the watertight compartment. Two releases were provided, one in the rear cockpit and the other on the tail unit, either of which operated the piercing head on the carbon dioxide cylinder. As the dinghy inflated, it forced open the panel and was expelled from the locker. It was anchored to the fuselage by a 15-foot length of cord to prevent it drifting away before the crew could board.

The Skua carried a methyl bromide fire extinguisher installed on the starboard side of the rear cockpit. A pipe from the nozzle seating was connected to a spray mounted above the carburettor. An upward movement of the lever released the contents of the bottle to the spray, or alternatively, the bottle could be removed from the mounting and directed at the blaze by hand.

The Skua's oxygen supply was simultaneously drawn from a pair of cylinders mounted on each side of the bomb compartment in the rear cockpit. These cylinders were connected to a pressure regulator and flow meter fitted in each cockpit, whence the supply was taken to bayonet sockets 'conveniently' mounted for the attachment of the face mask when required.

The front cockpit seat accommodated a standard seat-type parachute. A stowage rack for a pack-type parachute was provided on the port side of the rear cockpit. Originally, provision had been made for carrying a spin parachute in the rear fairings of the tail unit. From the front cockpit two cables were taken and connected, one to the parachute release door and the other to a catch, which, when opened, would jettison the parachute.

There was also a hinged, tubular frame provided on the starboard side of the rear cockpit to accommodate the standard Bigsworth Chart Board. When not in use, the frame, with the board attached, was stowed vertically against the side of the fuselage and secured with a simple clamp.

The Skua also carried a canvas 'hold-all' on the port side of the rear cockpit, which was divided into pockets to hold various navigation instruments. Separate stowage was also provided for the course and wind calculator. The two cockpits were provided with two-way speaking tubes, which ran along the port side of the cabin. Finally, there was a first-aid outfit on the inside of the port door of the wireless compartment. Also, a fireman's axe was stowed in the rear cockpit.

The target towers

A great many Skuas ended their days performing the lowly duty of target tug. This seemed to be the fate for dive-bombers in Great Britain, for while other nations used them daily in combat, most British aircraft of this type were relegated to this second-line chore. So the Skua joined the ranks of the Hawker Henley, Brewster Bermuda and Vultee Vengeance.

Provision had already been made for fitting towed target gear to the Skua in the rear cockpit compartment. The various items that made up this equipment depended on whether the towing was for anti-aircraft gunnery or machine-gunnery practice. The installation comprised the winch gear for an AA winch, Type B, mounted on the coaming, guide pulleys for the cable, a flag target container and three Bowden control levers. The flag target container was installed in the bomb trunk, and release of the targets was controlled by the three control levers, painted respectively red, white and green. Provision was also made for carrying three sleeve targets, two of which could be carried in a sling on the port side of the bomb trunk, while the third was stowed under the wireless equipment. The halyards for these targets were stowed on three magazine pegs, which were also painted red, white and green. Leg guard tubes were fitted, which could be folded and stowed in order to facilitate access to the door in the cockpit floor.

A knife, wire cutters and a marline-spike were included in the equipment, together with a special outer tube for the wing-folding stay; this tube was longer than the standard stay and permitted the plane to be folded with the winch in position. To prevent the towing cable from fouling the tail unit, a guard tube was fitted to the tail-wheel fork, and guard cables were fitted on the underside of the tail plane. When the MG triple drum winch, Type D, was fitted instead, a winch mounting (DFT 306) was fitted to the coaming brackets, using the existing cockpit side panels.

When the AA winch was used, the installation allowed the following target arrangements to be utilised:

1. Three vertical 5 feet 5 inch flag targets (not exceeding 57 lb) or
2. Three horizontal 5 feet 5 inch flag targets (not exceeding 57 lb) or
3. Three 4 feet sleeve targets (not exceeding 55 lb).

When the triple drum winch was employed, the installation permitted the following target arrangements.

1. Three 4 feet astern attack targets (not exceeding 23 lb) or
2. Three 3 feet astern attack targets (not exceeding 16 lb).

The power plant

During the first tentative discussion on a replacement aircraft for the Hawker Osprey in 1933, the DNAD had called for a float version to operate from the trade protection cruisers of the fleet as a combined reconnaissance/strike aircraft, able to glide-bomb targets. A specification for this latter type was complicated by restrictions on dimensions to fit the hangar space aboard such ships, which limited it to a 16 feet 2 inch folded wingspan, a length of 36 feet and a height of 14 feet. The unfolded wingspan was finalised at 46 feet. The other limitation was imposed by the weight capability of the launching catapult on these cruisers, which was 5,500 lb (later raised to 6,000 lb). The Air Ministry calculated that the only available engine able to meet these requirements was the proposed Bristol Aquila II, a nine-cylinder, single-row engine rated at just 500 hp. However, this would only give the new aircraft a top speed of 179 mph, absurdly just 5 mph faster than the aircraft it was due to replace!

To raise the new aircraft's maximum speed to a more useful (and realistic) 209 mph, at 14,500 feet, the Bristol Pegasus II engine was considered, but this would have pushed the aircraft's all-up weight to 7,210 lb, again, ruling it out for cruiser launching.[3] Fortunately, the Admiralty's decision to go for a carrier-based dive-bomber finally obviated that complication. Even so, finding the most suitable power plant proved difficult, due to the old problem of priorities,' and the decisions taken fatally affected the Skua's final performance.

The Bristol Engine Company's[4] Perseus (designed by Roy Fedden, with Leonard Butler as his chief draughtsman), had first appeared on the scene in 1932, the year before the embryo Skua's discussions process. Following the successful radial engine, the Mercury, the Perseus became that firm's first sleeve-valve type engine to be successful enough to go into production. The concept of the sleeve-valve engine had been championed by the RAE in a series of papers published in 1925/6. The principle offered the prospect of both a simpler and more efficient engine especially at high rpm, by utilising a rotating sleeve inside the cylinder instead of the then conventional poppet valve. This sleeve had holes in it, which, as it rotated, lined up with those in the cylinder and opened and closed the valve. Such a method also did away with the need for space-consuming push rods or rockers. The theory was fine, but finding a practical way through the problems involved, including bursting sleeves, took a further 6 years and much money and sweat, but the arrival of the Aquila and the larger 580 hp Perseus was fortunate. The Perseus had an all-up weight of 1,026 lb (466 kg), and was rated at 540 hp (400 kW) at 2,400 rpm. The engine's bore by stroke was 5.75×6.5 inches (146×165 mm) and the displacement was 1,520 in^3 (24.9 litres). This engine was followed progressively by improved marks, which took the Perseus to 810 hp in 1936 and to 930 hp by the eve of the war, and later led to the highly successful twinned Hercules and Centaurus developments of later years.

Both the two Skua prototypes were powered by the more conventional Bristol Mercury IX nine-cylinder, air-cooled, poppet-valve, radial engine, rated at 840 hp, which was also fitted to the RAF's Gloster Gladiator biplane fighter. However, the Mercury engine was shortly afterwards allocated exclusively to the RAF for their Bristol Blenheim programme and was no longer available for Royal Navy aircraft.

The version of this engine finally utilised to haul the Skua through the sky was the Bristol Perseus XII aero-engine. This engine was a nine-cylinder sleeve-valve radial type, with the cylinders themselves equi-distance around a nine-sided crankcase. Immediately in front of the crankcase was situated the front cover, by means of which the drive for the sleeve mechanism was enclosed. The reduction gear, which provided a speed reduction of 0.5 to 1, was mounted on the forward face of the front cover. Behind the crankcase was the gear-driven supercharger and astern of this was the rear cover, which formed the base for some of the auxiliary components. The rest of these auxiliaries were mounted on an accessory gearbox, which was totally separate from the engine, but was driven by it through a drive shaft connected to the auxiliary drive shaft in the engine rear cover. A two-piece crankshaft was fitted, the joint between the halves being made at the crankpin, which enabled a solid master rod and a one-piece big-end bush to be employed. An inertia starter jaw was fitted at the rearmost end of the crankshaft.

The cylinder barrels were machined from aluminium-alloy drop-forgings, with each barrel being equipped with three inlet and two exhaust ports. Special steel-alloy sleeves were employed for the barrels and each sleeve was provided with two inlet ports, one exhaust port, and one combined inlet and exhaust port. The cylinder heads were of cast alloy and were retained at the upper end of their respective barrels by studs. The two spark plugs of each cylinder were screwed into adaptors located close to the centre of the head.

The AVT 85MC master control carburettor incorporated a three-stage variable datum automatic boost control unit and a two-stage automatic mixture control unit. As the carburettor was fully automatic in its functioning, the responsibilities of the pilot were reduced to the minimum and the danger of engine damage resulting from incorrect setting was obviated.

A high initial oil pressure device was incorporated in the oil pump unit, which was located at the port side of the rear cover, the purpose of this being to ensure adequate lubrication of the engine during the early stages of running. During normal operation, the device automatically went out of action.

The basic particulars of the Bristol Perseus XII were as outlined in Table 6.[5]

Table 6   Bristol Perseus XII engine

Type of engine	9-cylinder sleeve-valve air-cooled radial, supercharged
Bore	5.75 in
Stroke	6.5 in
Swept volume	1520 in^3
Compression ratio	6.75 to 1
Reduction gear ratio	0.5 to 1
Direction of rotation of airscrew shaft	Left hand
Direction of rotation of crankshaft	Left hand
Supercharger gear ratio	7 to 1
Weight, dry, less inertia starter and auxiliary drive gearbox	1,093 lb
Cylinder numbering (viewed from rear)	1, 2, 3, 4, 5, 6, 7, 8, 9 counter-clockwise Cylinder No. 1 vertical

Performance

International power rating	715/745 bhp at 2,400 rpm at 6,500 ft and +1¼ lb/in^2 boost
Maximum power rating	905 bhp at 2,750 rpm at 6,500 ft, and +2½ lb/in^2 boost
Maximum take-off power	795/830 bhp, at 2,650 rpm, at +2½ lb/in^2 boost
Minimum take-off	2,180 rpm at full throttle

Limiting operational conditions

(1) Maximum take-off (3 minutes or 1,000 feet)
Maximum rpm	2,650
Minimum rpm	2,180
Boost	+2½ lb/in^2

(2) Maximum climbing (30 minute limit)
rpm	2,400
Boost	+1¼ lb/in^2
Cylinder temperature	250°C

(3) Maximum level flight (5 minute limit)
rpm	2,750
Boost	+2½ lb/in^2
Cylinder temperature	260°C

(continued)

Table 6   (*continued*)

---

(4) Maximum cruising (with automatic rich mixture)
    rpm   2,400
    Boost $+1\frac{1}{4}\,lb/in^2$
    Cylinder temperature $230°C$
(5) Maximum cruising (with automatic weak mixture)
    rpm   2,400
    Boost $-\frac{1}{2}\,lb/in^2$
    Cylinder temperature $230°C$
(6) Maximum for TV dive (maximum 20 seconds)
    rpm   3,120
    Boost $+2\frac{1}{2}\,lb/in^2$

Fuel

Type: Specification DTD 230
Consumptions:
(1) At maximum take-off conditions at   73.5 gallons per hour
    sea level (830 bhp at 2,650 rpm)
(2) At maximum climbing conditions at   60.3 gallons per hour
    sea level (745 bhp at 2,400 rpm)
(3) At maximum cruising (automatic   0.65 pints per bhp hour
    rich mixture) conditions at sea level
    (as above)
(4) At economical cruising (automatic   0.494 pints per bhp hour
    weak mixture) ($-\frac{1}{2}$ per in^2 boost at
    2,400 rpm)

Oil

Type   Specification, DTD 109
Pump pressures
    Normal $80\,lb/in^2$
    Minimum (5 minute limit) $70\,lb/in^2$
Consumption   8 to 14 pints per hour at 2,400 rpm
Inlet oil temperatures
    Take-off (minimum for cold starting) $5°C$ or $15°C$ (with early type oil pumps)
    Maximum for continuous cruising $70°C$
    Maximum for climbing $80°C$
    Emergency maximum (5 minute limit) $90°C$

Ignition

Firing order   1, 3, 5, 7, 9, 2, 4, 6, 8
Magnetos   Two BTH C2SE-9S or C3SE-9S
Direction of rotation   Counter-clockwise
Speed of rotation   1.125 engine speed
Ignition timing   Fixed at 13° before TDC
High-tension leads   Marconi harness

(*continued*)

Table 6   (*continued*)

Carburation	
Carburettor	AVT 85 MC
Chokes	Two, 76 mm
Main jets (cc)	Two, 2,350, 2,400, 2,450, 2,500 or 2,500
Power jet (cc)	One, 1,700
Power bleed jet	Inoperative – blind jet was fitted
Slow running jets (cc)	Two, 400
Enrichment jet (cc)	One, 700
Restrictor plug for delayed action pump (cc)	One 700
Air box jets	
Upper	Two 3.5 mm
Lower	Two 4 mm
Starting systems	Cartridge starter (Skua I and Roc)
Airscrew	Variable-pitch

NOTES

1. *The Blackburn Skua I*, in National Archives RTP 4618/291.
2. The rules for parking aircraft equipped with differentially controlled brakes were contained in AMO A114/30 and had to be carefully followed in the case of the Skua.
3. Aspects of Skua development are contained in National Archives ADM 1/10103, *op cit.*
4. The engine division of the Bristol Aircraft Company at Weston-super-Mare.
5. From Air Ministry Pamphlet AP 1589C, Vol. I. (M24019/18. January 1940. C&P) (copy in author's collection).

5

AFLOAT AT LAST

As we have seen, the first six Skua-IIs to enter service in October 1938, were assigned to No. 800 Squadron at Worthy Down. They went on to join one other front-line squadron, No. 803, before the outbreak of war just a year later, on 3 September 1939. No. 801 Squadron was formed at Donibristle with six Skuas in January 1940, under the command of Lieutenant Commander H. P. Bramwell, RN, who led them until April. A fourth squadron, No. 806 Squadron, was designated to receive the Skua. The Commanding Officer, Lieutenant Commander D. R. F. Cambell, had been designated as early as November 1938, but the squadron did not actually form at Eastleigh with eight Skuas and four Rocs, until February 1940.

No. 800 Squadron had transferred from the carrier *Courageous* to the new carrier *Ark Royal* in November 1938, when the existing Nimrod aircraft were replaced by the six Skuas from Worthy Down. The Commanding Officer was Lieutenant Commander G. N. Torry, RN (initially a Flight Lieutenant, RAF), and he led the unit from November 1938 to April 1940. The Osprey flight was retained aboard the carrier until the eve of the war, when the whole squadron was disembarked at Hatson RNAS in the Orkneys. The last days of peace saw the squadron conducting search missions between the Orkneys and the Norwegian coast, in the hope of tracking German warships breaking out into their 'waiting' positions in the Atlantic, and merchant ships scurrying home. The outbreak of war found this squadron, still equipped with just six Skuas on its strength, back aboard the *Ark Royal*, which was lying at the main fleet base of Scapa Flow with units of the Home Fleet under Admiral Sir Charles Forbes.

Finally, No. 803 Squadron had three Ospreys replaced by six Skuas aboard *Ark Royal*. In March 1939, Lieutenant Commander C. A. Kingsley-Rowe was appointed as their new Commanding Officer, and on 3 September 1939 the squadron had nine Skuas on its strength. Even with two squadrons of Skuas embarked, the new carrier was very lightly equipped compared with carriers in the United States or Japanese navies. Thus, although it had been calculated that the *Ark Royal* could accommodate a maximum of twenty-two Skuas (along with forty-two TSRs) for a total complement of sixty-four aircraft, their most likely opponents, the

new Japanese *Hiryū* of similar displacement, could carry seventy-three
aircraft and the American *Yorktown* ninety-six.[1]

Gaining the new dive-bomber was one thing, learning the correct techniques to apply when using it was another. Major Alan Marsh, Royal
Marines, recalled that dive-bombing did not feature much in pre-war
training:

> Checking through my own log books and diaries I can only trace a
> modest amount of very elementary practice in Harts and similar.
> Basically this consisted of diving at the target at an angle of about
> 45 degrees using the gun sight for aim – at about 500 feet you pulled
> out of the dive, counting three as the target disappeared and then
> releasing the bomb. One developed one's own technique by practice.
> This was before the Skua came into service and so far as I can
> ascertain any training in the Skua was done with the Squadron.[2]

This was not always so, but certainly right up to the eve of the war training
had to be done with biplanes, all that were available, which proved to be a
very different technique to that demanded by the Skua. Captain T. W.
Harrington, DSC, described just what this involved as late as 1939:

> I see from my log book that the final Pre-War Dive-Bombing
> Training was on February 9th 1939, in one of the old [Hawker] Hart
> variants. By April of that year at practice camp, I achieved a
> grouping of 29 yards with eight practice bombs, which seemed to
> satisfy the experts at Sutton Bridge. I do recall, we all used to cheat a
> bit, by going down as low as we dared (from both the Range Safety
> Officer's viewpoint, as well as from a personal view!) This habit was
> to exact a nasty penalty in War conditions. The military objective of
> doing this dive-bombing was simply that it was then the best method
> of achieving accuracy. The exchange rate of aircraft vulnerability was
> recognised generally, but what was not very widely foreseen was the
> limitations imposed by the bombs available then and the methods
> that would be needed to achieve target destruction. Here I have in
> mind the differing needs of, say, a heavily armoured target (capital
> ship or fortification) or just of personnel or even very lightly con-
> structed targets (merchant ships, small bridges or radar systems).
>
> From the UK point of view, I think that the Admiralty was the first
> British service to achieve a specific aircraft with designed (and
> achieved) dive bombing characteristics. This was the Blackburn Skua
> (named after a formidable seabird, that dives bodily into the sea after
> its food) but it was somehow intended to fill both that role and that of
> a fighter. The Royal Air Force had also put out a staff requirement
> for a dive bomber and Hawker's famous Sidney Camm produced a
> typical Camm solution, the Henley, with his classic lines, as remem-

bered and seen in the Hurricane, Tempest and Sea Fury. The Henley flew beautifully, had excellent dive brakes and no doubt would have been a formidable strike aircraft. However, the fates and conflicts of priority in this defensive period had the effect of turning the excellent Henley into a target-towing workhorse – a great pity in the event.[3]

The arrival of the Skua made relatively little difference to the training methods, at least initially, as Colonel F. D. G. Bird recalled:

In March 1939, No. 800 Squadron was flying twelve Hawker Ospeys, having changed from nine Nimrods and three Ospreys because the Nimrod's wings did not fold and the lifts of her parent ship *Ark Royal*, would not accept a Nimrod. At the end of the month we were re-equipped with twelve Skuas, three of which were later replaced by Rocs which had a four-gun turret in the rear cockpit.

The Skua was described to us as a fleet fighter/dive-bomber and was the Navy's first monoplane. As a fighter it belied its title, being too heavy and unmanoeuvrable for that role, but, as a dive-bomber, it was well designed [and] steady in the dive. Visibility for the pilot was good for both dive-bombing and deck landing.

Bombs were carried on external bomb racks and the method of attack was to approach from up-sun, half rolling into a dive of between 70 and 80 degrees. If the sun offered no advantage, four flights of three aircraft each would approach the target in a four-leaf clover pattern, synchronised to arrive in succession from directions 90 degrees apart.

When re-equipping with Skuas, the squadron was stationed at Worthy Down, which had operated Royal Flying Corps bombers in the First World War. There was a target in the middle of the grass airfield and quadrant positions on the perimeter. We used to do a good deal of practice bombing with 3½lb practice bombs, which we also used when embarked to bomb a target towed by the carrier or by her attendant destroyer.

The bombs for use in earnest which we have cause to remember was called a Cooper. For all it was worth it could well have originated from a Marmalade factory in Dundee. Most of its puff went up-wards![4]

Others were to be thrown into action with no dive-bombing knowledge whatsoever. Vice-Admiral Sir Donald Gibson was trained as a naval pilot at Donibristle and Eastleigh, flying both the Sea Gladiator and the Skua, but he was to recall of the Skua:

It was one of the poorest fighter aircraft in history but at times it had success as a dive-bomber in the hands of well worked-up crews. I was not one of them, I had never dive-bombed anything, neither had dive-bombing been taught at the fighter school, nor was there any chance to train new crews in 803 Squadron.[5]

Early colour schemes

The standard pre-war colour scheme used by the Fleet Air Arm was a silver dope overall finish, the exhaust collector rings in front of the cowlings being a 'dirty bronze' shade. While No. 800 Squadron was operating from *Ark Royal* before the war, its Skuas were identified by three coloured bands around the rear fuselage. Typical serials and markings at this time were:

L2874 – coded A7C
L2880 – coded A7H
L2881 – coded A7L
L2887 – coded A7F
L2889 – coded A7G[6]
L2961 – coded A7? (aircraft letter not recorded)

The serials were painted in black and repeated under the wings, to read from the front below the starboard wing, and to read from the rear below the port. The coloured fuselage bands were roundel blue/red/roundel blue in that order. The i/d codes were white, painted across the bands.

No. 801 Squadron was fitted out with Skuas in the late summer of 1939 and went to *Ark Royal*. The squadron was disembarked to Hatston in September 1939, then re-embarked for North Sea operations on 25/26 of that month, before moving to the carrier *Furious* on 3 October 1939. Its Skuas were painted dark green/dark earth with pale (non-standard) grey undersides. The all-silver pre-war finish was apparently limited to No. 800 Squadron's machines.

Some Skuas were later seen in Target-Towing finish, and at least one was flown in 1938 in a silver finish with bright red diagonals painted on all surfaces, conforming to the style of later Target-Tug stripes. Yet another aircraft was L3007, a much photographed and publicised aircraft, which was finished in deep blue as for Target-Tug types. The exact purpose of these experimental finishes does not appear to have been recorded, although they were not from any operational unit and more than likely served as gunnery-trainers or similar operations.

Comparison with contemporary dive-bombers

It may be instructive at this point to compare the Skua with other dedicated dive-bombers in service, or about to enter service, with other air arms. Most of these machines were naval aircraft, like the Skua, only the

Luftwaffe among the land-based air forces (if one excludes the United States Marine Corps), adopting the method.[7]

So how does the Skua rate against these foreign dive-bombers of the same vintage? Immediately it is obvious that range is a principal factor in naval aircraft. Compare the German Ju87 Stuka with any of its naval rivals and it is obvious that this dive-bomber was built for close support of the army from airstrips and bases close to the front line. Carrier-based aircraft have reach as an important requirement, especially so in the wide wastes of the Pacific, where the American SBD Dauntless had more than twice the range of the Ju87. It far exceeded the Skua's range, even though the British aircraft's principal target was to be Japanese aircraft carriers. But looking at the reach of the Japanese Val, it can be seen how, typically, right through to 1944, the Imperial Japanese Navy could always find the American fleet long before the Americans, with their 'superior' technology, could locate the Japanese.

With regard speed, it is perhaps sobering to realise that the Skua was actually slower than almost every one of the other nations' specialised dive-bombers, even the Ju87 Stuka! This was an aircraft that was supposed to double, even to only a limited extent, as a fighter aircraft! Considering its potential enemy, a duel between the Blackburn Skua and a Mitsubishi Zero for control of the skies over opposing fleets presents the bleakest of scenarios, and surely puts the lid on any serious continuing attempt to classify the British aircraft as a true fighter plane.

In delivery of an effective payload to an enemy target, both the Ju87 and the SBD outclassed the Skua. Indeed, it was acknowledged by the Admiralty that a 500 lb bomb was far from ideal, but they were resigned to the fact that this ordnance would have to wait for the next generation of dive-bombers before it could be realised, if they wanted a dive-bomber at sea before 1941.[8] Against the right target (i.e. an aircraft carrier deck or an unarmoured light cruiser) lack of punch could, to a certain extent, be compensated for by accuracy. All dive-bombers were crewed by elites who strove for accuracy above all else, and most attained it.[9] But sending a dive-bomber armed with a 500 lb bomb against the *Scharnhorst* or the *Richelieu* was a futile exercise, which was only done due to insufficient knowledge of the capability of the weapons system itself, or because of a lack of any viable alternative.

Despite all the extra fittings and fixtures that the Royal Navy insisted on festooning the Skua with, weight-wise she did not compare too badly with most of her rivals, but her effective altitude limit was the lowest of them all. However, as things were to develop with the Skua, this did not turn out to be too much of a handicap. The Skua's wing area of $312 \, \text{ft}^2$ ($29.0 \, \text{m}^2$) was less than the Junkers Ju87B's $343.3 \, \text{ft}^2$ and the SBD's $325 \, \text{ft}^2$, while her wing loading of $26.4 \, \text{lb/ft}^2$ ($128 \, \text{kg/m}^2$) contrasted with the Stuka B's $27.1 \, \text{lb/in}^2$ and the Dauntless $33.4 \, \text{lb/in}^2$. The Skua had a power/mass

Table 7   Comparison of contemporary dive-bomber aircraft, 1940

	Skua-II	Ju87B	SBD Dauntless	D3A1 Val	LN410
Nationality	Great Britain	Germany	United States	Japan	France
Engine (hp)	1×905	1×1100	1×1010	1×990	1×690
Span (ft/in)	46' 2"	45' 3½"	41' 6"	47' 7¼"	45' 11"
Span (m)	14.07	13.79	12.64	14.52	14.01
Length (ft/in)	35' 7"	36' 5"	32' 2"	32' 4"	32' 0"
Length (m)	10.84	11.10	9.80	9.88	9.66
Height (ft/in)	12' 6"	13' 2"	12' 7"	12' 7½"	11' 5"
Height (m)	3.81	4.01	3.83	3.86	3.47
Max speed (mph)	225	238	253	240	220
Max speed (kph)	363	383	407	386	354
Weight (lb)	5,490	5,908	5,903	5,309	6,250
Weight (kg)	2,490	2,680	2,677	2,408	2,835
Ceiling (ft)	20,200	26,250	29,600	30,050	31,168
Ceiling (m)	6,157	8,001	9,022	9,159	9,500
Range (miles)	760	370	860	915	746
Range (km)	1,223	595	1,384	1472	1,200
Main bomb (lb)	1×500	1×1100	1×1200	1×551	1×496
Main bomb (kg)	227	499	544	250	225
Crew	2	2	2	2	1
Designed base	Aircraft carrier	Land	Aircraft carrier	Aircraft carrier	Aircraft carrier*

*The Loire-Nieuport LN410 was designed for operations from the new French aircraft carriers *Joffre* and *Painlevé*, but as they were never completed, only flew from land bases.

ratio of 0.11 hp/lb (0.18 kW/kg). Her rate of climb was only 1,580 ft/min (481.58 m/m) and her cruising speed just 114–187 mph (183–301 km/h).

But, despite being almost 2 years late on delivery, the Skua was still in service ahead of most of her foreign equivalents. Had she been on time, she would have outrated the equivalent naval dive-bombers (all biplanes) by a considerable margin – and that was her tragedy.[10]

NOTES

1. This disparity rapidly worsened for the Royal Navy as the inclusion of the armoured deck in the Illustrious class restricted hangar space yet more, while the *Indomitable* could only accommodate forty-eight aircraft, when her contemporary American equivalent, the *Essex*, could carry almost twice that number.
2. Major Alan Marsh, RM, to the author on 23 March 1977.
3. Captain T. W. Harrington, DSC, RN, to the author on 29 June 1977.
4. Colonel F. D. G. Bird, RM, to the author on 14 June 1977.
5. Vice-Admiral Sir Donald Gibson, *Haul Taut and Belay*, Spellmount, Tunbridge Wells, 1992.
6. This machine is illustrated on page 56 of Owen Thetford's book, *British Naval Aircraft*, Putnam, London, 1967, but is incorrectly captioned as belonging to No. 803 Squadron, but this was *not* the case. She served in No. 800 Squadron.

7. The RAF had a highly potent dive-bomber in its grasp in the late 1930s, the superlative Hawker Henley, a monoplane of the highest quality, but converted it into a target-tug! The Italian *Regia Aeronautica* and the United States Army Air Force were both late converts following the success of the German Junkers Ju87 in Norway and France in 1940; but the Italian Savoia-Marchetti Sm85 twin-engined aircraft was an abject failure, while the excellent North American A-36 *Apache*, forced through by General 'Hap' Arnold against the majority wishes of the USAAF, was restricted to just 500 machines in total (see Peter C. Smith, *Straight Down!* Crécy Publishing, Manchester, 2000). The fastest land-based dive-bomber was the Soviet Union's Petlyakov Pe-2 *Peshka*, made over from a high-altitude fighter aircraft and faster than most fighter aircraft of her day. But she did not enter full combat service until 1941. (See Peter C. Smith, *Petlyakov Pe-2 Peshka*, Crowood Press, Ramsbury, 2003.)

8. In the event, that aircraft, the Fairey Barracuda, suffered exactly the same fate at the hands of the RAF as did the Skua, and for much the same reasons, and did not join the fleet until 1943.

9. Though few could match the 80 per cent plus hit rate achieved by the Japanese Navy's Lieutenant Commander Takashige Egusa in 1942. (See Peter C. Smith, *Fist from the Sky*, Crécy, 2006.)

10. The famed American aircraft designer Ed Heinemann made the following claim when comparing the Northrop BT-1 (the predecessor, and in many ways, the prototype of the famous Douglas SBD Dauntless), and the Blackburn Skua: 'The Skua didn't make its first flight until February 9, 1937, even though the manufacturer had been incentivised (*sic*) by receiving a production contract for 190 planes in the July of 1936. The Northrop BT-1 had been ordered five months earlier and flew 19 months sooner, and the first production BT-1 was delivered 11 months earlier than the first production Blackburn Skua. Northrop was less than six years old as a company and the BT-1 was only their second attempt to design a carrier-based aircraft. Blackburn was an old, long established, manufacturing firm that had specialised in building naval aircraft since the First World War. Viewed from this perspective, the development of the Northrop BT-1 was an outstanding achievement.' (Edward H. Heinemann and Glen E. Smith Jr, *Sugar Baker Dog: The Victor of Midway*. Original draft manuscript, 1987, made available directly to the author by Ray Wagner from the N. Paul Whittier Aviation Library at the San Diego Aerospace Museum, 28 March 2006)

6

INTO BATTLE

From the outbreak of war, Nos 800 and 803 Squadrons were embarked aboard the aircraft carrier *Ark Royal* and operated both from her and from the RNAS airfield, and HMS *Sparrowhawk*, at Hatston, near Kirkwall in the Orkney Islands, alongside the main Home Fleet anchorage of Scapa Flow. This early period was also to witness several sorties into the North Sea and North Atlantic, and included the first taste of German air power, with the attempted sinking of the *Ark Royal* by a Heinkel He111, which dropped a 2,000 lb bomb, 'a very near miss with a very big bomb', as Dickie Rolph described it later. On 7 September the *Ark Royal* sailed from Scapa Flow to conduct patrols off Norway. On conclusion of these operations, she left again on 12 September to carry out anti-submarine patrols in the North-West approaches, these operations continuing until 17 September.

On the outbreak of the war, No. 800 Squadron, with nine Skuas, was still commanded by Lieutenant Commander (Flight Lieutenant RAF) G. N. Torry RN; No. 801 Squadron by Lieutenant Commander C. A. Kingsley-Rowe, RN, also with nine Skuas; and No. 803 Squadron by Lieutenant Commander Dennis Royle Farquharson Campbell, RN. Earlier that year three of No. 803 Squadron's Hawker Osprey biplanes had been replaced by six Skuas, giving a total strength of nine Skuas.

The Fanad Head *incident*

One of the first incidents of the war, in which the Skua featured prominently, was a story with so many twists, coincidences and strange turns of fortune, that, even today, it seems hardly credible.

On 14 September, an SOS call was received at 1240 hours from the merchant vessel SS *Fanad Head*. Her location was about 300 miles off the Icelandic coast. The ship reported that she was under attack and torpedoed but afloat in position 56° 45′ North, 15° 21′ West. She added that the enemy submarine was pursuing her on the surface. This submarine was later found to be the *U-30* (*Korvettekapitän* Fritz Lemp). Her position placed her some 200 miles distant from the *Ark Royal*. While four of her screening destroyers, HMS *Bedouin*, *Eskimo*, *Punjabi* and *Tartar*, were sent on ahead at their best speed to give assistance, the carrier prepared to recall her existing air patrols and land them back aboard. She retained three destroyers, the *Faulknor, Firedrake* and *Foxhound* to escort her and once her retrieval had taken place, she and her remaining destroyers altered course to 225° and increased speed to 24 knots in order to close the gap as quickly as possible.

By 1432 hours, with the gap shortened to 180 miles, the carrier prepared to fly off a fresh section of Skuas to search ahead for the U-boat. These, all from No. 803 Squadron, were led by Lieutenant Commander D. R. F. Campbell, RN, with the squadron observer, Lieutenant Michael Charles Edward Hanson; with Lieutenant Guy Beresford Kerr Griffiths, RM, and Petty Officer George Vincent McKay; and Lieutenant R. P. 'Thirsty' Thurston, RN, with Acting Petty Officer James 'Jock' Simpson as his observer, flying Skua L28723 (A7M). Each of the Skuas was armed with a single 112 lb A/S (Anti-Submarine) bomb and four 20 lb Cupar bombs (also known as Coupar or Cooper bombs),[1] two under each wing.

In order to save time, deliberate risks were taken. To turn into the wind for the fly-off, the *Ark Royal* was required to make a 180° turn off course, and her captain decided to 'save time' by not readjusting his destroyer screen to comply. The Senior Officer of the screen, Captain C. S. Daniel, RN, aboard the *Faulknor*, was instructed to maintain his destroyer's course and speed. The *Ark Royal* was thus rapidly left exposed without a protecting ring of Asdic underwater detection apparatus searching ahead of her, and was relying totally on her 26 knot speed, and a lot of luck, to keep her safe.[2]

In the event, the Skuas were despatched without incident, but as the carrier resumed course to rejoin her escorts, now 4 miles away, a second submarine, the *U-39* (*Korvettekapitän* Glattes) made a determined attack on the *Ark Royal*, firing a salvo of two torpedoes. However, their wakes were seen approaching by Leading Signalman J. E. Hall, whose prompt reaction saved the ship. The *Ark Royal* had her helm put over smartly and managed to avoid the spread. It was a very close run thing, but all the torpedoes missed their target, although one was so close that it exploded in the turbulent waters of her wake.

The destroyers were soon on the scene and in a determined hunt they attacked her with depth charges and blew the submarine to the surface. Boats were lowered and her crew were taken prisoner as the *U-39*, scuttled before she was abandoned, sank.[3] This was the first U-boat destroyed in the Second World War.

Far over the horizon, another drama was taking place. The three Skuas had located the island of Rockall together and had then dispersed to search different sectors. In the intervening 90-minute period the U-boat had finally closed her prey near enough to fire warning shots from her deck gun. Clearly, the Germans did not want to waste another expensive torpedo on finishing her off. Her passengers and crew, who took to the ship's two lifeboats, now abandoned the *Fanad Head*. The submarine, not expecting aircraft in such a remote location, had towed one of the boats clear, and had informed the captain that a neutral vessel was *en route* to rescue them. Then the submarine was taken alongside while a search was made for secret papers and a scuttling charge was prepared. The arrival of the first of the Skuas, Thurston's, awoke the complacent German submarine to its situation. Thurston was equally amazed to find the submarine alongside, and instantly reacted, releasing his bombs in a low dive.

In a desperate attempt to score bomb hits on the fast-disappearing U-boat, both Thurston and later Griffiths made diving attacks. For a long time it was assumed that, in their eagerness for a 'kill', they had pushed down to too low an altitude before bomb release. In fact, the Skuas were armed with the standard 112 lb A/S bomb, which should have been ideal, but it would appear that these had been wrongly fused with too brief a time lapse. As a result of this error the weapons detonated almost instantaneously.[4]

The bombs detonated almost directly under Thurston's Skua, and shrapnel set her fuel tank alight, forcing Thurston to ditch. Both aircrew survived the water landing, but had severe burns. They abandoned the sinking aircraft and started to swim, as best they could, toward the wallowing liner.

In the meantime, Campbell's aircraft was not too far off, having also sighted the ship. The explosions were seen by Lieutenant Mike Hanson, who assumed that the Germans were shelling the ship. It took 10 minutes for the Skua to close the scene of the action and, while still some distance away, Hanson sighted what he took to be a submarine conning tower. This object Campbell engaged, making two deliberate attacks, first with the small bombs, which again, unknown to the crew, damaged the underside of the aircraft, but not terminally in this case. Campbell was able to return for another attack, this time dropping the A/S bomb, but this failed to detonate at all! What they had wasted all their weaponry on was not *U-30* however, but most likely the wreckage of Thurston's aircraft still awash.

Turning back toward the *Fanad Head*, they saw two men swimming, which they later reported as being two of the U-boat's crew left behind when the submarine had crash-dived.[5] The swimmers were, of course, Thurston and Simpson. The real *U-30* then came back to the surface and, having no bombs left, Campbell was reduced to making a strafing run, which caused the submarine hastily to crash-dive once more. Their fuel was now running out and, after Lieutenant Hanson had radioed a brief report back to the carrier, they made one last turn over the two lifeboats, while Hanson used his Aldis lamp to flash the message 'Help Coming'. They then set a course back to base, and on the way met two sections of Swordfish TSRs[6] on the way out from the *Ark Royal* to the scene of the action.

The cold water, coupled with the injuries received, proved too much for Jock Simpson, and he never made it to the *Fanad Head*. Thurston, equally hurt, somehow found the strength to swim the mile and reached the ship, before he blacked out. Fortunately, one of the submarine boarding party had seen him, and a volunteer went over the side after him. Keeping him afloat, the Germans managed to haul Thurston back on board and tried to resuscitate him. The *Fanad Head* proved but a temporary sanctuary, however, for, with the departure of Dennis Campbell due to lack of fuel, the *U-30* resurfaced. The submarine had earlier sent an inflatable over to the ship to search for secret papers and ships documents, and she now closed the derelict in order to recover her boarders and their unconscious prisoner.

Fate had not finished with them yet for it was now that the third Skua put in a belated appearance. Having searched their own sector, Griffiths and McKay were making their way back to the *Ark Royal*, when McKay spotted the drifting *Fanad Head* on the horizon, and they altered course toward her. Not knowing what had occurred before, they made a low sweep around the ship to enable them to read her name and port of registration on her stern and, as they circled her, a bizarre rerun of earlier events was triggered when they sighted the hitherto obscured U-boat alongside. Once more the Skua made an immediate attack, Griffiths releasing both the Cupar and the main A/S bomb all in one salvo. Once more, the resultant explosions failed to harm the enemy, but damaged the Skua so badly that she fell into the sea, the weight of the Pegasus tearing the whole forward section of the aircraft away. The remnants of the Skua quickly settled, and George McKay was unable to get clear before it sank. Griffiths was more fortunate, and got out in time. Like Thurston earlier, Griffiths swam to the merchantman, and was able to climb the rope ladder left by the crew when they had abandoned her. Here, he was also taken prisoner by the boarding party.

The *U-30* then closed and, in order quickly to embark the men and find safety again from the troublesome aircraft that kept appearing in the middle of the ocean, they ordered them to jump into the sea. Thurston had finally woken up, and he and Griffiths were told the only option open to them. The whole group, submariners and aviators, leapt back down into the water, and were all roughly hauled aboard the U-boat. The Skua pilots thus became unwilling passengers aboard the very submarine they had not long before been doing their best to sink a short time before! The *U-30* then submerged once more and, all thoughts of economy now abandoned, Lemp fired a deliberate torpedo into the *Fanad Head* to put her under without further ado.

It was at this dramatic moment that the Swordfish arrived on the scene. Following the wake of the torpedo track, they made repeated attacks on the submarine, and she was severely damaged. Two of the crew had been thrown about and injured, while the submarine sprang numerous leaks. The U-boat took on a pronounced list, but, to the relief of Griffiths and Thurston, she survived the best efforts of their countryman to destroy her. Later, *U-30* also survived further attacks, this time from the four Tribal class destroyers sent after her earlier. They had located the drifting life-boats and, while HMS *Tartar* rescued the passengers and crew, the others had hunted the submarine, which, through a navigational error, had returned close to the scene of the action.

Having escaped by the skin of her teeth yet again, the damaged sub-marine set a course for Iceland, where she landed her two injured crew members. But Campbell and the badly burned Thurston were retained aboard, although well-treated, during a nightmare 2-week voyage back to Germany. *U-30* finally broke down and was towed into port. But even here, there were complications upon complications. Far from being a straight-forward case of hospitalisation followed by transfer to a POW camp, the two British pilots were seized by the *Gestapo* and interned at Brunswick.

The reason for this treatment was gradually pieced together later. Lemp in *U-30* had torpedoed and sunk without warning the 13,581-ton British liner *Athenia* in the same area in the first few hours of the war, an action that aroused a clamour in the civilised world as an early example of German barbarity in the new conflict. Among the 1,300 passengers and crew were many Americans, and the whole incident recalled the *Lusitania* sinking in the First World War, which brought the USA into the war against Germany. Not wanting such bad publicity, the Germans had denied all involvement, accusing Churchill of ordering a British sub-marine to do the deed to whip up hatred. Now, however, the whole cover-up would be exposed because the two British pilots had probably learnt of the *U-30*'s role in the atrocity, so they had to be kept silent, and hence the *Gestapo*.

Really, you could not make up such a plot, but this was real! Griffiths and Thurston were therefore interned in a camp with many senior Polish army officers (many of whom were to be brutally murdered by their captors later) and no word of their capture was given out to the British authorities. Indeed, yet further complications were involved when, in a mix-up following their grilling, the names of their two observers, McKay and Simpson, were broadcast in error by German radio, which claimed that *U-30* had shot them down and taken them prisoner!

It could not go on. Yet, a further strange twist of fate led to a group of RAF officers being mistakenly sent to the Brunswick camp. Griffiths persuaded one of these POWs to write a letter home to his wife, but under the RAF officer's name to fool their captors. It worked, his wife naturally recognised the handwriting and eventually, via the involvement of the Red

Cross, the two Skua pilots were finally granted proper POW status and the mystery cleared up.[7]

First blood

During the period 25 to 26 September, both No. 801 and No. 803 Squadrons were embarked aboard *Ark Royal*, which was operating in the North Sea. She accompanied the fleet, which put to sea to provide heavy cover for a cruiser squadron that had been sent to escort to safety a damaged British submarine, HMS *Spearfish*. They had pushed right into the North Sea toward the Heligoland Bight and, not surprisingly, attracted the lively interest of the *Luftwaffe*. The Skuas were flying continuous patrols over the fleet, managing to intercept three enemy aircraft, and were able to bring two of them down.

Initial contact was made at 1100 on 26 September, while in position 57° 36' North, 02° 36' East. A German flying boat, later recognised as a Dornier Do18, appeared low on the horizon and three Skuas from No. 803 Squadron took off from the *Ark Royal* to try and catch her. The Skuas managed to get close enough to fire some bursts, which they claimed damaged this aircraft. Later a report was received that a Do18 had landed in Dutch territorial waters, no doubt damaged by the Skuas and trying to reach her home base at Borkum Island off the mouth of the Ems River.

Some 30 minutes later another section of No. 803 Squadron's Skuas was launched when a second Do18 sighting was made. This time their target was less wary and she had the dubious distinction of becoming the first German aircraft to be destroyed by any British service in the Second World War. This aircraft fell to the Skuas of Lieutenant B. S. McEwen, with Petty Officer B. M. 'Horse' Seymour and Lieutenant C. L. G. Evans, with Lieutenant W. A. Robertson. After a brisk chase and skirmish, she was finally shot down by 'Horse', a Telegraphist/Air Gunner (TAG), from the back of his aircraft. The German floatplane was forced down on the sea reasonably intact and stayed afloat until the destroyer HMS *Somali* closed with her and took off the crew before sinking her.

Nor was this the end of the excitement. Yet a third Do18 was sighted and chased away by a section of No. 800 Squadron at 1230 hours.

On 3 October, No. 801 Squadron transferred to HMS *Furious* for operations off the Shetland Islands and then sailed with her to give protection to the First Canadian Troop convoy. On their return to Plymouth from this duty, on 29 February, the Squadron disembarked, moving back up to Wick with Fighter Command once more on 25 March, before transferring to Hatston for fighter defence duty.

On 17 October, the *Luftwaffe* launched an air attack on Scapa Flow by four Junkers Ju88 bombers of the I/KG 30 under *Hauptmann* Doench.

These were the fastest bombers the *Luftwaffe* possessed and were considered able to show a clean pair of heels to a Skua. Nonetheless, the Skuas carried out several interceptions and got in some brief attacks, but without claiming any definite results. Near misses only were made on the old training ship *Iron Duke*, which the German airman reported as an operational unit. In reply, one Ju88 was destroyed.

North Sea patrolling

On return to Scapa Flow, No. 803 Squadron was disembarked to Wick airfield and placed under the operations of Fighter Command for the defence of the fleet base at Scapa Flow. A small number of Rocs were on the unit strength at this time. On 30 January, Lieutenant Commander Campbell addressed a report to the Admiral Commanding Orkney and Shetland, in which he listed the unit's strength as eight Skuas and four Rocs. Campbell pointed out that, since that establishment had been authorised back in November, the operational duties of No. 803 Squadron had been changed:

> Until the middle of December, this squadron was solely responsible for the fighter defence of the Orkneys and Scapa Flow, and it had therefore been necessary to consider this squadron's effectiveness chiefly from the armament aspect. From this consideration only, the Roc was, and is, considered slightly superior to the Skua.

However, he pointed out that the duties No. 803 Squadron subsequently had to perform on occasion were not quite those that had been anticipated. Enemy aircraft formations had not approached Scapa Flow after 18 October, whereas No. 803 Squadron had to deal with enemy reports considerably farther away than Scapa, including against shadowing aircraft over the Home Fleet, convoys and trawlers under air attack and so on. When such requests were received, it was found that, should a standing patrol be a mixed one, then, due to the ranges involved, the Roc's short endurance (cited as low as 2 hours and 45 minutes in some instances) was a terminal handicap. Simply put, the Rocs had to be returned to base while the Skuas dealt with the situation, but in reduced numbers:

> In one particular case, the Commander-in-Chief, Home Fleet, ordered fighters to be sent to his assistance, a distance of 210 miles. The two sections standing by each contained a Roc, and therefore only four aircraft could be despatched instead of six.

Campbell stated that, now that interceptor squadrons were being added to the defence of Scapa Flow, the function of his own squadron, operating out of Hatston, was once more being changed. The RAF Sector Commander of Fighter Command was proposing that No. 803 Squadron be used for fighter duties at distances over the sea to which he would not despatch his own fighter units. An outer patrol line was under consideration for No. 803 Squadron to maintain. Campbell therefore stated:

> For the above functions, the Skua's endurance renders it a most suitable aircraft, but the Roc (with its shorter endurance) will be unable to carry out such duties. It is therefore requested that approval be sought to replace all Roc aircraft of this squadron with Skuas.[8]

South Atlantic interlude

Two German pocket-battleships had escaped into the Atlantic oceans before the war had broken out, and soon set about their task of sinking unescorted British and Allied merchant ships. The presence of two powerful raiders loose on the Atlantic trade routes caused grave concern. Early in October, several hunting groups were formed to try and track down one of these vessels, the *Admiral Graf Spee*, and destroy her. One such was Force 'K', which comprised the battle-cruiser *Renown*, the aircraft carrier *Ark Royal* and the destroyers *Hardy*, *Hasty*, *Hereward* and *Hostile*. These ships rendezvoused off the Butt of Lewis on 2 October, the *Ark Royal* having sailed from Loch Eribol and the *Renown* from Scapa Flow. They set course for Freetown, Sierra Leone, in West Africa. This steamy port became their main base until early March 1940, and from there they ranged far out into the South Atlantic.

Their first voyage from Freetown was a ten-day patrol, which took them across to the island of Fernando Noronha, north of the easternmost hump of the Brazilian coast and back again, but they found no trace of the enemy. A second patrol as far south as Ascension Island between 28 October and 6 November, proved as fruitless. Each day at dawn and dusk the squadrons went to action stations, but every tropical day followed another in a succession of hopes and disappointments as they beat up and down the empty ocean. Apart from the oiling of the destroyers, which had to be topped up by *Renown*, nothing broke the monotony until the penultimate day.

On 5 November one of *Ark Royal*'s patrolling aircraft was returning from another boring sortie when they sighted a lone merchant ship. On investigation this turned out to be the German blockade-runner *Uhenfels*, and the destroyer *Hereward* was despatched at top speed to collar her. This was well done and she was boarded before she could be scuttled, so there was something to be shown for all their patience, but it was not the enemy they were looking for.

During this period wide air searches were conducted in the central and south Atlantic. While it was mainly the Fairey Swordfish TSR that were used for deep searches twice a day, the Skuas were fully utilised closer in

and were readied to conduct dive-bombing attacks on the German battleship once discovered, with the aim of damaging her before the *Renown*
finished her off.

The *Graf Spee* proved elusive, carrying out a raid into the Indian Ocean
off Madagscar, on 15 and 16 November, before doubling back into the
South Atlantic once more. She was supported by a series of supply ships,
and replenished from one of these, *Altmark* on 26 November. Meanwhile,
in an effort to tighten the net, Vice Admiral d'Oyly Lyon at Freetown reorganised his forces, sending Force 'K', now reinforced by the light cruiser
Neptune, to assist Force 'H' (the heavy cruisers *Shropshire* and *Sussex*).
They probed south to the Cape, leaving their short endurance destroyers
to guard the Mozambique Channel, but again missed the main quarry.
Again, other German ships were swept up in the process, the *Neptune*
intercepting the blockade-runner *Adolf Woermann* near Ascension Island
on 21 November. Then followed a patrol between the Cape and Latitude
38° South, which found bad visibility and rough weather, which ruled out
all attempts to continue any kind of flying. After some days of this the
force turned northward once more, the *Watussi* being caught on 2 December by the *Sussex*.

The *Ark Royal* put into Simonstown naval base to refuel and re-
provision before taking up the search once more, and the Skuas flew
ashore for a short spell. Three more sinkings were made by the German
pocket-battleship in early December, this time in the area between St
Helena and the Brazilian coast and, leaving behind the fleshpots of South
Africa, Force 'K' was sent north again to this area. The *Ark Royal*'s force
sailed from Cape Town for the River Plate estuary, and, but for an order
from the Admiralty ordering them to alter course to due north, they
would have located the elusive *Admiral Graf Spree* before she became
involved in the running battle with the smaller and more lightly armed
British cruisers *Exeter*, *Ajax* and *Achilles*. Still, on 13 December the enemy
was finally cornered off the River Plate. In the event the cruisers, by
brilliant tactics and brave handling, won the day.

After the battle, the German ship was forced to flee to the neutral
sanctuary of Montevideo. Force 'K' heard news of the fight while still
sweeping north off Pernambuco and was ordered at once to refuel at Rio
de Janeiro, where the destroyer screen rejoined them from Freetown,
before the whole force then headed south at top speed toward the Plate
Estuary.

However, before they could reach the area, the captain of the *Admiral
Graf Spee* took his ship to sea and blew her up rather than face another
battle. This was the first great naval victory achieved by the Royal Navy in
the Second World War. The *Ark Royal* was sent down to 10° South to
meet and help escort the *Ajax* to Freetown and then, at the end of
January, did the same for *Exeter* after she had been patched up at the

Falklands. With the successful conclusion of their mission, Force 'K' was recalled home.

No. 806 Squadron arrives

No. 803 Squadron had been established in March 1939, with Lieutenant Commander D. R. F. Campbell, RN, as assigned commanding officer. By February 1940, the Squadron had on its books eight Skuas and four Rocs aircraft, when Lieutenant W. P. Lucy assumed command.

Meanwhile, another Skua squadron had joined the Royal Navy. On 15 February, No. 806 Squadron was formed at Eastleigh with eight Skuas and four Rocs. Their Commanding Officer was Lieutenant Commander C. L. G. Evans, DSC, RN. However, sufficient aircrews to man these aircraft were not ready until the next intake from the fighter training school had been trained. Among this intake was Graham Angus Hogg.[9] After gaining his wings in a Tiger Moth trainer and Hawker Hart, Hogg 'Marked time at Lee-on-Solent waiting for fighter course to start'. Midshipmen RN who had not long finished fighter school, waiting for an operational unit, told him:

Oh, you'll like Gladiators, but a cow could fly those. But, Hell, Skuas, it's no use trying to fly them, you'll just have to pray. They stall at 100 miles per hour and spin if you turn with the flaps down. They killed one third of our course.

Hogg recalled:

I thought, at the time, that they must be clever pilots still to be alive but, later, at fighter school, I came to think that they and their dead friends must have been ham-fisted elephants. Nevertheless, there was a Skua in a hangar at Lee and the first time I saw it, I nearly deserted. The Hart had looked big after the Tiger Moth; this looked an impossible size. With its high undercarriage and cockpit windscreen it resembled some kind of bird, a Crane perhaps. I sat in the cockpit and gaped at thousands of levers and dials, wondering how one possibly remembered the position and use of them all.

On joining No. 803 Squadron, Hogg commented:

At any rate, the CO expressed himself satisfied that we would not disgrace the Squadron completely.

As for ourselves, we felt that we had landed in as fine a crowd of fellows as could be found anywhere. There were twelve of us: the CO Nick, senior flight commander; Bill, second flight commander; V. J. senior observer; Ivan the adjutant, who had not long left Fighter School and the seven of us, Stanley, Eric, Lew, Daisy, Jack, Dick and

myself. All were doing their best to become smart and efficient, so
that when the Squadron went into action, and it was going in soon,
we should be ready for anything. During our fortnight at West
Freugh we continually practised dive-bombing and air-firing. The
CO warned us not to expect too many hits on the air-firing drogue.

'It's a very small target and the best score yet is eight points.'

Lew and Dick took off and returned with a score of twenty-four
points apiece – they had proved our worth as pilots.

On return from some leave in Edinburgh they found:

The Squadron was in a terrific 'flap'. It was to fly North to the
Orkneys as soon as possible to join HMS *Glorious*. No one thought
much of the idea; we were obviously going to assist in the Norwegian
campaign, which probably meant landing on a frozen lake or something equally frightening. It was impossible to get near a telephone
for officers saying good-bye to their wives and families. I bid my fare-
wells lying on a stretcher in the sick-bay, using the doctor's telephone.
On all sides of the wardroom, pilots and observers were writing last
letters and composing heart-rending telegrams.

The ground crews and equipment were sent off that night by
special train, the aircraft having been left ready for a hurried take-off.
We 'stood by'.

Scottish weather, however, ordained that we should not take off
until 2 days later [28 March]. When we did, the clouds were only at
about 1,500 feet, which is not great height when aviating in the North
of Scotland.

We took off singly and joined up on the CO as he became airborne.
I was flying a heavily loaded Roc on the left of the leader, which was
about the best position I could have been considering the flight that
followed. We flew up the west coast, finding it extremely bumpy, until
we reached the Caledonian Canal, up which we headed.

The clouds were down on the mountain sides and we were flying up
a natural tunnel. The Squadron went into sections, in line astern
stepped up, the leading section being fairly low. The air was full of
pockets and sometimes we would rise or fall 300 or 400 feet, stopping
at the denser air with a body-shaking crash. If the cloud had come
down to sea-level there would have been no turning back, the mountain enclosed us on both sides. The last sections spent a large part of
the trip in the clouds.

Everyone was extremely thankful when we emerged from the
mountains and saw Inverness ahead. A short trip over some small
hills and we were at Evanton, where the CO had decided to land for
the night. The sections broke up and came in to land independently.

Being heavily loaded, my Roc had to be brought in fairly fast.
It was a very rough landing.

The following morning they were surprised to be told that Lieutenant
W. P. Lucy, RN, had left the squadron, and that, Lieutenant Commander
J. Casson, RN, had become the new commanding officer. Changes had
been in the air; January 1940 had seen the arrival of Lieutenant Com-
mander H. P. Bramwell, RN, to take over command of No. 801
Squadron, but he had in turn been temporarily replaced by Lieutenant
E. G. D. Finch-Noyes, RN, in May, until Captain R. T. Partridge, RM,
could take over permanently.

South-west approaches

On 10 February, six German blockade runners left the port of Vigo to run
the gauntlet to Germany. To hunt them down the old team of *Renown* and
Ark Royal, joined by the light cruiser *Galatea* and destroyers, was organised by Admiral Dunbar Nasmith, C-in-C Western Approaches. Only one
of the six German blockade runners managed to reach Germany. Their
next job was to meet and escort safely home the damaged *Exeter*, which
they did between 10 and 14 February in the South-Western Approaches.
German radio intercepts gained knowledge of this mission and the *Ark
Royal* had gone on ahead and thus avoided a trap laid by a force of three
U-boats (*U-26, U-37* and *U-48*), which an easterly gale frustrated. On
16 February, on return to Scapa Flow at the conclusion of this duty, the
Skua squadrons were then all disembarked once more before the *Ark
Royal* sailed to the Mediterranean for training exercises.

No. 800 Squadron was soon in action, for, on 20 March, the squadron
intercepted a force of Heinkel He111 bombers off the north-east coast of
Scotland, who were endeavouring to attack a convoy. Although No. 800
Squadron itself did not claim any kills, they did help break up the enemy
formation. Their sister squadron was more fortunate and the unit's CO,
Lieutenant William Paulet Lucy, RN, with Lieutenant Michael Charles
Hanson, RN, the squadron observer in the rear seat, hit one He111 and
claimed it destroyed.

NOTES

1. One speculation for the name suggests that it refers to Cupar, Fife, which is on the
   northern side of the Firth of Forth and south of the Firth of Tay. At Grange in the Carse
   of Gowrie, the RNAS had a bombing range on the marshes, and it was here that the
   practice bomb of the same name took the name from nearby Cupar. But there is no
   confirmation of this theory from local sources. Whatever the origins of the name, these
   small, dart-like bombs were very common, being manufactured in Australia, Canada and
   the USA, as well as in Great Britain. Over the years the name metamorphosed into

Cooper through incorrect spoken usage of similar-sounding names, and the latter became generally accepted.

2. Analysing this decision later, the Director of Anti-Submarine Warfare commented that the *Ark Royal* had '. . . slipped her destroyer screen whilst turning into the wind to fly off'. He thought that while the value of the Asdics during such high-speed alterations of course was limited due to the turbulence, the actual *physical* deterrent and obstruction of the destroyers moving at high speed to keep on station, had they been retained, would have been '*considerable*'.

3. The full account of this sinking is contained in Peter C. Smith's *Destroyer Leader: HMS Faulknor 1935–1946*, Pen & Sword, 2004. The First Lieutenant of the U-boat talked a lot about the destroyer that picked him up, and revealed many details of German methods. This lucky escape was a warning, but it was ignored and, a few days later, a U-boat in similar circumstances sank the aircraft carrier HMS *Courageous*.

4. This vital fact was not realised at first, nor indeed, for quite a considerable time. Efforts by Guy Griffiths to inform the Admiralty of this fact in a coded message incorporated in one of his letters home from the *Oflag IX A* POW camp of Spangenberg Castle on 2 November, were not understood. A letter sent by Rear Admiral, Lee-on-Solent, to Simpson's widow on 20 September asked her not to confide in anyone other than immediate relatives, adding: 'It is in the public interest that information of the incident of war which has led to the loss of your husband should not find its way to the enemy . . ..' Griffiths was later to be joined in captivity by another Royal Marine Skua flyer, Richard Partridge, and they were both involved in a successful tunnel escape, although they were later recaptured. Griffiths rejoined the Fleet Air Arm at the end of the war, and became the first Royal Marine officer to fly a helicopter, a Sikorski Hoverfly, and he also served aboard the aircraft carrier *Glory* off Korea in 1951–52, before retiring from the Corps in May 1958.

5. This version of events is still being peddled 60 years on.

6. One section each from Nos 810 and 821 Squadrons.

7. Their adventures did not end there, and they became players in 'The Great Escape' *Stalag* breakout, but that is outside the scope of this book.

8. Lieutenant Commander Campbell, *Roc and Skua Aircraft – Squadron Establishment*; Memo dated 30 January 1940, Ref: O 7 (contained in National Archives ADM 1/10749).

9. Hogg had titled his unfinished autobiography, written in self-deprecating style, *The Camouflaged Coward* (hereafter cited as Hogg manuscript), but nothing could be further from the truth. The latter part of this manuscript was probably lost in the bombing of HMS *Illustrious* in January 1941. His brother (D.I. Hogg) retrieved as much as he could, edited it in 1965 with additional comment from their father and presented it to the FAA Museum. Graham Hogg had gone straight from Melville College into the RNVR in February 1939, joining the Fleet Air Arm and being awarded his Wings on 13 November 1939. He later became of the top-scoring FAA Fulmar fighter aces, but was tragically killed in a flying accident when an Avro Anson he was taking passage in crashed on take-off in the North African desert.

7

KILLING THE *KÖNIGSBERG*

There was no such thing as 'The Phoney War' for the Royal Navy. This trite piece of American journalese was phonier than what had been actually happening at sea during the first 7 months of the Second World War, but ashore the term might have had some relevance. Hitler's audacious invasion of Norway, against the formbook when Germany did not control the seas, changed all that for ever.

Despite all the earnest internet 'debate' that currently takes place 65 years after the event, on how ready or not the Royal Navy was for a face-to-face combat with a modern first-class air power, one thing is true, the naval aircraft of 1940 had never been expected to tackle such a force head on. The Royal Navy had not been expected to have to fight the *Luftwaffe*, virtually unaided by the RAF, on a plane-to-plane basis. But, due to unforeseen circumstances, that was just what the Skua had to do. Little wonder then, that losses were heavy. What should be more surprising to these shallow armchair critics, is just how much the Fleet Air Arm actually achieved in these totally unexpected circumstances.

The RAF persisted with its pre-war line for long into the war. As Captain Stephen Roskill, RN, was to write in the official history, on the failure of British air attacks on ships:

> Another factor was that at the outbreak of war the belief had prevailed that a good percentage of hits would be obtained on ship targets in medium- or even high-level bombing attacks. Disillusion came quickly, but the mistake resulted in neglect of the dive-bomber and in our fighting the first 2 years of the war with no aircraft of that type except for a handful of naval Skuas. The change from medium- to low-level attacks was slow and, even when accepted, did not produce results comparable to those regularly obtained by German dive- or low-level bombers. There was also the persistent denial of a properly equipped striking force to Coastal Command, and the claim of Bomber Command to be responsible for all bombing operations, which brought about a period of divided responsibility for attacks on shipping.[1]

Norway

That spring both sides had their eye on the little neutral state of Norway. Winston Churchill, then First Lord of the Admiralty, was eager to put a stop to the transport of iron ore from Swedish mines to Germany. The ships carrying this vital commodity used the neutral waters of the Norwegian coast to make their journey in safety, which infuriated Churchill, and he eventually persuaded Prime Minister Chamberlain to allow the mining of the Inner Leads off Narvik and elsewhere to force these ships out into the open sea where the Royal Navy could sink them. The British named this minelaying mission, Operation *Wilfred*. At the same time, with a view to gaining vital strategic bases for his *Luftwaffe* that would outflank the British defences, Hitler had been persuaded by Grand Admiral Raeder to occupy both Norway and Denmark prior to the launching of the main land offensive in the west through the neutral states of Belgium, Luxembourg and The Netherlands. With the help of the Norwegian traitor Vidkun Quisling, plans were made to use practically the whole of the German Navy, with the aid of a *Luftwaffe Fliegerkorps*, to make a surprise descent and occupy the principal ports and airfields of Norway before the British could react.The Germans allocated the equally asinine code name *Weserübung* (Weser Exercise) to this invasion. Both plans came to fruition at almost the same time.

Wrong-footed

The German landings caught the Admiralty unprepared with regards to air operations. The only aircraft carrier in Home Waters and able to be utilised was HMS *Furious*, and she was ordered to join the Home Fleet in company with the battleship *Warspite*. Unfortunately, a carrier is only as good as the aircraft embarked in her, and *Furious* only had two squadrons of Fairey Swordfish TSR aboard when she was rushed to sea from the Clyde. Her allocated Skua squadron, No. 801, was still ashore at Evanton and, in the panic to get her to sea, they were left behind. The two other big carriers, *Ark Royal* and *Glorious*, were in the western Mediterranean at the Alexandria naval base in Egypt. Both ships were immediately recalled home. Of the rest of the carrier fleet, HMS *Eagle* was in the Indian Ocean area on convoy protection and raider hunting duties and the two small carriers, HMS *Hermes* and HMS *Argus*, were both considered unsuitable for use in front-line operations.

Meanwhile, the *Luftwaffe* took the initiative by making a probe against the Royal Navy's main base. The Skuas of No. 804 Squadron, on fighter defence duties, were scrambled away to intercept. Yellow section, under Lieutenant F. M. Fell, RN, made contact with one group and attacked, claiming a Dornier Do17 hit and probably destroyed. However, although damaged, this aircraft, actually a Heinkel He111 of KGr 100, eventually made it back home. Red section, led by Lieutenant R. H. P. Carver, RN, also made contact and similarly thought that they had fatally damaged another He111, but this aircraft, although damaged, also survived the encounter. Blue section, under Lieutenant R. M. Smeeton, RN, claimed a third enemy, but again post-war records show none of the enemy was destroyed.

The *Königsberg* herself was part of one of the German task groups that had transported troops to Bergen on 8 April. Group 3 had consisted of two light cruisers, the gunnery training ship *Bremse*, two destroyers and five E-boats with their depot ship and two naval auxiliaries, *Schiff 9* and *Schiff 18*. Aerial reconnaissance had revealed that two light cruisers were present in the port and the RAF despatched twenty-four twin-engined bombers to deal with them. These aircraft duly attacked, but failed to score a single hit on either of the German ships, after which one, the *Köln*, returned to Germany. The sailing of her sister, *Königsberg*, had to be delayed, *not* because she had suffered slight damage from three shell hits by a Norwegian coastal artillery battery during the invasion, which was not serious and did not require much in the way of repairs, but due to her unreliable machinery.[2] This had to be fixed before she could face the long sea voyage home.[3]

The commanding officer of the *Königsberg*, Captain Heinrich Ruhfus, had not liked being left behind when his commanding officer, Rear-Admiral Schmundt, had scurried back south with the rest of the squadron, leaving him to face British retribution alone. During the night the ship's engine-room staff continued to work to rectify the faults and at midnight had reported to Ruhfus that the cruiser could sail at a maximum speed of 26 knots. Before dawn the ship's Nos 1 and 2 boilers were being fired up, in readiness for a dash south to safety, but it was already too late.

The target

First commissioned in March 1929, this middle-aged light cruiser was a 6,650-tonner, armed with nine 5.9 inch (150 mm) 60 calibre guns in three turrets, one forward and two *en echelon* aft, plus four twin 3.5 inch (88 mm) anti-aircraft guns and many lighter weapons. She was only lightly protected, having just a 2 inch belt of side armour with deck armour of 1½ inch maximum. In size, she had a length of 570 feet and a beam of 50 feet. While the three armoured turrets reduced the vulnerable area to the bow and quarterdeck, with the amidships mass of bridge, funnels and midship deckhouse where most of her anti-aircraft batteries were located, as good secondary aiming points. This meant that her magazines, ready-use ammunition, and her large machinery and boiler room spaces, were highly vulnerable to hits or near-misses. Being a static target, no 'aiming-off' or other adjustment was necessary and, being alongside the jetty, any bomb scoring a close detonation alongside would maximise the shock caused by the 'water-hammer' effect against her hull beneath the water. In short, she was an ideal target for the Skuas.

As always, the effect of her defensive fire would be minimised by achieving surprise, and no defending fighter aircraft need be taken into the equation for, at this early stage of the German invasion, the most forward units of the *Luftwaffe* were some 150 miles to the south at Stavanger/Sola airfield. Recognition of the target, with her unique 'staggered' rear turret formation, was easy, and Lieutenant Commander Geoffrey Hare, RN, the Senior Observer of No. 800 Squadron, on loan to RAF Coastal Command added to the knowledge by stating that she had a white band painted across both her fo'c'sle and quarterdeck, with a prominent white band and swastika painted atop her fore turret. The only thing that turned out to be beyond Senior Observer Lieutenant Geoffrey Hare's knowledge was that, during the interval since he had last seen her, *Königsberg* had shifted her berth and now lay with her starboard side secured alongside the Skoltegrund Mole, with her bows facing shoreward, to the east.

The attack plan

It was not until 9 April that rumours began to circulate in the Skua squadrons of these momentous events taking place across the North Sea. Hare had been aboard the first aircraft to overfly Bergen earlier and had identified the two German light cruisers. RAF reconnaissance aircraft 'H' for Harry had landed back at Lossiemouth at 1508 hours, and Hare transferred to another aircraft and was flown across to Hatston, convinced the Skuas had a target worthy of their efforts. On his return to base, Hare found that news of his sightings had already prompted the Commanding Officer of *Sparrowhawk*, Commander C. L. Howe, RN, to gain permission to use the Skuas based there in an attack. Hare and Howe went into a huddle with Captain Richard Thomas 'Birdy' Partridge, RM, the Commanding Officer of No. 800 Squadron, and Lieutenant William Paulet Lucy, RN, the CO of No. 803 Squadron, studying ranges, fuel capacity, payloads and the like.

With a nominal range of 760 miles and with a round trip to Bergen of approximately 660 miles, there was not much room for error. The fuel required for the aircraft for taxiing out, take-off and landing had to be added, along with adjustments for forming up, wind resistance and drift, search for the target, flight to the exit rendezvous, re-forming and so on all added small, but crucial, factors to be considered.

Richard Partridge later recalled that:

> I pointed out to Bill that Bergen was about 2 hours flying each way in still air for Skuas and that our official endurance was only 4 hours 20 minutes; to which he replied that we both knew that we could stretch this a bit and that if we didn't hang around over the target too long we should be able to make it.[4]

Soon it began to emerge that such a mission was 'on the cards'. However, it was plain that, due to the tightness of the mission, precise navigation was the key to success. Bergen lay some 30 or more miles from the coast, and Hare's knowledge, having been there, was vital to the operation. He knew the exact location of the target and could take the Skuas to it by the most direct route. A secondary consideration, ignored by the young pilots when they heard of their assignment, was the lack of up-to-date training practice in dive-bombing. Their long time in the South Atlantic carrying out a reconnaissance role, had not been conducive to keep up their expertise in their main mission. The Director of the Naval Air Division at the Admiralty made some play of this lack of preparedness later, but his aircrews did not let him down. This rustiness was not allowed to stand in the way, and the precise planning went ahead at top speed.

With the most up-to-date information in front of them, the team planning the attack produced a simple 'in-bash-out' scenario. With extra input from the Air Staff Officer, Lieutenant Commander Aubrey St John Edwards, RN, Hare and Lieutenant Michael Hanson, RN, the two Senior Observers, plotted a meticulous track designed to combine the minimum air flight time with the most advantageous approach and withdrawal routes. Careful timing was called for to get the whole force across the North Sea and up the Norwegian coast with the alarm being raised that they were on their way.

The final plan had two groups of Skuas, nine in the first wave and seven in the second,[5] timed to arrive over the target at first light. To achieve this, take-off from Hatston was planned for 0445 hours, but, due to the weather condition prevailing, this despatch time had to be delayed to 0515 hours. Once airborne, the Skuas were to rendezvous at the departure point from Auskerrey and, maintaining visual contact at all times between the two waves, steer a course of 074° (True) for Marsten. This had them crossing the coast of Norway at an altitude of 12,000 feet in latitude 60.09° North. They were instructed to maintain strict radio silence throughout the whole approach and to ensure no slip ups their IFF (Identification Friend or Foe) equipment was not carried on the mission. They were allocated a W/T (wireless telegraphy) frequency of 366, but were only to break silence once the attack had been completed, in order to transmit a brief result summary report.

Once they found themselves inside the coast island chain off the main Norwegian coast, the two forces had only to steer along a track of 360° to bring them up the fiord. Should they make landfall south of this datum point, such a course would still take them to the target, but, if north, then it would lead them westward to the open sea.

Whatever the outcome of the actual dive-bomb attacks, the survivors had to get back quickly and, again, by the most efficacious and economical route. Each pilot was to assess his fuel situation once the attack had been completed. Those with less that 50 gallons remaining were given permission to ditch in Norway itself, but to keep well away from the Bergen region. If the aircraft could be landed in a serviceable state, then the Norwegian authorities were to be notified in the hope that the aircraft could be made airworthy enough to take off and complete their homeward leg the next day. Any aircraft forced to ditch that were damaged in the process, were to be totally destroyed to prevent them falling into enemy hands.

For those aircraft that came out both undamaged and with sufficient fuel to make the return leg, a rendezvous point was fixed above Lyso Island, some 6 miles, 270°, up the coast from Bergen. A 10-minute 'linger' window was all that could be allowed for the survivors to assemble here. Once this time was up the Skuas were to steer a course 260°, which would take them over Sumburgh in the Shetland Islands. Those aircraft that reached that haven with less than 30 gallons remaining fuel in their tanks, were given permission to land there. Special refuelling facilities had been laid on to cater for such an eventuality. Again, the return leg was to be flown in strict W/T silence, only to be broken when the force reached a position 60 miles from Sumburgh, where either the group leader, or individual aircraft if separated, could broadcast their ETA.

A last instruction, that no aircraft was to land back at Hatston with her 500 lb bomb still aboard, seemed (and proved) to be a totally unnecessary warning. Thus all was ready, but still the aircrew themselves were unaware of it. As Dickie Rolph was later to recall, in those days:

> TAGs were the last to be told, except that, being Chief TAG of 800 I was allowed in on the fringe. We did have three rating Observers on the Squadron, (our two original Petty Officer Observers having become casualties in September). A great deal of secrecy was apparent and it wasn't until we observed our armourers loading up with 500 lb bombs that we were then convinced that 'something was in the wind'.[6]

The approach

After a final briefing at 0330 hours, followed by a quick breakfast from 0400 hours onward, finally, at 0515 hours on the morning of 10 April, the Skua-IIs hauled themselves and their bombs down the narrow runway and into the cold, murky half-light of a far-northern sky. Some aircraft only just managed to clear the perimeter fence as their wheels retracted. Dickie Rolph remembered:

> The Skua, when fully loaded, needed all the runway that Hatston could provide, and, once airborne, it behaved like a pregnant porpoise, so it needed some flying .... It is about 325 miles from

Hatston to Bergen each way, and the maximum range of the Skua was about 675 miles, so there was no room for mucking about.[7]

They formed up as arranged and set course for Norway, steering a track of 074°. In total, sixteen heavily laden Skua-IIs took off from Hatston that morning, seven from No. 800 Squadron and nine from No. 803 Squadron. The composition of the force is shown in Table 8.

On leaving Shapinsay the formations ran into a rain shower and, while diverting around this, one aircraft became separated. White Leader, Lieutenant Edward Winchester Tollemache Taylour, RN, and Petty Officer Cunningham flying L3020, eventually carried out the entire mission entirely on their own.[8] They conducted their own navigation and their own separate attack just 10 minutes after the main force had struck.

Everything else proceeded as planned, most of the journey being made through heavy cloud. This thinned to a thin layer at 8,000 feet as, at 0700 hours, the Skuas approached the coast at an altitude of 12,000 feet. They made landfall over Kossfiord, almost spot-on and just 30 seconds behind schedule and headed up toward Bergen harbour from the south-east, with

Table 8　The destruction of the *Königsberg*, 10 April 1940

Unit	Section	Pilot	Rear-seat Man
800	Yellow	Captain Richard Thomas Partridge, RM	Lieutenant Commander Geoffrey Hare, RN
		Petty Officer (A) H. A. Monk	Leading Airman L. C. Eccleshall
		Petty Officer (A) Jack Hadley	Leading Airman M. Hall
	White	Lieutenant E. W. T. Taylour, RN	Petty Officer (A) H. G. Cunningham
		Lieutenant J. A. Rooper, RN	Petty Officer (A) R. S. Rolph
	Spare	Lieutenant Kenneth Vyvyan Vincent Spurway, RN	Petty Officer (A) C. J. E. Cotterill
		Acting Petty Officer J. A. Gardner	Naval Airman (1) A. Todd
803	Blue	Lieutenant William Paulet Lucy, RN	Lieutenant M. Charles. E. Hanson, RN
		Captain Eric D. McIver, RM	Leading Airman A. A. Barnard
		Lieutenant Alexander Beaufort Fraser-Harris, RN	Leading Airman George Scott Russell
	Green	Lieutenant H. E. R. Torin, RN	Midshipman (A) T. A. McKee
		Lieutenant L. A. Harris, RM	Naval Airman D. A. Prime
		Lieutenant (A) William Coutenay Antwiss Church, RN	Petty Officer (A) B. M. Seymour
	Red	Lieutenant Bryan John Smeeton, RN	Midshipman (A) Frederick Watkinson
		Lieutenant Cecil Howard Filmer, RN	Naval Airman (1) F. P. Dooley
		Acting Petty Officer T. F. Riddler	Naval Airman (1) H. T. Chatterley

a rising sun just glinting above the mountain tops. Although their target was not where it was expected, it only required a brief scan of the harbour before Partridge identified 'a cruiser of the *Köln* class' berthed alongside the Mole. The two sections then formed into single line astern and began their final phase of the approach dive, clearing a thin cloud layer at 8,000 feet as they did so. Under this flimsy veil, there was excellent visibility for at least 20 miles, with every detail of the target area clearly etched and sharp.

Dickie Rolph recalled:

> We formed into attack formation when crossing the mountains just north of Bergen, before turning towards the target, our diving point, and the harbour. My pilot, Lieutenant Rooper, RN, said, 'Keep a good look out for the bomb.' Now, I ask you, diving at 65–70 degrees, 290 knots and then pull out![9]

Thankfully, the German defenders were caught totally flat-footed as the long line of dive-bombs came barrelling down out of the sun like beads on a necklace. The German air raid alarm had already sounded at 0630 hours when a Lockheed Hudson reconnaissance aircraft from No. 233 Squadron RAF had alerted the defences at just the wrong time by making two runs over the harbour. This brought the *Königsberg*'s gunners tumbling out of their quarters to open fire, but, with her departure, most stood down again. Captain Ruhfus also retired back below, but almost at once the air raid warning sounded again and he rushed back to his bridge. At once he observed 'twelve to sixteen single-engined aircraft' making a circuit of the harbour. Initially, Ruhfus was not unduly alarmed, the *Luftwaffe* liaison officer had previously advised him that the British had no single-engined aircraft within range of his ship, so he rather naturally assumed that these newcomers were German fighters arriving overhead from the earlier alert.[10] Indeed, this self-delusion was shared by the pilot of the cruiser's own catapult aircraft who had joined him on the bridge to assist identification. Both he, and observers ashore, confirmed the captain's initial assessment, claiming he could see the German national black *Balkenkreuze* markings on the underside of their wings!

Both men were almost immediately disillusioned of this false comfort.

The destruction of the Königsberg

Having 'eyeballed' and confirmed the target, Partridge led the Skuas round in a turn east-south-east, gaining altitude as they went to regain their 12,000 feet plateau. By 0718 hours they were in line astern with the sun at their backs. They then made an initial approach dive down to 8,000 feet and, with the speed building, tipped over in the final attack dive. The majority of the Skuas went into the final 60 degree attack dive from a height of 6,500 feet, releasing at around 2,000 feet altitude, in what was then termed 'High Dive Bombing'. This gave the bomb time to arm itself on the way down and to have sufficient terminal velocity to penetrate the decks of the target and do meaningful damage to her innards. There were obviously a number of variations to this average, with some pilots releasing at 2,500 feet, and two of them, Lieutenant Rooper and Lieutenant Harris, recording 'Bombs Off' at 3,000 feet. Other pilots elected to press on further down in order to ensure hitting, with both Lieutenant Spurway and Lieutenant Lucy releasing at 1,500 feet. Richard Partridge went down to 1,800 feet, at which height, he recalled, he could quite clearly distinguish the swastika painted on her turret.

Young Lieutenant Church showed even more composure. During his initial dive he found himself out of position and, rather than waste his bomb, took the calm decision to go around and try again. This he did, making his second run from stern-to-bow of the target in a shallower, 40 degree attack. He dropped his bomb at just 200 feet through considerable flak as the *Königsberg*'s gunners were, by this time, definitely awake! He escaped unscathed for his audacity and clawed his way back up to 3,000 feet with bursting shells following his track. Church was later to report that his Skua suffered nothing more that, '... one large hole in mainplane close to fuselage'.

While Church's second attack was the shallowest approach, and most of the Skuas went in at a 60 degree angle, several attacked at 70 degrees and a few aircraft dived at a 50 degree angle. Of the first seven Skuas, all save Church, attacked the cruiser bows-to-stern and the majority of the bombs landed toward the after part of the vessel. The first eight Skuas actually met no flak at all down to 4,000 feet, with only one solitary anti-aircraft gun seemingly being manned and firing accurately at 5-second intervals initially. The ship's defensive fire with lighter automatic weapons only slowly increased as the second half of the attack continued. Three Skuas made their attacks in over the cruiser's starboard bow, and one more adopted Church's stern-to-bow approach.

'Flak opposition was not very heavy,' recalled Dickie Rolph, 'and we did our getaway at about 50 feet. I was able, to my satisfaction, to machine-gun a boat-load of German soldiers crossing the fiord. I believe I scored a few hits.'[11] The *Königsberg*'s gunners were soon joined by fire from neighbouring warships, including one motor fishing vessel described as a 'Flak ship',[12] and from guns ashore to the south-west, but none of the pilots were deflected in their aims by any of the flak.

On the receiving end of the Skuas' attentions, it was a very different story. The cruiser soon became enveloped in the smoke and flames of explosions as the 500 lb bombs rained down in quick succession. There were no 'wides'; every bomb was a hit or a very near miss, either in the water astern or on the Mole close alongside. The resulting clouds of smoke, dust from the rubble and the fires aboard the target were intense and made observation of results difficult. Few of the pilots could get a clear view of results. One of those who did, Petty Officer Riddler, confessed his bomb had missed the ship but started a large fire in a warehouse on the jetty alongside. Leading Airman Russell stated that his pilot, Lieutenant Fraser-Harris, quite definitely hit fair-and-square on the cruiser's forecastle, punching through and leaving a large black hole from which vomited flames and white smoke. Lieutenant Spurway noticed his bomb detonated inside the ship, and resulted in clouds of debris and smoke. Finally, Captain McIver scored what was probably the decisive hit of the attack, amidships between the *Königsberg*'s two funnels, which penetrated her engine room and blew open her hull on the port side, lethal damage that was almost immediately compounded by a near miss just a few feet away.

The concentration of this dive-bombing attack deserves much more attention and merit than it has ever received. The DNAD later recorded that the estimated Mean Error for this attack was 50 yards, which compared 'very favourably' with a 1939 practice attack, which had only achieved a 70-yard spread. So much for 'lack of practice'.[13]

The last pilot over the target was, of course, the intrepid Taylour, making his lone assault well after the rest. Arriving some 10 minutes late, he found the target shrouded in smoke, but nonetheless made his 70 degree attack dive from 6,500 feet, releasing his bomb at 2,000 feet. He scored a close miss on the Mole alongside. The smoke cleared long enough for him to get a good look and he reported that the cruiser was badly hit. There was a fire amidships, she was listing to port and oil was leaking from her tanks staining the water alongside.[14] The final witness of *Königsberg*'s ultimate demise proved to be none of her assailants, but came from the captain of the American freighter *Flying Fish* anchored in the harbour, who had a grandstand view. According to this eyewitness the German cruiser began sinking by the bow, with flames soaring up to 100 feet into the sky and she went deeper and deeper. Eventually, her stern rose up and her screws could be seen. Some 50 minutes after the departure of the last dive-bomber, the *Königsberg* rolled over and capsized.

The bomb tally

From the subsequent German report, we can piece together a reasonably accurate assessment of bomb strikes.[15] The report admitted that, although the ship's guns were in action throughout the assault, even continuing by manual control once the electric power had been cut, the speed of the attack and the machine-gunning of the upper decks by the diving aircraft, made detailed records difficult. Nonetheless, the subsequent analysis gave the following details.

Hit No. 1

This bomb landed between the Mole and the cruiser, abreast the ship's aircraft catapult. Splinters scythed through the hull and oil bunkers at this point and pierced No. 2 boiler-room, wrecking the feed-pump situated there. Immediately the boiler-room began to fill with steam. Oil from the opened up bunkers also poured into the boiler-room and ignited, and a hasty evacuation by the surviving duty personnel into No. 1 boiler-room next door followed. The fires in No. 1 boiler-room were dampened down in order to minimise further escaping steam.

Hit No. 2

This may, in fact, have been two hits in close succession. One bomb passed straight through the signal bridge intact, and skidded off into the water off the port beam close alongside before detonating below the surface. The resultant explosion ripped open a large hole in the side of the ship and crushed part of the ship's double-bottom. Water at once began to flood No. 4 boiler-room and auxiliary machine room and nearby compartments. The ship's wireless room and transmitting station were also immediately inundated, and, although some men escaped from the latter, the radio operators were trapped and drowned at their posts. The duty watch men were also got up from No. 4 boiler room, but found that the hatch had distorted by the blast and could not be shut behind them. Water bubbled up through this aperture, rapidly filling portside compartments to deck-head level. The cruiser began to lurch over to port almost immediately and this angle steadily increased.

Hit No. 3

This bomb took the route straight through the ship's after control position and detonated between decks, starting a big fire. Splinters from this hit penetrated bulkheads and caused heavy losses among the ammunition supply parties of the 88 mm anti-aircraft guns, whose fire subsequently rapidly fell away.

Hit No. 4

The bomb went straight through the starboard side of the quarterdeck aft, abreast the sternmost 88-mm gun position. After plunging on down via the senior engineer's cabin, this weapon exploded above the starboard auxiliary machine room. The detonation caused widespread damage and several men were wounded.

Hit No. 5

The bomb entered the fiord off the port side of the ship, abreast the after 5.9 inch gun turret. The water-hammer effect was strongest from this blast and severely whipped the hull of the ship, springing internal joints. Numerous splinters came inboard, opening up compartments to limited flooding.

Hit No. 6

This bomb struck dead on the ship's centreline amidships, entering the upper deck between the after funnel and the ship's catapult. It continued down and exploded between decks, causing considerable devastation and inflicting casualties.

Königsberg *abandoned*

At the end of the attack the Port Forward boiler-room (No. 4) was totally out of service and filled with water. Splinter holes in the Starboard Forward boiler-room (No. 3), which had been filled by the damage-control team, were again sprung by subsequent concussion of near misses, and slow but steady flooding resulted. The Starboard After boiler-room (No. 2) had been totally abandoned and the only intact boiler-room, No. 1, had to be shut down. The total close down of any steam power had a knock-on effect on damage control. While splinter damage had knocked out many of the pumps entirely, even those that could still function, were without power. Consequently, the big fire amidships steadily gained ground.

The alternative propulsion plant, the cruising diesel engines, had been damaged by the bomb explosions aft and were not functional. All electrical power failed and only small hand-operated fire extinguishers remained available to the fire-fighting teams, who consequently fought a hopeless battle of containment and limitation. Hopes that hydrants ashore might substitute proved in vain because the several bomb hits on the Mole had cut the water main. The big fire spreading through the torpedo flat clearly threatened even larger explosions should the torpedo warheads explode.[16] Fearing more casualties, Captain Ruhfus ordered 'Abandon Ship'. The wounded crewmen were lifted ashore over the bow of the ship.

A subsequent tally found that only eighteen men had been killed outright, an amazingly low number considering the number of hits, and that a further twenty-four were wounded, half of them seriously. The ship's surgeon and medical team had been forced to abandon the sickbay during the attack, but continued to work as best they could both aboard the ship and subsequently ashore in an emergency medical post. Many of the injuries were serious burns and scalding. Their efforts were supplemented by an Army medical team, which soon arrived to assist.

On the material side, desperate attempts to launch the ship's aircraft[17] failed due to the list and splinter damage to the aircraft itself, and she was lost with the ship. However, more successful was the saving of four light 20 mm automatic anti-aircraft guns, which were hastily unbolted and manhandled ashore, along with some ready-use ammunition. These were later used to bolster the harbour's defences.

With the crew ashore, the fires were free to rage unchecked throughout the ship, the flames all the time being fed with fresh oil from the leaking bunkers. The torpedo warheads did finally ignite, causing a considerable explosion, which the Norwegian civilians ashore thought was the ship's main magazine blowing up, but this did not happen.[18] Instead, at 0951 hours the gutted hulk of the *Königsberg* rolled slowly over to port and vanished beneath the waters of the harbour, leaving a huge oil slick and a column of thick black smoke that rose to a height of 100 feet. It was a major achievement, the first major warship to be sunk by dive-bombing alone.

The return

The cost for this striking victory was modest for the result attained. Nonetheless, it was tragic. Dickie Rolph witnessed it: 'Shortly after leaving the entrance to the fiord I saw a Skua dive vertically into the sea from about 1,000 feet. This turned out to be Lieutenant J. B. Smeeton, RN, and Midshipman F. Watkinson, RN, and proved to be our only casualty of the trip.'[19] This aircraft had survived the attack, seemingly unscathed, and the cause of the loss was a mystery. Both aircrew died.

Over Lyso Island, the re-forming of the surviving aircraft took place, and course was set west again. The aircraft re-entered the area of heavy cloud, down to 2,000 feet above sea level, with visibility just 2 to 3 miles maximum. Not surprisingly, the squadron cohesion gradually lost its shape in these conditions, and individual aircraft began to straggle, some losing touch with the leaders completely. But all except Smeeton, made it home.

Dickie Rolph remembered that:

> Some aircraft were force to make for Sumburgh in the Shetlands due to shortage of fuel, others of us managed to make Hatston, arriving with the proverbial spoonful of fuel in our tanks. After a debriefing session shortly after our arrival back at Hatston, we were told that the American Consul in Bergen had managed to get through to the Admiralty and reported that the *Königsberg* had sunk some 2 hours after our attack.[20]

Evaluation

While the Skua crews, at their debriefing, had meticulously made no outright claims to having actually sunk the *Königsberg*, they were sure that they had damaged her badly, if not terminally. They were right of course, but an RAF Hudson 'D' for David, from No. 224 Squadron at Lossiemouth, overflew Bergen at 1515 hours, and reported seeing no sign of the cruiser, but a large patch of oil stretching from the Mole for 2,000 yards out in the main harbour. Only when the American Consul's report came in was the Skuas' victory confirmed.

It is also pertinent to note that, back in Berlin, they were equally ignorant of the loss of the cruiser at this moment. *Grandadmiral* Raeder, head of the *Kriegsmarine*, was busy detailing progress of the invasion to the *Führer* himself based on information given by the various Group commanders. On the whole it was favourable, the German Navy had got away with a very audacious plan, not scot-free, but remarkably lightly so far. One thing that did cause concern was the lack of adequate air defences at Bergen and the threat this meant to the *Königsberg* should she fail to sail that day!

It is refreshing to read the report on the sinking of his vessel submitted by Captain Ruhfus. It is both clear and unambiguous and shirks no blame. The conclusions he reached were different to those assumed by the British at the time, for he discards McIver's hit amidships as being the vital blow. On the contrary, Ruhfus states that this hit, although 'spectacular', did not penetrate far into the ship, but only detonated in the torpedo flat and vented out sideways. In his estimation, it was the one, or perhaps two, very near misses off the ship's port side that did the real damage. These tore open a large section of the ship's bottom.

Analysing the cumulative effect of the repeated blows, he concluded that these destroyed the ship's capability to fight the fires and take damage control measures to any effective extent. Compartments flooded by the near misses, could not be pumped out due to damage caused. Even those bombs that missed the ship altogether and exploded on the Mole alongside, added to this neutralising effect, for the fragments and debris that came inboard from these explosions smashed water mains, severed hoses and pipes and cut down the crew in exposed positions.

He recorded that the two or three shells from the Norwegian coast battery that had hit the ship the day before, while not being serious in themselves, had been concentrated on her starboard side on the waterline abreast her after funnel. This weakened the very point opened up by the two bombs that exploded aboard almost at that very same spot. One of these was in line with her after-deckhouse, in line with her sternmost 3.5 inch gun mounting, but the other was midway between the funnels, just forward of the patched-up shell damage, which caused uncontrollable flooding.

She had sunk by the bows in 30 minutes.[21] Her subsequent fate can briefly be told. The wreck remained *in situ*, her magazines intact but a latent threat to the surrounding anchorage. In 1941, the Germans finally got around to raising her from her shallow grave, though she remained inverted. They towed the hulk away to Nyhavn but later returned her to Laksevaag, and managed to turn her upright. She still leaked like a sieve and had to have a pumping vessel constantly alongside to keep her afloat.

In 1944 she was moved into a floating dock, but fell over when she was subsequently raised, causing much damage and causing the dock itself to list. In February 1945 she was again towed away to Berlandsundet Bay, where she again keeled over and sank to her side in shallow water and the Germans gave up. Eventually, in 1947, a Norwegian specialist team finally broke both sections up for scrap.

Postscript

A final word is in order to place the brave men who carried out this attack in a true perspective and enshrine their place in history. Captain A. V. S. Yates, MVO, RN, who happened to be at Hatston that day, many years later was to recall his impressions of this outstanding operation,[22] nowadays almost totally unknown:

When the Second World War started both Admiral Somerville and I were mobilised. He incidentally, was my cousin and was given the job of supervising new miscellaneous weapons. Among these was radar then called RDF, in which I had acquired some knowledge first having met Watson Watt at Bawdsey in my pre-retirement days and secondly during my near 2 years with Sperry; so James asked me to join him.

In April 1940 I had been investigating RAF uses of radar with a view to reporting how they could be adapted to Naval requirements and further how they could be replaced in due course. This took me to the Orkneys, Shetlands and Fair Island and it was on return from Fair Island that I was staying, I think, in the Kirkwall Hotel investigating Hatston among other places in that area. [There follows an extract from his diary of the time.]

10 April 1940: What a day! I awoke at 0430 to the roaring of the Skuas as sixteen of them took off for Bergen, and I was on the aerodrome to welcome them as fifteen out of sixteen returned soon after 9.00. Brave gang in old aircraft, which cannot catch a modern bomber, let alone escape from a fighter, they all attacked the one German cruiser (with staggered turrets) in Bergen. They estimated three if not four hits and of course hits on the jetty alongside may well have been effective.

Anxiously we counted as they came back, most in perfect formation, two with crumpled wings, the last one very groggy, banking widely as he came into land and having to make a second shot at it. No heroics, no press photographers here as in the RAF. They fell in outside Headquarters and as they were dismissed, I heard one sailor chuckle to another 'What do we do now mate? Bomb up again?' 'Shouldn't be surprised', came the answer. As they walked away little Dick Bell-Davies, their Admiral, with the VC ribbon on his breast, said, 'Well done' to one or two of them. That was all!

Not quite all.

That evening the BBC went on the air to broadcast the victory in their own inimitable, and (still today) their arrogantly *ignorant* manner, 'The RAF has done it again!' they thundered.[23]

NOTES

1. Captain Stephen Roskill, RN, *The War at Sea. The Defensive 1939–1941*. HMSO, London, 1954.

2. The *Königsberg*'s propulsion plant was a mix of both steam and diesel machinery, with a pair of double-acting four-stroke ten-cycle MAN diesels supplementing the normal geared turbines. This combination proved 'unpredictable' in action.

3. Captain Ruhfus, *Über den Einsatz des Kreuzers 'Königsberg' bei der Besetzung Bergens am 9. April und den Untergang des Schiffes an 10 April 1940*. (Official Report on the damage to the cruiser *Königsberg* on 9 April and the sinking of the ship on 10 April 1940.) 1.Abt. Std. 307683; Xerox copy of original German typescript in author's collection.

4. Captain Richard T. Partridge, RM, to the author on 28 March and 12 April 1977, originally quoted in Peter C. Smith, *Into the Assault*, John Murray, London, 1985, and also his memoirs, *Operation Skua*, Yeovilton, FAA Museum, 1983.

5. In the event, one aircraft of the second group became separated and instead of a nine and seven attack formation, the attack was delivered as a nine, six and one sequence.

6. R. S. Rolph, *The Königsberg Story*, draft article for *TAG Magazine* (presented to the author prior to publication).

7. *Ibid.*

8. For which dedication and bravery, Lieutenant Taylour was eventually to receive the distinction of being awarded a much-merited DSC, Bar and Mention, all on the same day!

9. Dickie Rolph, *The Königsberg Story*, *op cit.*

10. Ruhfus, Report, *op cit.*

11. Dickie Rolph, *The Königsberg Story*, *op cit.* Lieutenant Filmer also reported sighting this boatload of troops and Naval Airman Dooley also subjected it to some accurate bursts of machine-gun fire.

12. This was probably *Schiff 18*, one of the auxiliary vessels that had remained at Bergen. Cunningham was one pilot taken under fire by this vessel as he made his getaway. He recorded that this made him belatedly realise that a hazily remembered reference to a 'Flagship' at the early-morning briefing, had probably actually meant '*Flak* ship'!

13. Admiralty, *Notes by Director of Naval Air Division on Report on sinking of Königsberg*, dated 25 April 1940. X/L04326. Contained in National Archives ADM 199/478.

14. The intrepid Taylour was later to serve with No. 808 Squadron aboard *Ark Royal* in the Mediterranean, being credited with the destruction of one CR 42 and one Ju87, for which he got a Bar to the DFC awarded for the Bergen attack. One who flew with him in No. 800 Squadron, where he was the Junior Flight Commander, remembered him as 'a typical RN flyer, tall, dark, slim, smoked fags at the 3.00 am briefing like a chimney using forced draft!' He went on to serve with No. 802 Squadron on Russia Convoys, where he was killed in action on 13 September 1942, during the battle for PQ 18.

15. Ruhfus Report, *op cit.*

16. The *Königsberg* was equipped with twelve torpedo tubes in four triple mountings.

17. The normal complement of the cruiser was two Arado Ar196 floatplanes, but only one appears to have been aboard at the time of her sinking.
18. One post-war British account, which is *still* being circulated, stated that the *Königsberg* blew up and broke in half, which is total nonsense.
19. Dickie Rolph, *The Königsberg Story, op cit.*
20. *Ibid.*
21. In stark contrast to Captain Ruhfus's Report, a revisionist description of the attack on the *Königsberg* published in London and New York in 1980, claims that she was only 'set on fire and put out of action'. It adds that she was decommissioned and broken up in 1943. It says absolutely nothing at all about the witnessed and photographed fact that she capsized and sank within 30 minutes of the attack! *Conway's All the World's Fighting Ships, 1933–1946.* German section by Erwin Sieche. Edited by Roger Chesneau. The book is claimed to be 'definitive'.
22. Captain A. V. S. Yates, MVO, RN, to Commander Dennis White, RN, Fleet Air Arm Museum, Yeovilton, 13 February 1984. Copy kindly made available to the author by the late Dickie Rolph, BEM.
23. John Dell has pointed out an equal irony with regard the results of the RAF's pre-war policies, in that, the Fleet Air Arm had been allocated Hawker Henleys as target-tugs and that there were actually several Hendons at Hatston at exactly the same time as the attack on the *Königsberg*. He adds: 'Thus, while the Skua crews were making their way over the North Sea at the limit of their range, in danger of running out of fuel, back at the base they had flown from were aircraft that, in their original designed role, were dive-bombers with 50 per cent greater range, twice the bomb-load and at least 50 mph higher top speed (and probably 100 mph faster cruising speed). Madness!' John Dell to the author, 19 August 2002. We can but agree.

8

LONG ODDS

After the euphoria of the first attack, the war in Norway deteriorated into a long, hard slog, with the Royal Navy taking on the *Luftwaffe* almost unaided for the first time, but, unfortunately, not the last. Already, the naïve predictions that naval aircraft did not need to be as good as land-based aircraft because all their battles would be fought out at sea, had proved so much pie-in-the-sky. It was the young Skua pilots who had to fight a type of war nobody had foreseen.

The Bergen blitzkriegs

On 11 April the Skuas conducted nothing but routine convoy patrols, but the arrival of No. 801 Squadron, moved up to Hatston on the way to try and join the *Furious*, brought the potential striking force up to a peak strength, twenty aircraft being available.[1]

There were ample shipping targets reported as still in the harbour at Bergen and so a mass dive-bomber attack using all three squadrons was despatched from Hatston at 1405 hours on 12 April. The force went off in three waves, and the first comprised seven Skuas from No. 803 Squadron, again led by Lieutenant W. P. Lucy, RN; the second wave had Acting Major R. T. Partridge, RM, leading six aircraft from No. 800 Squadron, while the third wave, commanded by Lieutenant Commander Hugh Peter Bramwell, RN, consisted of seven Skuas from No. 801 Squadron. Again, the bomb load for each machine was a single 500 lb SAP. The whole force of twenty aircraft had cleared the runway by 1430 hours. Partridge took Lieutenant Commander (O) K. W. Beard, a very experienced naval observer.

They crossed the Norwegian coast, which was covered with 10/10th cloud at 6,000 feet. This protected them on the approach. The sky was clearer over the harbour and as they drew closer they observed several large transport ships alongside and moored out in the harbour. A line-astern dive approach was made against the latter, machine-gunning on the way down, and each aircraft dropped one 500 lb SAP bomb. Unfortunately, although many near misses were reported, there were no direct hits scored on any vessel. An enemy MTB was strafed by Green section repeatedly.

Petty Officer Jimmy Gardner's aircraft was hit by anti-aircraft fire and forced to ditch in a bay, at Kors Fiord. Both Jimmy and Naval Airman (1)

Table 9   Composition of No. 803 Squadron Bergen strike, 12 April 1940

Section	Aircraft	Pilot	Navigator
Blue	F	Lieutenant W. P. Lucy	Lieutenant M. C. E. Hanson
	G	Lieutenant C. H. Filmer	Leading Airman G. S. Russell
Green	A	Lieutenant H. E. R. Torin	Midshipman T. A. McKee
	B	Lieutenant L. A. Harris	Naval Airman D. A. Prime
	L	Lieutenant W. C. A. Church	Naval Airman A. J. Hayman
Red	M	Lieutenant K. V. V. Spurway*	Petty Officer A. C. J. Cotterill
	Q	Petty Officer J. A. Gardner	Naval Airman (1) A. Todd
	R	Petty Officer T. Riddler	Naval Airman H. Chatterley

*On loan from No. 800 Squadron.

Todd were fished out of the drink by the crew of the American freighter that he had earlier machine-gunned. America was supposed to be neutral, but the crew did not seem to hold a grudge and soon Jimmy was allowed considerable freedom. Eventually, after being cared for by first the Americans and then the Norwegian authorities, Jimmy found himself staring in a shop window in Bergen, while a member of the German occupation forces earnestly tried to engage him in conversation in bad Norwegian about the goods on display in the window! Gardner decided it was high time to make a departure and find his way back to the UK, and eventually ended up at Molde as we have seen. Both he and Todd finally got back to the UK via a Norwegian fishing boat and returned some time later to Hatston. On arrival at Headquarters, '... he was treated to some of the "Pussers best"[2] and then was sent for by the C-in-C at Scapa. Before he got word Jimmy was lifted aboard the flagship in a euphoric state, that really was excusable', recalled Dickie Rolph.[3] No doubt Admiral Sir Charles Forbes turned a blind eye under the circumstances.

Gardner's aircraft was the sole casualty of this operation.

The operation was repeated again 2 days later by two squadrons, six Skuas from No. 800 Squadron making their attack 1 hour ahead of nine from No. 803 squadron. Again, the latter unit's composition this day was as outlined in Table 10.

The first wave departed Hatston at 0500 hours and the second 50 minutes later, with No. 800 Squadron reaching the coast of Norway at 0700 hours and commencing their attack 12 minutes later.

The first strike bombed large freighters moored alongside the quay at Bergen and also, as targets of opportunity, machine-gunned a pair of enemy submarines, *U-7* and *U-60*, and two E-boats, *S-23* and *S-25*, seen in the harbour.

During the interval between the departure of the first wave and the arrival of the second, the weather closed in and the second strike crossed

Table 10   Composition of No. 803 Squadron Bergen strike, 14 April 1940

Section	Aircraft	Pilot	Navigator
Blue	F	Lieutenant W. P. Lucy	Lieutenant M. C. E. Hanson
	G	Captain E. D. McIver	Leading Airman A. A. Barnard
	H	Lieutenant A. B. Fraser-Harris	Leading Airman G. S. Russell
Green	A	Lieutenant H. E. R. Torin	Midshipman T. A. McKee
	B	Lieutenant L. A. Harris	Naval Airman D. A. Prime
	K	Lieutenant W. C. A. Church	Leading Airman F. Coston
Red	C	Lieutenant K. V. V. Spurway*	Petty Officer Andrews
	Q	Lieutenant C. H. Filmer	Naval Airman F. P. Dooley
	R	Petty Officer T. F. Riddler	Naval Airman H. Chatterley

*On loan from No. 800 Squadron.

the coast at 8,500 feet, again with 10/10th cloud cover to shield them. However, this prevented them from observing any reference points. The whole nine-strong squadron then dived, in formation, through this thick cloud, coming out into clear skies at an altitude of just 400 feet. However, Red section lost contact with the rest during this dangerous manoeuvre. The rest located Marstein and completed three complete circuits in section line astern. Green section lost contact with Lucy at this point and both Torin and Spurway decided together to abort the mission due to the adverse weather conditions.

However, Blue leader continued to take his section up the fiord to Bergen and carried out a dive-bombing attack on one large transport anchored in the harbour, claiming to have hit and destroyed her. This was the German freighter *Barenfels* (7,560 BRT), which was loaded with a cargo of war supplies, including the vital anti-aircraft guns that Raeder was so anxious to see emplaced around the port. Lucy himself made this their target and made a low-level glide-bombing attack, his bomb scoring a very near miss, detonating between the after part of ship itself and the jetty alongside, which stove in her hull underwater. The *Barenfels* sank by the stern despite all attempts to save her, taking her cargo, and those crucial guns, to the harbour bottom.

A Dornier flying boat was also seen moored in the harbour and the three Skuas circled her then conducted a strafing attack. This was tempting fate too much, and Captain of Marines Eric Donald McIver's aircraft was hit by flak at low level, crashing in flames into the harbour. Both McIver (who was later Mentioned in Dispatches) and Leading Airman Albert Alexander Barnard, were killed outright. The remaining pair of Skuas exited safely, and they noted that the wind direction had altered 180 degrees during the mission.

Long-range armed reconnaissance

Naturally, the success of the first mission, coupled with these reinforcements, proved too tempting to resist. What had been done once, could be done again. Much has been said of how out of touch with reality the Admiralty were at this stage of the war under the ceaseless prodding of the First Lord, Winston Churchill. His political skills were considerable, as he was soon to prove, but his tactical decisions, especially those with an air/sea element, were often disastrous, and amounted to little but action for action's sake. Major Partridge was to put on record that he felt at that period, his Commanding Officer, Acting Captain Howe, was put under considerable and continuous pressure to mount such operations, in the cause of 'offensive at any cost regardless of reality'. Daily offensive reconnaissance sorties by single Skuas were to become one manifestation of this 'Posthumous VC' type of mission.

The first such mission was a reconnaissance of the outlying defences of Bergen, which was conducted by just two aircraft, F – Lucy/Hanson and A – Torin/McKee. They took off at 0500 hours on 15 April, and again, flying at an altitude of 4,000 feet, they ran into very bad weather on the way to the target, but then split up at 0650 hours. They reached the coast at 0705 hours, and made individual and independent final approaches up to Bergen, Lucy from the north, Torin from the south. In the fiord a German patrol boat, the *Tarantel-18*, was attacked by Lucy, the Skua dropping a single 250 lb and eight 20 lb bombs, scoring hits. The *Tarantel-18* was thought to have sunk immediately, but was only badly damaged. Torin sighted the surfaced German submarine *U-58* in the southern approaches, which he reported as 'probably the same submarine seen the day before'. An attack was made, and one hit with a 20 lb bomb was claimed on this vessel, which prevented her from diving, but even if correct, this would not have been sufficient to cause much damage. Both aircraft returned safely to the *Ark Royal* independently at 0925 hours. On conclusion of this operation No. 803 Squadron was disembarked from the *Ark Royal* at Hatston.

The second of these armed photo-reconnaissance sorties over Bergen was arranged for 17 April. Again, a pair of Skuas, this time from No. 800 Squadron, was sent off together. The original time of departure was delayed from 0515 to 0945 hours due to the weather conditions. Again, the aircraft both carried a single 250 lb SAP and eight 20 lb Cooper bombs. Splitting up as before, both aircraft made alternative low-level approaches to the port, descending from 5,000 to 1,000 feet.

A good target, claimed to be the 1,535 ton German Training Ship/Minelaying *Bremse*, was observed secured to the Dokajeer pier and a dive-bombing attack was made against this vessel at 1150 hours, but with no obvious results.

On the return journey, the same reversal of the wind direction almost proved fatal to Birdy Partridge. Battling against this caused his Skua's fuel situation to approach the critical and he decided to divert to the allocated 'Emergency' airstrip at Sumburgh at Shetland. However, to his dismay, on making his final approach, Birdy received the wave-off because the strip itself was unserviceable. By this stage the aircraft had been airborne for a total of 4 hours 35 minutes, so carrying on to Hatston was just not an option. Birdy had to get his machine down on terra firma as best he could and did so! The aircraft was a total write-off but Partridge and his observer walked away from the wreckage intact. A Swordfish was eventually despatched to collect them and, on their eventual return to Hatston, Birdy was 'forthright' in his protest at such hazards being forced on the Skua aircrew, but in vain![4]

Operation Duck

German Junkers Ju87 Stuka dive-bombers had also been operating from Sola airfield near Stavanger, with considerable success, and it had been decided to conduct a naval bombardment of that base to try and stamp the nest out. The heavy cruiser HMS *Suffolk*, with four escorting destroyers, had been despatched from Scapa Flow to carry out this attack on 16 April. In the early hours of 17 April *Suffolk* had fired 202 rounds of 8-inch high-explosive shells from her eight main guns into the target area, destroying two fuel dumps, but causing little other damage. For this minimal disturbance the *Luftwaffe* were to exact a heavy penalty. For almost 7 hours the cruiser was subjected to repeated air attacks; she had really stirred up a hornets' nest. She was near-missed innumerable times, and then hit by a heavy bomb aft, which did enormous damage.[5]

Frantic signals for air cover to the RAF were made in vain, and eventually the FAA was called upon for aid. The plea for help finally reached RNAS Hatson at noon on 17 April and Green section of No. 803 Squadron was immediately scrambled to help. The three Skuas eventually sighted the crippled ship struggling along with a heavy list, some 150 miles from the coast. Within a few minutes of their arrival she was attacked yet again by a gaggle of Heinkel He111 bombers. Lieutenant Lucy led his section to the attack and they managed to drive the enemy off, badly damaging one of the Heinkels in the process. After about an hour, both Blue and Yellow sections arrived to provide further protection. Almost at once, Yellow section sighted a Dornier Do17 bomber some 1,000 feet above them, and at once pulled up after her. The Dornier jettisoned her bombs, put her nose down and left the Skuas standing! While continuing the fruitless chase, however, another He111 was seen and they managed to surprise her, carrying out a stern attack. Yellow 1 and 2 attacked repeatedly, and were joined by Blue 1 and 2. Finally, with thick white smoke

Table 11 Skua protection of HMS *Suffolk*, 17 April 1940

Section	Aircraft	Pilot	Navigator
Blue	F	Lieutenant W. P. Lucy	Lieutenant M. C. E. Hanson
	G	Lieutenant A. B. Fraser-Harris	Leading Airman G. S. Russell
	H	Lieutenant J. M. Christian	Naval Airman S. G. Wright
Green	A	Lieutenant H. E. R. Torin	Midshipman T. A. McKee
	B	Sub-Lieutenant I. Easton	Leading Airman F. Coston
Red	K	Lieutenant L. A. Harris	Petty Officer Andrews
	L	Sub-Lieutenant G. W. Brokensha	Naval Airman A. J. Hayman
	M	Sub-Lieutenant P. N. Charlton	Leading Airman A. Ashby

issuing from both her engines, the Heinkel dived into thick cloud and they lost them. Meanwhile, yet further He111s, witnessing the attack, retired from the scene and the *Suffolk* continued on course for Scapa.

At 1440 hours the patrolling fighters were relieved by No. 801 Squadron, with Red section under Lieutenant R. L. Strange, RN, and Yellow section led by Lieutenant Commander H. P. Bramwell, RN. At 1520 hours Strange's team drove off a reconnaissance aircraft, while 13 minutes later Bramwell managed to surprise what was probably the same aircraft, a Dornier Do18G from the I/KuFlG 406, and shot her into the sea.

Meanwhile, Yellow section of No. 801 Squadron landed, refuelled and then led a section of Sea Gladiators to *Suffolk*'s position, which by then was just some 40 miles from safety. Blue leader proceeded back to the *Suffolk*'s position independently, but no further enemy aircraft appeared and the *Suffolk* finally dragged herself into the Scapa Flow, where she was beached.

Once too often

On 20 April the weather continued to be poor to bad, but limited Skua operations were still managed. A long-range striking force made up of Skuas from both No. 800 and No. 801 Squadrons was sent to accomplish this, but poor weather made the attack unsatisfactory and nothing was achieved. One of this group, Skua L2999, failed to return from the mission. The fate of her veteran aircrew, Midshipman (A) John Richard Crossley, RN and Petty Officer (A) Maurice Hall, DSM, MID (2), was never discovered. It was a lonely and pointless demise, which Partridge, campaigning against such missions, especially during bad weather, felt deeply.

Birdy Partridge himself was out that day with Lieutenant Bostock, on a solitary armed reconnaissance flight to Larvik, south-west of Oslo. The Admiralty orders were to attack shipping targets located there, so Birdy's

Skua was loaded up with a 500 lb SAP bomb instead of the usual 250 lb bomb normally carried on such operations.

Although the distance was considerable, Partridge opted to add an additional 80 miles to the flight time by diverting around the principal *Luftwaffe* fighter base of Sola airfield near Stavanger, rather than risk overflying. At 12,000 feet the coast was crossed and course was set to Larvik itself. However, much to their frustration, someone had got it very wrong, for, on reaching their target area, nothing of any significance was found and they turned to flog their way home again. However, a fleeting opportunity did occur with the bonus of being able to rid themselves of the 500 lb bomb, when a speeding German E-boat, *S-22*, was sighted. Birdy attacked this fast and very elusive target. He made the attack with some confidence, but in the end he missed the zig-zagging boat by some 100 yards. As he later confessed to the author:

> I can remember pre-war bombing targets towed by armoured motor-boats off Singapore for simulated dive-bombing, with similar results.[6]

To his lasting chagrin, soon after wasting his only bomb on such a slippery customer, Birdy found a potential target much more worthy of his attention, a surfaced U-boat sailing sedately along a straight-and-narrow course. He could do nothing more than carry out a quick strafing run, which did not seem to worry the submarine in the slightest. Partridge told me, 'It was like peppering a rhinoceros with an airgun.' There was no time to tarry for any further action, not that machine-gun fire was ever going to do much damage to a stoutly constructed U-boat.

The carriers return

The long-awaited return of the carriers *Ark Royal* and *Glorious* took place on 21 April and preparations were made for the Skua squadrons to re-embark in these and the *Furious* as soon as she returned from Norway.[7] In readiness for this, an additional Skua section was authorised to be added to the six Skua-IIs and two or three Rocs[8] set-up maintained by Nos 800 and 801 Squadrons. These aircraft rejoined the *Ark Royal* from Hatston at Scapa Flow on 23 April, but only after some very hasty deck-landing practice had been conducted. Many of the Skua pilots had, in fact, never made a landing aboard a carrier in this aircraft. One of those that had not was Richard Partridge! He confided to me many years later:

> I kept that fact to myself as I thought it might be bad for morale. Actually, I was not very worried about it because of certain charac-teristics of the Skua.[9]

A Glorious *interlude*

After their short period ashore, No. 803 Squadron also went back to sea again on 22 April. This time their host was the aircraft carrier *Glorious*, which was commanded by the former submariner, Captain Guy D'Oyly-Hughes, DSO*, DSC, RN, who knew little of aircraft operations and who constantly clashed with his Commander (Air), J. B. Heath.[10] *Glorious* already had aboard seventeen Gloster Gladiator-II biplane fighters from No. 263 Squadron, RAF, which, under Operation *DX*, she was to convey to Norway to work from a frozen lake airfield, then under preparation.

The composition of the squadron for the move is seen in Table 12.

Unfortunately, the fly-on was marred by a bad accident. Midshipman Griffith's aircraft (8R) crashed over the port side of the carrier while landing, and although the pilot was recovered, his air gunner, Ken Brown, was killed.

Romsdalen Valley combat

On the later afternoon of 24 April, *Glorious* flew off a six-plane force to cover the Andalsnes area. The Skuas were from Blue and Red sections composed as in Table 13.

The two sections took off from the carrier at 1740 hours and proceeded direct to Andalsnes. At 1830 hours they flew up the valley at 8,000 feet, sighting many bomb craters from Andalsnes to Dombas, the work of the ever-present *Luftwaffe*. The snow had been swept on Lake Lesjaskog,

Table 12   No. 803 Squadron on transfer to HMS *Glorious*, 22 April 1940

Section	Aircraft	Pilot	Navigator
Blue	F	Lieutenant W. P. Lucy	Lieutenant M. C. E. Hanson
	G	Lieutenant A. B. Fraser-Harris	Leading Airman G. S. Russell
	H	Lieutenant J. M. Christian	Naval Airman S. G. Wright
Green	A	Lieutenant H. E. R. Torin, RN	Midshipman T. A. McKee, RN
	B	Lieutenant G. R. Callingham, RN	Naval Airman D. Prime
Red	P	Lieutenant L. A. Harris, RM	Petty Officer K. Baldwin
	Q	Midshipman A. S. Griffith, RN	Naval Airman K. A. Brown
	R	Sub-Lieutenant I. Easton, RN	Naval Airman A. J. Hayman
Yellow	K	Sub-Lieutenant W. P. Lucy, RN	Lieutenant M. C. E. Hanson, RN
	L	Petty Officer A. G. Johnson	Leading Airman F. Coston
	M	Sub-Lieutenant P. N. Charlton, RN	Naval Airman Culliford

Table 13   No. 803 Squadron – Romsdalen Valley combat, 24 April 1940

Section	Aircraft	Pilot	Navigator
Blue	F	Lieutenant W. P. Lucy	Lieutenant M. C. E. Hanson
	G	Lieutenant A. B. Fraser-Harris	Leading Airman G. S. Russell
	H	Lieutenant J. M. Christian	Naval Airman S. G. Wright
Red	P	Lieutenant L. A. Harris, RM	Petty Officer K. Baldwin
	Q	Lieutenant C. H. Filmer	Naval Airman H. Pickering
	R	Sub-Lieutenant I. Easton	Naval Airman A. J. Hayman

which had been christened 'Gladiator Lake' in readiness for the arrival of the RAF fighters who, it was hoped, would finally bring the hard-pressed troops ashore, offering some relief from the endless air attacks.

Within 10 minutes both section leaders sighted a formation of Heinkel He111s approaching, and proceeded to carry out section attacks on two of these, and also against a Dornier Do17. The first Heinkel was a confirmed kill, and was seen to crash among the trees on a mountainside. The second He111, despite being seen to be hit repeatedly by Browning fire, refused to go down, and, once more, humiliatingly outpaced the pursuing Skuas. The Dornier also escaped unscathed after a brief attack. At the end of this skirmish Blue section had expended its ammunition, and re-formed on the leader.

Meanwhile, Red section had attacked two further He111s, in both cases opening fire on them from 400 yards range, but they were unable to close the gap and get nearer than that. Although Lieutenant Harris managed to get in two good bursts at the second aircraft, the enemy seemed impervious to the bullets and no results were observed. However, Sub-Lieutenant Easton stated that he positively saw one He111 crash at Andalsnes while he was on the return flight back to the carrier after the two sections had re-formed.

Ark Royal had earlier contributed two sections of Skuas to this duty, one from each of her squadrons. Unfortunately two of these Skuas, L3050 (6M) piloted by Midshipman (A) C. Treen, RN, with Naval Airman A. E. T. Goble, and L2877 (7K) flown by the new Commanding Officer of No. 801 Squadron, Lieutenant Colin P. Campbell-Horsfall, RN, with Petty Officer (A) A. E. Suggett, ran out of fuel on the way back and had to ditch. Both aircrews survived the icy water, were plucked out of the sea by escorting destroyers and later returned to their carrier, very much the worse for wear. Colin Campbell-Horsfall (who had only taken over the squadron on 17 April), had been very badly hurt during the ditching. On the squadron's return to Scapa Flow, he was replaced as the unit CO by Lieutenant Ian R. Sarel, RN.[11]

Gladiator guides

Meanwhile, having confirmed their makeshift landing ground was ready for them, the RAF Gloster Gladiator fighters, under the command of Squadron Leader Dondaldson, were flown off the *Glorious* in two sections of nine aircraft each, each led by a Skua. The first group was guided to Lesjaskog by Yellow Leader, Sub-Lieutenant G. W. Brockensha, with Petty Officer (A) S. Andrews in L2905 (8K), who took off at 1730 hours. The second group was led by Green Leader, Lieutenant H. E. R. Torin, DSC, RN, with Midshipman (A) T. A. McKee, RN in L2903 (8A), who left at 1815 hours. Both parties landed without incident and were soon in action that same evening and claimed to have destroyed fourteen enemy aircraft.

The success was a brief one, however, for the lake was bombed the following afternoon by Junkers Ju88s from 2/KG 30 escorted by Bf110s from the I/ZG 76 and Ju88Cs from the Z/KG 30. These arrived overhead while the Gladiators were still trying to start their engines, and thirteen Gladiators were destroyed, while the lake had over 130 bomb craters. The surviving five Gladiators were moved to the airstrip at Andalsnes, where they were later destroyed.[12]

Three strikes and you are out![13]

On 24 April the *Ark Royal* was enshrouded in a blinding snowstorm, but this later cleared and a section from No. 800 Squadron was able to take off. The change was dramatic and the mountains of the Norwegian coast could clearly be seen more than 50 miles off, outlined against the deepest of blue skies. The Skuas were ordered to maintain a patrol over Namsos and provide Allied troops with at least a modicum of air protection. At their best economic speed this gave the patrolling aircraft an overall endurance of about 5 hours, which meant they could cover the port for approximately 3 hours. They approached Namsos and maintained a tight Vic formation over the town, which could be seen ablaze and smoking from earlier *Luftwaffe* visitations.

They patiently plodded up and down without any sign of enemy aircraft, and, after a considerable time, as such strict station-keeping was heavy on the throttle, fuel began to be an anxiety. The flight therefore made its way back out to sea and eventually the first two aircraft managed to land back aboard the carrier. However, as the rear aircraft, L3050 piloted by Midshipman Treen, with Naval Airman A. E. 'Doc' Goble as his rear-seat man, started to turn into the final landing circuit, the last drop of fuel was consumed. The Perseus cut out with a sigh and the Skua descended unceremoniously into the sea.

As Doc much later recalled, the Skua, whatever other faults she might have, did float well and they had plenty of time to launch the onboard dinghy. However, the dinghy's connection wire came loose and their salvation floated gently out of reach, forcing the two aircrew to make an undignified scramble for the aircraft's tail. The escorting destroyer 'crash boat' stormed up in traditional style to effect their rescue, but made its final approach at too high a speed, swamping the Skua with her wash. As their faithful mount sank beneath them, Treen and Goble had to make another fast exit and swam to the destroyer's whaler, which had been lowered just in time.

After being landed in the Shetlands they were flown to Inverness in a Sunderland flying boat, and collected a replacement Skua, L3055, which they flew, via Hatston, back aboard the *Ark Royal* on 4 May. She was heading back to Norway, and they were airborne once more the following afternoon 'spending 4 hours chasing shadows'. During the course of this their new machine developed an oil leak, and the prospect of another dip in the briny loomed. The engine actually seized up as she slid over the round down astern, but they got down, and the RAF fitters[14] worked during the night to change the engine. The weather worsened and the Skuas remained stuck down throughout 6 May, but the next day they were flown off at 0600 hours to patrol the Narvik and Halstead areas.

Apart from being engaged by 'friendly' anti-aircraft fire at intervals, nothing much occurred to inconvenience the section. However, once more, Treen and Goble's aircraft engine suddenly went silent on them. There was no opportunity to reach the fiord for another water landing. Instead, they made a glide approach to an upward snow-clad slope, the useless engine breaking away as the bolts sheared on impact, with the rest of the aircraft slithering to an undignified halt about 100 yards further along. Goble described the effect thus:

> Now, for those who don't remember, in the Skua rear cockpit you sat on a covered crossbeam with no back to it and to use the gun you stood up and used a thick strap, known as the fighting strap, across your back and pulled the gun up with its arc mounting. This was the position I was in when the crash came, and, in consequence, my back took all the impact while I held on to the gun. This caused severe damage to the muscles so that my head dropped and I couldn't straighten up. My pilot, Midshipman Treen, appeared to be OK but you don't crash like this without some damage.

After getting themselves clear of the wreck, the two men attempted to set fire to it before the Germans, who were all around in the nearby mountains overlooking Narvik, could arrive on the scene. They tried burning Very lights at the front, but this had little effect. Treen bravely went back to the rear cockpit and used the onboard axe to split open the fuel tanks. Once done, another Very cartridge was fired directly into the aperture, which did the trick, igniting the aircraft satisfactorily and igniting Treen's clothing with equal vigour. He had to roll in the snow to put the flames out and did not appreciate Goble's reaction, laughter, which he later attributed to shock. Soon the ammunition began exploding so they beat a hasty retreat.

The choice was then either to plod through the snow to the Swedish border, some 3 miles off to the eastward, or to reach the shore, an unknown distance to the west. After about 3 hours of sliding and stumbling they reached the top of the Rombaks Glacier with Narvik in sight in the far distance, but no way of descending. They eventually jumped and slid down about 500 feet to the ice-stream at the bottom, which they also navigated. Finally, they found a lone house, with an English-speaker, who rowed them out to the usual ubiquitous patrolling British destroyer in return for 1,000 cigarettes. She eventually landed them back at Orkney where they were transferred to a hospital ship, then home. Third time lucky?

Attack on Trondheim

On 25 April the *Ark Royal* and *Glorious* were wallowing through 35-foot waves in the teeth of a north-westerly, in their launching location, 65° 12′ North, 8° 24′ East. The *Glorious* despatched the bulk of No. 803 Squadron against Trondheim in early morning raids. First off the deck at 0315 hours, were Blue and Red sections, each Skua carrying a single 250 lb General Purpose (GP) bomb and eight 20 lb bombs. They arrived over the target area an hour later and, at 0430 hours, Lieutenant Lucy led all five machines in dive-bombing runs against nine German floatplanes moored in Trondheim harbour. They witnessed at least one direct hit and many close misses on these aircraft. Lieutenant J. M. Christian forgot to activate his master switch so could not release his main bomb.

The Skuas then gained altitude and switched roles, carrying out a fighter patrol, on the arrival of nine Swordfish from the *Ark Royal*, who were to bomb the frozen lake behind the town; they provided top cover during that mission. Once the TSRs had completed their attack, the Skuas returned to Trondheim harbour to finish their earlier work, strafing the surviving floatplanes and leaving only three afloat, one of which was burning fiercely and in sinking condition. While they were thus engaged, Christian had the satisfaction of finally making his dive-bombing run, successfully this time, taking as his target a larger freighter alongside the main stone jetty of the harbour. His bomb was later confirmed to have missed the ship, but exploded close alongside her on the jetty.

The five Skuas then re-formed, but Lieutenant Fraser-Harris's engine seized up. He managed to make a forced landing in Stjornfjorden, some

20 miles north-west of Trondheim, while his four companions arrived safely back aboard *Glorious* at 0730 hours.

Lieutenant Fraser-Harris and George Russell meanwhile, had found that not only was their aircraft so damaged that she was sinking rapidly, but the dinghy was also useless. There remained nothing for it but to swim ashore. In his official report Fraser-Harris wrote:

> The water was extremely cold, and we had great difficulty in walking up the beach to a group of Norwegians. They were very unfriendly,[15] but had mistaken us for German airmen, two of whom they had killed the day before. As soon as our identity was established, their attitude changed completely and we were given warm clothing and food. We were only a short distance from the German forts, and German patrols were on the roads. So, dressed as Norwegians, we were led by a guide to a small farm in the mountains. Shortly after our arrival several Norwegians came in from the vicinity of the German forts and also from Trondheim. From them I collected what appeared to be valuable and urgent information and decided to try to get through to British Headquarters forthwith.
>
> We travelled in Norwegian dress. A guide who spoke English and knew the way to the British lines arranged the journey. We left at 2200 and walked to the head of the valley, where we got a sleigh from a farm. On this we travelled for 5 miles up to a lake in the mountains. Here we left the sleigh and at 0330 set off on skis up a river valley to the north. Our efforts at this art were not a success, and we finally walked, going being fairly good on the frozen snow ....[16]

After an 8-mile slog, they had breakfast in a farmhouse, boarded a second sleigh at 0800 hours and finally reached another fiord where they boarded a small boat, which transported them to Folafo. Here, the obliging Norwegian police hired them a taxi, which carried them the final short distance to the British Brigade Headquarters of General Carton de Wiart, in some style. They had travelled a total of 69 miles in 24 hours. They finally rejoined the squadron aboard *Glorious* courtesy of the anti-aircraft cruiser HMS *Calcutta*.

At 0425 hours, Green section, led by Lieutenant Harry Ernest Richard Torin,[17] was despatched to search for an enemy cruiser, which had been reported in the area. They quartered to the northern approaches to Trondheim, but found no warships whatsoever. Torin therefore took his section to Trondheim harbour, where there were ample targets in the form of supply vessels and transports at anchor. After their attack they found one of the Heinkel He115 floatplanes, which had managed to survive the earlier assault and get airborne, and promptly shot her down.

This solitary victim proved to be dearly won however, for all three Skuas were lost on this sortie. They flew into bad weather on their return and became lost. Sub-Lieutenant Easton in L3010 (8B) became detached from his colleagues and although he endeavoured to find *Glorious*, he failed. With fuel failing he returned to the coast at Osen, and ditched safely close to a British destroyer. Both he and Naval Airman A. J. Hayman, a New Zealander,[18] were picked up safely. In a similar manner both his companions, Lieutenant Harry Torin in L2903 (8A) and Lieutenant Callingham in L3048 (8B) returned to Namos due to petrol shortage, and both made force landings in the vicinity, at Roan and on Namos beach respectively.

Meantime, Yellow section had flown off *Glorious* at 0430 hours, and likewise had proceeded to the coast in a hunt for the German cruiser, this time looking through the southern fiords. This tempting target turned out to be mythical, but two larger tankers were found lurking there alongside the oiling jetty at Thamshavn, at the southern end of Orkedalefiord, and these were attacked and set ablaze.

The full composition of the Trondheim attack force can be seen in Table 14.

While these units had been thus engaged, *Ark Royal*'s Skuas had also made a contribution to the full day's work. Starting at 0415 hours, two aircraft of No. 800 Squadron and seven from No. 801 Squadron, under the overall command of Lieutenant Commander H. P. Bramwell, were launched. They were armed with the single 250 lb GP bomb and eight 20 lb Coopers and joined in the search for enemy shipping thought to be lurking in Trondheim's approaches. They eventually conducted individual attacks

Table 14   No. 803 Squadron Trondheim attack force, 25 April 1940

Section	Aircraft	Pilot	Navigator
Blue	F	Lieutenant W. P. Lucy, RN	Lieutenant M. C. E. Hanson, RN
	G	Lieutenant A. B. Fraser-Harris, RN	Leading Airman G. S. Russell, RN
	H	Lieutenant J. M. Christian, RN	Naval Airman S. G. Wright
Red	P	Lieutenant L. A. Harris, RM	Petty Officer K. G. Baldwin
	Q	Lieutenant C. H. Filmer, RN	Naval Airman H. Pickering
Green	A	Lieutenant H. E. R. Torin, RN	Midshipman T. A. McKee, RN
	B	Lieutenant G. R. Callingham, RN	Naval Airman (1) D. A. Prime
	C	Sub-Lieutenant I. H. Easton, RN	Naval Airman A. J. Hayman
Yellow	K	Sub-Lieutenant G. W. Brokensha, RN	Petty Officer S. E. Andrews
	L	Petty Officer A. G. Johnson	Leading Airman F. Coston
	M	Sub-Lieutenant Philip N. Charlton, RN	Naval Airman F. Culliford

against six merchant ships in the harbour, scoring one direct hit and many near misses. A Junkers Ju88 and a damaged He111 found on a frozen lake, were machine-gunned on the way out.

A second three-Skua launch took place at 0455 hours, with Red section led by Lieutenant G. E. D. Finch-Noyes, RN. They claimed to have attacked and put to flight both a Heinkel He111 and a Junkers Ju88 that morning, without damage to themselves. A third despatch was made at 0555 hours, again of three Skuas, but in the deteriorating weather, they made no contact and returned aboard at 1015 hours.

Aalesund patrols

The following day No. 801 Squadron's first mission of the day saw two sections maintaining a fighter patrol over Andalsnes and Leskasjog. The *Luftwaffe* was much in evidence and in an engagement with a trio of 5/KG 4's He111s, one bomber was claimed as shot down, and a second damaged.

No. 803 Squadron from *Glorious* mounted an afternoon fighter patrol over Aalesund, the Skuas of Blue section taking off just before noon. The composition of the force can be seen in Table 15.

Soon after they had started their patrol over the little town, they saw a formation of He111s from I/KG 26 approaching and at 1308 hours, steered to engage. As the Skuas moved in, the German bombers closed their formation up and concentrated their fire. Despite this Lieutenant C. H. Filmer, flying L2991 (8Q), continued to close and his aircraft was caught in the cross fire and terminally damaged. Filmer's Skua was last seen diving away with smoke pouring from her engine. His two companions, undeterred by the fate of their colleague, carried out a beam attack on the right-wing Heinkel of the formation, managing to shoot it down, but the rest made good their escape at high speed.

Yet another He111 was then seen at 1350 hours, busy attacking an Allied transport ship below and the duo transferred their attentions to this machine. They were joined in the attacks by Lieutenant Commander H. P. Bramwell, the Commanding Officer of No. 801 Squadron, who also managed to score some damaging hits before being wounded by return fire and having to break off his attack.[19] Again, the German aircraft

Table 15   No. 803 Squadron Andalsnes patrol, 26 April 1940

Section	Aircraft	Pilot	Navigator
Blue	F	Lieutenant W. P. Lucy, RN	Lieutenant M. C. E. Hanson, RN
	H	Lieutenant J. M. Christian, RN	Naval Airman S. G. Wright
	Q	Lieutenant C. H. Filmer, RN	Petty Officer K. G. Baldwin

demonstrated a remarkable ability to absorb punishment but, after repeated forays, the Skuas had the satisfaction of seeing this aircraft, from the 9/LG 1, make a forced landing in the fiord, where it quickly sank. By that time all the Skuas were out of ammunition and duly returned to the ship. Their place was taken by Yellow section, but they encountered no enemy aircraft during their patrol.

But what of Lieutenant Cecil Howard Filmer and his crew? He recorded both the battle and his subsequent experiences in his official report, which is reproduced here:[20]

Took off from HMS *Glorious* at 1200, Friday 26 April, to carry out a fighter patrol over Aalesund and Andalsnes, Lieut. Lucy leading, myself No. 2 and Lieutenant Christian No. 3.

At about 1300, flying at 8,000 feet, I observed three Junkers 88s travelling in the opposite direction, to the Southward. I immediately rocked my wings to draw the Leader's attention and set off in pursuit. The enemy aircraft were about to make a bombing attack on Aalesund and were flying fairly slowly, so I caught up with them in about 5 minutes.

As I got within range and fired a burst they turned, still in formation, down to the right and in the opposite direction. I followed, firing all the time at the left-hand aircraft until I was within less than 100 yards range. As I broke away to the left and downward I felt my aircraft being hit. Petrol flooded the cockpit, getting in my eyes before I could pull my goggles down, and there appeared to be an oil leakage somewhere.

The aircraft I had attacked was by this time losing height rapidly with smoke pouring from the starboard engine. The other two machines were circling over it.

My engine suddenly began to run very roughly indeed, so much so that I thought the engine would tear away from its mountings. The throttle was useless, moving the lever either way made no difference to the revolutions. I then saw smoke coming from beneath the instrument panel so I switched off the ignition. No more smoke issued, but the airscrew continued to turn at 1,600 revs. Until I was down to 4,000 feet, when it suddenly stopped completely.

At about 1,000 feet, I switched on the ignition momentarily, but the smoke appeared once more so I switched off finally.

During this time I had tried to obtain an answer from my observer, Acting Petty Officer Baldwin, but with no success. Looking through my rear window I could see him lying on his back so assumed he was either killed or wounded.

I could see no fields below large enough to have made a good landing, so decided to force-land in the sea in Aalesund harbour, near enough to the jetty to enable my observer to be rescued quickly.

I pancaked on the water with the undercarriage up, undid my straps and climbed aft to help Baldwin. He was dead however, having received a burst in the head. I then pulled the dinghy release grip, but no dinghy appeared and before I had time to lever open the compartment the nose sank quickly, air pouring out of the flotation tank in the port wing, which had been hit.

I was now in the water holding on to the fuselage, and tried to put more air into my lifesaving jacket, but found this impossible as the coldness of the water had taken my breath away.

I then tried to climb onto the tailplane, but this was also impossible as the fuselage was too slippery and my legs and arms were paralysed by the water. I hung onto the parachute release wires until help came. I was taken to hospital and was very kindly treated.

The aircraft was later salvaged through the kindness of the Norwegians and with the help of Major Lumley, R.M. and Lieut. Copeland-Griffiths, RN. It was hoisted on a pontoon, the engine was removed, and the wings were folded in order to deceive the enemy.

Norwegian engineers had only partly examined the engine when I left for Molde, but the carburettor induction pipe had been shot away, one cylinder had seized up, and one bullet had passed through twelve fins without entering the cylinder.

The fuselage was fairly well preserved except for approximately sixty bullet holes, one group of which tore a large hole in the starboard petrol tank. The forward tank was pierced, the remainder of the bullet holes being scattered from below the pilots seat to the after end of the cabin.

All important gear in the aircraft was removed, the five guns being added to the defences of the British forces in Aalesund.

I placed myself under the orders of Major Lumley, Royal Marines. I was occupied in salvaging my aircraft on Saturday 27 April and in the evening Petty Officer Gardner and his Air Gunner, Todd, arrived in Aalesund with important information from Bergen. On Sunday 28th I was sent with this information to the SNO [Senior Naval Officer], Molde.

I travelled by car with an interpreter and an official of the Norwegian Secret Service to Vestnes, where we embarked aboard a small motor boat for Molde. This journey by boat was very hazardous as numerous enemy aircraft were flying overhead, some attacking us and others attacking a sloop (HMS *Flamingo*) in the vicinity.

I arrived at Molde in the middle of an air raid, but reached the Headquarters safely and reported to the SNO, Captain Denny, who placed me under his orders to help in the operations.

We were bombed continuously in Molde, both with 1,000 lb bombs and with incendiary, which were falling about 100 yards from HQ. After each bombing attack the enemy aircraft machine-gunned the woods immediately above and behind HQ.

Both at Molde and Aalesund the enemy machines did exactly what they liked. The lack of friendly aircraft above sapped the morale of the troops and civilians practically more than anything else.

By midday Monday the whole of Molde was in flames, but this did not deter the Germans from making more attacks.

We embarked about the [light cruiser] HMS *Glasgow* early on Tuesday morning.

Meanwhile, the rest of the Skuas were getting on with the war in a more conventional way. Return fire from an attacked enemy also smashed the windshield of Petty Officer (A) J. Hadley's machine, but, though badly cut about the face and head, he managed to land back safely aboard the carrier.

The third sortie consisted of a mixed gaggle of Skuas from both the *Ark Royal*'s squadrons commanded by Lieutenant Finch-Noyes, RN, and Lieutenant Church respectively. The former, leading Red section, manages to get astern of a patrolling He115 floatplane and get in some damaging bursts before she escaped in the murk.

Carrier task force

On the following day, Saturday 27th, Vice-Admiral Wells held the carrier force well out to sea in position 64° 40′ North, 04° 48′ East. He concentrated on maintaining fighter patrols over the army bases of Namsos and Andalsnes and the RAF airfield ashore, while seeking to mount attacks on enemy targets afloat and ashore at Vaernes and Trondheim. What the Royal Navy was in fact originating, and using in combat for the first time, was the concept of the Carrier Task Force. The two big carriers with their fighter, dive- and torpedo-bomber potential, were protected by a fast battleship, HMS *Valiant*, a heavy cruiser, HMS *Berwick*, and a flotilla of ten screening destroyers. Although to be expanded and perfected firstly by the Japanese and then the American navies in the Pacific 2 years later, the Royal Navy off Norway in the spring of 1940 provided the blueprint.

Get-together at Grotli

No. 801 Squadron, commanded by Lieutenant R. L. Strange, was airborne from the *Ark Royal* with a fighter patrol flying off at 0820 hours to cover Andalsnes. They ran into a pair of bombers from the 4/LG 1 and attacked, reporting hits and a fire in one engine of a He111, which crashed-landed.

Ark Royal sent her second Skua section of the day aloft, three aircraft from No. 800 Squadron, under the command of Birdy Partridge flying L2940. They witnessed the attack on the *Flamingo*. The He111, from KF 26, had a head start of 2 miles and a height advantage of 1,000 feet. It seemed hopeless, but Birdy Partridge described what happened next.

> I guess our speed advantage over the German bomber was only 10 to
> 15 knots. After 10 minutes with throttles jammed wide open I was at
> the same height as my quarry and gaining slowly but surely on him.
> Some 600 yards astern of him now and his rear gunner started firing
> at me, though I was hardly within his range for accurate shooting,
> but the thought did cross my mind that he might have a lucky shot.[21]

After a long stern chase of about 25 miles Partridge eventually got up to within 400 yards astern of his quarry and fired a long burst from his Brownings, but to no obvious effect. Another 100 yards was gained, and then the whole 600 rounds were pumped into the Heinkel, and smoke started billowing from her starboard wing. This enabled Birdy's two wing-men to close up also and take over the attack, but the leader himself had taken return fire into the temperamental Pegasus. In fact, a fuel line had been severed. He considered the enemy bomber doomed and called back his colleagues while himself turning his Skua toward the coast, hoping to glide to a suitable area for an emergency landing. And, at some 90 knots, the Skua whistled down and down, hitting the snow and ice of the frozen Lake Breidal and remaining in one piece. Both Partridge and Robin Bostock got out safely. Their two wingmen, having followed them down and noted their location, headed back to the *Ark Royal*, while Partridge and Bostock attempted to destroy as much of their faithful mount as they were able.[22]

Eventually, they sought refuge from the cold in a small wooden hut and awaited rescue. A little while later there was knocking on the door and voices could be heard in a foreign tongue. Norwegian? No, German, it was the three aircrew of the Heinkel that they had shot down, asking if they could share their warmth. The Germans had a Lüger, the British had nothing at all, but Partridge, by gestures and such, persuaded the Germans that they were his prisoners, which they seemed quite content to accept. Only later were they all located by the Norwegians, and, after many adventures eventually found their way to the coast, where they were taken off by the cruiser HMS *Manchester*, and once more rejoined the *Ark Royal*.[23]

Glorious had No. 803 Squadron aloft early from 1030 hours that day. Both Blue (F – Lieutenant W. P. Lucy/Lieutenant M. C. E. Hanson and R – Petty Officer A. G. Johnson/Leading Airman F. Coston) and Yellow (K – Sub-Lieutenant G. W. Brokensha/Petty Officer S. E. Andrews, and L – Lieutenant Leslie Alban Harris, RM, and Naval-Airman F. Culliford) sections flew reduced fighter patrols over the same area once more. While Blue section met no enemy at all, Yellow was more fortunate. The duo sighted a solitary He111 from the 7/KG 26, which they engaged and managed to destroy. Both sections were unscathed and all four Skuas landed safely aboard the carrier *Ark Royal*, as *Glorious* was unable to recover them because she had her Sea Gladiator fighters spotted on her flight deck in case of *Luftwaffe* attack.

The afternoon launch from *Ark Royal* was three Skuas from Red section of No. 800 Squadron, under Lieutenant G. E. D. Finch-Noyes, RN, which took off at 1515 hours. These Skuas were followed by two more from No. 801 Squadron, led by Lieutenant H. P. Bramwell, RN. These five aircraft soon found themselves heavily engaged with strong formations of Heinkel He111s from the KGr 100 and Junkers Ju88s from the KG 30 who were making a determined attack on the ships. From 1600 hours the Skuas were almost continually engaged fending off at least seventeen bombers and they managed to break up the attack before expending all their ammunition. No kills were claimed but several enemy were thought to have been damaged in this encounter. None of the ships were damaged so the Skuas had achieved their main objective.

To replace this group a further section from No. 801 Squadron was launched at 1645 hours, led by Lieutenant (A) William Coutenay Antwiss Church, RN, piloting L2931 (7L). The main enemy group, having been beaten off the unit, still found a target in the lone form of an He111 from the 2/JGr 1000, which they duly engaged. Eventually, they managed to shoot this aircraft down, but Church's aircraft was heavily hit in return and crashed in flames. Neither Church nor Acting Sub-Lieutenant David George Wills, RN, survived.

Mêlée over Molde

The fighting on shore was going badly. The two British army forces landed to capture Trondheim in a pincer movement, were both heavily defeated and outflanked, suffering many casualties. Under almost continuous air assault, both forces were retreating back to the sea, and the Royal Navy was ordered to rescue them. This gave the supporting fleets even greater responsibilities at a time when combat and accidents had reduced the number of Skuas fit for combat to just eighteen. These were: No. 800 Squadron – seven Skuas; No. 801 Squadron – seven Skuas; No. 803 Squadron – four Skuas. There were also five Rocs embarked, two from No. 800 Squadron and three from No. 801 Squadron, but these had little or no fighting value. These aircraft were all concentrated aboard the *Ark Royal*, while the *Glorious* was sent back to Scapa to refuel and embark reserve aircraft before returning to the fray.

On 28 April *Ark Royal* was in 64° 58′ North, 08° 07′ East. Fighter patrols were allocated to No. 803 Squadron. Blue section (F – Lieutenant W. P. Lucy/Lieutenant M. C. E. Hanson; K – Sub-Lieutenant G. W. Brokensha/Petty Officer S. E. Andrews; R. Petty Officer A. G. Johnson/ Leading Airman F. Coston) of this squadron had an eventful day. At 1220 hours a Junkers Ju88 was seen carrying out a dive-bomber attack on an Allied sloop. Lucy immediately made a beam attack, while Brokensha and Johnson could not close the gap in time, and made attacks from astern the enemy aircraft. This had the effect of making the German pilot jettison his bombs as he quickly dived his fast bomber out of range of the Skuas. But Lucy had made his mark, and Petty Officer Johnson, who followed the Junkers as best he could, witnessed it lose height and crash in flames on an offshore island. To bring down a *Schnellbomber* was indeed a major victory for the team. But they were not done yet!

Some 10 minutes after this episode, the section had re-formed and then sighted three Heinkel He111s some height above them. Johnson was able to make an immediate attack, which caused his target aircraft likewise to jettison her bombload and make good an escape. Lucy and Brokensha laboriously climbed to gain some height above the remaining pair of Heinkels, and made successive stern attacks on both. One of the enemy received damaging hits, which stopped one engine and caused the under-carriage to drop before it finally crashed spectacularly into the fiord below. Two down!

Lucy and Brokensha continued their patrol over Molde and were again rewarded with the sight of seven further Heinkel He111s heading out to sea to the north-west, possibly seeking to attack the fleet. This group pre-sented a tough, close-knit target to tackle in a strong, defensive formation, but the two British pilots spotted that the starboard wing bomber was slightly out of station from the rest. They concentrated their attacks on this straggler and were rewarded with hits and the inspiring sight of a third enemy bomber flaming down into the sea. Three down!

The two Skuas again managed to climb above the remaining six bombers and Lucy carried out a stunning vertical attack against the leading Heinkel. This was sufficient to persuade the whole formation that enough was sufficient and, again jettisoning their bombs harmlessly into the ocean, the formation broke up intent on escape, with every man for himself. Although both Skuas tried to keep in contact with at least one enemy bomber, they had soon fired away what little ammunition re-mained to them. As this ragged group made its way back inland they ran into the indefatigable Johnson, who homed in on one in a series of rear attacks. Almost unbelievably on that remarkable day, he reported that the port engine of his target burst into flames and the Heinkel dived into cloud and was not seen again. Four down? Well, maybe, but even if this last enemy escaped, the incident over Molde was undoubtedly the Skua's greatest day as a fighter aircraft! The whole section returned safely, landing aboard the *Ark Royal* somewhat jubilant.

With his Commanding Officer absent, Lieutenant G. E. D. Finch-Noyes, with Petty Officer H. G. Cunningham as his observer, had taken over from Partridge as the temporary Officer Commanding No. 800 Squadron. With two companions in Red section, Finch-Noyes took off from the carrier to provide standing fighter cover for the evacuation ships, Convoy TM 1. They soon met opposition, including Junkers Ju88s from the KG 30, which they harassed sufficiently to spoil their attacks. They then discovered an He111, which both Finch-Noyes (flying L3000) and L2934 duly despatched. Both Blue 803 and Red 800 were recovered back aboard the *Ark Royal* at 1540 hours.

Even the Rocs had bestirred themselves, and three of them, under the leadership of Lieutenant R. C. Hay, were flown off to intercept a shadower just after midday. This enemy was hit and damaged by the fleet's AA fire and slid away before the Rocs could make their first-ever contact with the enemy. But at least they had seen action from a carrier deck.

The Skuas were very much involved in offensive action also, joining the TSRs in a strike. While the Swordfish launched at 0317 hours to attack the *Luftwaffe* airfield at Vaernes, No. 800 Squadron, led by Lieutenant K. V. V. Spurway, and No. 801 Squadron, under Lieutenant R. L. Strange, both had three Skuas apiece airborne from 0400 hours. Their bombload was the single 250 lb SAP plus eight 20 lb Coopers, and their target allocation was ships at Trondheim, and then fighter protection to cover the withdrawal of any surviving Swordfish.

They crossed the Norwegian coast at an altitude of 13,000 feet and surprised three large freighters anchored in Trondheim roads. They also observed whole squadrons of floatplanes at anchor in the harbour. The ships were tackled first, attack dives commencing from 8,000 feet concentrated on delivery of the main bomb against these targets, one direct hit being made. The smaller Coopers were dispersed among the bobbing seaplanes, along with some judicious machine-gun fire and then the Skuas turned for their rendezvous with the Swordfish. This part of the mission was accomplished without hindrance and the Skuas returned to the carrier at 0630 hours. But there were only five!

In leaving the attack area and attempting to find the TSRs, Midshipman (A) L. H. Gallagher, RN, with Naval Airman G. W. Halifax, found themselves alone, so headed back out to sea on their own. However, after beating up and down where they expected to find *Ark Royal*, they saw only empty ocean. With fuel levels dropping, Gallagher decided to return to shore and landed at the primitive Setnesmoen airstrip, where in the confusion of the impending evacuation, he still managed to get his aircraft refuelled and ready to go. His plan was to fly direct to

Hatston, as the whereabouts of the *Ark Royal* was still unclear. (She had, in fact, gathered in her aircraft and departed the scene, temporarily retiring out of range of the *Luftwaffe* and prematurely mourning the loss of another young aircrew.) But there is a certain law, and this kicked in when the sole remaining Coffmann cartridge, used to start the Pegasus engine, did not do its job. They turned to the RAF Gladiator unit for help, but these aircraft were hand-cranked and they could not help. It looked like Gallagher's mount would have to be destroyed before the Germans arrived at the port.

They spent an uncomfortable night sleeping under the wing of their aircraft. The next day, they found that everyone else had pulled out while they had been sleeping and left them to it. They therefore prepared to set fire to their aircraft and head for the evacuation area. But while getting ready to do this, they discovered a few old and rather corroded Coffman cartridges among the aircraft's effects that they had overlooked the day before. Using these, they managed to start the engine after all, to their enormous relief, and made a precarious take-off even as Heinkel He111s were bombing the strip.

They were back in the air, but possessed no maps. Undeterred, this most resourceful 18-year-old made best guess on the most direct route to Hatston. Fortune finally smiled on them for, after a journey of around 3 hours, they reached the Orkneys and landed successfully without a scratch.

Shuffle and deal

The Skuas of No. 803 Squadron continued to switch flight decks, with Lieutenant Christian acting as Temporary Squadron Commander aboard the *Glorious* while the CO led the rest of the unit from *Ark Royal.* On 30 April, Christian flew Lucy's 'resurrected' aircraft ashore to Hatston, returning to the carrier with a new aircraft, together with Sub-Lieutenant P. N. Charlton, Lieutenant G. S. Russell and Petty Officer Heard in a Roc fighter.[24]

On 1 May, although *Glorious* rejoined the force, the scheduled naval attack on Trondheim was cancelled. The fleet survived an attack by seven Junkers Ju87 dive-bombers in the late afternoon. At the same time fighter patrols were despatched to cover the ports. Blue and Yellow sections of No. 803 Squadron were flown off *Ark Royal* at 1800 hours and proceeded together to Namos, where they then split up and patrolled independently. Lucy and Harris encountered no enemy and landed aboard the *Glorious* at 2115 hours. Brokensha and Johnson were equally denied combat, but not action! Having left Namos at 1950 hours also to rejoin their parent carrier, the pair were flying above low cloud when heavy anti-aircraft fire was suddenly opened up on them. The fleet had taken no chances, on hearing aircraft they let fly regardless and Brokensha's aircraft disappeared from

Johnson's view as it vanished into low cloud. The Yellow leader's aircraft had received crippling damage from this 'friendly fire' and crash-landed. Fortunately, both aircrew survived the occurrence and were rescued by the destroyer *Nubian*. Despite the zero visibility, Leading Airman Coston navigated Johnson safely back to the *Glorious*, and without the use of her beacon.

Meanwhile, Christian, Russell and Charlton had also taken off from *Glorious* and conducted a similar patrol over Namos and all three managed to return safely to her. At the end of the day's flying, all surviving Skuas were back aboard *Glorious* and Lucy resumed command of the Squadron.

The fleet now started to retire to Scapa. During the preceding 8 days the Skuas had mounted ninety-eight sorties (seventy-two from *Ark Royal* and twenty-six from *Glorious*'s squadron working from both carriers) and had lost nine aircraft to all causes. The *Ark Royal* replenished her air group and No. 803 joined Nos 800 and 801 Squadrons aboard, all being brought up to a strength of nine aircraft each. The port of Narvik was still scheduled to be assaulted by the Allied forces, even though ports further south had been abandoned and preparations were made for RAF reinforcements to be sent. The *Glorious* was to ferry eighteen modern Hawker Hurricane-I fighters over to Norway and *Furious*, once her repairs had been completed, a further eighteen Gloster Gladiators.

On 3 May No. 803 Squadron's aircraft and stores were embarked in *Ark Royal*, while Petty Officer Heard flew his Roc to Donibristle and exchanged it for a Skua. The following day, Petty Officer Glover, recovered from Norway, flew from Hatston to rejoin his unit. He landed aboard *Ark Royal*, which had sailed from Scapa escorted by the anti-aircraft cruiser *Curlew* and six destroyers, to take up her covering position of 70° 17′ North, 16° 98′ West. From here, two sections of Skuas at a time were flown off to maintain daily fighter patrols over the main British army HQ at Harstad throughout the day from late on 6 May onward.

Thus, from 0800 hours on 7 May Skuas were launching and recovering all day. The first Skua patrol encountered no opposition, but one aircraft was badly damaged in a crash-landing aboard on their return. The poor weather conditions cut into the patrol programme and it was not until 1330 hours that a further pair of aircraft from No. 801 Squadron led by Lieutenant T. E. Gray, RN, was airborne and they were joined by three more from Blue section of No. 803 Squadron. This trio, commanded by Lieutenant W. P. Lucy, RN, launched and were soon back patrolling over their old stamping grounds off Narvik once more. Throughout the day No. 803 Squadron's contributions were arranged as seen in Table 16.

Blue Section took off at 1450 hours and made landfall at Aandenes. The three Skuas climbed up to 12,000 feet and immediately spotted a pair of He111s from the 8/KG 26 above Ofotfiord, which they attacked. One of

Table 16   Composition of No. 803 Squadron fighter patrols, 7 May 1940

Section	Pilot	Navigator
Blue	Lieutenant W. P. Lucy	Lieutenant M. C. E. Hanson
	Lieutenant G. F. Russell	Naval Airman H. Pickering
	Petty Officer H. Glover	Naval Airman H. Chatterley
Yellow	Lieutenant L. A. Harris, R.M.	Lieutenant J. H. R. Medlicot-Vereker, RN
	Petty Officer A. G. Johnson	Leading Airman F. Coston
	Sub-Lieutenant P. N. Charlton	Naval Airman F. Culliford
Green	Lieutenant J. M. Christian	Midshipman V. K. Norfolk
	Sub-Lieutenant I. Easton	Naval Airman A. J. Hayman
	Midshipman A. S. Griffith	Naval Airman F. Dooley

the German bombers made the standard hard dive away and escaped; the other was engaged in a series of brief bursts by Lucy, but again, simply outran him. Lucy gave up the hopeless chase and returned to the patrol area and once again ran into another brace of Heinkels (Mk 5s), but after one short attack ran out of ammunition. However, two 'probables' were claimed and one Heinkel was damaged, making a crash-landing back at Vaernes. Return fire wounded Lieutenant (A) G. F. Russell. The section then returned independently to the carrier. Yellow and Green sections patrolled over Narvik itself, but were not engaged.

Good work over Narvik

The following day the *Ark Royal* launched six separate fighter patrols from 0540 hours onward. The fourth patrol, by No. 803 Squadron's Blue section, got away at 1305 hours, the Squadron being organised as in Table 17.

Blue section was aloft at 1305 hours, and an hour later was on its beat over Narvik. Some 20 minutes into the patrol the *Luftwaffe* duly put in an

Table 17   Fighter patrols over Narvik, 8 May 1940

Section	Pilot	Navigator
Blue	Lieutenant W. P. Lucy	Lieutenant M. C. E. Hanson
	Lieutenant T. E. Gray	Naval Airman H. Pickering
	Midshipman A. S. Griffith	Naval Airman F. Dooley
Yellow	Lieutenant L. A. Harris. RM	Lieutenant J. H. R. Medlicot-Vereker, RN
	Petty Officer A. G. Johnson	Leading Airman F. Coston
	Sub-Lieutenant P. N. Charlton	Naval Airman F. Culliford
Green	Lieutenant J. M. Christian	Midshipman V. K. Norfolk
	Sub-Lieutenant I. Easton	Naval Airman A. J. Hayman

appearance and was sighted by Griffith, who Lucy ordered to lead the attack. The Midshipman followed the enemy, firing short bursts, but his two companions lost him in thick cloud. Griffith was forced to break off his futile attacks as the enemy drew away, but almost at once nearly ran into another target, a Junkers Ju88, that he engaged head-on in the brief interval that the two aircraft passed each other, without a positive result. The section eventually re-formed over Harstad at low altitude, and returned to the *Ark Royal* without further incident.

At 1600 hours Yellow section was airborne to continue the Narvik cover, but over Aandenes found 10/10th cloud cover stretching up from 4,000 to 7,000 feet. The three Skuas climbed to 7,500 feet to clear it and continued to the Narvik area. Almost at once Petty Officer Johnson caught a glimpse of a large flying boat. The whole section swooped down on this prey, making stern and beam attacks on the lumbering target. Again, the German machine showed a remarkable ability to absorb machine-gun fire, and finally vanished in a shallow dive through the thick cloud, heading towards high mountains.

Soon after this incident Sub-Lieutenant Charlton flying L2916 (8M) reported falling oil pressure and then the Skua's Pegasus stopped completely. Charlton took his only available action, he dived down through the cloud barrier, with Lieutenant Harris following him and attempting to maintain contact. Charlton managed to make a successful forced water-landing close by Tovik. Both the pilot and his air gunner, Naval Airman Culliford Harris, survived and Charlton signalled this fact to the anti-aircraft cruiser *Curlew* out at sea, and she promptly despatched a des-troyer to rescue the two men.[25]

When Harris and Johnson were debriefed aboard *Ark Royal* their target was identified as a Dornier Do26 seaplane. It was later learned that this big floatplane, from KGrzbv 108, had to make a force-landing itself in a nearby fiord near to Narvik. In addition to her four-man crew, this machine was packed with two-dozen Austrian ski troops, reinforcing the German garrison. They were unharmed and remained composed enough actually to capture the crew of a small boat sent over by a trawler to investigate. A platoon of Royal Marines had to be despatched to rescue the unfortunate crew and destroy the flying boat.

By strict contrast with all this excitement, Green section conducted an uneventful patrol.

On 9 May the fighter patrols continued as before, without incident, but the routine was enlivened by the mounting of a nine-Swordfish strike against German forces at Hundalien, Nordalsbroen and Sildvik in aid of the army. Three Skuas from No. 800 Squadron, under Lieutenant K. V. V. Spurway, were assigned as escorts for this force and then estab-lished a standing patrol. No enemy aircraft were encountered during the mission, but the weather remained universally dismal. During the return flight Midshipman (A) C. Treen, RN, with Naval Airman A. E. T. Goble, flying L3055 (6H), were forced to make their second emergency landing ashore. They got down safely, destroyed their aircraft and then found their way to the coast. They were eventually taken to safety aboard the destroyer HMS *Bedouin.*

Nor was that the only Skua action of that day. Back at Hatston, No. 806 Squadron was now fully worked up and ready for action. Captain Howe decided to utilise them in full by launching another long-range attack on Bergen, which was thought to be still full of suitable ship targets and bereft of much AA protection. Therefore eight Skuas, under the command of Lieutenant C. P. Campbell-Horsfall, RN, each armed with a 500 lb SAP, were despatched. They made their attack in conjunction with six Coastal Command Blenheim twin-engined bombers, with naval observers embarked.

The Skuas claimed to have scored one direct hit on a freighter and another on an oil tank in the port area, while some escort vessels were strafed. Return fire shot down one Blenheim, and damaged the Skua (L3014) flown by Petty Officer (A) A. Jopling and Naval Airman K. L. Jones, which returned safely with both men uninjured.

Young Sub-Lieutenant Hogg was one of those who took part in this attack, it was his first combat mission and he described it this way:[26]

At 4 o'clock we received our orders and instructions and were airborne by 4.30. It was a lovely evening with light, wispy clouds and 200 miles of North Sea stretching in front of us.

What lay on the other side? As I flew, I looked at my body – my hands on the control column and my legs and feet on the rudder bar. Would they be slashed and torn by flying steel? Could I stand the awful agony?

For just under 2 hours we flew over the grey menacing North Sea, with anxious eyes on our engine gauges. A line loomed up on the horizon – the coast of Norway. Crossing over it a few minutes later, we went into line astern. My heart was thudding like a steam hammer and I had a funny feeling in the pit of my stomach. We swept round the back of Bergen and came in at 5,000 feet, through a thick black cloud.

The bay lay below us; it was filled with shipping. I picked my target, two large ships anchored alongside one another, and dived down with my diving brakes lowered. At 2,000 feet I released my bomb and pulled up my flaps, continuing in a shallower dive to keep up a good speed. As I screamed down the fiord I espied a German sloop escorted by three MTBs [e-boats]. I immediately made towards them and machine-gunned the decks of the largest ship. To get away I had to cross over the MTBs, and climb to avoid a hill. Slowly! Oh, so slowly, I left them behind. Tracers were flying past my right wing. Would I never get over that hill? That mass of earth became indelibly printed on my mind – I can see it now.

At last I was over and, finding some more of our aircraft, flew back with them to Sumburgh, in the Shetlands, where I successfully landed.

I saw Stanley make a doubtful touch-down and noticed that his aircraft was covered in oil. As soon as I could get hold of him, I asked him how he had fared.

'Well', he said, 'when we went through that cloud over Bergen, instead of flying by my instruments I tried to follow the man in front. I lost sight of him and while peering round, the aircraft stalled and I fell 4,000 feet on my back. I turned the right way up at 1,000 feet to find myself a few miles from Bergen. I climbed up slowly and dived from no great height. Ack-Ack was bursting all round and I heard one or two nasty clangs. Crossing the enemy coast on the way back I was somewhat disturbed to find that the engine would only run with the throttle in the take-off position – imagine the amount of petrol it was using! I was practically growing grey hairs all the way across the North Sea. As I was circling the aerodrome here the engine coughed and stopped. I put the nose down to land in the sea and the motion must have pumped the last drop of petrol into the carburettor. The engine lasted long enough for me to land – my prop stopped as I finished my landing run. There seems to be a hole in the air intake – and a few other places.'

We flew back to Hatston in the failing light and landed in semi-darkness, using lights. I landed and was very proud to discover that the man before me had 'pranged'. I had not.

The whole squadron was waiting to welcome us and I am sorry to say that some of the officers had become inebriated to celebrate our safe return or mourn our loss. I went to bed a thankful man.

A total transformation of the war came on 10 May with the opening of the long-delayed main German assault in the west. 'Hitler has missed the bus!' Prime Minister Chamberlain had announced shortly before, the last of many fatuous statements by that worthy as the combination of Panzer and Stuka started its incredible crash-through to Abbeville. Immediately the focus of the combat shifted south, but in Norway, the Allies stubbornly clung to their mission, with both *Glorious* and *Furious* still embarking RAF fighter aircraft, and the army preparing for the Narvik attack.

This day found *Ark Royal* riding out a full gale in position 70° 50′ North, 16° 30′ East. Conditions were bad and not conducive for aircraft operations. Nonetheless, by early afternoon the winds were easing, and in

Table 18   No. 803 Squadron claims, 10 April to 10 May 1940

Date	Claim
10.4.40	1 *Köln* class cruiser (shared with No. 800 Squadron); 1 warehouse
12.4.40	4 transports; 1 MTB damaged
14.4.40	1 large transport; 1 flying boat
16.4.40	1 auxiliary patrol boat; 1 U-boat damaged
17.4.40	1 Heinkel He111
24.4.40	1 Heinkel He111
25.4.40	9 floatplanes; 1 warehouse; 2 large oilers; 1 Heinkel He115
26.4.40	1 Heinkel He111; 1 Junkers Ju8
28.4.40	1 Junkers Ju88; 2 Heinkel He111
18.5.40	1 Heinkel He111; 1 Dornier Do26

response to a radar warning from *Curlew* of incoming enemy aircraft, three Skuas were launched at 1320 hours, but they failed to locate the enemy, which apparently turned back. Time was also found to send off the first of several standing air patrols for the Narvik area, a trio from No. 801 Squadron led by Lieutenant W. H. Martyn, RN, being got away at 1400 hours. The usual He115 shadower was encountered above Harstad and engaged, but took full advantage of cloud cover to evade destruction. The patrol was taken over by three aircraft from No. 803 Squadron under Lieutenant W. P. Lucy, an hour later. Lieutenant Gray was the only one of these to sight any enemy aircraft, a Heinkel He111, but, once more, this machine escaped by using her superior speed. Two later patrols were quiet and uneventful, and deteriorating weather again brought operations to a halt.

No. 803 Squadron's claim sheet for the period 10 April to 10 May is shown in Table 18.

Attack at Asko

Back at HMS *Sparrowhawk*, the comparative success of the previous mission led to another combined attack on 11 May. This time the target was an oil farm, whose existence had for some reason only just been revealed to the planners. The tanks complex was situated on Asko Island and Captain Howe considered it a prime target for the Skuas. The lighter 250 lb SAP bomb, plus four 20 lb Coopers, were considered the most suitable weaponry to deal with the tanks, and were fitted to six Skuas. At 0510 hours these aircraft took off under the command of Lieutenant Commander C. L. G. Evans, RN. Accompanying the Skuas was again a three-Blenheim force from No. 254 Squadron, RAF, armed with incendiary bombs.

The crossing was uneventful and the attacks were virtually unopposed. The Skuas reported several tanks hit and gutted, and this was confirmed by photographs. The complex was left burning well and there were no casualties among the attacking force.

Sub-Lieutenant (A) Graham Angus Hogg later provided an eyewitness account of this attack:[27]

> I felt that I had been sufficiently frightened for some time to come but on arriving at the hangar the next morning, I discovered that I was due for another trip to Bergen at dawn the following day.
>
> Strangely enough, I slept like a top but did not feel so good creeping around in the half light at 4 o'clock in the morning. We repeated the same manoeuvres as before and successfully fired some oil tanks without damage to any of us. It was a goodly blaze. I certainly enjoyed my breakfast at 9 o'clock.
>
> Photographs that came in that morning showed that in our first raid we had sunk a training cruiser. She had received three direct hits – one forward, one amidships and one astern. My bomb looked uncommonly like the splash plume in the middle of the harbour.[28]
>
> Two Norwegians who had just rowed across from Bergen, said that the last bomb in the first raid had been an unqualified success. It must have been Stanley's. German Officers of occupation had been entertaining some local Quislings to a big party in a hotel on the dockside. Just as the President rose to propose a toast, a large and beautiful bomb spoilt the whole proceedings by landing smack in the middle of the room. The majority of the revellers are now, undoubtedly, 'toasting' in Hell.
>
> I take the opportunity, here, of noting how one feels before any action. Prior to take-off I, personally, have a horrid sensation in the pit of my stomach, which soon goes away until the lead starts to fly. Then it comes back again but I am like a man possessed and completely ignore it. To my knowledge, very few people are unfrightened (*sic*) in action but the majority hide or overcome it extremely well. I know one or two pilots who are impervious to fear but I consider that they are the exceptions.

Meanwhile, *Ark Royal* was launching fighter-escort patrols endeavouring to protect two separate troop convoys (the Scots Guards for Mo and the French Foreign Legion for Bjerkvik) and their naval escorts (the cruisers *Cairo* and *Enterprise* and *Effingham* and *Aurora* respectively), as well as a bombarding force headed up by the battleship *Resolution* and cruiser *Penelope* off Narvik itself. As the troops took priority over the naval force, the convoys were given priority and No. 803 Squadron despatched three aircraft at 1000 hours and two further Skuas at 1035 hours for these missions. Both sorties were uneventful and subsequent patrolling, although scheduled, was weathered out for a time. When flying did resume at 1630 hours, No. 800 Squadron (two Skuas) and No. 803

Squadron (two Skuas) sent out further cover for a brief period before darkness descended.

A similar story followed on 12 May, with *Ark Royal* again despatching five No. 800 Squadron aircraft as fighter escorts to the troop convoys. Of these, a three-plane section commanded by Lieutenant J. A. Rooper, RN, were the only ones to encounter the enemy. They sighted a Heinkel He111, which they drove off before turning their attention to a Dornier Do17, but both bombers escaped unscathed.

In conjunction with the preparation for the assault on Narvik itself, Operation *OB*, the *Ark Royal* also launched Skuas armed with single 100 lb bombs as fighter-bombers both to provide air cover to the troop-ships and assault force at Balangen, and also to attack selected targets ashore. One of these latter targets was the rail bridge at Nordalsbroen, where a German armoured train had been causing a nuisance. Three Skuas from No. 803 Squadron, led by Lieutenant J. M. Christian, RN, were sent to deal with the bridge, but weather conditions ruled out this attack. As an alternative, the Skuas bombed the railway at Sillvjik in an attempt to cut the link. A second attack against the Nordalsbroen bridge mounted at 1915 hours by a pair of aircraft from No. 800 Squadron, under Lieutenant G. E. D. Finch-Noyes, RN, also failed, bombs being jettisoned when they again met impossible cloud conditions over the target.

Missing a 'sitter'

Back at Hatston, No. 806 Squadron made an attack for the third day running, this time directed against shipping at Bergen. Intelligence had indicated a new attempt to run through a merchantman loaded with a fresh consignment of anti-aircraft guns to that port and it was hoped to catch her before she could offload this vital cargo. Lieutenant Commander C. L. G. Evans led six Skuas, each carrying a single 500 lb SAP bomb, into the air at 1000 hours. Again, three RAF Blenheims accompanied them. The Skuas did indeed catch the ship just entering the fiord at 1158 hours, under the close escort of two small destroyers, and made their attack in two waves of three aircraft each. Their lack of experience unfortunately told this day, both sections underestimated the speed of the target vessel and all six bombs missed astern. It was a bitter disappointment to have failed against such an ideal, and important, dive-bomber target.

Sub-Lieutenant Hogg wrote:

> About 2 days after our oil tank episode, we set off to attack shipping in the mouth of the fiord and discovered a medium-sized merchant ship steaming towards Bergen, escorted by two MTBs. Taking full advantage of a suitable cloud formation, we swept down one after the

other. As soon as they saw us coming, the two MTBs scuttled off as fast as they could go and away from the steamer. I was the last to dive and, to my alarm, saw that all the other bombs had dropped about 50 yards astern. It was all up to me. I dived down, taking extremely careful aim and released the bomb at 1,500 feet. I would like to be able to say that the ship heeled over, blew up and sank; she did no such thing. I missed by a good 100 yards and the enemy vessel carried on to Bergen!

If we had met any enemy aircraft on the way home I should have felt sorry for them. There were eight extremely annoyed and vicious Fleet Air Arm pilots flying in the North Sea air. We felt sorry for ourselves when we reported in the Operations Room.[29]

The Narvik circus

The day 13 May was relatively quiet for Skua operations, with two-plane fighter patrols mounted by No. 800 Squadron departing HMS *Ark Royal* at 0215 hours, led by Lieutenant K. V. V. Spurway, RN, and at 0425 hours under Lieutenant J. A. Rooper, RN. However, two of the Skuas, L2938 piloted by Petty Officer (A) R. E. Burston, and L3001 piloted by Rooper himself, were forced to make emergency landings ashore. Both sets of aircrew were rescued. Fog curtailed a third patrol mounted by three aircraft from No. 801 Squadron under Lieutenant R. L. Strange. RN.

The Allied push to take Narvik finally gained some momentum the following day, with the British pushing up from Harstad and the French getting a force ashore at Bjerkuick, north of the objective. The same day saw the departure of the carriers *Glorious* and *Furious* from the Clyde with their cargoes of RAF fighter aircraft embarked. But, off Narvik it was business as usual for the three Skua squadrons aboard *Ark Royal*. The tempo of the flying operations was increased this day, with the carrier herself moving in closer to the coast to provide more continuous fighter cover and give bomber support to the advance.

The first fighter patrol was mounted by three aircraft of No. 801 Squadron led by Lieutenant Commander H. P. Bramwell, RN, which left the deck at 1000 hours. No air opposition was met and, other than a strafing run against some derelict German transport aircraft at Lake Harvig, the patrol was quiet. The next trio of Skuas to get airborne was from No. 803 Squadron, led by Lieutenant W. P. Lucy. They also went north of Narvik to Lake Harvig, carrying 100 lb bombs to smash the ice and thus scuttle the enemy aircraft. This accomplished, they steered for the bombardment fleet supporting the landings, where they found the battleship HMS *Resolution* under heavy air attack by Heinkel He111s from the KG 26.

The Skuas attacked and drove off these raiders, so damaging one Heinkel that it had to force-land at Vaernes. The gallant Lucy then turned his section's attention to a further pair of He111s from the same unit observed making a low-level run. During their attack, return fire from the two bombers laced into Lucy's mount, L2925 (8F), which blew up at low altitude above Ofotfiord. Aghast at this sudden disaster, Lieutenant T. E. Gray flew across the fiord and contacted the destroyer HMS *Whirlwind*, leading her to the area where debris was still floating on the surface of the water. After a diligent search Lucy's body was recovered from the water, but the body of the Squadron Observer, Lieutenant Michael Hanson, DSC, RN, was not found. Meanwhile, Gray found he had used up most of his fuel during the rescue operation and was forced to put down his own aircraft, L2918 (8G), on the coast near Breivik. The destroyer HMS *Encounter* eventually picked up both him and his TAG, Leading Airman A. G. Clayton.

Three further Skua sorties were flown that day. In the first sortie No. 803 Squadron despatched two aircraft at 1535 hours under Lieutenant L. A. Harris, RM, and they, again after bombing Lake Hartvig, duelled with a large force of He111s from the II/KG 26, inflicting damage on two of them. In the second sortie three more aircraft from No. 803 Squadron under Lieutenant J. M. Christian, RN, flew off at 1700 hours. The third sortie, involved three aircraft of No. 800 Squadron led by Lieutenant G. E. D. Finch-Noyes, RN, which took off at 1900 hours. None met any enemy opposition.

By 15 May the operational Skua strength aboard *Ark Royal* had been reduced to just twenty machines, eight with No. 801 Squadron and six apiece with Nos 800 and 803 Squadrons. Despite their best efforts they could not be everywhere, and the Junkers Ju87 Stuka dive-bombers of the I/St.G 1 achieved a major victory when they bombed the Polish troopship *Chrobry* (11,442 tons) with a battalion of the Guards embarked, while she was on her way to Bodö escorted by just the destroyer *Wolverine* and a sloop. She quickly caught fire and had to be abandoned. Attempts by the TSRs later that day to sink the blazing hulk with torpedoes, all failed.

At 0710 hours, two Skuas from No. 803 Squadron, led by Lieutenant L. A. Harris, RM, escorted a TSR attack on German railway traffic near Hundallen. They became entangled with a pair of He111s and a Ju88 *en route* and during the fleeting fire-fight that followed before the enemy escaped intact, return fire damaged the Skua of Petty Officer (A) A. G. Johnson. Neither he, nor his air gunner, Leading Airman F. Coston, was harmed and 8L was able to land back aboard safely.

Three further fighter patrols that morning were relatively quiet affairs, with Lieutenant G. E. D. Finch-Noyes, RN, leading the final section, which had another brief brush with five Heinkels, but with no firm results.

No. 806 Squadron tries again

After their earlier debacle, No. 806 Squadron had been tethered while the lessons were digested and gone over in detail. However, on 16 May German warships were again reported to be at Bergen and the Skuas were despatched to strike once more. Strangely enough against warship targets, only the 250 lb/20 lb bomb mix was carried by each of the nine Skuas on this full-strength mission. Again, RAF Blenheims were supposed to have co-operated in the attack, but failed to make contact so the Skuas went in alone.

Again, Hogg provided a personal account.

One attempt was frustrated by bad weather but we eventually took off about 11.00 one morning. Two flights were to bomb oil tanks while we attacked a jetty. Owing to the position of this jetty our sec-tion had to fly further round behind the town than the others and, consequently, dived some 5 minutes after the remainder of the Squadron had finished.

The anti-aircraft fire was heavy but bursting behind us so we maintained an icy calm – what the eye does not see, the heart does not grieve over. When the others had finished their job, the AA gunners concentrated on us three, still getting into a good diving position. Unharmed, we dropped our heavy bombs on the jetty and then hurtled across the harbour at 1,000 feet, towards the oil tanks. We found these shattered by the rest of the Squadron.

In the event, no warships were in the harbour area, and, after scouting around for an alternative target, Lieutenant Commander C. L. G. Evans led his unit in an attack on oil storage tanks in the port area. All the aircraft returned safely to Hatston.

This proved to be the last such mission from the Orkneys for a while, for, with the increasingly disastrous news from Belgium, Holland and France, No. 803 Squadron was to be transferred south to Kent.

Back at sea, with the *Ark Royal* in position 67° 59′ North, 09° 8′ East, Lieutenant (A) W. H. Martyn led a force of three Skuas armed with a single 250 lb bomb each again to try to put down the hulk of the *Chrobry*. They found the target wallowing but still afloat and scored a direct hit, but this weapon was too small to have any instantaneous effect on so large a ship and she still remained afloat as they flew off. Yet another attempt was determined upon, this time with 500 lb bombs. Three more Skuas from No. 801 Squadron under Lieutenant Commander H. P. Bramwell were sent at 1040 hours to complete the job. However, by the time the section reached the location of the liner, she had finally disappeared beneath the waves, so these valuable bombs were jettisoned into the empty ocean and the Skuas took up fighter patrols over Harstad. Here, they soon sighted some He111s, which they engaged and dispersed without damage to themselves.

During a subsequent patrol by a pair of Skuas from No. 803 Squadron, commanded by Lieutenant L. A. Harris, RM, they engaged with two Dornier Do17s. It was later found out that far from being docile, if fast, bombers they had taken on, their opponents were a brace of Junkers Ju88C long-range fighters (*Zestroyer*), and these tough customers were soon joined by a couple more! Fast and heavily armed, these opponents were more than a match for a Skua, and Harris's aircraft, L2910 (8K), was soon so badly hit that he had to ditch in Rombaksfiord. Both Harris and his air gunner, Lieutenant J. H. R. Medlicot-Vereker, RN, survived their ordeal and were finally picked up by the destroyer HMS *Matabele*.

Marine Lieutenant 'Skeets' Harris (an old friend of Guy Griffiths and Dickie Owen, two other Marine airman 'characters' – they had attended the Brooklands Aviation Flying School at Sywell together in the summer of 1938) had been wounded in this scrap and took no further part in Skua operations.[30]

After a long period with no firm results, another Junkers Ju88 fell to the Skua, this time to Sub-Lieutenant A. T. Easton and A. J. 'Ginger' Hayman,[31] flying L3010 (ASB) on fighter patrol. They intercepted and hit this aircraft several times in a close-range attack. Their victim was seen to crash at Ofotfiord. Sadly, their faithful mount did not long survive their kill, for while on another fighter patrol on 21 May, they ran into thick fog and had to crash-land at Sandsoy Island, north of Harstad. Fortunately, both aircrew survived the experience.

During 17 and 18 May Skua activity from the *Ark Royal* was confined to providing fighter patrols over Allied shipping around Narvik. The Skuas could not prevent the Junkers Ju88s of the II/KG 30 from scoring a direct hit with a 1,000 kg bomb on the battleship *Resolution* on the latter date. This bomb penetrated three decks, but the tough old '*Resso*' withstood the insult and continued to operate undeterred. The same day a patrol of three Skuas from No. 800 Squadron damaged an He111 in a scrappy fight. Similar patrols on 20 May also proved unfruitful.

Ark Royal's final task before she and the *Furious* and *Glorious* returned to Scapa to replenish, was to provide air cover while they flew their RAF fighters ashore, and with all three carriers in company this began on 21 May. Six Skuas, three from No. 800 Squadron led by Lieutenant K. V. V. Spurway, RN, and three from No. 803 Squadron under Lieutenant J. M. Christian, were duly flown off at 0300 hours, but no enemy opposition over the Gladiators' landing site was encountered. This did not prevent yet another casualty, for in the low cloud and mist that prevailed, Lieutenant Christian's section lost contact with each other and had to find their own separate ways back to base. One of them, Sub-Lieutenant

Table 19   Other Skua losses, May/June 1940

Date	Serial	Marking	Unit	Aircrew	Location
13 May	L2938	6M	800	Petty Officer (A) R. E. Burston/ Naval Airman (1) G. W. Halifax	Tjeldoy, Harstad
13 May	L3001	6K	800	Lieutenant J. A. Rooper Petty Officer Wallace Crawford	Harstad, Slakstad
14 May	L2918	8G	803	Lieutenant T. E. Gray Leading Airman Clayton	Coast above Ramsa
16 May	L2910	8K	803	Lieutenant L. A. Harris Lieutenant J. H. R. Medlicot-Vereker, RN	Narvik, Sør av Øyord
21 May	L3010	8B	803	Sub-Lieutenant I. Easton Naval Airman A. J. Hayman	Harstad, Sandsøya

I. Easton, failed to find her and finally had to ditch his aircraft, L3010 (8B), ashore at Sandoya, near Harstad.

By 24 May, thick fog was delaying the *Ark Royal*'s entry to Scapa Flow itself, before she sailed on the Clyde. Meanwhile, the *Glorious* departed with more Hurricanes for Norway. This, despite a Cabinet decision that, due to the catastrophe in the south, Norway would have to be totally abandoned to the Germans, but not before Narvik was taken and the facilities there destroyed. Meanwhile, the brand-new aircraft carrier, HMS *Illustrious*, ran her acceptance trials off the Clyde. There was even some discussion that, fresh from this and without even working up, she should embark her squadrons, including a Skua unit (No. 806 Squadron), and be sent straight into the fight off Norway. Fortunately, this is one wild idea from the Prime Minister that Pound managed to squash! Instead, once her twelve Skuas and two Squadrons of Swordfish were aboard, she was under orders to sail to the West Indies to work up both the ship's company and her aircrews properly. In the event, *Illustrious* did not sail from the Clyde until 21 June.

Losses

During operations in the later part of the Norwegian operation, several Skuas became casualties. They are listed in Table 19.[32]

NOTES

1. The various details about the Skua squadron combat reports covering the Norwegian operations have, unless otherwise acknowledged, been extracted from the files at the National Archives, Kew, London, principally – ADM 199/479 and 480; AIR50, AIR 207, and AIR27/2387.
2. A rather larger than normal tot of rum.
3. Dickie Rolph, *The Königsberg Story*, draft article for *TAG Magazine*, op cit.

4. Partridge to the author, *op cit.*
5. The complete account of this operation can be read in Peter C. Smith, 'Sitting Duck: A Harsh Lesson Imparted', article in *Army & Defence Quarterly Journal*, Vol. 119, No. 4, Tavistock, October 1989.
6. Partridge to the author, *op cit.*
7. Unfortunately, the old *Furious* stripped two of her engine turbines around this time while working off Norway, and had to return to the UK for repairs. Claims on a Fleet Air Arm web site that she ran aground on the Norwegian coast are untrue.
8. Captain Eric Brown asserted that, to his knowledge, the Roc, 'was never deck landed or taken into combat' but neither of these statements is correct. Eric Brown, *Wings of the Navy: Flying Allied Carrier Aircraft of World War II*, Edited by William Green, Airlife Publishing Ltd, Shrewsbury, 1987.
9. Partridge to the author, *op cit.*
10. D'Oyly-Hughes was once alleged to have once stated that 'No aircraft has ever sunk a submarine, and no aircraft ever will', which, if he really did say such a thing, or believe it, besides being factually incorrect, reflected very badly on a Royal Navy Captain in command of one of the Royal Navy's precious few aircraft carriers!
11. Having made a partial recovery, and been awarded a DSC, Colin Campbell-Horsfall helped re-form No. 761 Squadron with Fulmar IIs in January and later set up the Advanced Fighter Training unit at RNAS Yeovilton, becoming its first CO on 1 August 1941. He took over No. 808 Squadron on 1 January 1942, and briefly embarked on the escort carrier HMS *Biter*. He was promoted to Acting Lieutenant Commander in 1943 (confirmed September 1945) and helped harmonise Naval and RAF forces in a combined control system at Lee-on-Solent, in readiness for air patrols for the invasion of Normandy a year later. Colin then became Wing Leader for No. 30 Wing, flying Seafires from Machrihanish in October 1944, and embarked aboard the carrier HMS *Implacable*. His command included his old unit, No. 801 Squadron, which must have delighted him. He went out to the Far East in March 1945, and took place in the final air attacks on mainland Japan with this outfit. After the war, he served at St Merryn on the Fighter Leaders' Course, and had great fun utilising his old dive-bomber skills on visiting rubber-neckers with Seafires from Nos 715 and 736 Squadrons.
12. Despite much post-war speculation, *no* Skuas were lost at Lesjaskog during this attack.
13. This incident is based on the article, 'Oh Calamity!!!' by the late A. E. T. 'Doc' Goble, first printed in *TAGS,* the Fleet Air Arm Telegraphist Air Gunners' Association Magazine, courtesy of the author and the then editor, Jack Bryant.
14. RAF personnel were still embarked in Royal Navy carriers at this period of the war, the change-over to all-naval crews still not having been completed.
15. Fraser-Harris later recalled that while they were attempting to paddle to the shore, this group of Norwegians bombarded them with rocks and abuse in about equal measure. It was not until Russell started to reply in kind with some good old Anglo-Saxon words, that the Norwegians became aware that they were 'friendly'.
16. Admiralty, *Fleet Air Arm*, Ministry of Information Pamphlet, HMSO, London, 1943.
17. Lieutenant H. E. R. Torin, RN, was to be awarded the DSC for his work in Skuas off Norway. He went on to become the first CO of No. 808 Squadron at Worthy Down, but was killed in a flying accident at HMS *Jackdaw* (the TSR training field, as Crail had become) on 30 September 1942.
18. Dickie Ralph to the author.
19. Lieutenant Commander H. Peter Bramwell was hospitalised and Lieutenant C. P. Campbell-Horsfall, RN, took over command of No. 801 Squadron. Bramwell was awarded both the DSO and the DSC for his work off Norway and later was fit enough to be appointed to command No. 778 Squadron, and then with the Service Trials Unit at RNAS Abroath between 1941–1942, being promoted to Commander in December 1942. He was instrumental in conducting the first Aerodrome Dummy Deck Landings

(ADDLs) of a tailhooked Spitfire VB there and flew one aboard *Illustrious* in December 1941; this became the genus of the Seafire.

20. Lieutenant C. H. Filmer, RN, 'Report of attack on three Junkers 88s and subsequent forced-landing of Skua L2991 in Aalesund Harbour', copy in author's collection. Happily, Cecil Filmer currently (2006) resides in Durban, South Africa.

21. Partridge to the author, *op cit.*

22. The bulk of the Skua survived this. When about a fortnight later, the ice melted, L2940 sank to the bottom of Lake Breidal, where she lay, preserved but undisturbed, for many years.

23. Operation *Skua*, the salvaging of Partridge's Skua many years after the war, and her restoration as a diorama at the Fleet Air Arm Museum, Yeovilton, as well as the re-uniting with one of the Germans, Horst Schopis in 1975, are the subject of many books and videos. See Bibliography. The search for more Skua wrecks continues at Bodo Museum.

24. The Blackburn Roc, the Skua's 'cousin' armed with a rear-turret, was said never to have served at sea. Heard's brief foray seems to prove that long-held assumption to be incorrect.

25. According to Vice-Admiral Sir Donald Gibson, Charlton was so used to Skuas ditching when out of fuel, that he regularly carried a screwdriver on long-range missions, in order that he could unscrew the clock from the aircraft 'dashboard' while his observer launched the dinghy!

26. Hogg manuscript *op cit.*

27. Hogg manuscript, *op cit.*

28. *Brummer*, was a German gunner training ship/minelayer, built in1936. She displaced 2,410 tons, and carried four 5.9 in guns, two 88 mm, four 37 mm, and could carry 450 mines. The official date of her loss has been given as 14 April 1940, to submarine attack!

29. Hogg manuscript, *op cit.*

30. Harris convalesced until January 1941, when he was sent to No. 805 Squadron operating in the Western Desert of North Africa. He survived Crete and ended the war as the Commander (Flying) at RNAS Ford. He got his DSC on 25 June 1940 'For daring and resource in the conduct of hazardous and successful operations by the FAA on the coast of Norway', and added an OBE in 1945 for his work in the Night Fighter Development Unit. After the war, he served with No. 705 (Helicopter) Squadron at Lee-on-Solent and retired as a Major in December 1957.

31. Albert John 'Ginger' Hayman (D/151230) was a regular Ordinary Seaman who had volunteered for Air training in 1939. He had been on the 1A Course at Eastleigh and completed his TAG course sometime at the end of March 1940, being posted straight to Hatston. After an eventful 4 weeks with Skuas, he was transferred and from September onward he was with No. 821 Squadron and participated in the Swordfish attack on the *Bismarck*. He later became an officer, going through as an Upperyardman. Lieutenant Easton was to ditch in Norway once more, this time in a Fulmar during the Petsamo raid on 30 July 1941 when he became a POW. Information from Ken Sims, DSM, who served with him.

32. Roy Stevens, the RAF armourer for Petty Officer Pilot E. Monk, gave the author this first-hand account of the job. 'The Skua was my favourite aircraft. The guns, Browning No. 4 Mk 2* N.T.5 were easy to get at. In action, they had to be cleaned *in situ*, loaded on the flight deck, unloaded in the hangar after the wings had been re-folded, and re-armed in the hangar, not a pleasant task with all our 4.5 inch guns and pom-poms chattering away and bombs falling all around the ship. All armourers helped to load up heavier bombs, but the 100 lb anti-sub bombs were carried on our shoulders. TAG's mostly looked after their own Vickers guns and magazines. In 1939 and 1940 we had to make up our own ammo belts and anyone with fingers was called on to help. A full squadron re-arm took 21,600 rounds (oh my poor, raw aching fingers).

9

LAMBS TO THE SLAUGHTER

The success of the attack on Narvik did not compensate for the fall of the Low Countries and the trapping of the British Expeditionary Force (BEF) at Dunkirk. The withdrawal of all Allied forces was secretly agreed, Operation *Alphabet*, and the Royal Navy was charged with saving the troops ashore in Norway, even as it was doing the same along the length and breadth of the English Channel. In accordance with this decision, the carriers *Ark Royal* and *Glorious*, escorted by five destroyers, sailed from Scapa on the last day of May, the former with her two embarked Skua squadrons, Nos 800 and 803, both built up to a strength of twelve aircraft. While the *Ark Royal*'s aircraft were to provide fighter cover for the evacuating convoys and other movements, the *Glorious* was to try and re-embark the Hurricane fighters she had so laboriously transported to Norway just a few days before. Meanwhile, back in London, Chamberlain had resigned and been replaced as Premier by Winston Churchill. He proved the man for the job, but if the Royal Navy thought there would now be less amateur political interference in the day-to-day operations of the service with Churchill's departure, they were soon to be disillusioned!

Alphabet patrols

By 3 June the *Ark Royal* and *Glorious* had reached their new operating station off Norway. Here, in position 70° 22′ North, 16° 00′ East, off Hinnoy, and with almost 24 hours of daylight, *Ark Royal* began launching Skuas to conduct two-plane, round-the-clock fighter patrols. For the next 4 days she followed a similar programme, maintaining a watch over the evacuation convoys, withdrawing almost 25,000 troops, as well as the Norwegian royal family and Parliament, all in the face of the enemy. Prominent was the Commanding Officer of No. 800 Squadron, Acting-Major Richard Partridge, RM, now safely returned to the fold after his soujourn ashore and collection of a new steed from Donibristle. Heinkel and Junkers probed the fleet's defences from time to time and had to be dealt with.

On his first patrol, which left about half-an-hour before midnight, Partridge lost his wingman almost immediately when his undercarriage would not retract, so Birdy carried on alone. Lieutenant G. E. D. Finch-Noyes, RN, followed him with two more aircraft at 0035 hours, and three further Skuas from the same squadron led by Lieutenant G. R. Calling-ham, RN, at 0345 hours. No. 803 Squadron then took over the job, with Lieutenant C. H. Filmer, RN, Lieutenant K. V. V. Spurway, and Lieuten-ant C. W. Peever each leading three aircraft patrols at 0550, 0645 and 0750 hours and finally Lieutenant Dennis Gibson, RN, with two Skuas at 1005 hours.

Interleaved with these patrols were a few more aggressive sorties. At 1115 hours Birdy Partridge was aloft again with a wingman to conduct an armed reconnaissance of the movements along the Drag to Sorfold road. Each Skua carried a single 250 lb SAP, one of which demolished a useful-looking pier off an enemy-held piece of the coast on their return journey. A patrol was also conducted by Lieutenant Finch-Noyes at 1145 hours and by Lieutenant Commander J. Casson, RN, at 2350 hours. Bad weather curtailed flying on 5 June, with just a single three-plane patrol by No. 800 Squadron under Lieutenant Callingham being flown. The next day the *Glorious* began to embark the Hurricanes aboard, flown by RAF pilots with no deck-landing knowledge and no tail hooks! Skuas were despatched to give them cover during this tricky operation. A trio of three-Skua fighter patrols was also sent to cover the troop evacuations from Bardufoss (Lieutenant K. V. V. Spurway, RN, No. 803 Squadron), Narvik (Acting-Major R. T. Partridge, RM, No. 100 Squadron) and Skaanland (Lieutenant G. E. D. Finch-Noyes, RN, No. 800 Squadron). On 7 June there was a continuation of the same scenario and, with the successful landing of the RAF fighters completed on 8 June, the *Glorious* and her two escorting destroyers, *Acasta* and *Ardent*, were detached from the force at 0253 hours to return to Scapa Flow. They never made it. Instead, they ran into the battle-cruisers *Scharnhorst* and *Gneisenau*, part of a German force that also included the heavy cruiser *Admiral Hipper* and four destroyers that were at sea conducting Operation *Juno*, the interception of Allied shipping, unknown to the British C-in-C.

Meantime, *Ark Royal* continued her established routine, but all the patrols were quiet. Only Lieutenant Dennis Gibson, RN, with three of No. 803 Squadron's Skuas, caught any sight of enemy aircraft, an He111, which, as so frequently before, outran them and was lost in the cloud cover. There were continuous patrols and one scramble, but no further sign of the enemy was seen.

The action hotted up a little on 9 June. As the *Glorious* had not answered any signals, it was assumed she was in trouble. Searches were flown by the TSRs and the Skuas joined in covering a sector up to 20 miles astern, but all drew a blank. Having disposed of several tankers, troop-ships and naval auxiliaries, as well as the *Glorious* force, but suffering a torpedo hit from *Acasta*, Admiral Marschall called off the operation and his force made for the safety of Trondheim.

Late in the afternoon the battleship *Valiant*, part of the covering force, picked up an enemy aircraft on her radar and reported the contact to *Ark Royal*. Immediately, three Skuas from No. 800 Squadron, led by Lieutenant G. R. Callingham, took off to hunt her down. Sure enough, not knowing it had been spotted, the He115 from the KuFlGr 506 was still stooging around the fringes of the convoy, sending back reports, and was caught by surprise. After a brief stern chase the Skua flown by Acting Sub-Lieutenant R. W. Kearsley, RN, got in some effective shots, which brought the float plane down, after a neat combined effort by all concerned.[1]

The three Skuas were still airborne at 2300 hours when a force of six Heinkel He111s from the II/KG 20 made a determined approach from astern of the *Ark Royal*. The Skuas managed to intercept, destroying one Heinkel and setting fire to a second, spoiling their attack. A second section, led by Lieutenant G. E. D. Finch-Noyes of No. 800 Squadron, was scrambled to assist and managed to chase and damage a third He111. Lieutenant C. W. Peever with three further aircraft of No. 803 Squadron flew off at 2355 hours, followed by Partridge's section from No. 800 Squadron. They successfully finished off the action, causing the enemy to jettison their bombs and make a hasty departure.

Attack on Sweden – the aborted operation Paul

Even after British soldiers had been evacuated at great risk from the shores of Norway, and indeed after the last British soldier had left the beach at Dunkirk, Winston Churchill continued to press for action to be renewed in Scandinavia. The export of iron ore had long been an obsession with the impatient Premier, and, indeed, had led to the original opening moves of the Norwegian fiasco with his plans to mine the Inner Leads. Now, like a dog with rat, which, although dead, it persists in shaking, Winston wanted to renew this action against yet another neutral nation. The original plan had been to stop the export of iron ore from the Swedish port of Lulea in the Gulf of Bothnia, and northern arm of the Baltic Sea. Daily, four or five ore ships loaded from special quays 9 miles south of the town and then sailed via either a mile-long channel to the east of Germando Island, or took a more tortuous route north of Junko Island. Either way, the vessels had to pass Tjuvholmsund via a 1 mile long, 200 feet wide and 25 feet deep dredged channel. The plan was to attack this port with carrier-borne minelaying and torpedo-carrying aircraft, but only after 1 hour's warning had been given by pamphlet-dropping aircraft to give the ships time to land their crews! The fact that the hour's warning would also aid the defenders seems to have been ignored. Furthermore, both the neutrality of Finland and Sweden also stood to be infringed.

The assessment was that the nearest German airfield was at Trondheim. However, there was also thought to be an advanced enemy airbase at Mosjoen, as well as the Norwegian airfields at Bardufoss and Skaanland, which were to be rendered unusable for 3 or 4 months by means of delayed action bombs.

In planning Operation *Paul*, a force of three aircraft carriers was originally specified, with cover and escort being provided by the Home Fleet. These were to launch their aircraft from one of three positions off north-west Norway: (a) And Fiord, some 270 miles from the target, (b) a position near 70° 40′ North, 19° 30′ E, at some 300 miles range or (c) from Porsanger Fiord, 345 miles from the entrance of the fiord. The aircraft were divided in four waves: local reconnaissance and defence of the carrier force; pamphlet-dropping and observer aircraft; a first wave of mine-dropping aircraft and Skua fighters; and a second wave consisting of minedropping aircraft, torpedo-bombers and Skua fighters.

The carriers selected to carry out the original attack had been:

Ark Royal – 30 TSRs and 18 Skuas
Glorious – 24 TSRs and 12 Gladiators
Furious – 24 TSRs and 9 Skuas.

Of these aircraft, six TSRs and six Gladiators were allocated to the defence of the carriers; twelve more Skuas were to provide the escorts for the thirty Swordfish (six carrying pamphlets) of the first wave with twelve more to protect the thirty-six Swordfish of the second wave. To reach Lulea, carry out the operation and return to the carriers, involved a long flight across both Norway and Sweden. To accomplish this the Skua was assessed as having a total fuel capacity of 166 gallons, with a consumption of 27 gallons per hour at 120 knots, or 30 gallons per hour at 130 knots. Its endurance was listed as: (a) Time – 6 hours 5 minutes at 120 knots, or 4 to 5 hours 30 minutes at 130 knots, (b) Distance – 730 miles at 120 knots or 715 miles at 130 knots. However, a note was appended that 'Full distance trials with the aircraft actually taking part in the operation will be desirable to ensure that no aircraft has an abnormally large consumption.'[2]

Churchill, was then still First Lord of the Admiralty and continued to interfere daily in operational matters. Impatient that the job had not yet been carried out, he had minuted his long-suffering First Sea Lord, Admiral Sir Dudley Pound, on 6 June, ending, 'Pray let me have report of how this is progressing, and when it is intended to begin'. Pound was fully extended overseeing Operation *Alphabet*, the evacuation of all British and Allied troops, plus the Norwegian royal family, in the face of German pressure. This fully involved every warship the Royal Navy could spare, including its precious carriers. Churchill, of course, had ignored this fact.

Pound patiently pointed out that when Operation *Paul* was first designed:

> ... there were no Germans in Norway at all, and it would therefore have been possible to operate the carriers as close in shore as we wished. Even when we knew that the Germans were in occupation of aerodromes on the coast of Norway, it did not appear that this would prevent Operation *Paul*, as it was hoped the range of the machines would be sufficient to enable the carriers to operate at a safe distance from the coast.

But things had now changed, 'it will not be possible now'. If the carriers (by this time reduced to just *Ark Royal*, *Glorious* and *Furious* and with the Skuas of Nos 800 and 803 Squadrons embarked, but for carrier protection only[3]) operated from Vestfiord 'it will almost certainly result in the loss or damage of both carriers to such an extent that the machines could not land on their return and would all be lost'.

Some 2 days later the *Glorious* was sunk by the *Scharnhorst* and *Gneisenau* and the operation was abandoned. With Europe falling like a house of cards, and Britain's allies disappearing like vapour in the sun, it is perhaps fortunate that Churchill was thwarted in using the Skua in an attack that would have brought yet another nation into the war against us.

The Scharnhorst *tragedy*

The loss of the *Glorious*, sunk on 8 June, along with her escorting destroyers *Acasta* and *Ardent*, by the German battle-cruisers *Scharnhorst* and *Gneisenau* while on her way back to Scapa Flow, was a stunning blow. The *Ark Royal* had been many miles away, still carrying out her escort duties under Operation *Alphabet* as the Allies cut their losses ashore and began to pull their troops out of Norway. Consequently, they knew nothing of the disaster until long after it was too late, but the Skua crews were soon to be caught up in the aftermath. They were still considering the possibilities of carrying out the long-delayed Operation *Paul*, but soon had a different set of problems to work out.

The first of these was effecting a rendezvous with units of the Home Fleet, the battleship *Rodney*, battle-cruiser *Renown* and destroyers, which was accomplished at 1440 hours on 10 June. This done, long-range air searches were mounted by the TSRs to try and find the two German capital ships. The *Luftwaffe* decided to gatecrash this particular party less than an hour later, and a pair of Skuas commanded by Lieutenant K. V. V. Spurway was flown off to search for an He115 snooper at 1550 hours, but the He115 escaped into cloud cover before they could close with her. However, she persisted in sniffing around the fleet, and so a second attempt was made to bring this gentleman to account an hour later. Lieutenant Commander J. Casson led a trio from No. 803 Squadron in another pursuit, but again, although they got in a few long-range bursts and claimed to have hit her, the He115 again remained nothing more than a 'possible' on the slate.

This routine continued on the following day, but the only excitement was the interception at 0830 hours of a RAF flying boat by three Skuas from No. 800 Squadron under Lieutenant G. E. D. Finch-Noyes, which had been mistaken for another enemy reconnaissance aircraft. The hunt for the German ships was called off after the weather closed in and prevented further flying. Later, they were found anchored off Trondheim.

Vengeance!

Angered by the loss of the *Glorious,* a revenge attack was decided upon against the damaged *Scharnhorst.* She had been discovered by aerial reconnaissance on 12 June, anchored and undergoing temporary repairs in Trondheim Roads, along with the *Admiral Hipper* and four destroyers. Accordingly, the *Ark Royal* and her accompanying warships altered course towards the Norwegian coast as Admiral Forbes complied with the Admiralty's wishes, while Vice-Admiral L. V. 'Nutty' Wells, DSO, RN, and his staff began planning how to carry out this very difficult task.

The German ships were under the immediate protection of two crack *Luftwaffe* fighter units stationed at the close-by Vaernes airfield, and to the naval pilots charged with the attack, it appeared to be a futile and suicidal mission. The ships lay 45 miles up the long approaches, with ample time for plenty of warning to be given to the German pilots. It was also June, so in order to make a concealed approach in any semblance of darkness, a midnight launch would be essential. Even if the attacking aircraft survived the long approach, the ships would be fully alerted and waiting with all anti-aircraft guns manned and ready. Finally, even supposing that all these hazards were overcome, the deck armour of the battle-cruiser could not be compared with that of a light cruiser like the *Königsberg.* The heaviest bomb the Skuas could carry could hardly be expected to penetrate through to the ship's vitals to inflict any worthwhile damage.

All these considerations were brushed aside by the overriding demand to exact a modicum of revenge for the humiliation of the loss of the *Glorious.* The plan was pushed ahead. As a sop to some of the protests, the RAF was brought into the equation; a striking force of Bristol Beaufort light bombers from No. 22 Squadron was to attack Vaenes airfield in a pre-emptive strike to prevent the enemy interceptors taking off. Moreover, an escort of RAF long-range Blenheim fighters from No. 254 Squadron, was to rendezvous with the Skuas on the way in to the target,

as added protection, and guard their withdrawal afterwards. Also discussed was the possibility of the two TSR squadrons joining the strike, as
their torpedoes were likely to be more effective against the big ship's 4½-
inch thick armour than the 500 lb SAP bombs. However, this idea was
abandoned as being too risky for the even slower biplanes to attempt.[4]

All these options were considered at a series of meetings held aboard
the carrier with Wells and his Commander Flying, Commander F. M.
Stephenson, RN, with both the squadron COs, Lieutenant Commander
Casson, RN, and Captain R. T. Partridge, RM, as the carrier, leaving the
area of bad weather behind her at 1600 hours, steadily closed the miles
between them and their target. Half-an-hour later, No. 800 Squadron put
up a fighter patrol of three aircraft under Lieutenant G. R. Callingham,
RN, over the fleet.[5] A second, two-plane patrol followed at 2230 hours.
The one thing that was in the striking force's favour, and it was the only
thing, was that the question of endurance could be omitted from the
equation; 'Beaky' planned to get in close before the launch to give them
some sort of chance. Both leaders were aghast at what was being
proposed. Casson said that, if the attack went ahead, he would expect to
lose at least half his squadron. Partridge pointed out that the weapons
they planned to drop would not do much more than dent a battle-cruiser;
Scharnhorst was no push-over like *Königsberg*.

These warnings were listened to politely, but the pressure from the
Admiralty was just too great. An attack *was* to be made, come what may!
There was nothing left for those aboard the *Ark Royal* charged with the
mission to do, but make their plans – and make their peace. Casson and
Partridge called in their senior Observers, Lieutenant R. S. Bostock, RN,
and Petty Officer (A) Wallace Crawford, and detailed work commenced,
Finally, at 1630 hours, the selected aircrew were briefed. The young
men had much to consider during the rest of the evening, and then the
final briefing was conducted at 2300 hours. Few had any illusions about
their chances of coming back from what all considered a suicidal mission.
Captain Partridge told the author that he fully shared his aircrews' appre-
hension, but tried to conceal it. He considered writing a letter to his wife,
Fay, but then had second thoughts because this felt, '. . . a bit melodramatic
and perhaps even courting disaster by anticipation'.[6] Even the usually
light-hearted Lieutenant G. E. D. 'Ned' Finch-Noyes, confided to his

Table 20   Air patrol, 12 June 1940

Aircraft	Pilot	Observer/Air gunner
6P	Lieutenant G. R. Callingham, RN	Acting Petty Officer W. Crawford
6Q	Midshipman R. W. Kearsley	Acting Petty Officer L. Eccleshall
6R	Petty Officer (A) W. J. Heard	Leading Airman J. Coles

friend Lieutenant Bob Everett, 'I don't know if I'm going to come back from this one, Bob. I want you to give these personal things my wife'.

The weather on 12 June slowly improved and became generally more suitable for flying, with the cloud lifting and the visibility extending. At 1650 hours three Skuas took off to maintain a defensive patrol over the fleet.

The full range of Skuas was readied, this being the maximum that could be accommodated on the flight deck of the *Ark Royal* to ensure a safe take-off with their bomb load.[7]

The RAF mission

The attack on Vaenes by the seven RAF Beaufort bombers, arranged to take place not earlier that 0200 hours on 13 June, was carried out earlier than ordered and under-strength, three of the bombers turning back. The four that reached the enemy field attacked at 0150 hours, a 10-minute error that proved deadly to the Skuas rather than the enemy. In fact, this strike, ahead of the agreed time, and too weak to do any real harm to the enemy, achieved the opposite effect to that intended. Rather than ensuring that the *Luftwaffe* fighters were pinned to the ground, the Beauforts merely stirred up the hornets' nest, so that, by the time the Skuas arrived, the sky was full of alert and vengeful Bf109s and Bf110s looking for targets!

Donald Gibson wrote:

> During the time that the Skuas were on the target six RAF Blenheims were to provide us with fighter cover. As I write this I hear retired German Air Force officers laughing.[8]

This attack also put all the German flak defences in the area, ashore and afloat, on high alert and readiness. The secret of success lay with surprise; the RAF ensured that there was none whatsoever. It was 20 minutes' flying time from the head of the fiord to the target, so no doubt the enemy would have been forewarned by observers on the coast anyway. But the pre-emptive strike made absolutely certain that there would be no repeat of the errors made by the Germans at Bergen earlier.

Given the odds, the DNAD retrospectively concluded that the attacking force had the right to expect no more than a single hit being obtained on the main target vessel, with maybe a 25 per cent chance of a second, but with at least 30 per cent of hits suffered from anti-aircraft fire and at least another 30 per cent from the defending fighter force.[9]

The Charge of the Light Brigade

The *Ark Royal* and her escorts arrived undetected at the pre-ordained flying-off position and the striking force was ranged up on her deck in the light of the northern summer sky. This comprised six aircraft from No. 800 Squadron and nine from No. 803 Squadron. Selection for inclusion in the operation was governed by the following factors:

1. Of the Skua pilots available, these fifteen had previous experience of dive-bombing with the aircraft, others had only fighter experience.[10]
2. The requirement of a standing air patrol over the fleet, meant that some Skuas had to be held back for this purpose, and fighter experience counted more for this duty.
3. As only light winds were prevailing over the task force, fifteen was the maximum number of aircraft that could be flown off *Ark Royal*'s deck in a single range.

Once the three fighter patrol aircraft had flown off the carrier, the Trondheim strike force began to be ranged aft. Ironically, because the wind had eased so much, only fifteen Skuas were readied for the mission, which was the maximum number that could be flown off with full load in one range. Vice-Admiral L. V. Wells considered that, 'the fleet reached the flying-off position undetected', which is probably correct. At 0002 hours, in position 64° 23′ North, 03° 19′ West, with the wind reduced to a Force 3 south-easterly over the bows, the Skuas began flying off. Details of the The strike are shown in Table 21.

Table 21   Attack on *Scharnhorst*, 13 June 1940

Aircraft	Pilot	Observer/Air gunner
7A	Lieutenant Commander J. Casson, RN	Lieutenant P. E. Fanshawe, RN
7B	Sub-Lieutenant G. W. Brokensha	Leading Airman F. Coston
7C	Petty Officer (A) T. F. Riddler	Leading Airman H. T. Chatterley
7F	Lieutenant C. H. Filmer, RN	Midshipman (A) T. A. McKee
7G	Midshipman (A) A. S. Griffiths, RN	Naval Airman F. P. Dooley
7L	Sub-Lieutenant J. A. Harris, RN	Naval Airman S. R. Stevenson
7P	Lieutenant D. C. Gibson, RN	Acting Sub-Lieutenant M. P. Gordon-Smith, RN
7Q	Sub-Lieutenant R. E. Bartlett, RN	Naval Airman (1) L. C. Richard
7R	Petty Officer (A) H. Gardiner	Naval Airman (1) C. H. Pickering
6A	Captain R. T. Partridge, RM	Lieutenant R. S. Bostock, RN
6K	Lieutenant K. V. Spurway, RN	Petty Officer (A) R. F. Hart
6C	Petty Officer (A) H. A. Monk	Petty Officer (A) R. S. Rolph
6F	Lieutenant G. E. D. Finch-Noyes, RN	Petty Officer (A) H. G. Cunningham
6G	Midshipman L. H. Gallagher, RN	Acting Petty Officer (A) W. Crawford
6H	Midshipman D. T. R. Martin, RN	Leading Airman W. J. Tremeer

A last word

Aboard the *Ark Royal* as the mission prepared to leave, there were some
poignant moments. One of the aircraft armourers, Ronald G. Jordan, was
to recall many years later, with great clarity, what took place:

> I was part of the armourer team of No. 800 Squadron aboard *Ark
> Royal*. There were teams who specialised in engines, aircraft rigging,
> armaments and electrics, all under a Squadron Maintenance section
> headed by an RAF Sergeant, and later by a Royal Navy Petty
> Officer. There were five or six of us in the armourer team, two navy
> people, the rest RAF, of which Corporal Long was the Main
> Armourer. He like, Corporal Kilmister the chief engine fitter, was a
> product of Lord Trenchard's Training Schools before the war, and
> real professionals who knew their job backwards. The 500 lb SAP
> bombs used to come up from the Bomb Rooms by continuous chain,
> we loaded them on the trolleys and took them to the aircraft. The
> bombs would be fused below, before they came up. The SAP bombs
> did not have nose fuses, they were all tail-fused, the firing pin over-
> coming the retaining spring by inertia, triggered by the second (CE)
> fuse, which would cause detonation.[11]

Ron also remembered the preparations for the Trondheim attack
clearly:[12]

> Life for the armourers was mostly cold [with inadequate clothing],
> wet, windy, highly pressurised and dangerous. Arming up bombs on
> a pitching flight deck was a difficult and dangerous business. Aircrews
> were often flying patrols for 8 hours a day at extreme range and
> sometimes they had to ditch in the sea because they couldn't be
> landed before their fuel ran out. [Ron said you could see the exhaust
> smoke turn ominously black.] The armourers had to strip all the
> ammo from the guns before the aircraft could be taken below deck.
> The *Ark* was a No. 1 target and subjected to frequent air attack,
> which meant the ship was often at action stations with the crew below
> deck trapped behind closed bulkhead doors – but not far from a great
> deal of av-gas. (Ron also recalled the time when the ship swerved so
> violently to miss a bomb that all the crockery in the mess shot onto
> the floor and was smashed. Life aboard was clearly no picnic.)

Ron explained the working procedures and how the squadron leader,
'always took off last so that the rest of the squadron could form up behind
the leader'. One of the armourer's jobs was to attend to any last minute
'stores' that the aircrew might want for a particular mission (apparently
this included the possibility of side arms, but the crews didn't always carry
them). On this day Ron recalled how Robin Bostock had made a request

for 'aluminium sea markers'. Ron had then gone to get these from the stores area. Ron pointed out that threading your way through the parked aircraft with their engines running was no easy task. He was in the process of handing the markers to Bostock in his cockpit, when Captain Partridge decided to check his engine at full throttle. This left Ron clinging to the side of the cockpit with his feet blown clean off the deck and in great fear that he was about to disappear over the back of the *Ark Royal*'s sloping rear deck![13] Ron was thus the last person to speak to Robin Bostock.

Take-off

The Skuas began flying off in position 64° 58' North, 04° 58' East, at 0002 hours on 13 June, each one armed with a single 500 lb SAP bomb, the squadrons being led by Lieutenant Commander Casson and Captain Partridge, RM. For a brief while the sections formed up, awaiting their escorts, but, as nothing materialised, the Skuas took their departure alone, gradually climbing to 11,000 feet as they did so. The departing dive-bombers were still dimly visible in the distance when the first RAF Blenheims belatedly arrived over the fleet later for the rendezvous. It transpired that they had seen the receding aircraft, but did not recognise them as the aircraft they were to escort. Nor could they communicate with either the now-vanishing Skuas or the *Ark Royal* herself.[14] Instead, they circled the ships for a while, then, making their minds up, decided to head for the target area anyway. By then there was no hope of them catching the Skuas or of being able to assist them in any way.

Meanwhile, all unaware of the RAF's double blunders, in two loose groups at 140 knots, the fifteen dive-bombers crossed the Norwegian coast over Froya island, to the north of the Halten light at 0123 hours at an altitude of 11,000 feet. (Gibson recalled noticing the lighthouse and thought it likely that someone from there, watching them pass, rang up Trondheim to tell them they were on their way!) Casson kept his eye on the clock, aiming to reach the target dead on 0200 hours. After another 10 minutes' flying time, some 25 miles down-fiord, the force altered course to the south and dropped to 1,000 feet, forming up in line ahead. Casson waggled his wings to attract attention, then jerked his thumb over each shoulder, which indicated adopt line astern, finally shaking his clenched fist toward the target area.

On arrival over the target, they found the weather fair and clear, but with slight low-lying round mist and haze. The German warships soon came into view, Partridge recalling the hunched shapes black against the sea in Strindfiord at 0157 hours. The bulk of the *Scharnhorst* was unmistakeable, her anti-aircraft guns already winking their greeting as flak hosed up.

The enemy warships they found at anchor were later analysed from the photographs taken. They revealed one battle-cruiser (this was *Scharnhorst*); one large cruiser (actually the heavy cruiser *Admiral Hipper*), one small cruiser (the *Nûrnberg*, which had only arrived that day) and four destroyers (*Karl Galster, Hans Lody, Erich Steinbrinck* and *Hermann Schoemann*).

The sky was crystal clear and there was no sign of aerial support. That would have been bad enough, but more than flak met the Skuas as they made their final approach through clear skies. The two squadrons split up ready to make their pincer attacks, Casson to port, Partridge to starboard. No. 800 Squadron elected to make a shallow dive-bombing run from the north, dropping down from an altitude of 8,000 feet in line-astern. The majority of No. 803 Squadron, save for the final section, made a south-to-north attack, bow-to-stern, against the battle-cruiser.

Well before the bulk of the Skuas got to the dropping point the waiting German fighters, single-engined Bf109s and twin-engined Bf110s and Ju88C-2s, were slashing in among them, with others queuing up to take their turn in the massacre. Partridge remembered seeing a Skua flaming down almost immediately. There was no sign whatsoever of the 'protecting' Blenheims as the dwindling numbers of dive-bombers pushed into this inferno. Planes began to drop away but the survivors pressed on and released, then tried to find an escape route that was not already barred by Messerschmitts or the wall of flak.

A Bf109 homed in on Partridge's aircraft, his observer shouting a warning, and the Skua was put into a tight turn, causing the attacker to overshoot. Then the next one came in and he was forced to jink again, but not before he caught sight out of the corner of his eye, of one Skua delivering a 'textbook controlled dive against one of the larger warships, but not making any apparent attempt to recover from its dive and plunging straight into the cold waters of the fiord at full tilt'. Given a small window free of enemy fighter fire, Partridge selected the nearest large warship and committed to the approach. At 260 knots going downhill, his aircraft was rock solid and, at 6,000 feet, Partridge raised the nose to shed some speed, pulled hard out of a stall turn with full flap down and went into the final attack dive. Flak from the battle-cruiser's forty-six anti-aircraft weapons of various calibres filled his windscreen and he pressed the bomb release at about 1,700 feet, lower than recommended. As the bomb came clear of the fork, Partridge turned sharply to port, raised his flaps and headed for sea level, while at his back Robin Bostock was shouting that they had scored a near-miss off the bow of their target, adding the fact that another pair of Skuas had barrelled into the fiord.

The Skuas that survived thus far had two options, follow Birdy's example and hit the deck to try and escape along the wave tops, or gain some altitude and weave their way out of trouble. The Skua could not do the latter, and all but one that tried to fight their way out by adopting this method lost their bet. Just about every dive-bomber of the few that made it out of that death trap did so at the very lowest of low levels, the German fighter pilots, not surprisingly, showing little stomach to follow them down there.

Donald Gibson recalled that when John Casson formed the Skuas up into line astern, he started to lead around the target in order to make a classic bow-to-stern attack, which involved a lot more time than Gibson considered they had left:

> Pat Gordon Smith, my observer, in his matter of fact voice, told me that four Messerschmidt [sic] 109s were astern of our section and I could see four Messerschmidt 110s on my starboard beam. I could also see Skuas going down in flames; being in a perfect position I therefore led my lot down, attacking from stern to bow.[15]

The attack

Lieutenant D. C. Gibson's official report stated:

> After having flown inshore for about 10 minutes, we turned to the south and approached the target at 10,000 feet, still proceeding at slow speed. Shortly after reaching Trondheim, 803 Squadron formed line astern and 800 Squadron broke away to carry out a separate attack.
>
> We carried out a shallow dive to 8,000 feet and made our approach. While still North of the target, which was one Battle Cruiser and one Heavy Cruiser, heavy anti-aircraft fire developed. By the time I was in a position to attack from North to South along the deck of the battle cruiser, the anti-aircraft fire was exceedingly fierce.
>
> Lieutenant Commander J. Casson was leading the squadron round to attack from South to North (from bow to stern). As I was the last section to attack, I considered it not worthwhile to expose my aircraft to an extra 5 minutes of anti-aircraft fire. We attacked from stern to bow of the enemy, being in a perfect position to do so. There appears to be only two survivors of the South to North (bow to stern) attack.
>
> Although we have no record of having hit the target, our bombs seem to have fallen close around it, one being estimated at 15 feet from its stern.
>
> With one exception, all the survivors escaped by low flying in the ground mist. The exception was Sub Lieutenant (A) G. W. Brokensha who circled the area twice to see if he could help anyone.
>
> Many Me109 fighters were seen to attack Skuas and four Me110 fighters were present, though they held off. I myself, was subjected to

a poor-spirited attack by the Me109s when in my dive. One Me110 was driven off by the Skua it attacked.

From what we saw, those who were attacked by fighters were those aircraft who climbed after attacking, and did not take advantage of the ground mist. As we had no height and negligible performance, it would have been suicidal to have gone to their assistance.

We gained the impression that the diversion created by the Beaufort bombers was a mistake. It appeared to take place a little too soon and destroyed any possibility of surprise. There are contrary opinions on this matter.

We did not see the Blenheim fighters until after we had left the coast.[16]

Lieutenant K. V. V. Spurway, RN, in 6K was directly astern of Captain R. T. Partridge, RM, in 6A as he dived in line astern, at a 60 degree angle of dive. Both aircraft released their bombs at a height of between 3,000 and 2,000 feet and he observed the mark of a close miss just off the *Scharnhorst*'s starboard quarter, and also witnessed 'a considerable flash'[17] just aft of the funnel, on the starboard side of the ship. He thought that Partridge appeared to continue his very low dive and was not seen to pull out. Spurway's observer also reported a flash on the port side, aft of the funnel, after his own aircraft had pulled out. He did not see either Partridge's or Spurway's bomb fall into the sea. Spurway commented that:

6K's bomb was released at 3,000 feet and on pulling away, the observer reported that he had seen a flash, possibly caused by 6K's bomb on the port side abaft the funnel. The photograph taken directly after 6K's bomb had fallen shows considerable smoke over the battle-cruiser.

6K pulled up to 5,000 feet until clear of the gun area and then dived low over the land to the Northward as an Me110 was observed on the starboard beam. An Me109 was observed some distance away. The fighters apparently failed to observe 6K against the dark ground. 6K subsequently returned in company with 6Q, which joined up on leaving the coast.

Other aircraft were observed to attack the *Hipper* class cruiser ... but no hits were observed. The weather was hazy with a clear sky, and the movements of aircraft were hard to follow against the ground or water. Two large fires were observed ashore. One in the vicinity of Vaernes aerodrome and the other further west. No Blenheim or Beauforts were sighted. A large number of He115s were observed in the water off the town, and two were seen in the air in the vicinity. A large ball of flame was seen in the sky over the ships by

Petty Officer Hart. It is possible that this was an aircraft shot down in flames.[18]

The enemy defences were fully manned and ready. Long-range AA fire was not accurate. Both ships and shore batteries used flak with coloured tracer up to an altitude of 8,000 feet, each ship using a different colour.

The effects of the enemy AA fire was mixed. Some Skuas were seen to become separated from their leaders when taking avoiding action, but that apart, the AA fire 'appears to have been disregarded'.[19]

The Official Report[20] stated that both squadrons 'pressed home their attack through intense and accurate anti-aircraft fire from ships and shore batteries. Many enemy fighters Type Me109 and Me110 engaged the Skuas during and after the attack'. During the approach, in line ahead, aircraft became detached from squadrons and sections due to heavy evasive action. The report noted that all the aircraft that returned, attacked *Scharnhorst* from the north-east adding, 'it appears that seven and probably eight bombs were aimed at *Scharnhorst* from this direction, of which one, or possibly, two, are thought to have been hits'.

The No. 803 Squadron leader led the remainder round astern of *Scharnhorst*, apparently with the intention of attacking from the south-east:

> None of these aircraft returned but it appears probable that they eventually attacked the cruisers, as a bomb was seen to fall 50 yards from the 'Hipper' class cruiser during the 'get-away' of the aircraft which attacked form the North-east.
>
> The losses of aircraft and personnel are particularly heavy ... though it is possible that some escaped into Sweden.

Two hits were claimed, and two explosions, but the Germans later stated only a single bomb struck the *Scharnhorst*. Even that solitary success was dashed from them, for although the bomb penetrated her upper deck, it failed to detonate. It may have been dropped from too low an altitude, or been a dud bomb, but the effect on the German ship was minimal.

Escape or die!

Now a heavy price was being exacted. While most Skua survivors owed their immunity to hitting the deck at near sea-level and seeking sanctuary in the mist conditions, the majority fell to the enemy guns. No fewer than eight of the fifteen Skuas were lost within the space of a few minutes. It was a disaster. His companions, observing Birdy's Skua heading straight down toward the sea, thought he was done for then and there, and reported that he had, 'continued his dive and not observed to pull out'. Hammering back up the fiord, Partridge almost wrote his aircraft off in a mid-air collision, avoiding by the narrowest of margins, colliding with a startled German floatplane that stumbled into his path. Birdy tried to snap-shoot this wanderer; the German, indignant, fired a Very cartridge, which attracted a pair of Bf109s' attention. Their number was up.

They could not outrun the Bf109Es, from the II/JG 77, and though he tried to shake them off by swerving all over the fiord, Birdy could not bluff two aircraft more than 80 mph faster than his own aircraft. Sooner or later, one of them would get in a position to make a clear shot, and sooner rather than later, one did. There was a last cry from Robin Bostock in the back seat, then a large section of the Skua's wing was chopped away by a cannon shell. The petrol tank ignited and Birdy had no choice but to bale out and trust he had sufficient altitude for the parachute to open. The Skua went into the water with Robin still aboard, impacting at the head of Stjornfjorden, south of Stallvik.

Partridge somehow survived the drop, but was badly burnt about the face. Local fishermen rescued him after he had spent some 20 minutes in the fiord and a Norwegian doctor tended his immediate needs. However, it was decided that he needed specialist treatment and they handed him over the German army for proper medical care. It was the start of a 5-year period as a POW, and a whole new series of adventures, but it was not to be the end of Birdy's association with the Blackburn Skua!

Twenty-six year-old Lieutenant Finch-Noyes, in L3000, had his premonition only too well realised. L3000 was hard hit and crashed into the rear yard of the Schøningdal farm, the propeller and undercarriage being thrown into the farmhouse itself. Finch-Noyes went down with his aircraft, but Petty Officer Cunningham managed to bale out in time and parachuted to safety. He was soon captured and became a POW. Midshipman Gallagher's aircraft was another victim of the II/JG 27 and both aircrew were killed.

John Casson, the son of Sir Lewis Casson and Dame Sybil Thorndike, and, at 30 the oldest man on the mission, with Peter 'Hornblower' Fanshawe the squadron navigator behind him, were in L2992. His rigger had taped a sprig of 'lucky' white heather to the instrument panel before they had taken off. It seemed to work! A Bf109 became glued to his tail so Casson dived to sea level and thrust the throttle forward 'through the gate'. Casson had a reputation as a stunt flyer, and now he exerted all his skill and tricks of the trade. Twice he flew directly at the cliff face hoping to make his pursuer chicken out. Once, he recalled, he flew down a village street 'seeing windows flash past each wing tip', and once his prop sheered several feet off a fir tree. But his opponent was as skilled as he, and had all the speed.

His dash for life was witnessed from below by a 14-year-old Norwegian schoolboy, Johs Halsen. He was later to recall:

> There were four 'planes – two British, two German; the Germans behind the British – flying very low down the fjord. Two came over the trees by my window, very fast, the German shooting ....[21]

A burst from the German fighter hit the Skua, wounding Peter in the shoulder and blowing open the petrol tank as L2992, her number finally up, hit the water in a cloud of spray. Both aircrew managed to climb free and inflated their Mae West life-jackets. John remembered he had a silver flask his wife had given him, and it was full of brandy. They took swigs of this, which helped a little in the icy water. Finally they were both hauled out of the water by Norwegians in a small rowing boat and taken ashore. Both men were well tended to in a nearby house close by, and then taken to the local hospital before becoming POWs.

Dickie Rolph was one of the lucky ones:

> Fortunately my pilot [Petty Officer Monk] had decided how to employ our only asset, i.e. we could fly slower than the Me109s and Me110s. However, after some hair-raising attacks against us we got away.[22]

Gibson also survived by a very low-level escape route:

> I always say that I left Trondheim by road at about 250 miles an hour. I do remember that on the outskirts I saw a horse above us – it was grazing on a bank – but by then we were alone and found the small island from which we were briefed to take departure and this we did.[23]

About 10 minutes' later twin-engined aircraft were seen overhead. They turned out to be the promised RAF fighter cover. As they were somewhat redundant by this time, Gibson had his observer signal them by Aldis lamp recommending them to go home!

Of the sixteen aircrew of the lost eight Skuas, six were killed outright, Harris, Bostock, Gallagher, Crawford, Finch-Noyes and Tremeer; one, Stevenson, died in hospital of his wounds in captivity on 31 May 1941. The remaining nine, Casson, Fanshawe,[24] Filmer, McKee, Bartlett, Richards, Partridge, Cunningham and Martin became prisoners of war. Effectively, this single attack had cost the Royal Navy a whole squadron of highly trained and combat-hardened veteran airmen, and for nothing.

Gibson's aircraft was the last one to return to the carrier. He recalled, shortly afterward, the fleet ran into thick fog and had to be led clear of it by a Skua of the standing fighter patrol, led by Sub-Lieutenant B. H. St A. Hurle-Hobbs[25] who could see the mastheads protruding from the top of the bank.

Table 22   Skua losses in the attack on the *Scharnhorst*, 13 June 1940

Number	Aircraft	Unit	Aircrew	Crash site
L2963	7F	803	Lieutenant Cecil Howard Filmer, RN Midshipman Thomas Anthony McKee, DSC, RN	Orkanger, Frøsetskjaeret
L2992	7L	803	Sub-Lieutenant (A) John Anthony Harris, RNVR Naval Airman Stuart Rex Douglas Stevenson	Orkanger, Tømmeråsen
L3000	6F	800	Lieutenant George Edward Desmond Finch-Noyes, RN Petty Officer Howard Gresely Cunningham, DSM	Trondheim, Møllebakken
L2992	7A	803	Lieutenant Commander John Casson Lieutenant Peter Evelyn Fanshawe, RN	Orkanger, Utenfor Langvika
L3047	6H	800	Midshipman (A) Derek Thomas Revington Martin, RN Leading Airman William James Tremeer	Trondheim
L2955	7Q	803	Acting Sub-Lieutenant Richard Edward Bartlett, RN Naval Airman L. G. Richards	Rennebu, Vagnillgrenda
L2995	6A	800	Acting Major Richard Thomas Partridge, DSO, RM Lieutenant Robert Southey Bostock, RN	Rissa, V/Bessholmen
L3028	6G	800	Midshipman (A) Leonard Henry Gallagher, RN Petty Officer Wallace Crawford	Hermstadheia Rissa

Fighter patrols

Back at the fleet, a two-Skua fighter patrol was flown off at 0130 hours. These were Lieutenant C. W. R. P. Peever, RN/Petty Officer (A) E. Andrews (7K) and Acting Petty Officer (A) Theobald/Naval Airman J. D. L. DeFrias. At 0210 hours reliefs for the fighter patrols over the fleet, which was now steaming westward away from Trondheim, were flown off. The three aircraft and crews were: Sub-Lieutenant B. H. Hurle-Hobbs, RN/Leading Airman V. H. Cordwell (6L); Petty Officer (A) L. E. Burston/Naval Airman R. H. Holmes (6M); and Midshipman (A) C. Treen, RN/Naval Airman D. H. Lowndes.

The fleet altered course to 170° at 0305 hours, into the wind, and prepared to land on the returning Skuas. The *Ark Royal* left the formation and proceeded ahead to carry this out, but 30 minutes later seven had landed back aboard and it seemed clear that no more would be coming back. In view of the submarine danger, *Ark Royal* therefore dropped back

and resumed her station within the destroyer screen once more. The whole
fleet adopted the 170° course in case there were any stragglers. But there
were none.

At 0424 hours the fleet ran into thick fog, but Sub-Lieutenant Hurle-
Hobbs was able to indicate a clear area to the C-in-C and the fleet was well
outside the fog bank by 0520 hours. Escorted by the destroyers *Escort* and
Kelvin, the *Ark Royal* then retrieved her three patrolling Skuas, and had
them aboard by 0550 hours. Some 10 minutes later *Ark Royal*, with
destroyer escort, was ordered to proceed independently to Scapa Flow.
The *Ark Royal* finally returned to Scapa Flow with the fleet, much
chastened by her losses, on the afternoon of 14 June.

Analysis

Vice-Admiral L. V. Wells felt the loss of so many of his young aircrew
deeply, and yet, of course, it was he that had planned the mission and
despatched them to their fate. In his report he noted that[26]:

> Owing to the conditions of light and sky which was clear except for
> some very light cloud, and to the 50 miles which lay between the coast
> and the anchorage, surprise was not achieved, and the Skuas were
> met with fighter opposition and intense A.A. fire.[27]

He also reserved judgement on other causes:

> It is difficult to judge whether the Beauforts' attack on Vaernes Aero-
> drome carried out just before the Skuas arrived served to distract the
> attention of the defence from the approach of the Skuas, or whether
> it had an adverse effect against surprise. Many enemy fighters were
> certainly over the anchorage at the time the Skuas dived to attack,
> but this may have resulted from the Skuas being reported during their
> passage from the coast.

The DNAD, Captain Clement Moody, commented that: 'Any attack
carried out on a battle-cruiser in harbour with fighter defence must expect
to suffer heavy casualties unless surprise is achieved.' He considered that
surprise might have been compromised by two events in particular:

1. The Squadron Commander of 803 Squadron who appears to have
   delayed his attack in order to work round the target. His last section
   of aircraft, who did not wait for him, suffered no loss.
2. It is possible that the Beauforts' attack on Vaernes aerodrome
   merely stirred up the hornets' nest. It would probably have been
   better for them to have attacked about 2 hours before. The Skuas
   attack might then have synchronised with the enemy fighters' refuel-

ling, and the return to bed of the AA guns' crews. As it was, all AA
Defences must have been fully manned.

He continued:

When the objective is very important, and conditions for surprise not
certain beforehand to prevail, it therefore becomes very necessary for
the main attack to be delivered in the greatest strength that can be
provided with the forces available. This not only results in a lower
percentage of aircraft casualties, but is necessary to ensure decisive
results. The Skua attack on this occasion had a right to expect (without surprise) only one hit and a 25 per cent chance of a second, and
30 per cent casualties from gunfire plus up to 30 per cent more from
fighters.[28]

Rear-Admiral J. W. Rivett-Carnac merely wrote, 'Noted with
interest',[29] and nothing more. The C-in-C, Admiral of the Fleet Sir
Charles Forbes, was more forthcoming. He thought that achieving
surprise was very difficult against Trondheim:

... and I think it is reasonable to assume that the Skuas were reported
by coast watchers at least 20 minutes before they arrived over the
target. In that time there could have been several fighters at 10,000
feet over the enemy ships.

He also felt that 'It is interesting to note that all but one of the survivors
got away by low flying tactics'. He was gracious enough to add his own
obituary to those who fell. 'The attacks were courageously pressed
home.'[30]

NOTES

1. As so often became the case, after the war Kearsley and the German pilot, who was
   rescued by another He115, made contact and became firm friends
2. Operation *Paul* contained in National Archives document, ADM 199/1930.
3. Admiralty Message timed at 1528 hours 5 June included the instruction, '(b) fighters will
   not repetition not accompany TSRs'. So *somebody* had been thinking.
4. For an interesting account of the ideas considered for this mission see: G. A. 'Hank'
   Rotherham, *It's Really Quite Safe*, Sunflower University Press, Manhattan, Kansas,
   1985. Dickie Rolph commented, '... fortunately, it was not laid on quite like he and
   others proposed, and it is just as well that the Swordfish were kept out of it'. He added
   that after the Skua attack, during the withdrawal towards the coast, 'I sketched the
   position of the German ships moorings and how they were protected on the only side
   open for a torpedo attack by anti-torpedo nets. After landing-on, at the 10-second
   briefing (!) I tried to show my sketches to one of the officers with the Admiral – he "didn't
   want to know" and nobody wanted to know how we managed to get away.'
5. Lieutenant Callingham was later to become the temporary Commanding Officer of
   No. 887 Squadron, equipped with six Fulmar IIs between May and August 1942. After
   the war he became Air Group Commander of the 13th Carrier Air Group aboard the
   light carrier HMS *Vengeance* from 1945 to 1946, and again of the 14th Carrier Air Group

aboard the light carrier HMS *Theseus* in the Far East from 1 January 1947, his appointment to Commander being confirmed in 1951. Possibly, he is most famous for making the first carrier landing of the Fairey Gannet prototype aboard HMS *Illustrious* on 19 June 1950.

6. Partridge to the author, *op cit.*
7. Rolph, *op cit.*
8. Vice-Admiral Sir Donald Gibson, personal memoirs, FAA Museum Yeovilton, with his permission. These he much later worked up into his biography; see Vice-Admiral Sir Donald Gibson, KCB, DSC, JP, *Haul taut and belay; The Memoirs of a flying sailor*, Spellmount, Tunbridge Wells, 1992.
9. Admiralty, *Notes by Director of Naval Air Division on Report on sinking of Königsberg*, dated 25 April 1940. X/L04326. Contained in National Archives ADM 199/478.
10. Just quite how this squared with Gibson being on the mission, when, as he later confessed, he, 'had never dive-bombed anything', is unclear.
11. Ron Jordan to the author, 4 February 2006. While SAPs were good weapons against armoured warships, Ron later recalled that the pilots told him that GP bombs were better weapons against merchant ship targets, against whose thin hulls and decks the SAP would go straight through without causing much lethal damage.
12. Mr Ronald G. Jordan to Mr Simon Partridge (Captain R. T. Partridge's son), 25 May 2005, by kind permission of both.
13. When the two men met in 1987 Ron mentioned this incident, and Partridge replied. 'I had other things on my mind!'
14. The RAF used wide circuits; naval aircraft used shorter circuits.
15. Vice-Admiral Sir Donald Gibson, *op cit.*
16. Report No. 11, *Attack on enemy warships in Trondheim Harbour*, dated 13 June 1940. (CAFO 3572/39, (contained in National Archives ADM 199/ 480).
17. *Ibid.*
18. *Ibid.*
19. *Ibid*
20. *Operations off Trondheim (Amended)* (contained in National Archives ADM 199/480)
21. *Vide: Telegraph Sunday Magazine* article, 1982.
22. Dickie Rolph in *The Society of Friends of the Fleet Air Arm Museum Newsletter*, No. 40, January 1997, p. 13, copy presented to the author by R. S. Rolph, BEM.
23. Vice-Admiral Sir Donald Gibson, *op cit.*
24. Fanshawe and Casson, became members of the famous 'Great Escape' team at *Stalag Luft III*, Peter being the 'sand dispersal specialist'. Casson served briefly in the post-war Royal Navy at HMS *Wagtail*, a shore base near Ayr, but resigned his commission in 1946.
25. Later to be lost aboard the escort carrier HMS *Dasher*, which blew up in the Clyde after a petrol fire in the hangar with heavy loss of life.
26. Vice-Admiral, Aircraft Carriers' No. AC 0565, dated 18 June, 1940. (No. 190/A.C. 0565 to Admiralty, contained in National Archives ADM 199/480.)
27. A pencilled note in the margin comments that Trondheim held 50 per cent of all *Luftwaffe* fighter aircraft in Norway.
28. DNAD, Comments on Submission MO 11951/40, dated 11 July 1940. (Contained in National Archives ADM199 480.)
29. DTSD, Comments on Submission MO 11951/40, dated 15 July 1940. (Contained in National Archives ADM199 480.)
30. Commanding-in-Chief, Home Fleet, HMS *Rodney*, Memorandum –*Dive Bombing attack by Skuas of 800 and 803 Squadrons on enemy warships at Trondheim on Thursday, 13th June, 1940*, dated 27 June 1940. (1118/HF 1359 contained in National Archives ADM 199/480.)

10

THE LAST DITCH

The German victory in Norway had been achieved, against all predictions, by the overwhelming use of air power. The *Luftwaffe* had dominated the air, the land, and, to a great extent, the sea. The Germans had demonstrated their new thinking in the swift conquest of Poland in September. Norway had reinforced the lesson, but the Allies still needed persuading. 'Hitler has missed the boat! crowed Neville Chamberlain. On 10 May the *Blitzkreig* broke over western Europe and proud nations collapsed like a house of cards within days. How could Royal Navy flyers possibly be involved with the collapse of continental armies? Impossible! Yet they were in the thick of it, and, when the nation's military fortunes were at their nadir, the Skuas brought one of the very few specks of comfort amid the general wreckage.

Dunkirk

Far, far away to the south, the BEF, the cream of the army, was in serious trouble. After weeks of non-stop retreat, outnumbered, outflanked and bombed non-stop throughout the hours of daylight, they had reached the Channel Coast hoping for salvation. This the Royal Navy was attending to with its usual efficiency, organising a fleet of destroyers, reinforced by a host of smaller ships and civilian craft, and was evacuating troops daily, but at very heavy cost. Into this bedlam, to provide the ships with what protection they could, flew the Skuas of No. 806 Squadron.

Lieutenant Commander Charles Evans, commanding No. 806 Squadron, now placed under command of RAF Coastal Command, reported with nine aircraft at Detling airfield from Worthy Down at 0500 hours on 27 May.[1] For the next few days the squadron carried out continuous fighter patrols, returning to Worthy Down when released each evening.[2]

Their first assigned mission was a fighter patrol over the evacuation fleet on 28 May, which covered the area North Foreland–Calais–Dunkirk, known as the Goodwin Patrol. White section provided this patrol with three Skuas (Lieutenant C. P. Campbell-Horsfall, RN/Petty Officer Observer Clare; Midshipman (A) G. A. Hogg, RNVR/Naval Airman A. G. Burton; Midshipman (A) J. Marshall, RNVR/Naval Airman A. G. Jones).

The patrol was a complete disaster, but the Germans played no part in their misfortunes. It started badly and progressively got worse. On take-off, No. 3, Midshipman (A) Marshall failed to allow a sufficient run for his aircraft to get airborne. There was no wind at all, and the run was conducted uphill, so the Skua did not even succeed in clearing the airfield boundary and crashed into some trees at the edge of the aerodrome. Both Marshall and Jones, his air gunner, were extracted from the wreckage and taken to the Sick Bay at RAF Detling, but neither man suffered any serious injury.

Now reduced to two aircraft, White section headed off to the Goodwin area to carry out the patrol. At about 0915 hours, the two Skuas were 'intercepted' by a full squadron of twenty-four Spitfires, who made attacks on them from astern, badly damaging both aircraft. Lieutenant Campbell-Horsfall's aircraft was hard hit and he was compelled to put down in the sea some miles from the coast. Fortunately, he spotted a British destroyer and pancaked alongside her.

The Skua sank almost immediately, both she and her dinghy being completely riddled with bullet holes. Campbell-Horsfall had wounds in one arm and a hand, which subsequently had to be amputated. Despite these wounds, the pilot somehow managed to keep Petty Officer Clare, who had been wounded in the leg, afloat, until the destroyer came up. She quickly lowered her whaler and rescued both men.

Midshipman Hogg's Skua, although badly shot up, managed to reach Manston RAF airfield, where he made a force-landing. The undercarriage of his Skua had been rendered inoperational and he put down belly-up. Hogg got out and went to drag Burton, his air gunner, clear, but found that the Spitfires had killed him outright.

Just what was it like to be attacked by your own side? Sub-Lieutenant Hogg was to later record this massacre, and its typical aftermath, in graphic detail:[3]

On 28th May 1940, I was flying in open formation, just off the French coast, when it happened. C. H. suddenly turned over on his side and dived for the sea, closely followed by myself – some twelve fighters were attacking us. As I screamed down I felt bullets striking the aircraft and I could see tracers entering the belly of the leader's machine. My gunner fired a few bursts and then stopped. I called to him on the inter-communication but received no reply.

We pulled out of the dive at 8,000 feet with the fighters still close behind. A hole appeared in the side of my cockpit; metal dust and splinters fell on to my head as a bullet whistled through the top of the back seat. We dived again and I saw tracer crashing through the leader's fuselage.

Our general direction had been towards the British shore and as we pulled out of this second dive the fighters left us. C. H. held up a bloody hand to wave me away, signalling that he was going to land in the 'drink'. I followed him down until certain that he would be picked up by some destroyers steaming just below us and then having watched him land, set off towards Margate. My intention was to land as quickly as possible, The aircraft was riddled and I could get no reply from the air-gunner; he would doubtless require medical aid.

I crossed safely over the coast and started looking for an aerodrome. I attempted to land at Margate but this was impossible, as it was disused and covered by old cars, etc. Worried stiff, in case my air-gunner was bleeding to death, I set course for Manston and arrived there within 5 minutes. Having circled once, I prepared to land. Only one undercarriage leg would come down!

I should have to come in fairly fast, with my wing down, the wing which had a leg down. The speed would keep my legless wing in the air until I had run some distance and lost flying speed when the wing tip would dip to the ground and the aircraft slowly slew round.

I carried out the fast approach and touched the ground at 80 knots. She immediately stood on her nose, the airscrew shattered, the leg gave way and I skidded to a standstill on the aircraft's belly. Later, I discovered that both my tyres had been deflated by bullets, causing the remaining wheel to act as a brake, thus bringing about the accident.

Throwing off my straps, I leapt out and looked in the back cockpit. I was very nearly sick. The air-gunner was huddled in a corner, obviously stone dead; the whole cockpit was drenched in blood. The fire-engine arrived, I climbed aboard and was taken to the Duty Pilot who sent an ambulance out to the crash.

Hogg continued:

When I had fully recovered from the shock I had lunch and went to the sick-bay to find out about my dead air-gunner. He never knew what hit him. I believe he was hit in six different places. To this day, I cannot understand how I escaped unscathed.

Strapping my revolver round my waist and carrying my maps and parachute, I took the train to London in order to return to Worthy Down. I was hatless, my cap having been in the back seat and soaked in blood. Arriving at Victoria, I whistled a taxi to take me to Waterloo.

'I'm afraid you'll have to come along with me.'

I turned round to see a London constable; I guessed that I must look rather suspicious.

'Do you think I'm a German parachutist?'

'No, of course not but you might be, so if I take you to the Railway

Transport Office, you can identify yourself there.'

I had no identification papers on my person and it took 30 minutes of telephone calls to prove my *bona-fides*. I missed the connection to Worthy Down. Eventually, the police gave me an identification slip with the parting words 'You must remember, there's a war on' – Heavens!!!

I caught a later train and shared a compartment with a dear old couple who wanted to know if I was returning from leave. They must have thought that the Navy had a hectic time on leave, judging from my scruffy condition. I arrived at the aerodrome without any more trouble and, having told my story at least fifty times, retired thankfully to bed. (The Fighters had, in fact, been Spitfires!)[4]

Lieutenant Campbell-Horsfall and Petty Officer Clare were later landed at Dover by their saviour and were sent to recover in Middlesborough Hospital; both had bullet wounds. The only uninjured man, Midshipman Hogg, was sent off on 48 hours' leave, before rejoining the squadron none the worse for wear. Undaunted by such gross stupidity, No. 806 Squadron carried on, with Sub-Lieutenant (A) I. L. F. Lowe taking over Campbell-Horsfall's role as section leader. He mounted patrols throughout the remainder of 28 May with three Skuas 'A', 'C' and 'H', airborne between 1616 and 1825 hours, while three further aircraft 'F', 'G' and 'B', were patrolling over an evacuation convoy off Ostend between 1750 and 1941 hours.

On Wednesday 29 May there were the usual Goodwin patrols operating. Three machines, 'G', 'F' and 'H', were up between 1450 and 1618 hours. They reported seeing large numbers of troopships in convoy steaming from Ostend to Dunkirk to pick up more troops. They also stated that there was 'Fire and Smoke' from Dunkirk itself. Three more No. 806 Squadron aircraft, 'C', 'Q' and 'M', were up from later that day. This patrol was mounted by Yellow section, with two Skuas (Lieutenant W. L. Le C. Barnes, RN/Lieutenant D. Vincent-Jones, RN, and Sub-Lieutenant Ayres, RNVR and a single Roc (Midshipman Day, RNVR/Naval Airman Newton).

At about 1830 hours, over the Ostend area, contact was made with five Junkers Ju88Ks at an altitude of about 1,000 feet. The Junkers were busy dive-bombing one of the evacuation convoys, and at first failed to notice the three naval aircraft. The two Skuas immediately attacked the leading enemy bomber from astern as it was in the midst of its dive. The Roc followed the Skuas down, and as the Junkers started to take avoiding action, the turret gunner managed to get in a long burst attack from astern. This is just about the only recorded occasion that a Roc managed successfully to engage the enemy. One of the Junkers was seen to go out of control, and crashed into the sea, while another fell away from the rest of the formation, and was last seen 'staggering towards the shore, losing height rapidly'.[5]

The rest of the Junkers broke off their attack and headed home, showing No. 801 Squadron's aircraft the usual clean pair of heels.

Another encounter took place on Thursday 30 May, when the same three aircraft ('F', 'Q' and 'R') were on the same patrol at 10,000 feet. Conditions were difficult, with low cloud and poor visibility. At approximately 1645 hours, some 12 miles north of Dunkirk, they made contact with a Heinkel He111K at an altitude of 1,500 feet. This aircraft was preparing to attack a 4,000 ton merchant vessel. They again attacked at once, and the enemy immediately jettisoned four bombs about a mile ahead of the ship, and was quickly lost to sight in the scud.

The whole squadron, nine aircraft, was airborne at 1000 hours on Sunday 2 June. They were passing in the vicinity of an anti-aircraft cruiser (thought to be HMS *Coventry*, but was in fact her sister, HMS *Calcutta*, which had been engaged throughout the Dunkirk evacuation). At around 1115 hours a Junkers Ju88K was seen to commence a dive-bombing attack on this ship and a stick of four bombs fell ahead of her. In order to deter this, Lieutenant Commander Evans in the squadron's leading aircraft, L2989, attacked the enemy head-on. He thought he scored some good hits and the Junkers disappeared into the clouds in a slow spiral. In a short while another Ju88k was seen and attacked by Yellow section, but also dived away into cloud cover and was lost to view. However, a Coastal Command Avro Anson was later to report seeing a Junkers Ju88K endeavouring to return over Dunkirk from the direction of the sea shortly after the time of the attack, and her port engine was on fire. This was No. 806 Squadron's last action over the Channel before No. 801 Squadron relieved them.

Throughout June and into July, No. 806 Squadron settled down at Worthy Down, where the pilots had already been familiarising themselves with the Fairey Fulmar, the squadron's future mount. There were only three Fulmars available at this time, which they took turns to fly. On 15 July, the squadron flew out to embark aboard its new home, the aircraft carrier *Illustrious*. Sub-Lieutenant Hogg recalls the event:[6]

Three sections of Skuas led the way with an upper guard consisting of the section of Fulmars. We were to meet the carrier at sea and land on as quickly as possible. We saluted Dartmouth Naval College, *en route*, with a passably good shoot-up and carried on over the sea until we could see the *Illustrious* taking on the Swordfish. We waited until these were on board and then started to come on ourselves.

It was the first time that the squadron had landed on a carrier and the first time that the carrier had taken aboard a complete fighter squadron, with the natural result that it was a somewhat lengthy

procedure. One by one we safely arrived and it came to my turn. I was
following Ivan up the wake of the ship, flying about 200 feet above
and behind him. He seemed to be getting rather low and suddenly, to
my surprise, he landed in the sea! I carried on and made a successful
landing.

It turned out later that his engine had stopped some 200 yards
astern of the ship and he had no option but to do what he did. His
air-gunner got out the dinghy and they filled this with the luggage
that they had in the back seat; they swam around, pushing the dinghy
until picked up by a destroyer. Because of some deck trouble, Eric,
the last one left in the air, was unable to land so he returned to
the shore and force-landed on a beach. These were the two only
accidents.

All aircraft onboard, the ship returned to port where she stayed for
a few days, making ready for her 'working up' trip.

801 relieves 803

On 26 May, the ten Skuas from No. 801 Squadron had been disembarked
to RAF Abbotsinch, along with eleven pilots, two observers and eight air
gunners. All the aircraft were swung and had their guns re-sighted. Some
2 days later, orders were received to proceed to RAF Detling and to
operate from that airfield under the direct order of No. 16 Group, RAF.
Due to the bad weather conditions prevailing, the squadron was unable to
comply with this order until 30 May, the move south being broken by an
overnight stop at RAF Sealand, again due to the weather.

No. 801 Squadron arrived intact at Detling at 1100 hours on 31 May
and immediately on arrival the Squadron Commander and the Senior
Observer made their way across to RAF Hawkinge. Here they went to the
Operations Room and received details of the first bombing target (*Black
Violet*).[7] They immediately returned to Detling and got things moving. All
the Skuas were bombed up there and flew over to Hawkinge to receive
last-minute updated instructions. The situation across the Channel was
dire in the extreme and very fluid, with friendly and enemy positions
changing by the hour.

Black Violet

The mission the squadron had been assigned, was a crucial one, calling for
both speedy execution and pin-point accuracy. The shrinking perimeter
had to be held for as long as possible, but was now under serious threat.

The 6th Battalion, The Black Watch, was the reserve battalion of the
British 12th Infantry Brigade that had been allocated to the extreme left
sector of the northern front, along the Nieuport Canal. They were only

expected to hold that northern flank for 24 hours, because although the bridge over the canal had been blown, they were repeatedly attempting to infiltrate across it. So serious did the threat become that the Royal Fusiliers were assigned the sole task of dealing with it, the South Lancs closed up with them and the Black Watch extended the line down to the sea.

Facing them across the canal was the German 256 *Infanteriedivision.* This division formed part of 26 *Korps*, 18 *Armee* which had crossed the German–Dutch border to the south of Nijmegen on 10 May. After crossing the river Maas on a captured bridge, by 12 May, 26 *Korps* had advanced across Holland to Moerdijk, where it relieved the paratroops that had captured the bridges there on the first day of the invasion. The *Korps* then reoriented itself to the south-west and, on 14 May, began an offensive aimed at capturing Antwerp in Belgium, which, by 18 May, was in German hands. The 26 *Korps*, then advanced west through Belgium via Ghent as the Allied troops in Belgium fell back towards Dunkirk. By the end of May, the division had come to Nieuport, which formed the easternmost edge of the Dunkirk perimeter. Over the next few days the division slowly pushed forward as the Dunkirk perimeter shrunk.

All through that night the Germans continued their attempts to push troops across the bridge, and indeed, did manage to move some 500 troops across and exploited their bridgehead during the day, which led to hard fighting to contain them. Movement was also made on both flanks of this position, which were threatening, but the British managed to hold on. Clearly, the key was the bridge and its demolition was essential.

At 1920 hours nine Skuas took off from Hawkinge and carried out a bombing raid on positions adjacent to Nieuport. Over the target area the formation searched hard for their assigned targets, but as their report subsequently emphasised, 'No pontoon bridge seen anywhere near canal'.[8] A large section of the old bridge still stood, however, which the pilots described as a 'reinforced pier on a small island on canal, N.N.W. of Nieuport'. This appeared to be the only structure across the water, and six of the Skuas, two sections, made it their target. The other section directed its diving attacks against 'two piers on the Nieuport foreshore'. Through the smoke of the bursting bombs they were able to report that, 'Several direct hits registered'.[9]

Mission accomplished, the squadron turned for home. The visibility, which had been good, became very hazy, with 8/10ths cloud at 18,000 feet, but the ship-dotted Channel itself, appeared very calm. This cloud was their undoing as it hid a large enemy fighter force (reported at twenty Bf109Es), until it was almost too late. These carried out high-speed interceptions of the Skuas as they made their way. In the resultant attacks two Skuas were shot down while the pilot and air gunner of a third Skua were wounded and the machine badly damaged, which necessitated an emergency landing at Detling being made with the undercarriage retracted. All seven survivors had landed by 2030 hours.

But the fight had not been totally one-sided. One Messerschmitt was definitely brought down by the Skuas. Petty Officer Reid was credited with the kill, and the evidence of rear gunners in a nearby formation of RAF planes, who witnessed the engagement, points to a second Bf109 being shot down in the sea.

A wartime booklet on Coastal Command, gave the following Air Ministry account of this mission:

> ... on 31st May, ten Albacores and nine Skuas, under the direction of Coastal Command, bombed pontoon bridges over the Nieuport Canal and piers on the foreshore. Direct hits were made. Going home the Skuas, their ammunition exhausted, ran into twelve Me109s. Two Skuas were lost but the remainder got away, for the Messerschmitts turned upon three Hudsons on patrol.[10]

R. V. 'Joe' Beckett later provided a much more prosaic, and accurate, viewpoint.

> I joined N801 from Worthy Down with Beardsley at 3am Friday morning, special transport to Detling (near Maidstone, on top of the North Downs) on 31st May 1940. Typical Navy. 'Who are you? – don't know anything about it!' The only TAG in the ground force party was Stan Hedger. 'The aircraft will arrive about dinner time!' They did. No time for grub, bomb up and away over the Channel. Hedger came back with the pilot shot and himself up the bottom as well. The bell tent had quite a bit more room that night! 'Blood' Reid was one TAG; he shot down a Jerry and was awarded the DSM. The following two more TAGS, who had also just finished the course, Ford and Crone, joined on the Saturday night at Detling to make the numbers up.[11]

Naval Airman R. Hedger's Skua, piloted by Midshipman R. M. S. Martin, had fought a running battle with some Bf109s on their return back across the Channel, and, as related, both men received serious wounds. What had been achieved?

Well, for a start the Bf109s did not have things all their own way as has been alleged. Reid's gallant last action, was matched by Petty Officer Kimber with his TAG Naval Airman L. W. Miles, flying in L3030, who also claimed to have shot down one of the enemy fighters.[12] This 'possible', although not confirmed, was witnessed by RAF Hudsons as last seen trailing smoke and losing height.

The commander of the 12th Brigade in his report to Major General D. G. Johnson at 4th Divisional Headquarters, recorded the Fleet Air Arm attack thus:

On the afternoon of 31st May this brigade was holding a sector from opposite Nieuport to the sea. Between 1500 and 1700 hours a determined attack was launched upon our front – the third within a period of 12 hours. The leading German waves were stopped by our light machine-gun and mortar fire, but strong enemy reserves were observed moving through Nieuport and on the roads to the canal north-west of Nieuport. At this moment some RAF bombers arrived and bombed Nieuport and the roads north-west of it. The effect was instantaneous and decisive – all movement of enemy reserves stopped; many of the forward German troops turned and fled, suffering severely from the fire of our machine-guns.[13]

In fact, there were no pontoon bridges, but the army had thought there were and so reported them. The actual time of the attack was later than he remembered. Also, of course, the army personnel could only know the aircraft were British, not that they were naval bombers. Richards (whose main objective throughout the book seemed to be dutifully to promote the strict RAF line) deliberately failed to point this out, so once again the RAF received the credit for a remarkable Fleet Air Arm achievement.

The Skua and Roc attack was a great morale-booster to the British troops grimly holding on in that sector. The Black Watch historian recorded that:

> ... the position was held and in the evening, after our bombers had had a go at the bridge, the day got really quite peaceful. This sight of our own aircraft for the first time caused great jubilation.[14]

The *Luftwaffe* itself, only claimed to have destroyed two Skuas during the whole period of the Dunkirk operation, both being shot down by the Bf109s of I/JG 20 on 31 May.[15] These two aircraft were L2917, piloted by Sub-Lieutenant J. B. Marsh with Naval Airman G. R. Nicholson, and L3005, piloted by Lieutenant R. Strange, with Petty Officer (O) N. 'Blood' Reid, all of whom were killed. As we have seen, a third Skua crashed on landing back at Detling, with both aircrew badly injured. The Bf109 destroyed by Reid was confirmed as a definite 'kill', while the second Messerschmitt was recorded as only a 'probable'.

Night patrols

It was not only Royal Navy Skuas that were based at Detling at this time. Included among the 'strange assortment' based there, thrown in to operate as best they could across the Channel, were such aircraft as ancient Gloster Gauntlets and Fairey Swordfish (both biplanes) and Westland Lysander army-co-operation aircraft. All these types were used as improvised dive-bombers in a desperate last-ditch effort to make up for decades of RAF neglect of the type. Some desolate Fairey Battles, the RAF's main light bomber before the war, were loudly heralded as the answer to the army's needs and totally discredited with enormous losses after just 3 days' operations. Other aircraft used were Avro Ansons, Coastal Command's main patrol aircraft of the day, and even more ancient relics.

On the evening of 31 May, a yellow-and-black striped, target-towing Skua from No. 2 Anti-Aircraft Co-operation Unit from Gosport joined this assortment. This aircraft was piloted by D. H. 'Nobby' Clarke with winch operator Leading Aircraftsman Phelan, and was accompanied by a similarly equipped Battle.[16] Both aircraft were unarmed and had had their wireless sets removed at Gosport. Clarke had earlier witnessed a demonstration of towing lighted flares, which generated 20,000 candle-power, and Sainsbury informed him that his mission was to conduct night patrols with this equipment. The area to be covered and the method to be used, as recorded by Clarke later, were 'between Dunkirk and the River Scheldt, about 10 miles offshore, lighting our flares one at a time until they are all used'.[17]

The idea was to illuminate the approaches to the evacuation route used by the Royal Navy, which had already lost a number of destroyers and lesser vessels to E-boat and surfaced U-boat attack during the hours of darkness when they were shielded from the ever-present Ju87 Stukas. The first such mission was flown on the night of 1/2 June. Led to the area by the Ansons, the Skuas streamed their 6,000 feet of towing wire and then Phelan fed a succession of 2-foot long flare tubes down it. On the tube reaching a toggle at the end of the wire, the firing pin was triggered and the flare illuminated. It was primitive, but, according to Clarke, it worked perfectly:

> Suddenly the night sky vanished; the faint horizon disappeared. A billion misty droplets of water, almost invisible in the darkness, hurled back the glare of 20,000 candlepower so that I could see nothing outside the cockpit. We were locked in a bowl of brilliant whiteness, and it was as if we had flown inside an electric light bulb – even the instruments showed their black and white faces.[18]

As each flare faded, another from the stock of twenty or thirty was fed down the line as the Skua quartered the allocated zone. Enemy night fighters were expected to be the biggest hazard to such an operation, but these failed to materialise. However, the sortie was brought to a prema-ture conclusion when an unknown aircraft flew through the towing wire and the Skua had to abort. On the way back to England at 4,000 feet altitude, Clarke followed the laid-down procedure of switching his navi-gation lights on and off several times before leaving them on, and then firing off a red and yellow Very recognition cartridge. This had no effect on the searchlight operators on the English coast however. Clarke's Skua was illuminated and he was dazzled. He stalled the engine and went into a series of spins that brought him down to sea level. He survived this to land safely back at Detling and the operation was deemed a success, the Ansons claiming to have sunk an E-boat.[19]

Channel action

For No. 801 Squadron this period was one of intensive and dangerous work. They had been ordered to re-form with six Skuas and six Rocs for their new role, the Rocs being ferried to Detling from IR Pools,[20] the theory being that the Roc's shorter range did not matter for cross-Channel and convoy escort work. Thus re-equipped, they went back to work.

On 2 and 3 June three Skuas and three Rocs were sent out to patrol at 4,000 feet. They covered the area from the North Foreland up to within 5 miles of Dunkirk, but there were no engagements to report. The sudden shift was brought about because with the last Allied troops taken off, the land fighting had moved far to the south and the *Luftwaffe* had followed.

R. V. 'Joe' Beckett was to recall:

I think our first trip across the Channel was on 3rd June (Sunday?), a fighter patrol Ramsgate/Dunkirk. The panic was over by now and nothing but wrecks and burning oil tanks along the French coast could be seen.

Beckett's mission was flown with Lieutenant Ronnie Hay in Roc L3161, and was of 2 hours 25 minutes duration.[21] On 3 June, four new pilots and two new observers joined the squadron. The establishment at this date was complete with six Skuas and six Rocs, with two IR Rocs and one IR Skua. Half the squadron were sent on 5 days' leave from 11 June, while from 6 to 8 June, local flying practice was conducted by the new pilots. Beckett's log showed he flew practice sorties with Sub-Lieutenant Lowe in Skua L3102 on 6 June and in L3161 the following day. Also, the new aircraft were swung, guns sighted and compasses swung.[22]

Now refreshed for the fray, between 9 and 11 June No. 801 Squadron's aircraft were used as patrolling cover over East Coast and Channel convoys. The aircraft were sent out singly and time in the air averaged 4 hours. However, Joe's photo reconnaissance flight with Lieutenant Lowe in L3161 ended in engine failure after only 5 minutes. Harrington was out with Lieutenant Collett in L2878 on convoy patrol twice that day, but they were plagued with intercom problems.

Bouncing Boulogne

Photo-reconnaissance (P/R) missions[23] now grew in importance as England braced herself for invasion and the Germans began their build-up along the facing coast. The Skuas added this to their convoy escort duties and took it in their stride. But from time to time they took the offensive to keep the enemy on their toes. One such mission was carried out on 12 June, when, in addition to two convoy patrols, four aircraft carried out dive-bombing attacks against enemy E-boats that had started to set up their bases in Boulogne harbour.

The aircraft took off at 1201 hours and, on reaching Boulogne, and, at 1235 hours, attacked at least five E-boats, which they identified as being, 'painted light grey in position south side of harbour'. Such targets were quite small, but, on this occasion, were stationary, and the men claimed, 'Two hits scored on crane jetty', while one Skua strafed all five vessels. They encountered no opposition of any kind and, on landing back at Detling at 1302 hours, the CO recommended launching another strike, but using smaller bombs against these unarmoured ships.[24]

This was duly approved and, at 1525 hours, a second strike of the same four ('F', 'H', 'B' and 'R') aircraft took off. Harrington was flying a new mount, Roc L3160, on this mission, with Naval Airman Clayton manning the ball turret. This time the machines were armed with, 'three 250 lb bombs and forty 20 lb bombs'.[25] On arrival back over Boulogne they found that the surviving E-boats had been moved from the south side of the crane jetty to a new location at the Promenade Quay, north of the Southern Railway terminal building. They duly attacked here and claimed to have scored direct hits on one E-boat and to have damaged two others. They also scored hits on the jetty itself. On the way out they machine-gunned a coastal battery 2 miles up the canal and also a group of parked army trucks, registering many casualties.

The next day a P/R flight was made to look at the damage they had inflicted, Skuas 'F' and 'R' overflying both the outer and inner harbours at 500 feet and encountering 'heavy pom-pom and HA fire'.[26] They could see no enemy warships left in either harbour, either visually or from the photos they took. Meanwhile, between 1422 and 1550 hours that same day, three further No. 801 Squadron aircraft, 'H', 'M' and 'F', carried out a similar mission over Calais, Gravelines and Dunkirk, receiving AA fire only from the first.

Among No. 801 Squadron's pilots at this time, destined for fame, was 19-year-old Midshipman George Clifton Baldwin, RN. He had flown Skua missions from both *Ark Royal* and Hatston before arriving at Detling, where, in July, he was promoted to Acting Sub-Lieutenant.[27]

A 'new boy'

Captain R. W. Harrington, RN, was appointed to No. 801 Squadron on 11 June 1940, having been operationally trained in the torpedo-bomber and seaplane roles, but having converted to the fighter role in March 1940.

I had, of course, flown the Skua in October 1939 and seen the remark 'very nice' in my log-book. Indeed, I also flew the Skua's sister aircraft the Roc, which apart from being aptly named was as real to life as the definition; I noted my log-book comment was 'not very impressive'. I think these two comments of mine, were made in the strictly 'flying' sense and accurately describe to some extent the two aircraft's military functional use. The Skua, once you could get to the target in the conditions necessary for a successful outcome to the particular dive-bombing you were trying to achieve, was a good dive-bombing tool; the main problem was to get there and, hopefully, to get back. All these elements were tied up in what range (power, fuel and speed) you were operating within, the defensive opposition you were up against and the type of target you were trying to destroy (a function of heights of dive-entry and of the pull-out above the target and the type of bomb and its fusing arrangements – instantaneous or delayed to allow penetration of target).

The Roc was a Skua with the observer's or wireless air gunner's compartment modified to hold a heavy Boulton and Paul hydraulically operated gun-turret. With this contraption of great weight and much wind-drag, it made the beast both difficult to fly and useless as an offensive weapon (with no military significance).

During the fall of France, our Skuas were operating from the RAF base at Detling, then under Coastal Command. Hectic days indeed, living under canvas in glorious weather and fed like fighting cocks by a local caterer. He really did his stuff for the 'boys' and did not stint us in any way, despite the Admiralty's modest monetary contribution for our victualling.

Our main role was to cut any bridges the army wanted 'done', any enemy installation or barges (which were found from our other role of taking part in a daily reconnaissance of the local French, Belgian and Dutch channel ports) and finally to provide 'fighter' cover for any special convoys off the Kent or Essex coasts. I won't digress on the reconnaissance or convoy roles, other than to say that in naval aircraft with sea camouflage, we seemed to form a legitimate target for both the German and British defences as well as a worthwhile target for both the Royal and German Air Forces. It is quite a novel experience fighting your way out of the country, weaving and dodging on the enemy side, and then forcing a passage back to your own airfield.[28]

U-boats, E-boats and batteries

On 15 June, No. 801 Squadron took part in another photo-reconnaissance mission, taking off at 1335 hours and landing back at 1514 hours, with 'B' talking the pictures and 'R' and 'H' providing escort. They covered Boulogne, Calais and Dunkirk at an altitude of about 200 feet, encountering heavy flak on leaving Boulogne. At 1810 hours, 'F' went out alone, covering Boulogne, Calais, Dunkirk and Ostend. This mission located three new AA batteries at Boulogne and 'a multiple pom-pom firing accurate bursts' near Ostend airfield. This aircraft landed at 2003 hours, but 'M', which went out alone at the same time, did not get back until 2034 hours, having been delayed by a U-boat sighting at 2000 hours. The aircraft attacked but the submarine submerged.[29]

Some 3 days later Lieutenant Lowe and Joe Beckett flew L3160 as part of an uneventful three-plane patrol over the French and Belgian coast.[30] Earlier, at 0413 hours, Lieutenant Savage ('F') had gone out alone for a P/R over Boulogne, crossing over the harbour at 0435 hours at a prudent height of 4,000 feet. This did not save him, for an effective burst of AA fire smashed the pilot's windscreen and injured him in the face. 'Owing to blood from injuries interacting with eyesight,' Savage was forced to return to base. His navigator, Lieutenant Hayes, was also struck by a piece of shrapnel, but only suffered a scratch on his face.

The next day, 19 June, the E-boats they had driven out of Boulogne made an unwelcome reappearance. At 0940 hours three plane BOULDS, with 'Q' and 'R' flying escort for the camera-loaded 'P', took off for that port yet again. Two E-boats were seen in the outer harbour at 1000 hours, picked up by their high-speed wash. The two escorts reported that the P/R Skua, 'was not seen after it had gone into Boulogne to secure photos', so the two aircraft proceeded slowly up the coast at altitudes between 7,000 and 12,000 feet as far as Calais, Dunkirk and Ostend. Nothing was going on at those places and both aircraft landed at Manston at 1045 hours.

Meanwhile, the 'missing' Skua was making all kinds of discoveries. After taking good shots of both the inner and outer harbour and sighting at least three E-boats underway there, the Skua 'proceeded towards Calais under heavy AA and pom-pom fire'. Here, it secured good pictures of a new heavy gun battery, being constructed south of that port at 40° 54' North, 01° 4' East. The freshly dug gun pits of the battery were reported as 'showing up plainly'. Not content with that coup, the pilot poked his nose into Calais harbour itself. Here, he received a warm welcome, consisting of, 'intense HA and pom-pom'. It proved rather too warm a welcome, as it was later recorded, 'Port wing almost completely destroyed. Port petrol tank on fire. Returned to Manston under extreme difficulty'.[31]

Study of the photos led to a decision to mount an attack on the new gun battery near Cap Gris Nez. On 20 June, a single Skua was sent off on a BOULDS over the area at 0613 hours; at 1031 hours another Skua, with a two-plane escort this time, was also despatched. The pilot reported thirty-five lorries 7 miles north-east of Calais and three enemy minesweepers at sea off Calais. But the focus of attention was the battery and, at 1337 hours, a nine-aircraft dive-bombing attack was mounted by No. 801 Squadron, with four Skuas and five Rocs. The RAF provided them with an escort of twelve Hawker Hurricanes. The attack was made from the seaward in line astern at 1445 hours. After several sorties with the Skua, Harrington had again switched mounts and was flying Roc L3117 with Naval Airman Crone.

The method used was dive-bombing down from 2,000 feet to 1,000 feet. The whole delivery took just 2 or 3 minutes, and the lead aircraft took photos as they went down. The squadron achieved surprise; no enemy gun opened fire on the first two sections at all, but by the time the third sub-flight reached their drop point, heavy flak was starting to meet them and one Roc H/801 piloted by Sub-Lieutenant Day, with Observer Naval Airman Burry, was shot down into the sea. In reply, the aircraft achieved a confirmed, 'four direct hits and several near misses'.[32] A P/R mission on 22 June, which took photos of the battery from 1,000 feet, confirmed these results.

R. V. Beckett recalled: 'We dive-bombed a new gun emplacement being built at Calais – lost one aircraft.' He flew with Sub-Lieutenant I. L. F. Lowe, RN, in Skua L3161. The flight time was 1 hour 30 minutes.

This was their grand finale, for soon they were ordered back north once more. Beckett recorded:

22 June – Test flight with Lieutenant Gray, in L3102. 20 minutes. We then went up to Hatston at the end of June and as you know, Norway was the objective (flight time 4 hours plus) official endurance 4½ hours!

Skua tactics over the Channel – Summer 1940

In an interview with Captain Harrington,[33] he gave details of how the Skuas operated at this period:

When we went to Detling, you see, we were working under Coastal Command,[34] not Fighter Command. And our main function was to do reconnaissance from Boulogne right the way up to beyond Zeebrugge, Dieppe and Dunkirk, because the threat at that time was that Uncle Hitler was going to get his troops barged up and start coming across. It was most interesting because the Blenheims of the RAF and ourselves used to do this thing completely differently. The Blenheims used to do their recce at about 6,000 feet, obviously to take advantage of the cloud and that sort of thing. Our experience taught us that you did your recce 1½ inches above the ground contour and nobody troubled you, you troubled them.

If you were going to do the Calais and Boulogne run you were going one way round the hills, and come down through the valley and go out through the harbour. You would be taking pictures; you'd take photographs because I mean, that's what you were there to do. It was most interesting; we learnt one or two little tricks .... For instance, Boulogne harbour; if you came down the valley with the hills on either side, you popped out into the harbour below the level of the cranes. There was a very good reason for this and that was that the dear old square heads would have their 37 mm light flak, red-hot golf ball-producing machine. He was a dedicated chap, he would aim at you and of course he'd forget about his chums on the other side of the harbour. So you'd go through there and you'd see cranes falling down and the like.

Indeed, on one occasion in order to try and get their 109s on to us, they had some of these fairly heavy calibre coastal defence guns which they were firing out to sea with these great water geysers; splash barrage. Just, you know, single shots, obviously they were not attempting to hit us, but point out where we were. You could see the 109s hunting us by the splashes. Of course, they had great difficulty, as we had sea camouflage, which was of great advantage to us. But all points had two sides, and the great disadvantage of our camouflage is that we used to get attacked just as much by the RAF, who hadn't a clue when it came to Skua recognition. Nor did they care very much, they just registered, 'who are these extraordinary, foreign-looking aircraft' and, eagerly looking for scalps to paint on the sides of their aircraft for the camera back home, were not too particular whose scalp they got!

As the RAF worked to different frequencies we could not express ourselves over the radio. We just went flat out. In a Skua that was a bit like going flat out in an Austin Seven! You just waited for them to come at you and then took counter-measures. You could just turn and play with your flaps; making them overshoot. Or, if you were unlucky enough to be flying a Roc, your rear gunner could fire a warning burst over them, which again, with a cloud of red-hot golf balls coming out of the back, would make the odd Blenheim or fighter, think twice and pause for thought. Then we'd just disappear as best we could again, at sea level.

Of course the RAF were officially notified every time we went out, but it was obvious that cross-communication between Coastal and Fighter Commands were not good. I mean, this early on in the war and co-ordination between one control unit and another of the same command was very much interrogative let lone between Fighter Command and anyone else. I think everyone was much on the defensive, in an aggressive backs-against-the-wall type of way at this period, and anything they couldn't see or understand, was just taken out.

It could be amusing, in that, even when you were doing convoy protection duty off Dover or somewhere like that, you would go and be relieved by a Blenheim and the first thing you knew of your 'Relief' would be the Blenheim shaping up to attack you! Their attitude was, 'There's a funny-looking aircraft over our convoy, it might not be on our side, let's hack it down!' Even the fact that we were docilely stooging around over the ships and not being fired at, did not deter them. This was probably because one of the aspects of convoy spotting with a single machine was not to destroy the whole convoy single-handed yourself, but to gather the intelligence sufficient to organise a proper, co-ordinated strike. So that a potential 'enemy' could be shadowing the convoy and not necessarily be showing it aggression in a direct way. But such an aircraft would still pose hostile intent.

Whether these cross-Channel excursions were mounted singly or in pairs, naturally depended on what we were out there to do. A convoy protection patrol would probably be a single aircraft, if you were doing a vital bit of reconnaissance, we'd sometimes go over in pairs. For instance, we did the first attack on the Cap Gris Nez gun battery. We spotted the Huns digging the gun positions. How that came about was because we were actually out looking at the German build-up of invasion barges, but stumbled on the construction work for the big guns.[35]

This experience was confirmed by another Skua pilot:

We were used to being shot at from bombers, from fighters, from the ground, from ships, even by our own Fleet on return from some-where. Our aircraft were full of shot holes, the rigger and fitter used to cover them with canvas and glue, then paint a swastika or other symbol on each one.[36]

Stan Orr was another pilot flying with No. 806 Squadron, and he appeared to have had a guardian angel watching over him at this time. He had started his flying career by volunteering for the RAF before the war, but had been rejected because he failed an eye test at the Kingsway, London, recruiting office. Nothing daunted, he applied for the Fleet Air Arm, sat exactly the same test in the same room, and passed with flying colours! On completion of his flying training in April 1940, Orr had been one of the young flyers allocated to replace losses and was assigned to Skuas, being sent to join HMS *Glorious*. Due to bad weather he was unable to fly aboard her, instead routeing to Hatston, flying his first missions from there, before moving down to Kent. Orr's luck continued to hold out, and, although he lost several friends shot down over the Channel by Spitfires around the time of Dunkirk and later, he survived.[37]

An RAF source gave some backing to this 'shoot-on-sight' attitude with regard to the Skua. Squadron Leader D. H. Clarke, DFC, AFC, then flying with No. AACU, recalled:

> I had been attacked by German and British aircraft (it was surprising how few of our pilots could recognise the unmistakable Skua or Roc), and naturally, by Army and Navy anti-aircraft guns.[38]

How it should be done!

Squadron Leader D. H. Clarke, DFC, AFC, who had no time at all for naval flyers, thought it was they, not the Skua, who were not up to the job.[39] Many years later, he was to give a graphic and boastful account of how he personally showed the Royal Navy just how the Skua should be flown! This terminated with a full-flap vertical dive ('vertically, not just steeply') from 3,000 feet, flattening out at 50 feet.

> ... lifting those wonderful flaps for a zoom to gain altitude; no sign of squash, or of high speed stalling. I used that trick many times in the early days of the war to dodge trigger-happy pilots (mostly allies) who were a bit vague on their aircraft recognition. Nothing could dive as slowly as a Skua, nor did I ever discover another aircraft which could pull out of a vertical dive at such low level so safely.

Clarke also stated that the complaint about the Skua being a killer in a spin, which had resulted in the fitting of the tail parachute, was an 'unjustified complaint'. He was apparently ignorant of the fact that it had been an RAF pilot during the pre-war flight-testing that had originally commented on it:

> When the emergency tail parachute cord was pulled (it was a typical 'bodge' assembly with a ring in the cockpit and a long wire, fabric doped to the outside of the fuselage, which tripped a spring-loaded hatch just behind the trailing edge of the rudder) it was as if you were suddenly hoicked up by the seat of your pants and suspended on a nail – that is, if the contrivance worked! It didn't always.
>
> But the real joy with the Skua was its diving abilities and after all it was designed as a dive bomber. The pilot sat in a low-sided cockpit with really excellent visibility and the seat-adjustment ranged from almost sitting on the floor to standing upright.

Clarke went on to state:

> I had always held that the FAA should attack targets – especially the German Navy – by diving vertically. Ships' anti-aircraft guns, I argued, can seldom bear on a vertically diving aircraft and if the ship is rolling or pitching the chances of scoring a hit are nil. But the

aircraft, especially a Skua, could easily hit the ship – and if the pilot knew that he was safe he could take plenty of time with his aiming.

He was gracious enough to demonstrate this to the Royal Navy, and also flying a dive-bombing attack against a British light cruiser with eight 1 lb flour bags, scoring seven hits out of seven dives. 'My eighth bomb hit exactly in the middle of the bridge – in fact it penetrated the chart table!'

New methods

Clarke's memories and their own recent combat experiences in Norway apart, the Royal Navy flyers were on a sharp learning curve with the Skua over the Channel at this period. Captain Harrington later detailed exactly how the Skuas of No. 801 Squadron developed their own special tactics, and how the lessons learnt then in that aircraft, had relevance even 30 years later.

Because the Skuas were not fast, even without bombs, we soon latched on to one or two fundamentals, which have since formed basic requirements for naval attack aircraft. The first of these was that, if aircraft were successfully to penetrate well-defended targets, for whatever purpose, then the first requirement to be achieved was surprise – almost rule one of any warlike operation. This meant, wherever possible, a low-level approach, below the enemy warning system. This technique we developed and our losses off the French and, later, the Norwegian coasts were significantly less than those of our Air Force friends in their Blenheims and the like. This method provided for another vital element, namely one of identification – was it the target, and was the target a real, worthwhile target. In a ship sense, was it theirs or one of ours that nobody knew was there!

The main problem about this technique was the final climb for the attack if one was in a rather under-powered old Skua. I guess this requirement led to the fundamental disagreement between the Navy and the Air Force staffs about sharing a joint requirement for a properly designed low level (thick air) attack bomber. This was ultimately to result in the Navy's Buccaneer and from the Air Force point-of-view, the never-to-materialise TSR 1 and TSR 2 requirements. Both of these never got into service and neither was primarily aimed at the key low-level requirement. They tried to meet low and high level conditions.

The other lesson we learned on the Skua was on the weapon-delivery side. One the one hand, if you had only traditional bombs, then you were committed to the classical 'dive' approach. In short, you had to arrive over the target at the right height for a 65 to 75 degree dive, release the bomb with the right sort of penetration speed (a function of height), then recover from the dive and make your way out like a 'half-tide' rock. With the limited range of weapons and their associated limited fusing arrangements, you were always facing fairly critical limitations; compromising between a really highly productive run with a high chance of target destruction and the maximum chance of getting home and hopefully be available for further strikes. In a carrier your replenishment of aircraft and crew takes time.

The final lesson we learned, apart from the need for an aircraft with a really high performance, was that the aircraft should have a really effective, balanced and flexible in-air braking system. The Skuas dive-brakes were really in the wrong position and they had the effect of pushing you forward and over your target. In other words, if you wanted to achieve a 70 degree dive, you had to start your dive at least at +80 degrees and aim somewhat short of your target, so that as the speed built up, you finished with your final release-point at the correct point of aim and at the right height etc. Correcting this floating forward effect also had another dividend for us, as the flak had a great problem in tracking you correctly, and anticipating this ever-increasing forward 'float'. It was comforting to see the stuff passing under your aircraft, which was good news to you and very bad news to anyone foolish enough to try and follow you down.[40]

By the time we got to mid-1941, we had become maids-of-all-work of all kinds of attack, both shore and carrier-based. Before some of us old hands of 801 were hived off and embarked with the Fulmar II fighter aircraft in the brand-new *Victorious*, we had reached the art of hitting ships pretty well indeed, for sure. We had all sorts of esoteric tricks in store for the wiley Hun, even to the extent of hitting ships tucked into the shelter of cliffs in the deep fiords of Norway. This entailed a splendid curved approach, where the bomb was implanted with a nice 'in-swinger' type of movement.[41]

NOTES

1. Six Rocs were allocated to Detling (L3103, L3105, L3106, L3118, L3154 and L3156) and were mainly used for anti-submarine patrols and as a makeshift dive-bomber.
2. See, Lieutenant Commander Charles Evans, RN, *Operations of No. 806 Squadron while working in conjunction with the RAF Coastal Command from May 27th to June 3rd, 1940*, dated 11 June 1940. (1712/155 contained in National Archives ADM 199/115.)
3. Hogg manuscript, *op cit*
4. Despite very positive identification by both survivors, this fact is still hushed up today, and in reference books written 60 years after the event in which the attacking aircraft are claimed to be French!
5. *Ibid.*

6. Hogg manuscript, *op cit.*

7. Commanding Officer, 801 Squadron, RAF Station Detling, Maidstone, Monthly Letter of Proceedings, dated 13 June 1940. (B/G 18/3 contained in National Archives ADM 199/115.)

8. No. 801 Squadron, *Operational Record Book*, 31 May 1940. (Contained in National Archives AIR 27/2387.)

9. *Ibid.*

10. Air Ministry, *Coastal Command – The Air Ministry account of the part played by Coastal Command in the Battle of the Seas 1939–1942*, Ministry of Information Booklet 70-411, HMSO, London, 1943.

11. R. V. 'Joe' Beckett, letter to Dickie Rolph dated 7 September 1998 and made available to the author.

12. Flying Log Book of Naval Airman L. W. Miles, No. 801 Squadron.

13. Denis Richards, *Royal Air Force 1939–1945, Vol. 1, Collapse in the West*, HMSO, London, 1953.

14. B. J. G. Madden, *A History of the 6th Battalion, The Black Watch, 1939–45*, D. Leslie, Perth, 1947.

15. Norman Franks, *Air Battle Dunkirk 6 May to 3 June 1940*, Grub Street, London, 2000.

16. See Squadron Leader D. H. Clarke, DFC, AFC, *Ghost Fighters – over Dunkirk*, article in *RAF Flying Review*, April 1959.

17. *Ibid.*

18. *Ibid.*

19. This claim, like so many others, was not authenticated by enemy records.

20. Commanding Officer, 801 Squadron, RAF Station Detling, Maidstone, Monthly Letter of Proceedings, dated 13 June 1940. (B/G 18/3 contained in National Archives ADM 199/115.)

21. R. V. Beckett letter to Dickie Rolph, *op cit.*

22. Commanding Officer, 801 Squadron, RAF Station Detling, Maidstone, Monthly Letter of Proceedings, dated 13th June 1940. (B/G 18/3 contained in National Archives ADM 199/115).

23. Known as 'Boulds'.

24. No. 801 Squadron, *Operational Record Book*, 12 June 1940. (Contained in National Archives AIR 27/2387.)

25. No. 801 Squadron, *Operational Record Book*, 12 June 1940. (Contained in National Archives AIR 27/2387.)

26. No. 801 Squadron, *Operational Record Book*, 13 June 1940. (Contained in National Archives AIR 27/2387.)

27. Baldwin was to go on to earn a DSC and Bar, and was among the first to take the naval adaptation of the Supermarine Spitfire, the Seafire, into combat with No. 807 Squadron during the North African landings in November 1942, becoming CO the following year. He served aboard the escort carrier HMS *Battler* at the Salerno landings, later moving ashore. Once the Germans started pulling back in October, Baldwin, true to his Skua lineage, proved that even the most aerodynamic of fighter aircraft could be adapted for dive-bombing. He later fought at the South France invasion and in the Aegean clear-up in 1944 with 4th Fighter Wing, then went out to the East Indies for the recapture of Singapore. Among his many post-war achievements were operating the Royal Navy's first jet aircraft, the Supermarine Attacker from HMS *Eagle*; angled-deck trials aboard the USS *Antietam* and flying an American Crusader in excess of 1,000 mph in level flight. After spells at Lossiemouth, the Defence College and Yeovilton, Baldwin became Director of Naval Air Warfare between 1964–6 and fought his hardest battle, cam-

paigning long, hard and vigorously against the RAF and Labour Government's attempts to destroy the Royal Navy's carrier fleet, for which he was passed over for promotion to Admiral. He retired from the service in 1968 with the consolation prize of the CBE. He was a founder member of the Fleet Air Arm Officers' Association and member of the Press Council. He died, aged 84, on 11 November 2005, having lived to see his predictions come true with the preliminary work being commenced, and by a Labour Government, on two new 'Super-carriers' for the fleet.

28. Captain T. W. Harrington, DSO, RN to the author on 29 June 1977.

29. No. 801 Squadron, *Operational Record Book*, 18 June 1940. (Contained in National Archives AIR 27/2387.)

30. R. V. Beckett letter to Dickie Rolph, *op cit.*

31. No. 801 Squadron, *Operational Record Book*, 19 June 1940. (Contained in National Archives AIR 27/2387.)

32. No. 801 Squadron, *Operational Record Book*, 20 June 1940. *op cit.*

33. Interview with Captain Tom Harrington, RN, at his home in Harpenden, on 13 June 1986.

34. RAF Detling was a satellite airfield, with lodging facilities and part of No. 16 Group. The Station Commanding Officer at Detling was Group Captain Sainsbury, RAF; the Air Officer Commanding Coastal Command at this time was Air Chief Marshal Sir Frederick Bowhill, KCB, CMG, DSO, RAF. The *Luftwaffe* twice bombed Detling, in August and September 1940.

35. Harrington interview, *op cit.*

36. Vice-Admiral Sir Donald Gibson, *Haul Taut and Belay*, *op cit.*

37. Stan Gordon Orr was to continue to ride his luck. He was a Fulmar pilot aboard the *Illustrious* when she was pulverised by Junkers Ju87s off Malta in January 1941, but was lucky enough to be in the air when six bombs hit her. He fought over Malta and then against Vichy in Syria. After a period as an Instructor he formed No. 896 Squadron with Grumman Wildcats (Martlets) in 1942, but developed polio. He was expected to die but, after 10 weeks in an iron lung, he cheated the grim reaper yet again and made a full recovery. He became CO of No. 804 Squadron flying Hellcats in 1944, taking part in the *Tirpitz* attacks and notching up his third DSC of the war. He resumed instructing at Boscombe Down, with the Naval Test Squadron. He also commanded the Interservice Hovercraft Trials Unit, retiring from the Navy in 1966 having flown more than 100 types of aircraft. He worked for Vosper's as their chief test pilot. He finally (and probably reluctantly) went to meet his maker on 19 August 2003, aged 86.

38. Squadron Leader D. H. Clarke, DFC, AFC, 'The Decision is Always the Pilot's', article in *RAF Flying Review*, October 1961.

39. Clarke claimed that, 'The Fleet Air Arm hated the Skua; it was one of the six best aircraft I have flown. I imply intentionally that the FAA didn't know what it was talking about and I do so vehemently. They didn't!' He also claimed that, early in the war, after three Navy pilots had spun in at Lee-on-Solent 'the first day (sic) the FAA flew Skuas' his target-towing unit at Gosport had been phoned up by the Navy and asked to put on a demonstration. Squadron Leader D. H. Clarke, DFC, AFC, 'The Shunned Skua', article in *RAF Flying Review*, December 1961.

40. Captain T. W. Harrington, DSO, RN, to the author on 29 June 1977.

41. It was typical of the Admiralty policy of the time that just as these bombing techniques had been perfected, the highly trained and motivated aircrew were transferred to fighter duties with the Fulmar. Although this aircraft had been converted from an original bomber design, it no longer had any capability for dive-bombing whatsoever! It was a total waste. In a similar manner, the American Vought SB2U Chesapeake dive-bomber,

although trialled, was never tested out in the role for which it had been constructed, viz dive-bombing, but only as an anti-submarine aircraft, for which task it proved, not surprisingly, totally unsuitable and was abandoned! By late 1941 the Royal Navy, having honed and perfected the technique in hard combat, had left itself without any major dive-bombing capability whatsoever, the 'new' Fairey Albacore biplane being a strange kind of throwback substitute to a former age of wires and struts.

11

NORTH AND SOUTH

For No. 801 Squadron, the next 10 months were ones of extremes. The men dealt with extremes of location, from the coast of Norway once more to the coast of West Africa, and had a final touch of *deja vue* when they were once more due to be sacrificed in a futile attack on the altar of their old enemies, the battle-cruisers *Scharnhorst* and *Gneisenau*. Happily, this time common sense prevailed – helped by a minor rebellion!

Norway again

At the end of June 1940, No. 801 Squadron, commanded by Lieutenant (A) Richard M. Smeeton, RN, moved back north to Hatston. The reason for the recall was the escape back to Germany between 20 and 23 June of the battle-cruiser *Scharnhorst* and eight destroyers. The *Gneisenau* took a torpedo hit from a submarine and had to return to Norway, along with the *Admiral Hipper*, and the Skuas were needed to maintain a close watch on this latter pair. Joe Beckett recalled: 'We then went up to Hatston at the end of June and as you know, Norway was the objective (flight time 4 hours plus) official endurance 4½ hours!'

The route taken was recorded in the log of Lieutenant Harrington, flying Roc L2890 with Corporal Webb as a passenger. On 25 June they took off from Detling and flew to Sealand and then, after a brief halt, flew on to Donibristle (which Harrington noted was 'Squalid'). Here, Harrington transferred to Skua L2890 and on 28 June conducted an air test in her, making a 'not very clever landing'. Then, with Naval Airman Crone as his rear-seat man again, but with no maps, he flew on to Hatston. Bedding in followed, Beckett flew a 30-minute test flight with Sub-Lieutenant (A) Lowe in L2889, on 1 July.

The first combat mission was a 'Blitz' to attempt to find what turned out to be a 'Phantom' German cruiser. The Armed Raider, *Komet* (*Schiff 45*) sailed from Gotenhafen, with the ultimate intention of breaking through the blockade, heading up the coast of Norway to the ports of Germany's ally, the Soviet Union, and thence reaching her distant field of operations, the Pacific, by way of Siberia. To find and sink her on the first leg of this journey, the Skuas were scrambled from Hatston on 5 July, and quartered the waters off the Norwegian coast in vain. Beckett was up in L3014 for 4 hours. Most aircraft had to refuel at Sumburgh after a fruitless quest, before returning to base. On 6 July the aircraft flew back to Hatston, a 40-minute journey.

The following day, 7 July, in anticipation that the 'cruiser' might have put into that port, a strike was launched against Bergen. Among the Skuas were Harrington and Crone in L2890 and Sub-Lieutenant I. L. F. Lowe and R. V. Joe Beckett with the ever-faithful L3014. Both aircrews recorded a 4-hour round trip in their logs.

Captain T. W. Harrington later gave this eyewitness description of the mission, and just how close-run a thing it could be with regard endurance:

We operated from Hatston[1] airfield, (mainly a small straight road with telegraph poles removed). From here, we could either fly direct to the coast of Norway at the extreme length of their range, or, embark on one of the few remaining aircraft carriers and thereby having a great choice of naval targets on the vast west coast of Norway, with its many offshore islands and deep fiords running inland.

That day six of us took off from Hatston in the dark (not too much of that during July) and we flew low across the north part of the North Sea (to avoid detection by the German radar). Our target was the shipping in the port of Bergen and our plan was to climb up to our most effective dive-bombing height (approximately 15,000 feet depending on the thickness of the target's building materials and the type of bomb we were carrying, i.e. semi-armour piercing etc.). On this particular party, we climbed to about 'ten grand' (10,000 feet), because we started to run into thicker and lowering cloud as we crossed the outer islands. This not only forced us to fly lower, but also meant that we were having difficulty to avoid 'bunching' together, which in turn meant an easier target for the enemy gunners and from our point of view, we had less 'room' to roll into our dive-bombing run, when we had selected a worthwhile target.

I found myself behind a friend of mine as he pushed his aircraft over into its dive and put out his dive-brakes (which allowed you to dive steadily at some 70 to 80 degrees towards your target). The effect of these dive-brakes is to make your aircraft steady, but also causes the aircraft to track forward during the dive. This means that when an anti-aircraft gun fires at you when he has you in his sights and fires, he will often miss you because of this forward moving and the shell often goes below you instead of hitting you. (Good News!)

Because of this cloud and the fact that I was stuck behind my chum, I was in fact getting all the flak aimed at him and this was whizzing over the top of my diving aircraft. Not a very comfortable situation. It also did not help too much in my tracking of my target (a ship alongside a jetty).

As you know, when things start going wrong, you often start experiencing the effects of 'sod's law' – when lots of not likely other things also start going wrong! In this case, I noticed that my fuel gauges were reading zero, and my flap indicators were showing the wrong reading (I smelt an electrical problem). When I selected my bomb release (another electrically operated button) the bombs did not release.

I did not have too much spare time left in my 75 degree dive, with clouds of red-hot 'golf balls' flying over the top of my canopy, so I had to screw my head round to my emergency bomb release levers on the right-hand side (starboard) of my cockpit, in order to grab them and when steady, release the bombs. All this came to pass, but while my head was bent down to the emergency panel, one of the 40 mm enemy shells hit the top right part of my canopy, passed over where my head would normally be and left my aircraft through the port-side of the canopy – making a nasty smashing noise!

Anyway, after letting my bomb release go, on its target, I found myself no longer chewing gum but munching some nasty-tasting 'sawdust'. So I lifted off my oxygen mask and blew out this newly created (non-chewing) material – which I blew all over the place, giving a rather new type of 'non-skid and high-traction' finish to many parts of the cockpit.

The trip home was not too comfortable – not so much because of the draught caused by the German shell – but because of the electric failure, which in turn meant that I had no physical indication of my fuel situation. We had three tanks and it was bad news to let any one of these tanks drain dry because the engine took a long time to come on-stream again. The flight out and back took 4 hours and 30 minutes, which in weak mixture meant that we were very, very close to nearly not making it! I made for Sumburgh airfield in the Shetland Islands, being the nearest base.

When I was filled up with petrol, I found that I had used all the capacity of the three tanks except for 7½ gallons (i.e. about 2 gallons in each tank left) – about 10 minutes' flying in weak mixture.[2]

Lowe and Beckett also had to put down at Sumburgh to top up before making the 40-minute trip on to Hatston.

The Squadron routine

The Skuas returned to Sumburgh on 10 July, for another attempt. The following day an attack force took off for Norway, Beckett's pilot on this occasion being Sub-Lieutenant (A) Martyn, flying L2959. However, *Komet* seemed to have all the luck; the weather closed in and became so bad that the Skuas had to return to Sumburgh after an hour's flying. They stood by, hoping for a break in the overcast, but finally gave up, returning to Hatston once more on 14 July.

Between 16 and 20 July, the Skuas, being rusty after so many weeks ashore, took the opportunity to brush up on their deck landing (ADDL) skills aboard the *Furious*, coupling this with extra dive-bombing practice against towed sea markers. Captain Harrington recalled the Skua's potential in this, her prime, objective:

> The only other characteristic the Skua had in a long steep dive, was that, as the speed built up, the aircraft tended to rotate round its axis. This was easily controlled and was caused by the setting of the ailerons being adjusted for normal flight conditions. One countered this by the controls, plus laying one's sighting to let a natural creep take place. The old girl also had a bomb-throwing crutch, which took the main bomb on the belly clear of the propeller, an essential for a steep dive.[3]

The squadron made further such attacks on 24 and 26 July.

View from the back seat

Dickie Rolph talked to the author at length about how things appeared from the rear seat.[4]

> I once flew with a tyro pilot, Midshipman L. H. Gallagher. We attacked a Dornier Do17 bomber, and he insisted on holding to a straight, steady course to get close in so he could do some damage. He forgot about the stuff coming back! He quickly used up all our ammunition. We somehow managed to land back aboard the carrier with three bullet holes through the spinner.
>
> On one occasion, when withdrawing at very low level down a Norwegian fiord after bombing oil tanks near Bergen, German AA gunners in positions atop the cliffs were actually depressing the guns and firing down on us. On another trip, I managed to empty my Lewis into a boatload of German soldiers as we zoomed over them, and felt pretty good about it! It made a change to be able to fire back at the enemy, instead of being on the receiving end all the time.
>
> My regular pilot, Petty Officer H. A. Monk, can lay claim to be the first (and perhaps only) pilot to land a Skua on a flight deck at sea, without a hook! We had returned from a mission and all seemed well, but the tailhook would not come down. Fuel was getting low so he decided to land aboard anyway. We flew slowly past the carrier, making the 'Thumbs Up' sign, indicating, 'Let me on!' Whether they understood or not, we went around and landed, without any mishap.

Ken King also told the author how things were viewed from the back seat of the Skua. Ken was drafted to No. 801 Squadron at Hatston early in July 1940. He recalled:

Although the Squadron was part of the HMS *Furious* strike force, most of our operations to Norway were from Hatston, with only a few trips from the carrier herself. The CO was I believe Lieutenant Saunt, the senior pilot was Lieutenant Savage and my pilot was usually Sub-Lieutenant Parsons

Initially our trips to Norway started at Hatston, to Norway, then return to Hatston. Later, the route changed: Hatston to RAF Sumburgh, Shetland Isles, to top up with fuel, then to Norway, return to Sumburgh, refuel then back to Hatston (Perhaps our targets were further afield). At RAF Sumburgh Lieutenant Sarel, the Senior Pilot was Lieutenant Savage and my pilot was usually Sub-Lieutenant Parsons. I can only recall when Sub-Lieutenant Parsons was not my pilot and both times we had unusual endings.

The Skua was a two-seater, with a pilot and usually a navigator or a TAG in the rear cockpit. The rear cockpit also had a Transmitter Receiver, TR 1082/83, but in those days there was little voice transmission, mostly WT (Morse). The Receiver-Transmitter was powered by five 2-volt Accumulators, the Aircraft 12 volt Accumulator and a 100 volt dry battery for the Receiver. The aircraft had a short fixed antenna, also a 200-foot trailing aerial, which you wound in and out on a reel, by hand. The rear cockpit was not too bad as we had a cupola, which could be pulled down to keep out some of the slipstream and cold, but it had to be opened to use the rear gun. The Skua also had a belt inside the rear cockpit that stretched from one side of the aircraft to the other, was also the station, which could be hooked up and which you could lean on reasonably comfortably (as when in a dive). When in an actual dive, one had to brace yourself well, to prevent becoming a heap on the aircraft floor, when the pilot pulled out of the dive. The Skua's top speed was about 225 mph and it was pretty reliable mechanically, as I don't recall any mechanical failures in all the trips we did to and from Norway. RAF Sumburgh, Shetland Islands, was also the station, which we could work the radio to obtain D/F bearings, providing we had a D/F code. The D/F code was a lifesaver if you happened to get separated and lost.

I can only remember two occasions when we went over as a full squadron. The first time I guess we were lucky as our aircraft could only keep up in Rated, and we were told to return to base, which we did. Unfortunately, we lost two aircraft to German fighters during that particular raid. We only lost three aircraft during the 3 months I was with the squadron. The other occasion was on my last trip from HMS *Furious*. I should mention that, in those days, the TAGs were never present in the briefings, for we were left outside the door waiting! The pilots were briefed and also given a point of departure from Norway and a course to steer to reach Sumburgh or Hatston, just in case they became detached from the flight or squadron.

The D/F code was a sheet, listing time of day and date and a combination of figures, which were changed periodically. If you asked for a bearing they would challenge you for the combination or figures for the day and hour. If you gave the right figures you would receive a bearing, if not you could cry all day! I should also mention that weather forecasting at that time was a little bizarre. Sometimes we would send an aircraft over to Norway in the morning and, depending on his report, we would go over early afternoon on a specific raid. Some of our raids were to Bergen, Stavanger, Dolvic and Trondheim, none of which were at night.

Our strategy always seemed to be: Sub-flights formed up; fly over just below the cloud base, until we sighted land; then we popped into the cloud and somehow managed to come out over the target. We dive-bombed Sub-flight Leader first down, followed by the Left wingman, then the Right wingman, turn out to sea and re-form for the return home. Although some pilots came back along on their return trip, our Sub-flight always flew out together and returned as a Sub-flight together. A Sub-flight Leader always had an Observer Navigator, but the wingmen always had TAGs.

On my first trip with a pilot other than Sub-Lieutenant Parsons, we became detached from the Sub-flight and were returning to Sumburgh alone. After quite some time, the pilot asked me for a bearing. I made contact with Sumburgh and got the bearing, and told him the course to steer, then shortly after that he said, 'It's OK, I see land'. So we flew around for a few minutes and he was not quite sure where he was. Our fuel was getting low, so he decided to land as best he could. I should mention that the course he would have to steer, would have taken him out to sea again, so sighting land he chose to force-land because his fuel was so low.

At that time in the UK there was the possible threat of airborne invasion from Germany, so many places were putting up poles etc. in the fields to deter enemy gliders from landing. These were what confronted my pilot, cows and poles in the fields where he was going to attempt a landing. He did a real neat job of clearing the cows, flew between two of the poles, and touched down all by the book. But we were running out of space and he had to swing the aircraft to port to avoid a huge hedge ahead. Even so, we tipped up on our nose with the tail up in the air for everyone to see. We both clambered out unhurt and, a few moments later, some RAF fighters flew overhead. We walked across some fields to a farmhouse and the lady answering the door got a shock to see two guys in flying suits. We found out we were in Scotland, not too far from an airfield, and we were back at Hatston in a couple of days. Unfortunately, I cannot recall the name of the pilot (who was a rating pilot), nor the place near where we landed.

Hunting in the fiords

Then they were off on ops once more. On 21 July they flew with a full bomb load, into Sumburgh, in the Shetlands, which they again found to be enshrouded by mist and cloud.They took off the next day for the Norwegian coast. Lowe and Beckett in L2907 had to abort with engine trouble, but the rest pressed on and Harrington recorded he had 'Bopped a Boat' before returning to 'Hateful Hatston' via another refuelling stop at Sumburgh. A convoy operation followed on 24 July, when Lowe and Beckett had to land at Dyce.

They embarked aboard *Furious* again and 2 days later, on 26 July, the squadron headed off once more to what Harrington termed, 'That Bane of My Life – Norway', where another enemy ship target was claimed hit, but he had to record of one of his closest friends, 'Johnny Missing'[5] after they ran into terrible weather conditions.

The attack was made despite these very poor conditions, thick cloud and heavy rain. Rating Pilot R. H. Williams, with Naval Airman Beardsley, was flying L2951 on this mission to Sogne Fiord, and they reported that Sub-Lieutenant J. E. H. Myers and Naval Airman S. A. Bass in L2906 failed to return, being posted 'missing, believed killed'.[6] It later transpired that, unable to locate the target vessel, the Skuas dive-bombed the oil tanks at Bergen. Conditions were abysmal and during the attack dive two of the Skuas collided, Myers' aircraft crashing about a ¼ mile offshore from Haugesundsletta, north of the town of Haugesund. The other Skua somehow miraculously survived the impact and managed to limp home to make a crash-landing at Sumburgh.

Between 25 and 28 July, the German battle-cruiser *Gneisenau*, having completed repairs after being torpedoed by the submarine HMS *Clyde* on 20 June, made her run south to safety in Germany, escorted by the light cruiser *Nürnberg* and four destroyers. Despite all the patrols, she evaded sighting and reached Kiel safely. On 26 July the squadron carried out an unsuccessful dive-bombing attack against an enemy merchant ship 40 miles north of Stavanger.[7] Petty Officer Kimber and Petty Officer Clayton failed to return from this sortie.

Routine training flights and dive-bombing practice were carried out on 27 July, then it was back to operations. In August the fuel tanks near Bergen were bombed four times. Bombing missions continued to be inter-spaced with reconnaissance sorties (HFX), like that conducted off

Stavanger on 1 August. By contrast with their previous bad weather experience, the Skuas found the visibility off the enemy-held shore, 'Too Bloody Clear for Comfort'. They were still operating at the extreme limit of their endurance in a 4 hours 30 minutes round trip. R. H. Williams with Naval Airman Beardsley in L2907 took part in a dive-bombing attack on Soletto W/T Station this day.[8] A meteorological flight carried out by Harrington, with Lieutenant Nedwell in the rear seat of L2907, the following day also found conditions, 'Clear as a Bell'. For the next few days the squadron was involved in training, air tests, fighter attacks, front and rear gun firing, formation flying and dive-bombing practice, and this period culminated in further deck-landings aboard the *Furious* on 6 August.

On 7 August a sortie was made to the Norwegian coast, but L2907 could not keep up with the formation and Harrington was forced to abort the mission. The rest of the force mounted a successful dive-bombing attack on the oil storage tank complex at Dobvik, 6 miles south of Bergen, returning safely after a sortie of 4 hours 50 minutes. On this mission the Skuas carried a mixed bomb load of one 250 lb, and eight 20 lb bombs.

A new mount had to be found for Harrington and, with Lieutenant Hayes and A. M. E. Spencer as passengers, L2890 was given air and bombing tests between 8 and 12 August. During another patch of rough weather on 14 August, one of the carrier's Swordfish, piloted by Lieutenant (A) Fryer, failed to return and a box search was flown to locate the wreckage, in vain. The next day, an HFX was conducted by Lieutenant Gray flying L3030, for the army, followed by further sea-marker bombing. The period from 18 August onward saw the squadron undertaking carrier take-off and fighter patrol, fighter attack and dive-bombing training.

Harrington returned to combat in his new aircraft, with the trusty Crone as his observer, on 21 August, when the squadron attacked enemy shipping in Haugesund. It turned out to be, as Harrington's log book recorded, a 'Dirty Trip, Best Forgotten'.

More intensive practice followed, with drone target shooting simulating astern chases, and eight hits were recorded on the target on 22 August. Dive-bombing practice, fighter practice, dog-fights and formation flying were conducted the following day. The unit was readied for an attack on 26 August, in support of a raid on German shipping off Bear Island by the heavy cruisers *Norfolk* and *Australia*, whose aircraft were also to attack Tromsø. Both the Skuas and the cruisers' floatplanes were recalled when already airborne and on the way to the target. R/T and oxygen testing followed and while the radio was poor, the oxygen was OK.

The Bergen beat

Then the squadron left Hatston for Sumburgh, from where an attack was launched on 28 August. Once more, the targets assigned were the oil tanks at Dobvik, a mission that Harrington recorded succinctly as, 'Miles up some fiord – Not much Good'. Again, the Skuas had to return via Sumburgh.

The squadron re-embarked aboard HMS *Furious* on 4 September, making the 55-minute flight out from Hatston without incident. The carrier then turned her bows eastward and during 5 and 6 September fighter patrols and dive-bombing practice kept the aircrews busy as the task force closed the target area. On 7 September a strike was flown off the carrier against German shipping off northern Norway, but without result, the aircraft returning direct to Sumburgh on conclusion of the sortie of 4 hours 10 minutes.

No time was lost for, after returning to Hatston for a quick refuelling and rearming, they were off again on 9 August, attacking Norwegian shipping targets.

On 13 September, another attack was made, this one directed against the oil tanks at Skålevik, near Bergen. This involved a 3 hour 50 minute round trip from Hatston and returning via Sumburgh. On this occasion L2912, flown by Petty Officer Edward G. H. Harwin, with Naval Airman John R. Maunder, was intercepted by a Bf109E and badly shot up, Maunder being killed. The Skua came down in neutral Sweden at Svartedalen, Andvik. Also shot down was L3030, piloted by Lieutenant T. E. Grey with Lieutenant J. C. W. Iliffe as his observer, who both became POWs.

Trondheim raid

On 20 September, No. 801 Squadron flew out to the carrier *Furious*, a 1-hour transit. Lieutenant Harrington, recently returned from sick leave, flew L2890, with Petty Officer Baker as his rear-seat man. On the morning of 22 September, the attack force was despatched against Trondheim, but the whole raid was a fiasco. (Harrington wrote despairingly in his log, 'Oh Boy/Oh Boy!') One Skua, L2942, flown by Sub-Lieutenant B. F. Wigginton, with Ken R. King as his TAG, ran out of fuel, and landed in a river near Ramselle, Sweden. Although they survived this incident, they were interned for a year. Ken told the author what took place:

My last trip in a Skua took place from HMS *Furious* on 22 September 1940, and my pilot was Sub-Lieutenant Wigginton. The night before, the TAGs had a meeting in the hangar with the Senior Observer, who told us that the carrier, after flying off the squadrons (there were also Swordfish squadrons on this raid), would turn around and head for home, but would leave a destroyer about 60 miles off the coast, on the same course as the *Furious* was steering. The pilots had been given a point of departure from Norway and a course to steer to rendezvous with the destroyer. I remember asking the Senior Observer, 'How about a D/F Code?' He replied, 'You won't need one, as the carrier will break W/T silence and give you a bearing.'

We flew off *Furious* about 0330 on a miserable, dark morning with mist and drizzle, forming up as a squadron, then into clouds for a while. Our target was shipping in Trondheim Harbour. When our aircraft [L2942] broke through the cloud there were no other aircraft to be seen, so we continued to Trondheim to drop our bomb. We then flew to the given point of departure, and set course for the destroyer, but we could not locate her. We called up the *Furious* for a bearing. There was no response. Of course, we had no D/F code to try and work our way to Sumburgh.

My pilot thought the best thing to do was try and make it to Sweden, so we flew easterly and tried to stay low over the water to avoid confrontation. He was not prepared to dump us in the wilds, and eventually he did a pretty smooth landing with the dive-brakes down, on a river, and neither of us was seriously injured. We tried to release the dinghy, but, as often happens, it wouldn't completely release. We then noticed two men coming toward us in a rowboat. We asked them where we were, but they did not understand English, but they did take us aboard and rowed to the shore.

Here we met the local Pastor, who informed us we were in Sweden. We had landed on the River Faxållven, outside Ramsele. He took us to his Parsonage where Swedish army officers then interrogated us individually. We stayed the first night there, then moved to the Grand Hotel in Ostersund. There, we met up with a Swordfish crew, also from *Furious*, who had also come down the same day. It was quite embarrassing to be in the best hotel in town, dressed in navy blue coveralls, white submarine sweater, flying boots, carrying a flying suit and helmet. We stayed there for a few days, having the run of the hotel for meals etc, and even went to the cinema, but were always accompanied by two Swedish soldiers with rifles (Our bills were paid by the British Legation).

Eventually, we were transported by train to Falun, then to the Internment Camp a few miles outside Falun, where I remained for 51 weeks, before suddenly being repatriated back to the UK. The Swordfish TAG, who was a New Zealander, and I became very good friends.[9]

Another strike was made on 28 September, while, on 3 October, the squadron attacked a ship off Bergen but the aircraft were bounced by five Bf109s and were lucky to escape.

The last missions flown were on 29 September, when a search was made for shipping off the Norwegian coast. Williams and Beardsley in L3023 reported 'Heavy flak, just made it back'.[10] Despite the continued attrition, the squadron was out again on 2 October, making an attack on assembled shipping at Haughesand, a 4 hour 20 minute mission, which proved their Norwegian swansong. Another loss was taken when the Bf109s struck again, this time shooting L2929 down in flames. The Skua came down in Bjourne Fiord and both crew members, Sub-Lieutenant A. Hartoch, and Naval Airman J. Adlam, were killed.

Tromsø attack

The aircraft carrier *Furious* sailed from Scapa Flow on 13 October 1940, to carry out a night strike against Tromsø. At 0430 hours on 16 October, eleven Swordfish TSRs from No. 821 Squadron, plus six of No. 801 Squadron's Skuas, were sent against the oil tanks and the seaplane base at Tromsø. The Skuas and crews included L2902 (Savage and Hayes), L2890 (Harrington and Crone) and L2930 (Lowe and Beckett), the last crew recording how they had flown out to the carrier on 11 October, a 45-minute flight.

The overall mission time was 3 hours 15 minutes for Lowe, but only 1 hour 55 minutes for Harrington. However, of this flight, only two Skuas returned to the carrier. The unit's Commanding Officer, Lieutenant E. G. Savage, with Lieutenant H. S. Hayes as his navigator, flying L2987, was forced by lack of fuel to ditch at Vassare Trask, Gallivarre. Although both men survived, they were captured by the Swedish army and interned for a year.

It later transpired that Savage's aircraft had released its bomb over the target area, but, for some unknown reason, perhaps because they had difficulty in finding their way back to the carrier, the decision was made to steer a course for neutral Sweden.

As soon as the Skua crossed the frontier, in the vicinity of the sensitive ore-mining village of Malmberget in the early hours of 17 October, the ever-alert Swedish anti-aircraft batteries started firing on her. They might have not known about Operation *Paul* and its ramifications, but as neutrals the Swedes were armed, vigilant and ready for attack from either side. Hayes and Savage tried to stop the shooting by firing off their Very lights, but in vain. The Skua eventually came down in the water in Lake Vassaratrask, close to Gallivare. Both crew members were able to launch their dinghy and paddle to the beach, where they were quickly picked up by a patrol of the Swedish army.

The two British aircrew were grilled by the local commandant, who then sent them under guard to Framby, where they were interned. However, this was of short duration and by December they had been repatriated to the UK. The aircraft itself had sunk in shallow water and was salvaged. The wreck was taken to the Royal Swedish air force base of

Fröson and stored there at the F4 facility. There it remained until late 1944, when it was put to scrap. The hulk was finally utilised for airborne gunnery target practice at the Ason Island range near Brynaset in the late 1940s, being shot up by J26 Mustang fighters from the *Flygvapnet's* F4 Wing.[11]

Voyage to Africa

The rest of October and early November at Hatston was spent in training. The weather in the far north was closing down and opportunities to strike at the enemy off Norway were proving more and more infrequent. So the usual round of formation flights, night landings, dive-bombings, drogue shooting, back seat firing, night-light fly-bys of *Furious* and R/T testing followed as grey day succeeded grey day.

A welcome change from this routine followed. On 6 November the squadron again embarked aboard *Furious* for the 'Southern Cruise', during which the men practised their dive-bombing skills against the escorting cruiser HMS *Dido*. By 27 November they reached Takoradi and the intense heat of Africa and carried out a patrol from the local airfield before re-embarking for the return voyage. On 21 December the Skuas conducted anti-submarine patrols, the first for many of the aircrews after a U-boat had been sighted in the vicinity. However, their searches were unrewarded. On Christmas Day there was little 'Peace on earth and Goodwill to all men' for the men of No. 801 Squadron as *Furious* was hauling her ancient hull through a full gale, with the deck rising and falling a full 40 to 50 feet as they tried to search for the German heavy cruiser *Admiral Hipper*.

Throughout early January the Skuas were employed daily on searches, reconnaissance and anti-submarine patrols in excellent visibility, before returning once more to Hatston.

On 27 December they made another unsuccessful attack on shipping off Norway.

On 5 January 1941 they attacked shipping off Norway, with two ships damaged. This was to prove to be the Skuas' final Norwegian mission and thus they ended their long wartime operational association with that country on a relative 'high'.

It was on 8 January that Harrington wrote off L3023 with a spectacular crash. Then, on 20 January the squadron moved down to the Coastal Command bases of St Eval and St Merryn in Cornwall.

Cornish interlude

Back under RAF control once more, the Skua aircrews found that nothing had changed to enlighten their new masters as to their proper role. As during the previous summer, most of their days were spent waiting to have a crack at the lurking German battle-cruisers *Scharnhorst* (their old foe) and *Gneisenau*, which were holed up in the French port of Brest after a commerce-raiding voyage. Plan after plan was made to try and disable these menaces, but the bad weather conditions thwarted every effort. Nor did their RAF superiors show any sign of enlightenment as to just what was, or was not, possible.

Captain Harrington recalled:

> Whilst on the subject of dive-bombing techniques, I have two incidents, which illustrate the problems. At RAF St Evel, waiting to have a go at the infamous 'Salmon and Gluck' pair of battle-cruisers holed up in Brest harbour, we were briefed to go in and attack them using 500 lb semi-armour piercing bombs. The conditions were very cloudy (cumulus) and it looked as though we would be lucky if we could even see them from above 7,000 to 10,000 feet.
>
> It was pointed out that we needed to make a dive-attack from a minimum height of 15,000 feet, with a dive angle of at least 70 degrees, and release these weapons at 7,000 feet. This was to achieve the right terminal velocity with the bombs in order to penetrate the targets' protective armour. An emotive hush greeted this technical dissertation! The RAF Group Captain was, for some reason, furious, and seemed to think it was a lot of technical nonsense – anyway our minimum figures were confirmed by Plymouth Naval Operations.
>
> Our CO and a few of the old hands volunteered to have a go in the hope that there might be some holes in the clouds, but this was turned down.[12]

Joe Beckett also confirmed this account:

> In January 1941, we were sent down to St Merryn to do a job on the German ships at Brest. Say no more. One brave man said he would not take his squadron in there and probably saved all our lives.
>
> We ended up attached to the RAF at St Eval doing convoy duty along the Bristol Channel (St Eval was only 5 minutes' flying time from St Merryn). Most of early 1941 was spent on convoying (did we ever get on with the RAF?).[13]

Captain Harrington continued:

> The opposite end of this story was an occasion when there was an invasion panic, and we were told by the local command to stand by to carry out some low-level attacks on a group of enemy transports, alleged to be making for the UK coast. The orders were to carry one 250 lb General Purpose Bomb with an instantaneous fuse and attack

at 100 feet. It would not take even a half-headed guy long to work out that such a trip would be a one-way one! When we suggested delayed fuses would be better, and thus avoid destroying ourselves as well as the enemy, much surprise was registered![14]

Instead, while they waited their fate, the Skuas carried out convoy protection missions (Scarecrows) and routine patrols, as a stormy February gave way to a blustery March. The poor visibility did not help with these roles either. On one occasion it took 2 hours even to find the convoy, and on arrival they were heavily fired on by all the ships they were supposed to be protecting. Night convoy patrols were also hazardous affairs, and Harrington had to make a forced landing at Cleve on the night of 20 March.

On 23 March the squadron made an attack on shipping at Alderney, in the Channel Islands. Some 4 days later Rating Pilot R. H. Williams and Petty Officer Baker in L2943 were part of a force that made a dive-bombing attack on shipping in 'Andalsnes', (the code name for Cherbourg), a 2-hour round trip.[15]

During April the squadron was but fitfully employed, spending its time on W/T exercises and formation flying, but No. 801 Squadron's days with the Skua were numbered. Joe Beckett recalled the end:

St Eval was bombed repeatedly at night and the aircraft suffered. The Skuas were pasted two or three times and finally could not muster enough aircraft to replenish the squadron.[16]

On 7 April they moved to Lee-on-Solent.
Beckett remembered:

Sent down to Lee-on-Solent – last entry in log Skua L2871, Pilot Lieutenant Briscoe, Test Flight 17th July 1941. Soon after this flight the tail fell off an aircraft and the CO was killed. I had flown 17 Skuas in all.[17]

On 19 April they flew to Yeovilton for night landing exercises. Harrington, with Lieutenant Wallace in the back seat, made his final Skua flight with L2895 on 20 April, when they flew back to Lee-on-Solent via Boscombe Down.

On 26 May the squadron was reduced to three aircraft to provide maintenance ratings for No. 800 Squadron. On the death of courageous Lieutenant (A) I. R. Sarel in a Skua flying accident at HMS *Heron*,[18] the new commanding officer became Lieutenant Commander (A) R. A. Brabner, MP, RNVR. However, it was not until 1 August that the squadron was fully re-equipped with twelve Sea Hurricane fighters, and moved to Skeabrae for fighter defence duties.

NOTES

1. Hatston was *not* the most popular of billets, and most notoriously primitive of all was the miserable Hut 9, where all officers of the rank Lieutenant and below, were confined.
2. Captain T. W. Harrington, DSC, RN, on 18 November 1985.
3. *Ibid.*
4. Dickie Rolph interview with the author, 21 July 1998.
5. Flying Log Book Lieutenant Commander Tom Harrington, RN.
6. Flying Log Book Lieutenant Commander R. H. Williams, RN.
7. Flying Log Book of R. H. Williams, MBE.
8. *Ibid.*
9. Kenneth R. King to the author on 17 February 1999.
10. *Ibid.*
11. According to Rolph Wegmann and Widfleldt Bo, *Making for Sweden. Part One – The Royal Air Force*, Air Research Publications, Walton-on-Thames, the aircrew comprised Lieutenant H. Hayes, and Lieutenant E. Graham. However, in Harrington's log book he recorded 'Savage & Hayes lost'.
12. Captain T. W. Harrington, DSO, RN to the author, 29 June 1977.
13. R. V. 'Joe' Beckett, letter to Dickie Rolph dated 7 September 1998 and made available to the author.
14. Captain T. W. Harrington, DSO, RN, to the author, 29 June 1977.
15. Flying Log Book of Lieutenant Commander R. H. Williams, MBE.
16. R. V. 'Joe' Beckett, letter to Dickie Rolph dated 7 September 1998 and made available to the author.
17. *Ibid.*
18. See Chapter 4.

12

WARMER CLIMES

We must retrace our steps back to the summer of 1940, to follow the fortunes of the Skua in combating Germany's friends, the collaborators of Vichy France and the boastful and posturing Fascist Italians, in both the Mediterranean and in West Africa.

Force H

The establishment of a special commander operating directly under the Admiralty, but based at Gibraltar where there was a flag officer already in place, was a clumsy arrangement. However, initially, with tact and give-and-take, the two Flag Officers, Vice-Admiral Sir James Somerville, commander of Force H and Vice-Admiral Sir Dudley North, Flag Officer Commanding, North Atlantic, managed to make it work reasonably well.

For the Skua, the battles in this period were conducted against the navies and air forces of the Vichy French and the Italians only. It was not until later that the *Luftwaffe* put in an appearance in the waters of the Middle Sea. After being directly pitted against the German Air Force in Norway and across the English Channel, the opposition the Skuas faced was certainly of a lesser calibre in many ways, but they were still heavily outclassed and totally outnumbered.

At the commencement of Mediterranean Operations in July 1940, No. 800 Squadron was led by her new commander, Lieutenant Richard M. Smeeton, RN, formerly of No. 804 Sea Gladiator Squadron,[1] with Lieutenant E. S. Carver as his chief navigator. The composition of No. 803 Squadron aboard the *Ark Royal* was as Table 23.

Mers-el-Kebir

The first Mediterranean operation that the Skuas were engaged in was the attempt to persuade the Vichy French fleet based at Mers-el-Kebir near Oran in Algeria, either to continue the fight against the Germans or neutralise their ships so that they would not fall into Hitler's hands. This called for delicate negotiations with the Vichy Admiral, Gensoul, who, in the event, refused all the alternatives offered to him.

Force H sailed from Gibraltar at 1600 hours on 2 July, to carry out Operation *Catapult*, with the *Hood, Valiant* and *Resolution, Ark Royal,*

Table 23   Composition of No. 803 Squadron Skuas *Ark Royal*, 3 July 1940

Commanding Officer Lieutenant (A) J. M. Bruen, RN
Senior Observer Lieutenant Godden, RN

Green Section	A	L2927	Lieutenant (A) J. M. Bruen, RN	Lieutenant Godden, RN
	B	L2997	Sub-Lieutenant (A) Brokensha, RN	Leading Airman Coston
	C	L2915	Petty Officer Riddler	Naval Airman Chatterley
Blue Section	F	L2953	Lieutenant Easton, RN	Sub-Lieutenant Gore-Langton, RN
	G	L2961	Midshipman Griffith, RN	Naval Airman Dooley
	H	L2996	Sub-Lieutenant Easton, RN	Naval Airman Irwin
Yellow Section	K	L2909	Lieutenant Peever, RN	Petty Officer Andrews
	L	L3017	Petty Officer Theobald	Naval Airman Defrais
	M	L2891	Petty Officer Glover	Naval Airman Burkey
Red Section	P	L2897	Lieutenant Gibson, RN	Sub-Lieutenant (A) Gordon-Smith, RN
	Q	L2874	Petty Officer Garmer	Naval Airman Pickering
	R	L2956	Petty Officer Peacock	Naval Airman Dearnley

light cruisers *Arethusa* and *Enterprise* and eleven destroyers. The French squadron comprised two new battle-cruisers, *Dunkerque* and *Strasbourg*, and two battleships, *Bretagne* and *Provence*, along with a seaplane carrier *Commandant Teste* and many large destroyers.

The next morning, off the French base, Force H went to action stations at 0845 hours; both reconnaissance Swordfish and Skua fighter patrols from No. 800 Squadron had been flown off the *Ark Royal* at 0600 hours. A second patrol from No. 803 Squadron relieved the first Skuas at 0930 hours. At 1050 hours the watching Swordfish reported that the Vichy squadron was raising steam. Other Swordfish laid mines across the harbour entrance, but negotiations continued. Blue section from No. 803 Squadron took off to conduct a fighter patrol at 1400 hours, Lieutenant Easton complaining that they were forced to operate at, 'the stupid height of 15,000 feet, where we obviously could not see any of the French aircraft beneath us'.[2] This group landed back aboard again at 1800 hours, at which time they first learned that the British heavy ships had been forced to open fire 6 minutes earlier. Force H fired at 17,500 yards range using spotter aircraft and within 10 minutes had blown up the *Bretagne*, and damaged the *Dunkerque*, *Provence* and *Commandant Teste*. Only the *Strasbourg* remained unscathed.

Somerville ceased fire at 1804 hours to give the French the chance to abandon their ships, but the Vichy shore batteries continued to engage and fighters swarmed up to drive the British aircraft away. In the skirmishing that followed two Skuas were lost, Petty Officer T. F. Riddler's aircraft spun into the sea during an engagement with the Vichy Curtiss Hawk 75A fighters and both he and his rear-seat man, Naval Airman H. T. Chatterly, were killed.[3] Riddler was observed to deploy his spin parachute, but went into the sea with it still deployed. A second Skua, that of Petty Officer H. A. Glover and Naval Airman J. A. Burkey, was forced to ditch due to a petrol blockage, but both aircrew were safely plucked from the sea by a destroyer. One Skua pilot later recorded:

> At Oran our squadron became entangled in dogfights with Dewoitine 520s. The Skua was no dog fighter and its spin recovery was doubtful, it being fitted with a spin recovery parachute. My section got involved in a fight with several Dewoitine 520s flown by very angry Frenchmen, and the matter was complicated by our instructions that we were not to fire at them unless they fired at us (rules of engagement so loved by politicians). On one occasion, anxious to rid myself of an infuriated Frenchman on my tail, I pulled hard back on the stick and the aircraft went into a spin at once, when I took a normal recovery action she came out almost immediately. My gallant observer, still Pat Gordon Smith, had his own pet K gun in the back and the Lewis gun, provided by the government, was stowed loose, but during the spin the Lewis gun had an argument with Pat, and on landing I was asked not to do it again.[4]

In return, a brace of Skuas from No. 800 Squadron, including the CO, shared the kill of a Vichy aircraft.[5] Sub-Lieutenant G. W. Brokensha with Leading Airman F. Coston, flying L2997, attacked and damaged a Breguet Bizerte flying boat. Meanwhile, the *Strasbourg* and her five escorting destroyers made a dash for it, aided by the fact that Force H had withdrawn down the coast. A striking force of Swordfish, with Skua escorts, was diverted to slow her down, but failed, as did a second TSR torpedo striking force.

There were still some Vichy ships aground but relatively unscathed and on the morning of 4 July, an aerial attack force of twelve Swordfish and nine Skuas was prepared to carry out attacks to finish these off. Blue section of No. 801 Squadron was at immediate notice from 0500 hours onward. There were several air raid warnings of approaching Vichy bombers, and twice the Skuas were ranged on *Ark Royal's* flight deck, only to be struck down again. Meanwhile, due to the weather over the target area, the planned British air attack was aborted. Blue section finally got airborne at 1300 hours and spent 1 hour and 40 minutes on patrol over the fleet, 'looking for what must have been an imaginary shadowing aircraft', while the rest of the squadron practised dive-bombing. The *Ark Royal* finally berthed back at Gibraltar at 1645 hours.

Table 24   Fighter patrols Mers-el-Kebir, 6 July 1940

L2961	G	Midshipman (A) A. S. Griffith, RN	Naval Airman A. F. Dooley
L2956	B	Petty Officer (A) G. W. Peacock	Leading Airman B. P. Dearnley
L2897	P	Lieutenant J. M. Charlton, RN	Sub-Lieutenant A. H. S. Gore-Langton, RN
L2953	P	Sub-Lieutenant (A) M. P. Gordon-Smith, RN	Lieutenant D. C. Gibson, RN

Force H, less *Resolution*, sailed once more on the evening of 5 July. The *Dunkerque*, which had been beached, was to be attacked by the Swordfish to make sure she was totally disabled. This was Operation *Lever*. By 0600 hours the next day Blue and Red sections of No. 801 Squadron took off to mount a fighter patrol to protect three waves of Swordfish TSRs, which attacked the stranded French battle-cruiser. The Skuas crossed the Algerian coast at 10,000 feet and were at once met by hordes of defending Vichy fighter aircraft, mostly Moraine-Saulniers (MS410), with a few American-built Curtiss H75s from GV II/5 and some Dewotines D520s.

Midshipman (A) A. S. Griffith, RN, flying L2961 (G) with Naval Airman A. F. Dooley as his air-gunner, gave this graphic description of the battle:

> My section broke up and I attacked a flight of three Moraines about to attack one of the Swordfish and succeeded in attracting their attention. Fired two short bursts at one from about 200 yards and it left the flight. The other two were joined by four more fighters and as things were then so hopeless I had to dive into a layer of thin cloud at 1,500 feet and escape seawards. Four aircraft pursued me for 40 minutes, three above the clouds and one below, so that at the end of that time my position was uncertain and after endeavouring to find the carrier by 'Square Search' Dooley obtained a D/F bearing and we were able to reach the ship with 30 gallons of petrol in our tanks after being in the air for 5 hours.[6]

Griffith also noted in his official report that 'French fighters appeared to be holding their fire'.[7]

Tough as it was, many of the Skua pilots involved, recorded the impression that many of the French pilots did not have their hearts in the job. This seemed to apply particularly to *L' Armée de la Air* pilots; the Vichy naval pilots were very different, reflecting the bitter and virulent anti-British attitude of their senior officers, and eager to kill. The air force aircrew seemed much more reluctant to make the best of their superiority.

Petty Officer (A) G. W. Peacock, flying L2956 (L) with Leading Airman B. P. Dearnley, who tangled with the naval airmen, commented: 'The Curtiss appeared to work in pairs. Quickly outurned Skua, one in rear, one above diving down. Holes in tailplane, holes and rent in rudder, large rent in fuselage.'[8]

These gentlemen obviously meant business. Sub-Lieutenant (A) M. P. Gordon-Smith with Lieutenant D. C. Gibson, in Skua L2897 (P), by contrast wrote: 'Dog-fight 30 minutes, own aircraft spun three times. French did not appear to put their heart into the fight.'[9]

A similar viewpoint was expressed by Lieutenant J. M. Churston, RN, flying L2953 (A) with Sub-Lieutenant A. H. S. Gore-Langton as his observer:

Enemy in every case seemed unwilling to engage our aircraft closely. Many situations arose when, due to vastly superior performance, the enemy could have inflicted casualties but reluctant to do so.[10]

On the combat front Petty Officer (A) G. W. Peacock, with Leading Airman B. P. Dooley as his air gunner in L2956 (R), observed: 'Curtiss Hawk seems to have blind spot 30 degrees forward.'[11]

Finally, Lieutenant I. R. Easton, leading Blue section from L2996 (H), with Naval Airman J. A. Irwin as his air gunner, left this blisteringly honest comment on the French fighter attack on himself, during a very uneven engagement. 'Enemy did not fire or often fired wide. If he had been trying, he could not have helped shooting Skua down.'[12]

None of the Swordfish was lost in the attack, which was estimated at the time to have scored six hits on the *Dunkerque*.[13] However, another Skua, piloted by Petty Officer G. W. Peacock and Naval Airman B. P. Dearnley, yet again a No. 803 Squadron machine, came down in the water, but, again, the crew were rescued. This reduced the unit's strength to just nine and the squadron had to be reorganised (as shown in Table 25).

No. 800 Squadron added to the tally, when Lieutenant Richard M. Smeeton, with Lieutenant E. S. Carver as his observer, leading Green

Table 25   Rearrangement of No. 803 Squadron Skuas *Ark Royal*, 8 July 1940

Green Section	A	L2927	Lieutenant Bruen, RN	Lieutenant Godden, RN
	B	L2997	Sub-Lieutenant (A) Brockensha, RN	Leading Airman Coston
		L2909	Lieutenant Peever, RN	Petty Officer Andrews
Blue Section	F	L2953	Lieutenant Christian, RN	Sub-Lieutenant Gore-Langton, RN
	G	L2961	Midshipman (A) Griffith, RN	Naval Airman Dooley
	H	L2996	Midshipman (A) Easton, RN	Naval Airman Irwin
Red Section	P	L2897	Lieutenant Gibson, RN	Sub-Lieutenant (A) Gordon-Smith, RN
	Q	L2874	Petty Officer Garner	Naval Airman Pickering
		L2956	Petty Officer Theobald	Naval Airman Defrais

section, shot down a Vichy flying boat. Not everything went our way, as Dickie Rolph recalled:

> I was there in 800 NAS flying protection patrols over the *Ark* and three battleships: French Dewoitine 502s were put up against us and at least one Skua (Petty Officer Pilot Riddler) was shot down by them.[14]

Force H returned to Gibraltar by 1615 hours, and at 1800 hours a large number of the young pilots, from both Swordfish and Skuas, were assembled in the stateroom and related their individual experiences to Admiral Somerville. He made a conscious effort to relate to his naval airmen and to try and understand their viewpoint on operations. Although not an airman himself, Admiral Somerville showed them the same empathy he did the crews of the little destroyers of the 8th flotilla, who were to be equally as hard worked in the months ahead.

The Regia Aeronautica

Force H again left Gibraltar at full strength on 8 July. The main aim of the operation was to draw some fire from Admiral Cunningham's main fleet operating from Alexandria in the eastern basin, by launching air attacks on the Italian naval base of Cagliari on the south-west tip of Sardinia, which had two neighbouring airfields, Elmas and Monserrato. Captain Cedric S. 'Dutchy' Holland of *Ark Royal* broadcast to the ship at 1215 hours outlining the plan.[15] The aim was to launch the TSRs in two sections from a position about 100 miles west of the target at dusk on 10 July to achieve surprise.

Force H proved most successful in the role of lure. Throughout the afternoon of 9 July Force H was attacked by wave after wave of Savoia-Marchetti SM79 *Spaverio* tri-motored bombers of the *Regia Aeronautica*, seventy-nine in total, formation-bombing the fleet from between 10,000 and 13,000 feet in tight patterns. This was the classic method adopted by the land-based air forces of the major powers as an article of faith, but, although accurate and awe-inspiring, very rarely scored any direct hits as the time of flight of the bombs was sufficient for the ships to take avoiding action. Nonetheless, it was sufficient to intimidate Somerville, who aborted the operation. Cunningham suffered even heavier attacks in the east, but held on and was rewarded with the sight of the Italian fleet, which he engaged and put to flight at the Battle of Calabria.[16]

The Skuas' part in this operation was pivotal. Throughout 8 July, Red section of No. 803 Squadron had been on stand-by for fighter patrols, but were not called upon. However, the following day was a very different story.

The day included one of the standing patrols of Skuas, Yellow section from No. 800 Squadron, sighting and pursuing an Italian seaplane reconnaissance aircraft. This was at 1530 hours, in position 39° 42′ North, 06° 20′ East. The section (A6A – Lieutenant R. M. Smeeton/Lieutenant E. S. Carver; A6B – Sub-Lieutenant M. F. Fell/Naval Airman D. H. Lowndes; and A6C – Petty Officer (A) A. W. Sabey/Leading Airman J. Coles) had been airborne at 1330 hours and were patrolling at 12,000 feet. While in a position 20° 060′ from Force H, Petty Officer Sabey sighted an aircraft, about 3 miles away to starboard at the same height. Lieutenant Smeeton formed the Skuas into line ahead and set off in pursuit. Their prey, having sighted them in its turn, had turned away immediately and began retiring on a course of 060°.

The chase was a long one; it took 30 minutes to overhaul her, but eventually the snooper, recognised as a Cant Z506B floatplane, was within range. Smeeton reported that she had Italian National markings on her rudder, with the white circles with three fascias on the upper surface of the mainplane and that her mainplanes had dull red camouflage dope on the upper surface, the remainder of the aircraft being uncamouflaged. The Cant was armed with two rear guns, one above and one below the fuselage and both sides opened fire when the range had come down to 800 yards, the Italian firing a good deal of tracer. Smeeton replied with short, 2-second bursts, 'In the hope of a lucky hit and slowing him down'. Then the section fired in turn, each aircraft remaining in the firing position astern long enough to fire off most of their ammunition. After a second attack by his two wingmen, the Cant went into a 30-degree dive and Petty Officer Sabey closed down to within 100 yards and got in a second short attack from astern.

The Italian seaplane dived to sea level and alighted with all airscrews stopped at the end of her run. The three Skuas circled above and one of his gunners let off a defiant burst of fire at Sub-Lieutenant Fell's aircraft. The Skuas re-engaged with both rear and front guns, which soon brought this misplaced bravado to a halt. One of the Italians appeared and waved a white cloth, as the Cant drifted, leaving a long trail of oil behind her. After 5 minutes, with fuel running low, the Skuas left their victim and returned to the *Ark Royal*, finally landing aboard at 1710 hours.[17]

Fighter duel

Meanwhile, three Skuas had tangled with an equal number of Fiat Cr42 biplane fighters, some 40 miles south-east of Cagliari. These agile little single-seater fighters were extremely manoeuvrable and formidable opponents. The Skua was no dog-fighter and the men were lucky to survive the encounter.

At 1530 hours, a two-machine patrol from Red section of No. 800 Squadron, had been reduced to one when the guns of one Skua 'froze', causing her to abort and return to the carrier. The solitary Skua was F, piloted by Lieutenant Rooper, RN, with Sub-Lieutenant (A) Woolston, RN, as his observer. This aircraft was at 12,000 feet, with clear weather conditions but a layer of cloud 1,000 feet above, and was fortunately joined by Green section, which had been reduced from three aircraft to just two due to the same problem. These were Lieutenant K. Spurway, RN/Petty Officer (A) Hart (K); and Petty Officer (A) Burston/Leading Airman Holmes (M).

Rooper's report of what happened next read:

We received an RDF report, and as a result, sighted a formation of three Fiat C.R. 42s, 10 miles from the Fleet and coming straight towards us. Green Leader attacked from head on; the enemy then pulled up in a spectacular 'Prince of Wales Feathers'. The centre Fiat continued in an upward roll and, as he was just about to stall-turn off the top, I got in a 3-second, no-deflection burst. I believe the enemy was hit – a small puff of smoke was observed from the fuselage, but this may have been caused by the pilot opening the throttle. By this time the other two aircraft had come round, one onto each quarter. I turned to port and carried out a beam attack on the No. 2 Fiat, firing a 2-second burst, range about 200 yards. By this time the other two enemy were out of sight behind me, so I half rolled. When I pulled out I found another Fiat in front and above me. He was on the tail of Green 3. I carried out a stern attack, firing a 2-second burst. He then turned violently away. I then broke away and rejoined the other two Skuas over the fleet. Enemy made no attempt to follow.[18]

He added, 'Sometime during the course of the engagement my Observer had cause to fire his Lewis gun. A stoppage occurred after one round'.

Lieutenant Spurway gave his viewpoint of the same encounter:

While on patrol over the fleet, Green and Red sections of 800 Squadron, reduced to three aircraft in all, due to gun freezing in the two other aircraft, were ordered to proceed to intercept enemy aircraft some 15 miles from the fleet. On approaching the position, Green Leader was forced by cloud to descend from 16,000 feet to approximately 13,000 feet and, on coming beneath the cloud, sighted a formation of three CR 42s about 500 feet below and on a reciprocal course to our aircraft. They were then too close for our aircraft to turn and carry out a stern attack, and probably saw our aircraft at about the same time as we sighted them.

Aircraft 6K therefore dived to carry out a head-on attack on the Leader, a manoeuvre which was helped by the enemy pulling up to meet him. The pilot fired a 2-second burst and passed just over the top of the Fiat, which carried out a 'Prince of Wales Feathers' and came round to attack from the rear. 6F got in a good burst at the Fiat Leader as he pulled up astern of 6K, and also at another. It is possible that the enemy leader was hit. Aircraft 6M was unable to get his sights on.

The enemy aircraft, after breaking formation, were on the Skuas' tails very quickly, and they were both more manoeuvrable and faster than our aircraft, in addition to climbing better, the engagement was broken off and our aircraft dived away. The enemy climbed away and did not attempt to continue.[19]

Chasing the bombers

Before she had gone down the Cant had obviously radioed in her sighting reports. Around 1830 hours that evening, with the fleet about 200 miles west of Sardinia, the Italian bombers began appearing in waves.

Between 1815 and 1835 hours, No. 803 Squadron's Red section (Lieutenant D. C. Gibson, RN/ Sub-Lieutenant M. P. Gordon-Smith, RN (A7P); Petty Officer (A) J. A Gardner/Naval Airman H. Pickering (A7Q); Petty Officer (A) A. W. Theobald/Naval Airman F. J. L. Defrias (A7L)), were heavily engaged against a formation of eleven Savoia S79, three-engined bombers. The bombers were camouflaged light brown and greenish-khaki, with green, white and red vertical stripes on their rudders. Although the weather was fine and clear, with no cloud, these aircraft were not sighted until on their final run in against the fleet in immaculate formation. Gibson's report described the Italian formation as:

Eleven aircraft flying in three sub flights in line abeam, stepped up from Port to Starboard, and one sub flight about a mile astern and above. Red section approached from ahead and attacked the left-hand sub flight from abeam. Red Leader turned too sharply and spun and when he recovered he attacked behind 'Q' and 'L'. All fired on left-hand aircraft of enemy formation, Leader expending all his ammunition. This aircraft jettisoned his bombs and all the remainder of his formation did the same. The rear enemy sub flight dived on Skuas, firing with front guns, and were engaged by 'Q' who chased them for 10 minutes. After attacking the left hand sub flight 'L' broke away downwards and pulled up under the centre sub flight, firing at the left hand aircraft, which broke away in a quick dive. 'L' broke away across the front of the sub flight and the rear gunner fired at the nose of the sub flight leader at 50 yards range. This aircraft went into a steep dive and one of the crew escaped in a parachute.[20]

As well as this one confirmed victory, another Sm79 was seen to fall out of formation, but not to go down. Both Gibson and Garner fired off all 2,400 rounds, while Theobald, who got very close and was affected by the slipstream, only got off half that amount. All were using the GMII sight-aligned Point at 250 yards. Defrais scored the fatal hits with his rear gun, finally bringing down the bomber, having expended 200 rounds.

Blue section (Lieutenant J. M. Christian, RN/ Sub-Lieutenant A. H. S. Gore-Langton, RN (A7F); Sub-Lieutenant I. Easton, RN/ Naval Airman J. A. Irwin (A7H); Midshipman (A) A. S. Griffith, RN/ Naval Airman F. P. Dooley (A7G)) took off at 1630 hours, with orders to proceed to 10,000 feet and remain in the vicinity of the fleet, closing *Ark Royal* at hourly intervals to report. It took the Skuas 10 minutes to climb to the desired altitude. The weather was clear, with extreme visibility, except into the sun.

At 1830 hours, Lieutenant Christian engaged a straggler from a group of four Savoia Sm79s in a quarter attack from 500 yards range. It soon developed into a stern chase, with the Skua steadily losing ground. The Italian tri-motor bombers simply maintained a straight shallow dive, keeping the formation in the main and returning fire from a single rear-facing gun mounted atop the fuselage. Christian gave his target a short burst, followed by two long bursts, firing some 2,400 rounds into her, before the enemy drew out of range. The Italian rear gunner soon ceased firing, and bits of the Savoia's tail could be seen falling away, but it did not seem to handicap her or reduce her speed.[21]

Over the fleet, young Midshipman Griffith described events as he saw them that afternoon thus:

> At 1630 Blue section was ranged at the 'stand by' and we were sitting idly in our cockpits when twin-engined enemy aircraft were observed overhead. How on earth they reached that position unnoticed is hard to say, but to grant all due credit,[22] before the first bomb had reached the sea, astern of the *Ark Royal*, the whole fleet AA armament had opened fire. I can remember starting up my engine with rather unsteady hands, listening for the sound of the bombs as they fell. We were quickly off the deck and climbed straight to 10,000 feet and once patrolling up there, we were able to assure ourselves that the fleet was unscathed. An uneventful hour passed before the main bombing force arrived and then it proved an awe-inspiring sight. I attacked one of a group of eight bombers and pursued it until, with [its] port engine stopped and flying unsteadily, I gave up the chase, leaving it in such a condition that it could never reach the coast. All my ammunition was expended and Dooley in the back had emptied the Lewis. On returning to the *Ark Royal* it was learned that the Skuas had shot down one bomber, badly damaged four and damaged three.[23]

Lieutenant I. Easton, with Naval Airman J. A. Irwin, flying as A7H, was also in action at 1825 hours, taking on a formation of eight Fiat heavy bombers at 10,000 feet. He attacked this bunch from astern and from below, opening fire at 300 yards with a 4-second burst. Easton fired off about 1,000 rounds, but the enemy was disdainful, and made no attempt to return fire. Having released their bombs in a tight pattern on the fleet, the bombers went into a shallow dive and simply left the Skua standing.[24]

Midshipman Griffith also attacked the same group, which he found at 12,000 feet. He made a stern attack, opening fire at 300 yards, with a 2-second burst, but got so close that the slipstream from his target put his aim off. He said three of the Italians jettisoned their bombs, but did not fire back. Using the GMII sight he fired some 1,900 rounds, and observed that the port wing engine of his target had stopped. When he had expended all his front gun ammunition, Griffith 'turned over top of enemy aircraft', enabling Air Gunner Dooley to contribute a further 125 rounds (one whole pan) at 300 yards. When last seen, this bomber appeared to be losing height and out of action.[25]

Blue section was in action again at 1905 hours. This time Lieutenant Easton closed a formation of eight Sm79s at 13,000 feet, developing a beam attack against one of a section of three. Again, the Skua closed to within 400 yards and opened fire with 5-second bursts, closing down to within 200 yards, before the enemy, again keeping immaculate formation, sped away at a speed the Skua could not match. The enemy replied at 250 yards range, firing explosive shells that made white puffs as they exploded ahead of the Skua, the enemy (understandably) over-estimating the speed of the pursuing machine.

Proposed attack on Bordeaux

On 23 July the *Ark Royal*, escorted by the light cruiser *Enterprise* and four destroyers, was despatched from Gibraltar to conduct a mission in the Bay of Biscay. Captain Holland announced to the ship's company that some large transports had assembled at the French port of Bordeaux and in the neighbouring Le Verdun Roads. The Admiralty feared these might be used by the Germans as troop transports preparing for the invasion of England, and ordered them sunk by pre-emptive air attack. Both the TSRs and the Skuas in their dive-bomber role were to be used. During 24 July two sections of Skuas from No. 800 Squadron took off to practise their dive-bombing skills in preparation for the strike. No. 803 Squadron was to be held for fighter defence, and the reasoning for this was as follows. The distance from Gibraltar to the target was 1,100 miles, which was only just within reach of the escorting destroyers. Once the strike had been made, therefore, the British force would, perforce, have no option due to fuel constraints, but to withdraw along its exact same track, which

would make its detection by any retaliatory *Luftwaffe* action comparatively easy. It was therefore expected the Skuas might see heavy action
against first-class opposition.

On 25 July it was the turn of No. 803 Squadron to practise fighter and
dive-bomber manoeuvres. Blue and Red sections stood by from 0600
hours for this, but they were not flown off until 2 hours later. One Skua,
piloted by Petty Officer J. A. Gardner, smashed its tail unit on a deck
projection while spotting. It was unable to take off and had to be struck
down for repair. Although Blue section carried out some practice dive-
bombing off the *Ark Royal*, persistent low cloud ruined the exercise. This
was followed by machine-gun practice and some cloud formation flying,
during which they lost Force H for about an hour! No. 800 Squadron's
Skuas then flew off and conducted similar practice, and then the remaining units of the squadron followed suit. Several Skuas experienced gun
failure, which was found to be due to defective 1938 ammunition.

In the end it was all to no avail, as the Admiralty cancelled the operation. More recent intelligence had revealed that there was no significant
assembly of transports off Bordeaux after all, and the force returned to
the Rock on 27 July.

NOTES

1. Lieutenant Richard Michael Smeeton had taken over command of No. 800 Squadron in June, just prior to her departure from Scapa Flow, as part of replenishment following the heavy casualties of the Trondheim attack. He served a year in this position, leaving the squadron in May 1941. After a distinguished career during which he rose to the rank of Vice-Admiral, Smeeton died on 29 March 1992.
2. Diary of Midshipman Griffith, RN, No. 803 Squadron, handwritten copy in author's collection (hereafter cited as Griffith Diary).
3. *Ibid.*
4. *Haul Taut and Belay, op cit.*
5. Assertions in the *Squadron Histories (1), 800 Naval Air Squadron*, that while flying, '... against the Vichy French at Oran, the squadron, in conjunction with 830 Squadron, shot down two Italian bombers', are totally incorrect. There were no Italian aircraft at Oran.
6. Griffith Diary*, op cit.*
7. Combat report extracts for No. 803 Squadron, *Mers-el-Kebir Action*, dated 6 July 1940 (contained in National Archives ADM/166).
8. *Ibid.*
9. *Ibid.*
10. *Ibid.*
11. *Ibid.*
12. *Ibid.* Not all the Vichy airmen were well disposed to the British fleet, however. Ron Jordan aboard the *Ark Royal* clearly remembers one Frenchman getting close enough to spray the carrier's flight deck with machine-gun fire!
13. In fact, although both the *Dunkerque* and the tug *Estérel* were badly damaged, the full brunt of the attack was borne by the 780-ton auxiliary *Terre Neuve*, which took four hits and disintegrated.

14. See *The Society of Friends of the Fleet Air Arm Museum, Newsletter No. 49*, January 1997, p 13. Copy presented to the author by R. S. Rolph, BEM.

15. Holland had been the British Naval Attaché in Paris before the war, and therefore knew both the Vichy fleet commander, Admiral Marco-Bruno Gensoul, and his irascible chief, Admiral of the Fleet Jean Darlan, well, which is why he was chosen to conduct the parley. However, his close association with the French brought with it not just friendship but sentiment, and Admiral Sir Dudley Pound, the First Sea Lord, thought it 'flawed' his judgement.

16. For a detailed account of the establishment of Force H, the battles of Calabria and Spartivento and the escape of the French cruisers ('The North Affair'), see Peter C. Smith, *Action Imminent*, William Kimber, London, 1980.

17. Smeeton's combat report, dated 10 July 1940 (contained in National Archives ADM 199/115). The Skuas had fired off 2,400, 1,815 and 1,800 rounds respectively from their forward guns (with their GMII sights aligned Point at 300 yards) and 194, 20 and 97 rounds from their Lewis guns aft. The Italian aircrew were *Capitano* Domenico Oliva and his radio operator from 287° *Squadriglia* R M.

18. Rooper's combat report, *ibid.*

19. Spurway's combat report, *ibid*

20. Gibson's combat report, *ibid.*

21. Christian's combat report, 12 July 1940 (contained in National Archives ADM 199/115).

22. The battleship *Valiant* was equipped with Type 279 air-warning radar at this time, but for some reason it did not always detect incoming attacks on this day.

23. Griffith Diary, *op cit.*

24. Easton's combat report (ADM 199/155 *op cit*).

25. Griffith's combat report, *ibid.*

13

LAST MISSIONS

Force H, under Vice-Admiral Somerville's inspired leadership, had now become a well-honed and efficient fighting force, considering itself an elite unit. Prodded by the ever-impatient Premier at home, who did not seem to realise just how much was being asked of the same few ships and aircraft, the Skuas were active in both the western Mediterranean and the North Atlantic, running almost non-stop. One special facet that developed at this period was the use of aircraft carriers to fly off reinforcing Hurricane fighter aircraft to Malta. This tactic had been pioneered off Norway by the fleet, and now became part-and-parcel of the constant fight to keep that island base in the fight. The Skuas played a dual role in this, both as protectors as part of the fleet escorting the carriers to their flying-off positions to the south-east of Sardinia, and as 'pathfinders', using the navigators to help guide the single-engine fighters long distances though the hostile skies of the central Mediterranean.

The first 'club run'

As a close-knit and independent squadron, Force H soon developed its own sense of *camaraderie*. Constantly on call for operations against both Axis partners in both the western Mediterranaean and Atlantic, both north and south, Somerville's command rightly considered itself a special force. The Force H 'Club' became part-and-parcel of the mythos of an elite defying the odds. It even had a mythical Club Tie, 'Mediterranean Grey with a pattern of Raspberries', allusions to the weather conditions and the total lack of thanks the men received for dirty jobs well carried out. Among the routine operations that became part-and-parcel of Force H's work, and over which the Skuas acted as protectors, striking force and guides, which included fleet operations, bombardments, fighting convoys through to Malta and the like, were escorting old aircraft carriers laden with RAF fighter aircraft, initially Hurricanes and later Spitfires, through the western basin to flying off positions for Malta. The first such operation took place on 31 July, Operation *Hurry*.

The aircraft carrier *Argus* had twelve Hawker Hurricanes embarked, destined for Malta. They were to be flown off some 500 miles west of that beleaguered island, and because they were single-seater, short-range interceptors, the navigation was to be in the hands of two Skuas, which were to guide them safely through. As a diversion, the *Ark Royal* was finally to carry out the earlier planned air attack on Cagliari at night.

By 1 August the whole fleet, *Hood, Valiant, Resolution, Ark Royal, Argus,* light cruisers *Arethusa, Enterprise* and ten destroyers were south of Majorca heading east on course 060° at 15 knots. A force of nine Skuas was flown off from 0515 hours[1] to provide escort for the return strike of TSRs that had hit Cagliari. As usual, other Skuas were assigned to fighter patrols and were stood by on deck from an early hour and managed to badly damage one enemy shadower. On return of the striking forces, six Skuas were flown off after noon, when Green section of No. 803 Squadron commenced their vigil over the fleet at 15,000 feet. The two squadrons alternated in keeping Skuas aloft and overlapping at all times, keeping three Skuas above and three to the rear of the withdrawing fleet. For No. 803 Squadron's part, Blue section replaced Green section at 1414 hours. After 2 hours without any sight of the enemy, they landed back aboard to refuel and Red section took over.

In the event, the Italian Sm79s arrived late in the afternoon in two distinct attacks, from 1815 hours onward. They were met by heavy AA fire, which forced many to turn away without dropping their bombs. Those few that did press on again dropped heavy bombs 'uncomfortably close', but once more the whole fleet came through without a scratch. One Skua pilot, Donald Gibson, recalled:

> In our time most of the air opposition was Italian and we had many combats with Italian bombers and reconnaissance aircraft, but even though we were flying Blackburn Skuas we had the measure of them and many brave Italian airmen were killed, and so were some of our people. With some remarkable exceptions, such as the occasion when every aircraft of a large Italian formation jettisoned their bombs when attacked by Petty Officer Theobald and me, the Italian Air Force showed great bravery and determination, achieving spectacular near misses on HMS *Hood* and *Ark Royal.*[2]

At dusk the fleet split up, *Valiant, Resolution, Arethusa* and *Argus* with three destroyers, continuing to the launch position, while *Hood, Ark Royal, Enterprise* and seven destroyers stood closer to Sardinia. During the night, while the cruiser was later detached to make diversionary signals, the main force moved to about 150 miles south of Sardinia, and the TSR striking force of nine Swordfish began to take off. One of these, piloted by Lieutenant (A) Robins, RN, crashed over the starboard side of the carrier while taking off in the dark. One of its bombs exploded on striking the water and, although the destroyer *Forester* made a careful search, no survivors were found. The remaining eight Swordfish duly bombed Elmas and laid mines in the Cagliari harbour entrance, but lost another machine, piloted by Lieutenant Humphries, RN, which had to force-land ashore.

Meanwhile, the *Argus* flew off the Hurricane fighters in two sections of six aircraft, each led by their faithful Skua. Although the promised RAF Sunderlands failed to turn up, both groups successfully made their way through to Malta without incident.Both formations then re-formed and fully expected to be bombed all day long. Nos 800 and 803 Squadrons again maintained continuous air patrols over the fleet at 14,000 feet, each section having two periods of 3½ hours duration on this duty. But there were no heavy attacks, which they put down to either the damage done by the night air attacks on the Italian base or that the enemy was searching for them further east, expecting them to be moving toward Malta still, when they had, in fact, reversed course.

Nonetheless, the Skuas saw some limited action. Lieutenant K. V. V. Spurway[3] leading Blue section of No. 800 Squadron (Lieutenant Smeeton/ Lieutenant Carver; Lieutenant Spurway/Petty Officer (A) R. F. Hart; Sub-Lieutenant Fell/Naval Airman Lowndes; Sub-Lieutenant B. H. Hurle-Hobbs/Leading Airman E. E. Bell and Petty Officer (A) L. E. Burston/Naval Airman R. H. Holmes) shot down in flames a shadowing Cant Z501 *Gabbiano* seaplane in the late afternoon.[4] Lieutenant G. R. Callingham, RN,[5] with another section of No. 800 Squadron (Lieutenant G. R. Callingham/Midshipman H. Morris; Midshipman R. W. Kearsley/ Leading Airman L. V. Eccleshall and Petty Officer (A) W. J. Heard/Naval Airman Hills) destroyed a Cant Z506B *Airone* shadower.[6] Also, Blue section of No. 803 Squadron engaged a lone Italian bomber that flew over the ship at about 17,000 feet, opening fire at long range and driving it away without it being able to drop any bombs. The Skuas took damage also, Lieutenant Christian, No. 803 Squadron's Blue section leader, crashed into the *Ark Royal's* superstructure while landing, and completely wrecked his machine.

On the way back to the Rock on 3 August, the force was again surprised, an enemy flying boat passing about 5 miles astern of *Ark Royal*, but it was far away before the standing section of Skuas was tardily accelerated off the deck in pursuit and it escaped scot-free. The Admiralty sent Somerville their congratulations at the success of the mission. They also recalled him to London for further consultation of Force H's mission and several of the ships of the force were due to be replaced.[7]

Excursions and exercises

The *Ark Royal,* escorted by the cruiser *Enterprise* and five destroyers, remained at Gibraltar. She sailed again on 25 August, to meet the ships from home waters, and took the opportunity to conduct flying exercises the following day. Three Skuas from No. 800 Squadron were flown off the carrier and sent back to land on the racecourse, which formed the only airstrip the fortress possessed. No. 803 Squadron, now just seven Skuas strong, was on stand-by to fly from 0745 hours. They were to attempt to intercept an incoming high-level attack mounted by nine Swordfish, which were flown off at 0830 hours. In this they were only partially successful. Next, they rallied to practise dive-bombing. This was done in line astern formation, but Midshipman Griffith recorded that this was considered by many of the young pilots to be 'a fatal disposition for a squadron, as proved in the Trondheim raid of the 13th June'. He added, 'I hope that we will be able to practise section bombing instead'. However, the exercise concluded at about 1300 hours that day without this being done.

The following day they rendezvoused with the incoming ships. As the *Illustrious* was carrying two squadrons of Fairey Fulmar fighters,[8] the opportunity was taken for combined exercises on the lines of the previous day, but with more aircraft involved and with the radar bearings of the 'attackers' being passed to the defending fighters by W/T. This much improved interception rates, although some pilots were perhaps too enthusiastic, Griffith himself reporting that his windscreen was cracked by an aerial trailing from one of the Swordfish he attacked!

Operation Hats

The next major movement in which the Skuas took part in the Mediterranean proved to be a big disappointment. Between 30 August and 3 September, Force H (now comprising *Renown*, *Ark Royal*, *Sheffield* and twelve destroyers), accompanied reinforcements for the Mediterranean Fleet, *Valiant*, the new aircraft carrier *Illustrious*, anti-aircraft cruisers *Calcutta* and *Coventry* and five destroyers, on their passage through the western Mediterranean, laying on two further air attacks on Elmas airfield and Cagliari on the night of 1 September. Due to the heavy anti-aircraft capability of the force, the inclusion of two fleet aircraft carriers and four radar-equipped ships,[9] enemy air attack was welcomed in the hope that heavy casualties could be inflicted. In readiness, the fleet maintained two fighter patrols of six aircraft each all day, but the Italians refused to take the bait.[10]

Lieutenant Gibson, DSC, and Midshipman Griffith amused themselves 'playing round huge columns of cumulous cloud, much to the consternation of the fleet gunners who twice opened fire upon us'.

Lieutenant (A) K. V. V. Spurway, DSC, of No. 800 Squadron was aloft at 1240 hours leading his section on fighter patrol, when he was ordered by the *Ark Royal* to intercept a shadower picked up on the radar. The Skuas set off in pursuit at 10,000 feet, and 8 minutes later, some 25 miles off the fleet's starboard bow, had closed sufficiently to identify an Italian Cant Z506B floatplane. The chase lasted some 55 miles, but Spurway finally managed to get in a single 2-second burst from his Brownings, which sufficed to do the job. The Cant immediately caught fire, then broke up in the air, two of the doomed aircraft's crew baling out on one parachute.[11]

This feat was then matched by No. 803 Squadron when Lieutenant (A) J. M. Bruen, leading Green section, was also homed onto and, at 1640 hours, eventually shot down a second floatplane, during his first engagement. '... the wreckage burnt so fiercely that it was seen from the Fleet.'[12] The Skuas performed well, particularly as the new Fulmars from *Illustrious* were totally unsuccessful.

All day they waited for the enemy, which did not appear. Lieutenant Gibson and Midshipman Griffith took off on patrol at 0745 hours but, 'search as we might amongst the rose-tinted early morning clouds we could not find a single enemy shadower'. A section of Fulmars was also up at 12,000 feet. The Skuas landed back at 1030 hours, being photographed by news cameraman Roy Kollino as they touched down. It proved a most difficult landing, up-sun, and Gibson had to go round again. He queried the wave-off and was told he would, in theory, have wrecked himself on the imaginary barrier, to which he replied immediately, he had not imagined that the imaginary barrier was there![13] By 3 September Force H was back at Gibraltar.

Dakar

Meanwhile, back in London a plan, Operation *Menace*, had been hatched for General de Gaulle to hoist the Free French standard in the French West African colony of Senegal, where there was a strong Vichy base at the port of Dakar, which outflanked British convoy routes, round the Cape to the Red Sea and beyond. The Royal Navy had to provide the covering force (Force M), but could only spare a limited number of ships, so the battleship *Resolution*, along with the *Ark Royal* and part of the 8th destroyer flotilla, was sent to join the battleship *Barham* and her destroyers from home, to make up the numbers. This force sailed on 6 September *en route* for Freetown, Sierra Leone. The initial plan hoped for a peaceable occupation, but the Vichy garrison, emboldened by the brand-new battleship *Richelieu* and reinforced by a squadron of three light cruisers and three destroyers, which were allowed to pass through the Straits of Gibraltar by Admiral Sir Dudley North without challenge, elected to resist.

As usual, the long days at sea heading south were used as opportunities for further exercises. From 1345 hours No. 803 Squadron, with six Skuas airborne, carried out mock interceptions and then conducted both simulated high-level bombing runs and dive-bombing attacks on the *Ark Royal* to exercise the fleet's gunnery. Midshipman Griffith recorded:

The interception of a Dornier Do18 by L2873, one of the classic Skua 'moments' of the war, is e-created in this magnificent painting by Chris Golds. (*Fleet Air Arm Museum, Yeovilton*)

Skua targets. The German freighter *Barenfels*, laden with anti-aircraft guns and other war supplies, was subjected to a second attack on Bergen by the Skuas. Here is shown a very near-miss close aft. She was duly holed and sank by the stern, but unfortunately, the enemy were able to salvage much of her cargo. (*MOI via Author's collection*)

Operations off Norway in the summer of 1940. One Skua is mounted on the *Ark Royal*'s accelerator ready for launch, while a second awaits her turn to engage. The wind indication smoke can be seen drifting to starboard, from the front of the flight deck, and the port wind deflector baffle is raised to aid the operation.
(*MOI via Author's collection*)

Skua targets. The oil tank farm at Dobvik near Bergen under intense bombardment. A Skua can be seen at the top of the photograph pulling out of her dive while her bomb detonates plumb centre beneath her.
(*MOI via Author's collection*)

Skua targets. Bergen harbour crowded with shipping as the German build-up and consolidation of Norway continues. The Skoltegrund Mole can be seen towards the top right hand of the photograph. The half-sunk wreck of the *Barenfels* can be made out on the southern side, but there is no trace of the sunken *Königsberg* off the northern side. She is totally 'out of action', being beneath the water! (*National Archives, London*)

Skua targets. The oil tank farms at various locations around Bergen were continually attacked. Here, a low-level photo clearly shows the target on the way in.
(*National Archive, London*)

Skua targets. The oil tanks at Bergen were continually struck and made a satisfactory amount of smoke when hit.
(*National Archive, London*)

Skua targets. Bridge-busting also called for accurate bombing, which only the Skua was able to deliver. The logging wharf was left untouched, but enemy communications suffered from this type of demolition. (*National Archive, London*)

Tom Harrington and Naval Airman Crone returning in L2890 from an attack on Bergen on 7 July 1940, with a hole through the pilot's windshield and another through the upper fuselage in the centre of the cockpit, just abaft the two main fuel tanks, cold, but otherwise intact!
(Captain T. W. Harrington, DSC, RN)

The attack on the *Scharnhorst*, June 1940. The fifteen Skuas can be spotted aft on *Ark Royal's* flight deck, the maximum number she could configure due to the weather conditions prevailing.
(R. J. Rolph, BEM)

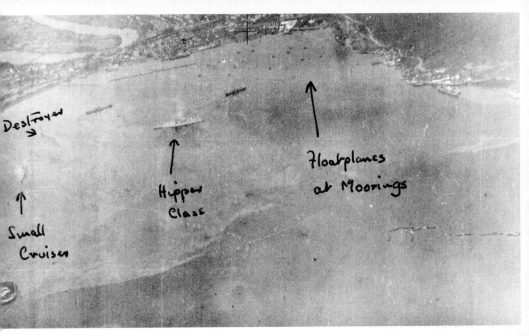

Another Skua-eye view of the full anchorage off Trondheim, with the *Nurnberg*, identified as 'small cruiser' to port, with a destroyer behind her, the *Admiral Hipper* centre, with two merchant ships beyond and a flotilla of He115 seaplanes from the *Luftwaffe*'s 2/506 beyond. (*National Archives*)

The attack on the *Scharnhorst* at Trondheim, on 13 June 1940. The German squadron is shown anchored off the town. The battle-cruiser is flanked by four destroyers and an auxiliary unit, the small cruiser is the *Nurnberg*, just arrived from Germany and the 'Hipper' class cruiser is the *Admiral Hipper* herself. (*National Archives, London*)

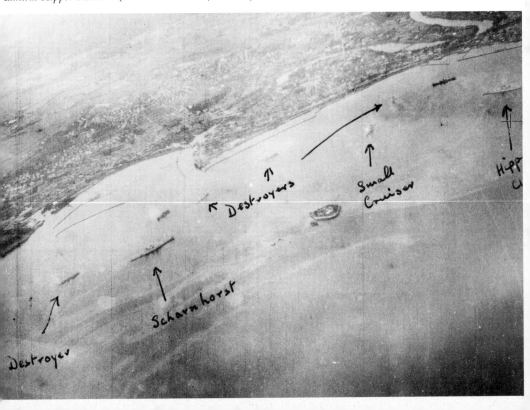

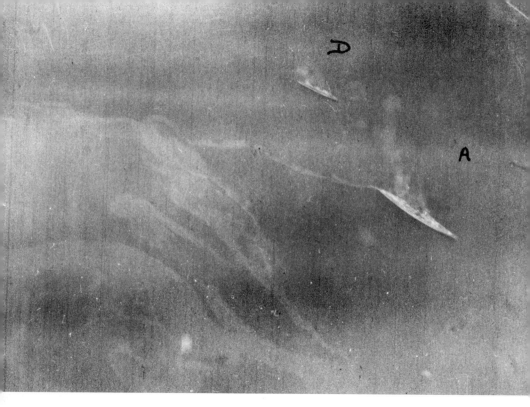

The attack on the *Scharnhorst* at Trondheim, on 13 June 1940. Two columns of smoke can be seen from the target, the right hand one is from her funnel as she is raising steam, the left hand column is from the bomb hits on her quarterdeck, which unfortunately failed to penetrate deeply enough t cause her serious harm. Seen astern of the battle-cruiser is a destroyer (marked 'D' with a small auxiliary unit (marked 'A'). (*National Archive, London*)

The attack on the *Scharnhorst* at Trondheim, on 13 June 1940. Seen astern of the withdrawing aircraft, is the battle-cruiser, while the fire on the shore behind her marks the demise of one of the Skuas, hacked down by defending Bf109s. (*National Archive, London*)

e Blackburn Skua 7F/803 (L2963) from the aircraft carrier HMS *Ark
yal*, on display after being salvaged by the Germans after the attack
the *Scharnhorst* on 13 June 1940. (*Franz Selinger*)

lose-up detail of the pilot's cabin and forward upper fuselage of the Blackburn Skua II 7F/803
2963) from the aircraft carrier HMS *Ark Royal*, on display after being salvaged by the Germans
ter the attack on the *Scharnhorst* on 13 June 1940. Note the cartoon of a Naval Officer's gun
ooting down a Hitler-headed wasp-like aircraft. This machine was flown by Lieutenant G. H.
lmer, (P), RN, with Thomas A. McKee (A), RN, DSC as his observer and crashed at Frostsiejaevet,
vneset, near Trondheim. (*Franz Selinger*)

Camouflaged Skua L2928 of No. 801 Squadron presents a well-worn appearance. She is operating from Detling under the auspices of RAF Coastal Command and undertaking hazardous missions across the English Channel, facing *Luftwaffe* fighters and flak over the target and RAF fighter interceptions on the way to and from the combat zone. (*Author's collection*)

Two flights of Skuas of No. 800 Squadron spotted and chocked, ready to fly off. Of interest is the mix of Royal Navy and RAF personnel, the bombs and their open containers on the starboard side of the carrier adjacent to the seated pipe-smoking officer. (*Imperial War Museum, London*)

In the spring of 1941, the
Mediterranean Fleet, based at Alexandria, Egypt, had
a rare glimpse of the Skua, when two from No. 803 Squadron, embarked aboard
HMS *Illustrious*, exchanged flight decks and landed aboard HMS *Eagle*, as seen here.
(*E. B. MacKenzie*)

.ua L2987 down on Sicily. During one of Force H's
-ing-off operations, Petty Officer Stockwell was leading a flight of six Hawker Hurricanes
ghters at Malta, but, due to a combination of misfortunes, including changes in wind direction,
ilure of rendezvousing aircraft, and the failure of the Skua's radio, the group ran out of fuel and
ery fighter was lost, while Stockwell had to crash-land on enemy territory.
Jicola Malizia via Mark Anthony Vella)

Operations at Dakar, Senegal. During Operation *Menace* when the Free French under General De Gaulle attempted but ultimately failed, to take over the French Colony from the pro-German Vichy regime with help from the Royal Navy. The Skuas provided constant air cover, both as fighters and as dive-bombers against the powerful French naval forces concentrated there, which included the battleship *Richelieu*. Here Skua L2933 with a mixed bomb load is being prepared for a mission by a deck crew in a wide variety of garbs and dress vaguely appropriate for the tropics. (*Courtesy Fleet Air Arm Museum, Yeovilton*)

The Skua combat missions with Force 'H' in the western Mediterranean included covering vital supply convoys to Malta, the flying off of Hurricane fighters to that island and the bombardment of the Italian port of Genoa, right uder the noses of the enemy fleet and air power. Here a Skua is seen with tail wheel up and engine running in January 1941. Note the bombs with their shackles on the deck in the foreground and the escorting destroyer in the background over the tip of the flight deck on the right-hand side. (*Courtesy Fleet Air Arm Museum, Yeovilton*)

battle said she was damaged, but, strangely, this does not appear to have actually been the case. Admiral Somerville in his battle summary also claims she was damaged in her boiler room. One Skua pilot stated he attacked the *Trento* of the same heavy cruiser squadron, while the Squadron's report gives their targets as light cruisers of the *Condottieri* class, but none of these were present at the battle that day. Whatever the individual ships singled out that day, No. 800 Squadron's attack on the Italian 8-inch cruiser squadron was the last such dive-bombing attack at sea carried out by the Skua. (*Ufficio Storico, Roma*)

No. 800 Squadron was the last to fly the Skua in combat from the deck of the *Ark Royal*. After an offer by the Admiralty to base the squadron at Gibraltar so that it could be re-embarked from time-to-time as a dive-bomber unit for special operations had been turned down by Admiral Somerville due to lack of facilities ashore, the squadron flew over to HMS *Furious* on 5 April 1941, to return home to the UK. Here the very last Skua is seen taking off from *Ark Royal* for the change-over. (*Courtesy Fleet Air Arm Museum, Yeovilton*)

During the early months of 1941 No. 801 Squadron was once more placed under the command of RAF Coastal Command ashore at St. Merryn, Cornwall. The principal reason was to participate in attacks on the German Battlecruiser *Scharnhorst* and *Gneisenau*, which were in Brest harbour. However, the techniques of dive-bombing were not understood by Coastal Command who ordered what would have been suicide missions in unsuitable conditions. The squadron's C.O. Lieutenant (A) Ian R. Sarel, bravely, refused to take his aircrew into such obviously stupid missions, although he volunteered to 'have a go' himself.

Here the *Scharnhorst* can be seen alongside the quay, with camouflage netting draped across stagings to alter her outline, with an anti-torpedo boom outboard of her (3) while the *Gneisenau* can be seen to the right, in dock, similarly clad (both(1), Camouflaged buildings are at (2), and oil tanks demolished in the repeated futile RAF heavy bomber attacks can be seen at (4). (*MOI, London*

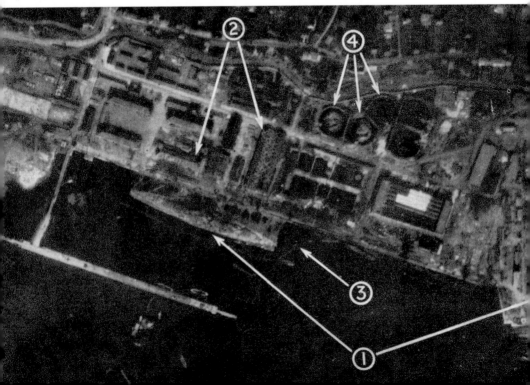

One of the last missions undertaken by No. 801 Squadron operating under RAF Coastal Command, was participation in Operation *Aandalsnes*, the bombing of German supply tankers and other shipping in dock at Cherbourg on 27 March 1941. Here bombs can be seen exploding on the inner harbour jetty close alongside the tankers. (*MOI, London*)

Skua L3006, coded L6G, used by
Blackburn for target-towing trials at Brough in the
two-tone 'Sea' scheme. (*Ray C. Sturtivent*)

Most Skuas, this is L2951
serving with No. 10 MU at Hullavington, were delivered from
Blackburns painted in an all-over silver livery. The Royal Navy repainted their
aircraft in the two-tone, upper and lower, dark and light grey scheme for carrier operations
(*MOI via Author's collection*)

In addition to the use of 'retired' Skuas in the
target-towning capacity, many Skuas were later completed as Target Tugs from the outset. This
aircraft, with here striking experimental Red Banding markings, is L30076, which was employed
by No. 20 Maintenance Unit, RAF, at Aston Down from 8 August 1939.
(*A. M. McKinnon via Ray C. Sturtivent*)

On landing, I learned from my elated parachute packer, Blatchford, that the CO Lieutenant J. M. Bruen,[14] had taken up with him the parachute that I had packed for practice this morning. A Sub-Lieutenant England flew in the back with me. He is a TSR pilot. The sky was completely overcast but I have never sweated so much in an aircraft.[15]

On Saturday 14 September the *Ark Royal* was totally unescorted, steering 340° at 26 knots to join the 1st Cruiser Squadron.[16] Griffith recorded that he awoke to find that they, '... were travelling at high speed across a glassy sea, so evidently something was amiss'.[17] A striking force of torpedo- and dive-bombers from Nos 820 and 803 Squadrons was being made ready. What was amiss of course, was the Vichy French squadron, now well on its way to Dakar. Lieutenant Christian, with Lieutenant Ennever as his observer, borrowed Skua L2961 from Griffith and flew a reconnaissance mission over Dakar to see if the cruisers had arrived there, but found only the *Richelieu* and a few colonial sloops were present.

The 'headlong dash' continued through the day until the rendezvous was made. On Sunday 15 September, the Skuas 'stood by for action', with No. 800 Squadron readied as the dive-bombing force and No. 803 Squadron for fighter patrols and reconnaissance missions. Lieutenants Christian and Ennever again overflew Dakar on two occasions, early morning and later afternoon, taking photographs, which revealed a good amount of shipping and two of the Vichy cruisers.[18] No action was taken, however, and *Ark Royal* commenced retracing her steps back toward Freetown once more, at a more sedate speed, with five accompanying destroyers. Meanwhile, life continued. A squadron notice was posted up aboard *Ark Royal* in Freetown harbour, for Nos 800 and 803 Squadrons, to the effect that the Admiralty had ordered the Skuas' Browning machine-guns to be harmonised on a pattern once more. If they objected, they were to do so in writing to the CO. Midshipman Griffith recorded that he, for one, did just that, citing as his reason the experience gained in Norway.[19]

On 21 September the *Ark Royal* was at sea with the fleet (*Barham, Resolution, Dragon* and six destroyers) heading back toward Dakar, her MLA being 287° at 13 knots. The next day saw this fleet reinforced by the heavy cruisers *Devonshire* and *Cornwall*. A solitary Skua was launched and made a photo-reconnaissance sortie over Dakar.

For a time Operation *Menace* was abandoned as it was considered impracticable, but after a few days it was (unfortunately for all concerned) revived and dawn of 23 September found the whole force, troopships, store ships and Force M, back off Dakar ready to negotiate or fight. They found a fogbound coast, resolute Vichy gunners manning the guns of numerous forts and the anchored warships, now less one cruiser, but reinforced by the large destroyers *L'Audacieux*, *Fantasque*, *Le Malin* and *Hardi*, and three submarines. In the air the Vichy defenders could call on nineteen modern Curtiss Hawks from the two pursuit squadrons based at Ouakam airfield and twenty-two Glenn Martin 156F twin-engined bombers at Thiès.

Midshipman Griffiths was airborne with his section at 0630 hours to carry out a fighter patrol over Force M, and this continued until 0930 hours. Griffiths recorded: 'Visibility was bad due to the large amount of dust in the air and this later proved to be responsible for the loss of several aircraft.'

Two Vichy submarines also sortied out of harbour to threaten the force, and Lieutenant Everrett claimed to have bombed and sunk one of these as she returned to harbour (This may have been the *Persée*, which was certainly sunk that day). Between 1230 and 1530 hours Griffith's section conducted a second Fighter Patrol, this time over the *Ark Royal*, but the enemy air force made little impression.[20]

The *Ark Royal* had embarked a total of twenty-one serviceable Skuas and thirty Swordfish TSR biplanes. She also had embarked two Free French Luciole light aircraft manned by French pilots who tried (but failed) to persuade the Vichy fighter pilots not to resist.[21] In the event, the fog caused total confusion among both attackers and defenders and operations were fragmentary, piecemeal and failures. A brief bombardment was ineffective and called off in case it caused loss of life. Attempted parleys were fired upon or ignored, and attempted landings were repulsed or simply went amiss. The end of a frustrating day found nothing accomplished save that the Vichy garrison was fully alerted and ready for battle. The Free Frenchmen aboard *Ark Royal* were far more phlegmatic about fighting their countrymen ashore than the squeamish British. One example, cited by Admiral Jameson, had a Free French officer patting a 500 lb bomb as it was being wheeled across to be loaded on a waiting Skua, with the words: '*Aha! Voilà un joi petit déjeuner pour l'Amiral.*'[22]

The FAA took heavy losses this day. Petty Officer Sabey flying with Leading Airman J Goles in L2900, took part in the dive-bombing of the *Richelieu*. He noted in his flying log that day, '*Ark* lost nine Kites, six crews saved'. The losses included three Skuas. One of No. 803 Squadron's aircraft, A7K, became embroiled in a fight with some Curtiss Hawk 75s, but, during the engagement received a hit from an anti-aircraft shell and had to force-land in the sea, both aircrew being rescued by the destroyer HMS *Forester*. A second Skua, A6C, returning from a fighter patrol, also had to force-land, the crew being rescued by the destroyer HMS *Echo*, while yet a third Skua also ditched, the crew being saved by the destroyer HMS *Greyhound*.

By way of some small recompense, Lieutenant J. M. Christian, with Sub-Lieutenant A. H. St G. Gore-Langton as his observer flying L3033 on a 3 hour 25 minute patrol from 1100 hours, engaged and badly damaged a Glenn Martin bomber.

On 24 September a combined heavy ship bombardment and air strike was planned, both against the Vichy forts and the battleship *Richelieu*, but this was dependent on the weather. The *Barham, Resolution, Australia* and *Devonshire* had reached their positions some 16,000 miles from offshore by 0715 hours, but were unable to view their targets. No. 800 Squadron made two attacks on the Vichy-French warships at Dakar. Meanwhile, the first of three planned air attacks had got underway. Six Skuas flew off the *Ark Royal* at 0625 hours, when the assigned targets were the two Gloire class light cruisers, whose exact positions were recorded as 'uncertain'. The alternative targets were two of the principal Vichy forts, Point Emmanuel or Gorée Island. Each of the Skuas was armed with a single 500 lb SAP bomb.

In the event, the attack was made in fine weather, with no cloud, but with a calm sea. Vertical visibility was good, however there was a considerable dust haze, which made horizontal visibility difficult. The dive-bombers, flying in above the fog, met with no airborne opposition. However, one mistook the destroyer *Le Fantasque* for a cruiser and made her attack on that ship. Two Skuas correctly attacked the *Georges Leygues* and *Montcalm*, while the final trio chose the battleship *Richelieu* moored alongside the 'X' Mole, as their target. The six aircraft made dive-bombing attacks, at an angle of 65 degrees down to an average bomb release height of around 2,000 feet.[23]

They met with only light anti-aircraft fire, of which only that from the *Richelieu* was considered accurate, but received no damage other than a hit in the tail of one Skua by a rifle calibre bullet of no significance. Nor did they inflict any damage on the enemy in return. No hits at all were made on any ship (the sloop *Gazelle* was not even attacked), the closest placings were two bombs that fell into the water about 15 yards off the *Richelieu* port side. Even if these two bombs had hit the Vichy battleship, her 8-inch armoured deck would have been sufficient to prevent much damage.[24] Another near miss on *Le Fantasque* was noted, which might have done some good on this lightly protected vessel had it hit.

This first attack was followed by two more, both delivered by Swordfish, one against Fort Manuel. The other, launched at 0800 hours, was a high-diving attack against *Richelieu* again, this time with the Skuas in the escort role. By this time, naturally, Vichy were fully alert and ready, and a hot AA reception met the British aircraft from both ships and forts. The commanding officer of No. 810 Squadron described the defensive fire as 'very accurate and intense'. Worse, the French had got some fighter aircraft aloft in time to intercept. While the Skuas tangled with the Vichy fighters, losing three of their number in the process, another section of Curtiss H75-CL fighters homed in on the rear flight of the Swordfish. The

French fighters shot down two (A2L and A3L) instantly, and forced three others hastily to jettison their bombs in order to escape. This failed to prevent the French pilots nailing a third Swordfish (A2A), whose main bomb had 'hung-up' on him, as the survivors made their get-away over Gorée Island. Although hits on the battleship's fo'c'sle were claimed, none were made, and the whole attack was an expensive failure, as were the ship bombardments that followed.

One of No. 803 Squadron's Skuas, A7K, became embroiled in a fight with some Curtiss Hawk 75s, but, during the engagement received a hit from an anti-aircraft shell and had to force-land. Both aircrew were rescued by the destroyer HMS *Forester.*

On the third day the weather proved better, but the result was even worse, with the *Resolution* torpedoed by a Vichy submarine and so heavily damaged that she later had to be towed away by *Barham.* Yet another indecisive duel between the British ships and the French forts and the *Richelieu* finally petered out once more with nothing accomplished. The Skuas were again aloft early, being airborne by 0530 hours and there were continual skirmishes with the Curtiss defenders.

By 27 September, the *Ark Royal* was back at Freetown once more. Although Admiral Cunningham was lavish in his praise for the contribution of the Fleet Air Arm, writing that the men had 'supplied invaluable reconnaissance information' and that the *Ark Royal*'s striking forces attacked the objectives in the manner and with the spirit expected of the Fleet Air Arm until prevented from doing so by increasing fighter opposition,[25] her air group had suffered severely. Five of the Skuas were written off for the destruction of just one Curtiss. With just sixteen Skuas remaining, replenishment was obviously necessary before they resumed operations again; the Swordfish suffered even heavier losses.

Mediterranean forays

Thus the *Ark Royal* did not rejoin Force H but sailed for home to refit, and some of her Skuas were replaced by Fulmars. No. 803 Squadron was disembarked at Crail on 8 October and rearmed with twelve Fulmars, their place aboard the *Ark Royal* being taken by the No. 808 Squadron, also equipped with Fulmars. No. 800 Squadron was also temporarily disembarked at Crail between 8 and 31 October, but retained their Skuas. The *Ark Royal* did not rejoin Somerville's flag until 6 November.

Within a day they were sailing east once more, to carry out Operation *Coat*; *Ark Royal, Sheffield* and eight destroyers, escorting the battleship *Barham,* heavy cruiser *Berwick,* light cruiser *Glasgow* and four destroyers who were on their way to join the main Mediterranean Fleet, dropping troop reinforcements off at Malta *en route.* Between 7 and 11 November, fighter patrols were flown by the Skuas and a solitary Sm79 was destroyed. Another air attack was made on Cagliari on the night of 9 November. That day, while still south of Sardinia, the expected bombing attack was detected by radar coming in at 13,000 feet and the fighters were sent to intercept. However, the slowness of the Skuas, and even of the Fulmars, made for frustrating conditions, and despite the fact that they attacked the twenty bombers persistently, and claimed some hits, the formation remained intact and carried out precision bombing, with near misses on both the *Ark Royal* and the *Barham*. Somerville, as ever, was forthright in his criticism, stating: 'Our fighters engaged them as they came in but could not make any visible impression on them. A lot of the pilots were changed whilst *Ark* was at home and the new lots are still pretty green.'[26]

Hard training followed the force's return to Gibraltar, but within a short time they were heading back into the lion's den again with another flying off mission, Operation *White*, flying off a further twelve Hurricanes from the old *Argus* and covering the passage of the light cruiser *Newcastle* to Malta at the same time. Force H was back to full strength (*Renown*, *Ark Royal*, *Sheffield*, *Despatch* and eight destroyers) for this operation, which took place between 15 and 17 November. However, this particular reinforcement ended in tragedy. The weather was poor throughout the approach period. This proved a two-edge sword, making aircraft operations tricky, and causing the cancellation of a planned air attack on Alghero airfield, but at the same time shielding the fleet from enemy shadowers. During the outward passage *Renown* received information from Malta, which indicated that a powerful Italian fleet was at sea south of Naples. Somerville considered that they might be in a position to intercept his ships and made the decision to launch the two batches of six Hurricanes, each with the Skua guide, much earlier than originally planned. This meant a flying distance of 400 miles for the fourteen aircraft.

The first flight took off from the *Argus* at 0615 hours, in position 37° 29' North, 6° 43' East. The wind at 2,000 feet was 20 knots, 200°, and the forecast from Malta reported a south-west wind in the vicinity, which should have aided things.

There was an hour's interval and then the second flight was launched in turn, each half dozen Hurricanes being led by a Skua as navigation leader. Flying the Skua (L2987) of the second flight was Petty Officer William Stockwell, RN, a former Sea Gladiator pilot and veteran of Norway. Things started to go wrong from the very outset, as they failed to rendezvous as planned. Somehow their initial landfall, Galita Island, was missed, nor did the Glenn Martin Maryland bomber, sent from Malta and which should have helped escort them from north-west of Galita Island, turn up. The Skua's navigator made continual radio calls for assistance, asking for D/F Bearings, but the radio set proved faulty and he was not able to receive any replies. Things became desperate with the Hurricanes beginning to run out of fuel, and Stockwell had no option but to begin a desperate search for land, friendly, neutral or enemy, so that his charges could at least alight safely. While he searched, one-by-one the six Hurricanes fell out of the sky and into the Mediterranean; there were no survivors.

The Skua was the only aircraft still airborne, but even her fuel situation was becoming desperate, when through the mist, land was at last sighted. It turned out to be the south-west coast of Sicily and this was confirmed by the flak that started to arrive. Finally, Stockwell managed to crash-land on a flat stretch of beach at Punta Palo at the Isola delle Correnti, close to Syracuse, where the two aircrew were quickly made prisoners. The Skua herself ended up with the *Regia Aeronautica's Stabilimento Costruzioni Aeronautiche* (Aircraft Construction Establishment), at Guidonia in June 1942. It would be interesting to know what the experts there made of her!

In the event, only four of the Hurricanes and one of the Skuas[27] made it to Malta safely, the rest being lost.

A court of inquiry was held to try and establish the causes of this disaster. This exonerated Somerville, and blamed a combination of contrary winds and inadequate training of the pilots. Somerville himself spoke to Captain E. G. N. Rushbrooke, captain of the *Argus*, who told him that he believed the Hurricane pilots did not know how to run their engines economically. Somerville was to record: 'Apparently the Observer in the second Skua, the party who failed to find Malta at all, was a sub-lieutenant RNVR doing his first operational flight. That I consider a positive scandal.'[28]

Battle of Spartivento

Operation *Collar* was the next in the series of highly important convoy operations that Force H was charged with. Three large 16-knot supply ships were to be sailed through to the eastern Mediterranean; two (*Clan Forbes* and *Clan Fraser*) were destined to stop over at Malta, while a third (*New Zealand Star*) was to go right through to Egypt. They had as their cargo, stores, supplies and motor transport for the army in the Middle East, as well as troop reinforcements for Malta itself. They were to be met east of the 'Narrows' by ships of the main Mediterranean Fleet, who would take them on under their protection. Two light cruisers, the *Manchester* and *Southampton*, also with troops aboard, were to go through as well, along with four corvettes. Returning home from the eastern basin at the same time were the battleship *Ramillies*, heavy cruiser *Berwick* and light cruiser *Newcastle*, all with defects to be repaired in the UK. The whole complex series of operations was put in train between 25 and 27 November 1940.

Unknown to the British, the Italians had known of the sailing of Force H within 25 minutes of their leaving Gibraltar! Accordingly, their fleet, under Admiral I. Campioni, sailed in three groups to join up and offer battle. This force comprised two battleships, *Vittorio Veneto* and *Giulio Cesare*, six heavy cruisers and fourteen destroyers. The RAF air patrols from Malta failed to sight these powerful squadrons at all.

The *Ark Royal* sailed with Force H and, as usual, the Skua flew fighter patrols throughout the afternoon of 2 November and during 26 November. Although the enemy air force failed to turn up, the day was not without incident, or losses. Among them were two Skuas, both of which crashed while landing back aboard. A number of fresh faces among the aircrews at this time were indications of less experienced personnel diluting the veteran flyers. An early victory on 27 November was the shooting down of a Cant Z506 reconnaissance aircraft by the early morning fighter patrol, after another long stern chase, which helped restore morale somewhat.

When reports began to be received by the TSR search aircraft of the oncoming Italian fleet, it came as a complete surprise. Somerville had to ensure the safety of the convoy, but at the same time rendezvous with the *Ramillies* force before the enemy fleet could intercept. While the main force, *Renown, Sheffield, Manchester* and *Southampton*, with five destroyers, steamed to meet the enemy, the *Ark Royal*, with the destroyers *Kelvin* and *Jaguar*, was detached to operate independently and prepare air-striking forces.

It was after 1400 hours, when the surface battle had already been decided and the Italian fleet was on its way home at full speed, that the Italian bombers finally made a belated contribution to the action. Attacks continued throughout the afternoon, with interceptions being made. But the most severe bombing took place in the final assault by fifteen Sm79s in three groups of five bombing from 14,000 feet, well above the range of most of the fleet's anti-aircraft guns. These gentlemen concentrated their fury upon the lone *Ark Royal* and a whole forest of heavy bombs near-missed her, the *Ark Royal* surviving yet again by the skin of her teeth.

During these heavy attacks, one Skua from No. 800 Squadron single-handedly successfully broke up a formation of four bombers, one of the few successful fighter interceptions that day.

During the afternoon, seven Skuas, led by the CO, had been flown off from the *Ark Royal* at 1500 hours, and ordered to search for the 'disabled' cruiser reported earlier.[29] These included four aircraft from No. 800 Squadron: L3015 (A6F) piloted by Lieutenant (A) J. A. Rooper, RN, with Sub-Lieutenant G. R. Woolston as his Observer; L3007 (A6M) piloted by Petty Officer (A) L. E. Burston, with Leading Airman R. H. Holmes;

Table 26   No. 800 Squadron Battle of Spartivento, 27 November 1940

Lieutenant (A) R. M. Smeeton	Lieutenant (O) E. S. Carver, RN
Lieutenant G. R. Callingham, RN	Midshipman H. Morris, RN
Lieutenant (A) J. A. Rooper, RN	Sub-Lieutenant (A) G. R. Woolston, RN
Lieutenant (A) K. Spurway, RN	Petty Officer (A) R. F. Hart
Sub-Lieutenant (A) M. F. Fell, RN	Naval Airman D. H. Lowndes
Sub-Lieutenant B. H. Hurle-Hobbs, RN	Leading Airman E. E. Bell
Midshipman R. W. Kearsley, RN	Leading Airman L. C. Eccleshall
Petty Officer (A) W. J. Heard	Naval Airman Hills
Petty Officer (A) L. E. Burston	Leading Airman R. H. Holmes
Petty Officer A. W. Sabey	Leading Airman J. Coles

L2900 (A6C) piloted by Petty Officer (A) A. W. Sabey, with Leading Airman J. Coles and L3017 (A7L) piloted by Petty Officer A. W. Theobald, with Naval Airman F. J. L. de Frias. Instead of a crippled ship, the Skuas found a cruiser division under way, which they identified as comprising three Condottierie class ships.[30] These ships were steering northward off the south-west tip of Sardinia at high speed. The striking force of seven Skuas'[31] targets were actually the heavy cruisers *Trieste, Trento* and *Bolzano*, which had been sent by Vice-Admiral Iachino to cover the retirement of the damaged destroyer *Lanciere.*[32] No hits were obtained, but according to the Italian report[33] five bombs fell very close to the *Trento.*[34] This is confirmed in the Flying Log Book of Midshipman (later Lieutenant Commander) A. W. Sabey, of No. 800 Squadron, RN, who was flying Skua L2900 with Leading Airman J. Coles as his TAG. He recorded scoring a 'near miss' on a Trento Class cruiser. The overall flight time for the mission was 2 hours 35 minutes.[35] The Skuas attacked the rear ship of the group, but all they could claim for their efforts were two probable 'Near-misses'. And the ships continued on their headlong withdrawal from the field of combat with no lessening of speed.[36] This, in fact, proved to be the last ever dive-bombing attack made by No. 800 or indeed, any, Skua squadron.

On the return flight, all seven joined in destroying a Meridionali Ro43 biplane floatplane from the enemy battleship, which was attempting to find safety at Sardinia as she had too little fuel left to return to her parent vessel. This was their only success of the battle.

East and West

The *Ark Royal* accompanied Force H during a series of missions following their return from the Spartivento clash. These alarms and excursions took them out into the Atlantic, and back to the Mediterranean and ensured the run-up to Christmas and the New Year was very eventful. Rumours and intelligence hints were continuous, and London became convinced the

Germans were about to sail an expedition to capture and occupy the Azores (though how they would have held and supplied such a garrison is unclear). It was a sufficiently strong concept that Their Lordships ordered Force H to sea on 14 December to patrol the route between those islands and the French port of Bordeaux from whence the invasion force was reputed to be sailing. Force H duly quartered that section of the ocean without any sight or sign of as much as a German rowing boat, and returned to Gibraltar on 19 December.

The next mission took them west, this was Operation *Hide* and its purpose was to meet and provide cover for the battleship *Malaya* from the eastern Mediterranean and the two supply ships *Clan Forbes* and *Clan Fraser* from Malta, with an escort of five destroyers. Force H duly rendezvoused with these ships (less the destroyer *Hyperion*, which was sunk by a mine off Cape Bon) on 22 December and returned in company. No. 800 Squadron's Skuas maintained the usual fighter patrols and drove off enemy shadowers, but could not close sufficiently to engage them.

They were hoping for a traditional Christmas in harbour, but midway through the day news came in that the *Admiral Hipper* was loose in the Atlantic and had made an attack on troop convoy WS5A, being driven off by the three escorting cruisers. Although *Admiral Hipper* returned to Brest, this was not clear, and Force H was sailed to assist and round up the ships of the convoy itself, which had been ordered to scatter.

Included in the convoy were the aircraft carriers *Furious* and *Argus*, as well as the supply ships *Essex*, destined for Malta, and *Clan MacDonald*, *Clan Cumming*, *Northern Prince* and *Empire Song*, with military supplies destined for the army in Greece. They were to be accompanied by the cruiser *Bonaventure* and four destroyers, while Force H (*Renown*, *Malaya*, *Ark Royal*, *Sheffield* and seven destroyers) was to provide the usual protection through the western Mediterranean as far as the Skerki Bank. This was Operation *Excess*, but *Admiral Hipper*'s foray had caused a postponement, and a gale, which drove the *Northern Prince* aground so that her troops had to be transferred to the warships going east, caused another. Thus it was not until 7 January that the *Ark Royal* finally sailed.

As always, the Skuas of No. 800 Squadron shared the fighter patrols with the Fulmars during the entire passage. On 9 January the *Ark Royal* was sent ahead of the convoy in order to fly off five TSRs to Malta, but it was not until that afternoon that the Italian air force put in a belated appearance. The attack, when it came, was just a gesture; ten Sm79s bombed from 11,000 feet, but the Skuas were unable to get in meaningful attacks against this group. No further attacks took place during the return to Gibraltar, but, over in the eastern basin, German Ju87 Stuka dive-bombers announced their arrival in the Mediterranean with a blistering attack, which wrecked the carrier *Illustrious*.

Even on the rare occasion that the *Ark Royal* was in harbour, or docked, the Skuas were kept busy. For example, on 19 January, in compliance with a request from the Admiralty, two of No. 800 Squadron's aircraft were sent out from the Rock to carry out photo reconnaissance flights over Oran and Mers-el-Kebir. These missions were carried out without interception by Vichy fighters and the photographs, when developed, revealed that the battle-cruiser *Dunkerque* had no appreciable list or trim but appeared to be still aground with her stern in position 239°, 2,880 feet from the Mers-el-Kebir fixed 121-foot light, under the fort itself. Her head was approximately 285° and she was protected by three rows of anti-torpedo nets. The photographs were forwarded on to London and Whitehall had one less worry.[37]

Genoa

Early in 1941 an audacious plan was drawn up to strike at north-west Italy. Reports were received that the Italian Navy had concentrated their remaining battleships in the port of Genoa after the drubbing they had received at Taranto. They considered this area, well outside the Royal Navy's normal range of western Mediterranean operations, and shielded from approach by Vichy France's southern coast and Corsica, as well as northern Sardinia, to be inviolate. It was indeed a risky business, thrusting Force H's head right into the lion's mouth, but because it would be so unexpected, the element of surprise was relied upon.[38] It was hoped that a bombardment might catch the enemy heavy ships in dock, where they might be damaged, or even destroyed. As spin-offs a blow here would affect the already shaky Italian morale, might divert part of the Italian air effort north away from Malta and the central Mediterranean and strike a blow at the industrial north of the country.

In order that the bombarding squadron might get a clear run in during the early hours, despite the period of moonlight, a diversionary air attack was to be made by the *Ark Royal*'s TSRs against the Tiso Dam in northern Sardinia, which was thought (mistakenly as it turned out) to be virtually undefended. The original operation was to have been conducted at the beginning of February, the *Ark Royal* accompanying Force H to sea on 31 January and a small striking force of eight TSRs being flown off in the early hours on 2 February. However, these aircraft met unexpectedly stiff resistance, and their torpedoes failed to breach the dam structure. Bad weather brought about the cancellation of the other half of the operation and the ships returned to Gibraltar.

Although there was some indication that security had been compromised, another attempt was made on 6 February, when battle-cruiser *Renown*, battleship *Malaya*, *Ark Royal*, light cruiser *Sheffield* and ten destroyers again sailed to carry out Operation *Grog*. They made a series of elaborate feints to throw the Italian watchers off the scent. Again, the *Ark Royal* was detached and two striking forces (one of fourteen and one of four) of her TSRs made diversionary attacks on an oil refinery at Leghorn and laid mines at Spezia. Then the heavy ships, having met with no resistance whatsoever, opened fire off Genoa at 0714 hours. The Italian battleship *Caio Duilio* had been in dock, and was straddled, but unfortunately escaped being hit.

During the bombardment, the Skuas conducted frequent and continuous fighter patrols, but were themselves hardly disturbed. During the withdrawal the fighter sorties were maintained throughout the day.

It was later learnt that an Italian fleet, including the battleships *Vittorio Veneto*, *Andrea Doria* and *Giulio Cesare*, with three heavy cruisers and ten destroyers, had been at sea trying to cut them off, but had failed to locate them. Aircraft from both sides had been unable to make much of an impression. At 1140 hours two Italian bombers had approached the withdrawing British ships, but they only dropped three bombs, very wide, and then made off before the Skuas could engage them. However, two enemy shadowers did pay the price, one in the forenoon and the other in the afternoon. Skuas of No. 800 Squadron notched up another victory when Lieutenant J. A Rooper with Sub-Lieutenant G. R Woolston flying L3015; Lieutenant R. M. Smeeton with Lieutenant E. S. Carver flying L2900; and Petty Officer A. Jopling, with Leading Airman J. Glen, shot down one of two Italian Cant Z506Bs while they were still deep in the Gulf of Genoa. The Fulmars destroyed the other and the survivors from this aircraft were later retrieved from the sea by the searching Italian fleet, who only then realised that Somerville's force had eluded them.

This proved to be the Skuas last combat victory.

Convoys, raids and excursions

The Skuas were not given much opportunity to shine during the following 6 weeks, because Force H, with *Renown* and *Ark Royal* prominent, was preoccupied with its old adversaries, the German battle-cruisers *Scharnhorst* and *Gneisenau*, in the Atlantic. Having broken out into the North Atlantic, these two ships went on a sinking spree, massacring both merchant shipping and threatening convoys. They then moved south to threaten the vital troop convoys to the Middle East, on the way to Sierra Leone and the Cape. Most of this period was devoted to long-range searches by the TSRs, but the Skuas and Fulmars also took part as and when required.

On 12 February, a day after their return from Genoa, *Ark Royal* accompanied *Renown* and *Sheffield* and five destroyers out into the Atlantic to give cover to convoy HG 53. They were then transferred to take over the guardianship of convoy WS 6 from the battleship *Rodney*.

They plodded along until 21 February and were, in turn, relieved by the *Malaya*. The *Ark Royal* then set course for Gibraltar, the return passage being briefly interrupted by a false report that the heavy cruiser *Admiral Hipper* had sailed from Brest. The *Ark Royal* reached Gibraltar on 25 February.

While at the Rock, the *Ark Royal* took the opportunity to conduct flying exercises on 3 March. The Skuas shared fleet defence with the Fulmars, and then conducted dive-bombing attacks against *Ark Royal* herself.

The two 'ugly sisters' made a dramatic reappearance on 8 March when they approached convoy SL 67, only to find the *Malaya* and two destroyers in attendance, whereupon they quickly sheered off. The *Ark Royal* was hastily sailed from Gibraltar that same day, with the *Renown*, light cruiser *Arethusa* and two destroyers, making high speed towards the area north of the last sighting. On contacting the convoy, they took over escort duties from *Malaya*, which had in the meantime been damaged by a U-boat torpedo. Meanwhile, the *Furious* with the other remaining Skua squadron embarked, had hurried up from Freetown with the battlecruiser *Repulse*.

While *Furious* was sent into Gibraltar and then went home, *Ark Royal* continued to patrol. The two German battle-cruisers created more havoc to the north and then made for Brest, where they were sighted on 20 March by one of *Ark Royal's* Fulmars some 600 miles WNW of Cape Finisterre. Radio failure delayed the accurate reporting of this and thus, although their old enemy passed within 110 miles of the *Ark Royal*, No. 800 Squadron's Skuas were thus denied the chance to have another crack at them, this time at sea. Thus the *Scharnhorst* and *Gneisenau* entered Brest on 22 March and *Ark Royal* returned to Gibraltar.

Some 2 days later, the carrier sailed once more to help Force H institute a blockade of the French port in the old style, alternating patrols with Home Fleet units over the next 3 weeks to maintain a continuous watch over the three enemy heavy ships.

Operation Winch

A rare break from this wearisome and fruitless patrolling came with another sortie into the western basin, to conduct yet another Hurricane reinforcement operation. The *Furious* was to have carried this out. However, her engines were playing up yet again, when the *Argus* arrived with the twelve fighters, along with their two Skua guides. Although the *Argus* could have conducted the flying off at a pinch, her short deck would have meant that the aircraft would not have been able to take off with maximum fuel aboard. Using the *Ark Royal* instead, meant more fuel and a launch at a greater range, therefore they would be more secure from enemy attack. Therefore, the *Ark Royal* had to be withdrawn from the Bay of Biscay in order to do the job. To Somerville's fury, the authorities at home appeared to have learned absolutely nothing from the previous flying-off fiasco and subsequent loss of life. He recorded: 'Two crews had been brought out in *Argus* for the Skuas accompanying the Hurricanes to Malta. After hearing reports from the commanding officers of H.M. ships *Ark Royal* and *Argus*, I was satisfied that these crews were not sufficiently experienced to carry out the operation. I therefore informed the Admiralty that I intended to utilise two experienced crews from 800 Squadron in *Ark Royal*'.[39] And so it was. With *Renown* (later joined by *Sheffield*) and four destroyers, *Ark Royal* with the Hurricanes and Skuas duly embarked, sailed late on the evening of 1 April to carry out Operation *Winch*. The fighters and Skuas were flown off at 0600 hours on 3 April, when the carrier altered course to 250° into a light breeze. The twelve Hurricanes and two Skuas were flown off in two batches, in position 37° 42' North, 06° 52' East. The weather was fair with good visibility, with a slight wind from the west boosting the flight to Malta. All these aircraft arrived safely and Force H was back at Gibralter by the 4 April.

This little operation was the swansong of carrier-borne Skua operations. Admiral Somerville had sounded the death-knell of the Skua in his force earlier.[40] The Admiralty had asked him whether he would prefer to retain No. 800 Squadron as a Skua unit, as it would provide him with dive-bomber potential. This Somerville had rejected. He favoured the Fulmar because of its slightly higher speed. As for dive-bombing, Somerville felt that there would be few opportunities for offensive operations, so he could dispense with that facility.

Operation Tender

The final replacement of the last carrier-born Skuas with Fulmars took place on 5 April, with Operation *Tender*. The previous evening the aircraft carriers *Ark Royal* and *Furious*, docked at Gibralter, exchanged stores and then, at 1915 hours, *Renown*, *Ark Royal*, *Furious* and *Sheffield*, escorted by the destroyers *Faulknor*, *Fearless*, *Fortune* and *Foresight*, sailed eastward at 18 knots until 2200 hours, when the force reversed course and increased speed to 20 knots.

At 0330 hours the light cruiser *Fiji* was met and *Repulse*, which had left Gibralter the previous day with *Argus* and the destroyers *Fury*, *Highlander* and *Velox*, was sighted at 0730 hours. With the coming of full daylight an hour late, the *Ark Royal* and *Furious*, each screened by two destroyers, operated independently of the combined fleet and carried out the aerial transfer. Four ASV fitted Swordfish and ten Fulmars were flown from *Furious* to the *Ark*, and four Swordfish and nine Skuas were flown from the *Ark* to *Furious*. One additional Skua, that had become unserviceable just prior to take-off, had to remain aboard *Ark Royal*. The whole exchange was completed by 1045 hours and *Furious*, escorted by *Faulknor* and *Fortune*, steered to join the ships steering back home. *Faulknor* later rejoined Force 'H' after handing her charges over.[41]

Thus ended the Skua's seaborne career.

Summary of combat

The Skua was not a fighter! From the outset she was designed as a dive-bomber, but with limited ability to perform fighter duties over the fleet at sea. She was certainly never expected to be pitted, head-to-head, against the latest and the best that the *Luftwaffe*, the *Regia Aeronautica* and the Vichy French could offer. Yet that is what the Skua did, and it is on that, and not her dive-bombing abilities, that the majority of historians and critics have based their assessment of her ever since.[42] So, assuming that the basis on which they were judged is a false one, how did the Skua fare?

Although the maximum number of Skuas operational at any one time in 1940 was only thirty-three, they were engaged with enemy land-based aircraft on no fewer than 152 occasions. The breakdown was as follows:

Skua versus *Luftwaffe*   = 100
Skua versus *Regia Aeronautica* = 36
Skua versus Vichy-French   = 16[43]

Not too bad a record for a dive-bomber!

NOTES

1. Take-off had been delayed 30 minutes due to problems with starting-up one of the Skuas.
2. *Haul Taut and Belay, op cit.*
3. Lieutenant Kenneth Vyvyan Vincent Spurway, a great Skua pilot, tragically was later killed in a flying accident while serving at the Royal Navy's fighter base of HMS *Heron,* Yeovilton, on 12 November 1941.
4. In fact this aircraft, from 146° *Squadriglia* RM, made it back to Elmas with one dead and three wounded crew members.
5. Lieutenant G. R. Callingham went on to serve with No. 880 Squadron in 1941 and No. 882 Squadron in 1942. He was appointed Acting Lieutenant Commander in the following year and ended the war as a full Lieutenant Commander in 1945.
6. A confirmed kill, flown by *Sottotentente* Sigfrido Marcaccini of 198° *Squadriglia*, RM.
7. The battle-cruiser *Renown* replaced the *Hood* as Somerville's Flagship; the light cruiser *Sheffield* replaced the *Arethusa* among such movements.
8. The *Illustrious* still had four Skuas embarked with No. 806 Squadron as there had been insufficient Fulmars to bring it up to strength. These were to find their way to various destinations in the eastern Mediterranean, one or two at Malta, two briefly aboard HMS *Eagle* and in the Western Desert.
9. *Valiant, Illustrious, Sheffield* and *Coventry.*
10. However, Griffith recorded that the *Ark Royal* flew three Skuas from No. 800 Squadron ashore before they left, and that Lieutenant Christian, and Petty Officer pilots Glover

and Peacock from his squadron, were also left behind, as was the battleship *Resolution*. Armoured glass and armoured panels were fitted to the Skuas that remained aboard.

11. *The Somerville Papers, op cit*, p. 137.

12. *Ibid.*

13. Commander H. Trail, RN, No. 800 Squadron, CO, was considering the use of controlled barrier landings at this time. *Ark Royal* was not finally fitted with a crash barrier until her October refit back in Liverpool between 10 and 29 October 1940.

14. Lieutenant (A) J. M. Bruen, a Dubliner, later went on to command No. 803 Squadron flying Fulmars aboard the carrier *Formidable* in 1941, where he shot down a confirmed Ju88, for which he got the DSC. He was promoted to Lieutenant Commander at HMS *Daedalus* at Lee-on-Solent in 1942, and served aboard the carrier *Indomitable* later the same year in the Indian Ocean, at Madagascar and at the famous Operation *Pedestal* Malta Convoy in August. He also took part in the North African landings at La Senia, Oran, with No. 800 Squadron, when he got his revenge for Dakar by destroying a Vichy D-520. In 1943 he was serving at HMS *Shrike*, the RNAS Londonderry, and became Acting Commander in 1944.

15. Griffith Diary, *op cit.*

16. The heavy cruisers *Australia*, *Cumberland* and *Devonshire*.

17. Griffith Diary, *op cit.*

18. The three Vichy light cruisers, *Georges Leygues*, *Montcalm* and *Gloire* (but *sans* their destroyer escorts which had been dropped off at Casablanca), had arrived safely at Dakar at noon despite all attempts by Force H and Force M to head them off.

19. Griffith Diary, *op cit.* On 17 April the DNAD had circulated a Memo, which compared the machine-gun settings patterns of two of Skua squadrons engaged over Norway. It was found that each squadron was setting its own pattern, and 'the pattern used in each case, is not the pattern issued by the Admiralty, and it is in fact too concentrated at ranges between 300 yards and 500 yards'. The patterns were: 'At 300 yards it is 8 ft×8 ft (50% zone); at 500 yards it is 8 ft×12 ft (50% zone); and at 600 yards it is 16 ft×18 ft, with gaps in it. Below 300 yards the pattern has big gaps in it, in fact if one is not fairly exact at 300 yards, where the pattern is reasonable but small, the chances of hitting are remote.' DNAD promulgated a Memo giving lining up diagrams for all fighter aircraft, including Skuas, which stated that, 'no deviation from the alignments given is to be made without Admiralty approval', the reason being that, 'for besides failing, unnecessarily, to shoot down enemy aircraft, with squadrons using various alignments it is impossible to arrive at the best alignment, always supposing the best one is other than that laid down by the Admiralty'. DNAD 27 April 1940 (A.0288/40, contained in National Archives ADM199/115). As Griffith recorded, when this missive arrived with the squadrons, it aroused some heated response from the pilots themselves! There was nothing new in this, Ron Jordan recalled that he had many arguments on the subject during the fighting over Norway. He always maintained that a 'square' pattern of harmonisation at 300 yards range was best for the Mk IV Brownings, others disagreed.

20. Midshipman W. J. Griffiths Diary, *op cit.*

21. When Swordfish flew over the town later to drop leaflets, they were met by anti-aircraft gunfire and Curtiss fighters looking for a scrap!

22. Roughly, 'Aha! There's a good light breakfast for the Admiral'.– (The Admiral concerned was probably Vice-Admiral Marcel Alfred Landriau, the Navy C-in-C at Dakar and Equatorial Africa, who had ordered the firing on the Free French peace delegation, who were under a White Flag at the time.) Quotation from Rear-Admiral Sir William Jameson, *Ark Royal 1939–1941*, Hart Davis, London, 1957.

23. Note that Arthur J. Marder, *Operation Menace*, OUP, London, 1976, claimed that the Skuas made a 'level bombing attack', but the report of Lieutenant Smeeton, the Commanding Officer of No. 800 Squadron, clearly states a 65 degree angle of dive. (See

Smeeton, Lieutenant, *Confidential Report on Dive Bombing Attack on ships in Dakar Harbour by six aircraft of No. 800 Squadron on 24th September, 1940.* ADM199/907.)

24. 'We might as well have dropped bricks!' one Fleet Air Arm pilot was recorded as saying of these attacks. Marder, *op cit.*

25. Report of Proceedings, Operation *Menace* by Admiral Sir John D. Cunningham, contained in National Archives ADM 199/906/907.

26. M. Simpson (Editor), *The Somerville Papers*, The Navy Records Society, London, 1975.

27. This Skua remained at Malta, and was eventually incorporated into the RAF's famous No. 431 Flight, which became a highly successful reconnaissance unit, with such famous pilots as Flight Lieutenant (later Wing Commander) Adrian Warburton, DSO, DFC, RAF, among its pilots.

28. *The Somerville Papers, op cit,* p 188.

29. Each armed with a single 500 lb SAP bomb.

30. Wrongly reported as Montecuccoli class light cruisers by some, but not all, this error was further compounded in some post-war histories as being a place (Monte Cuccoli!) rather than ships, resulting in total confusion.

31. *La Marina Guerra Mondiale, Vol. II, La Guerra Nel Mediterrano Le Azione Navali Dal 1 Giugno 1940 all' 31 Marzo 1941.* G. Fioravanzo, *Ufficio Storico Della Marina Militare,* Roma, 1960. Ministry of Marine, Rome, Official Narrative, *The War at Sea* by Admiral G. Berenotti.

32. From: BR 1736 (6). Naval Staff History Second World War – Selected Operations (Mediterranean), 1940. No. 9. *Action off Cape Spartivento, Sardinia.* Historical Section, Admiralty, London, 1957, p. 68.

33. Sabey, Lieutenant Commander A. W., RN, *Flying Log Book.*

34. This ship was actually not a cruiser at all, but merely the destroyer *Lanciere,* which had been hit and taken under tow, but was misreported by the TSR spotter plane.

35. Again, ship recognition was poor and the three ships were, in fact, the 8-inch heavy cruisers *Trieste, Bolzano* and *Trento,* of Admiral Luigi Sansonetti's 3rd Cruiser Division and they suffered no damage.

36. Admiral Sir James Somerville, *Report of Proceedings*, contained in National Archives ADM 199/392.

37. Somerville Papers at Churchill College Archives, SMVL 7/6.

38. There had been precedents for this, including the main Mediterranean Fleet's audacious bombardments of Bardia in August and of Valona, Albania, in December, both of which had been similarly audacious, but which had been achieved without loss.

39. Somerville Papers, Churchill College Archives, Cambridge. SMVL 7/7. Also further remarks in FOH to Admy, No. 262/16, of 5 April 1941.

40. 13 January 1941. Michael Simpson sagely commented that 'Somerville may have been a little hasty in letting his Skuas go; a dozen well-trained dive bombers, used in conjunction with Swordfish torpedo-bombers in attack on enemy warships, would have given him another attacking option'. *The Somerville Papers*, p. 60, *op cit.* However, what Simpson failed to mention at all was that the Admiralty gave Somerville a second chance to retain the Skua. Admiralty Message 1231/19 to FOH (R) *Ark Royal* proposed retaining No. 800 Squadron as a Skua unit after they had been relieved by No. 807 Squadron's Fulmars in February, but for the dive-bombers to be retained at Gibralter itself in protected dispersal points with accommodation for the personnel. In his reply (FOH 1412/28 to Admy, (R) VACNA, *Ark Royal*), Somerville recorded that, '... on the whole, I was in favour of retention of the Skuas, as this would allow the fighter strength of *Ark Royal* to be adjusted to suit special operations, and it would add to some degree our control of the Straits'. However, the proposal foundered on the bureaucracy and general inertia found at Gibralta. The VCNAS (Vice Admiral Sir G. F. B. Edward-Collins) said that nearby accommodation, sanitary arrangements etc. 'could not be provided in time by February',

other than 'at some distance from North Front'. Even then, 'it was doubtful if protected dispersal points for the aircraft could be ready'. Moreover, the Acting Governor [Sir Clive Gerrard Liddell] wanted to consult with the War Office before giving approval, and also H.M. Ambassador in Madrid [Sir Samuel Hoare] would need to be consulted, indicating that these worthies considered that any increase in the effectiveness of the Gibralter garrison [a British Crown Colony] would somehow be dependent on General Franco's tacit agreement.

41. Somerville Papers, SMVL 7/7, *op cit.*

42. And not just historians. It is interesting to note that Vice-Admiral Sir James Somerville, one of the few World War II British Admirals that went out of his way regularly to familiarise himself with air operations, got rid of the Skua in favour of the Fulmar, because he wanted a more efficient fighter aircraft for his fleet's protection, and who can blame him, rather than have dive-bomber potential. Yet, here is that same officer a year later, bitterly complaining that the Japanese Navy had wiped two of his heavy cruisers (*Dorsetshire* and *Cornwall*) off the map within minutes by dive-bombing attacks from carriers. 'These Jap bombers certainly are the devil and we've got to revise all our ideas. You see we've never been up against carrier borne aircraft before ....' He wrote to the Admiralty in a similar vein, citing 'The novel aspect of attack, *viz.* using fighter dive-bombers ....' Actually he was mistaken, the Japanese used their standard Aichi D3A1/2 'Val' dive-bomber, but the Fighter Dive-Bomber concept was hardly 'novel', as the Skua had embodied the idea since 1935 and he had used them as such in Force H all the time! (See *The Somerville Papers, op cit*, pp 407 and 408.)

43. *Vide – FAA Official History, Volume 1*, contained in National Archives ADM/234/383.

14

TRAINING, TRAGEDIES AND TARGETS

With their withdrawal from combat service, the main duties of most of the surviving Skuas were training and target towing (TT), duties that had been performed from the very beginning for most. The first production Skua, L2867, had pioneered this work at Martlesham Heath in August 1939, with drogue-towing trials proving satisfactory. Improved TT gear was developed by Blackburn and later batches were built with this duty exclusively in mind. In October 1939, seven Skuas (L2987 to L2993) were shipped straight from the factory to No. 3 Anti-Aircraft Co-operation Unit (AACU) at Malta. This unit was followed by No. 2 AACU the following February, equipping with another eight Skua TTs at Gosport (A Flight), and four more at Eastchurch (D Flight).

Initially, these schools were along the south coast because of better weather conditions. Hamble airfield near Southampton, for example, was one small field used for training. But following an attack by a single Heinkel He111 on 12 July 1940, the base was considered too vulnerable and the schools moved away to Donibristle. However, a detachment of Skuas from HMS *Raven* at Eastleigh remained there at least until a second attack on 23 November.

In a similar manner, being too close to the war zone after the fall of France caused Lee-on-Solent to suffer heavily in two air attacks during the Battle of Britain.

No. 793 Squadron had been formed in November 1939 as an ATTU. Many aircraft were destroyed by enemy action in August 1940, so units moved north. No. 776 Squadron was one example. In 1941 the Lido at Ainsdale was taken over by the Royal Navy, converted into a gunnery school and named HMS *Queen Charlotte*. A series of guns was installed

Table 27   Skuas used by No. 757 Squadron, February 1941 to April 1942

L2893	L2935	L2978	L2993	L3027
L2908	L2959	L2983	L3007	L3033
L2913*	L2961	L2984	L3014	L3035
L2934	L2974	L2985	L3026	

* at Crail

facing the sea. Aircraft from No. 776 Squadron (Fleet Air Arm) flying from RAF Woodvale would tow targets past or dive-bomb the school to give the gunners AA target practice. The Squadron lost three Skuas during the war: L2933 flown by Sub-Lieutenant C. F. Leney, which crashed in bad weather on 26 August 1942; L3004, flown by Sub-Lieutenant G. D. Hoyland, due to a collapsed undercarriage when landing on 21 December 1943; and L3008, flown by Midshipman G. I. Frazer, due to engine failure while taking off. The Skua crashed into the sea off Southport Pier but Frazer survived his dip intact! At the end of January 1946 it was placed under care and maintenance only and then closed completely.[1]

TAG Training

Between February 1941 and April 1942, the large number of Skuas withdrawn from front-line service saw useful employ at Worthy Down, where they were utilised for Telegraphist/Air Gunner (TAG) training. During this period these aircraft were attached to (or 'Borne on the books' of) No. 757 Squadron. They included several aircraft that were survivors of those that had served at Yeovilton's Fighter Training Unit (FTU) (see Table 27).

One distinguished pilot who flew the Skua with this outfit was Lieutenant (A) Laurence Olivier, RNVR, later knighted for his services to the theatre. His colleagues found him 'a quiet, likeable person, somewhat reserved, and by no means a mediocre pilot'.

Although no longer in the front line, these Skuas were at instant notice for recall to it. They were expected to be 'available' in case of invasion, so they always flew their training missions with their four .303 Browning machine-guns fully loaded. In addition, the training pilots were expected to be 'reasonably proficient' in dive-bombing. Commander 'Bill' Sears, RN, took it upon himself to instruct the Skua and Roc pilots in this 'warlike preparation'.[2]

One pilot who took part in this 'training of the trainers' later remembered that the Skuas under instruction often used the airfield's target for practising dive-bombing, utilising four smoke (practice) bombs of about 14 lb. The method was loosely to peel off at about 5,000 feet and steer the nose onto the target, at an angle of about 70 degrees. These attacks were made into the wind; otherwise a 'dedicated' pilot could find himself beyond the vertical as the target drifted under the engine cowling. He recalled that the terminal velocity in the dive, with the flaps fully extended, was around 230 knots and that on reaching it, the pilot fell forward in his harness, as there was no further acceleration to push him back in his seat. Actual bomb release, followed by the pull out was ('for we tyros') at around 2,000 feet. One had to be alert in quickly checking the dive at this point, as it was invariably accompanied by a brief temporary loss of consciousness or blackout, 'with cheeks and jowls a-'dropping'. Once the horizon looked to be back in the right place (*sic*), the pilot raised the flaps, and the Skua responded very quickly. With what was described as seeming like terrific acceleration, the aircraft was climbed once more and the process was duly repeated, until all four practice bombs had been expended.

Blake himself clocked up a total of 362 hours 20 minutes on the Skua, which was pretty much a record in itself, so he was well qualified to comment. Skuas were regarded as good in a dive, and they were always (perhaps optimistically) regarded as very strong, 'although tail units did fall off at times, but not with us'. The Skua was reputed to be tough enough to make a forced landing ashore 'a good proposition', for the engine 'far away somewhere up-front' quickly became detached, thus reducing the risk of cremation in such eventualities. Thus, although one historian described the Skua as 'too dainty an aircraft for the rigours of naval warfare',[3] most of the aircrew that flew in her described her in a totally opposite manner. One pilot recorded that the Skua 'was built like a battleship'.[4]

One log book entry recorded 'dived at ASI approximately 320 knots', which must obviously had been done without flaps. They were also highly manoeuvrable, Blake recalling that they often '"took on" RAF Hurricanes, being able to turn inside them, perhaps with "not-so-good" pilots'. Actually stalling off a turn was unheard of in the unit and a pilot could be pretty fierce with the stick, 'providing it was a progressive pressure backwards'. They could also be slow-rolled without problems, as long as the speed was maintained, but nobody tried out a spin as these particular machines had been deprived of their tail parachutes. Overall, the verdict was that flying the Skua was easy, although three-point landings were tricky. Due to their design for carrier work, they could be landed at very slow speeds, but care had to be taken when applying the brakes, especially so at Worthy Down 'where some of the landing run was downhill!'[5]

Most accidents with the Skua in No. 757 Squadron were due to engine failures, but there were no fatalities. As for the ceiling, Blake recorded that he often took them up to 20,000 feet, even though these particular machines were no longer equipped with oxygen. Altitudes of 15,000 feet were normal, for which the heater was essential and worked without problems. However, one matter that did cause problems concerned the hood. Blake himself suffered broken and dislocated bones in his right hand when a hood came off its tracks with 'a noise like an explosion'. All the essential controls (undercarriage, flaps, throttle and so on) were mounted on the left-hand side of the Skua's cockpit so he was able to land without further problems. Nonetheless, he was aware of several 'very bad' in-flight accidents due to similar hood problems, and even one fatality in

Scotland in which this was suspected as the cause. Indeed, for a time during the depths of winter, the unit was ordered to fly without hoods! Fortunately the powers-that-be eventually relented.[6]

The much-maligned Perseus engine gave few problems in itself, 'but it was very obvious that the Skua was badly underpowered'. They were rugged though, one pilot, R. Parkhouse, RNVR, while carrying out an illegal 'beat up' of an army anti-aircraft gun position, hit and carried away about 20 feet of a top 'neutral' power cable. He nonetheless returned to Worthy Down with the whole rig wrapped around his propeller and landed safely. The Skua's range, moreover, was regarded as a plus for Royal Naval aircraft.

Overall, the consensus in the unit of the Skua was that 'we came to like them and were sorry when they moved on'. By contrast, the same pilot recorded that he once flew a Roc, target-towing at Crail and found it, 'a dreadful thing not a single redeeming feature, except that they would not easily "nose over"'. This part of the Skua's life came to an abrupt halt on 16 April 1942, when an entry in Lieutenant Commander Blake's logbook read: 'All Skuas withdrawn from (T) A/G training to be converted to target towing.' Some of these aircraft, once converted by the addition of a windmill winch and associated gear, were rumoured to have been sent as far afield as Sierra Leone and Ceylon (Sri Lanka).

Accidents and errors

Many Skuas came to an abrupt termination of their short lives through flying accidents and in the rough-and-tumble of combat operations, such attrition was commonplace among all aircraft and air forces. Many of those involving the Skua have been recorded already, but other losses were by no means attributable to the stress of combat. Some were due to inexperience, bad weather and the like, while some were just plain embarrassing.

High on the category of the latter was an incident that was alleged to have occurred to No. 803 Squadron, while aboard the brand-new aircraft carrier HMS *Illustrious* on 7 July 1940, during her 'shake down' cruise and in the comparative safety and idyllic conditions of Bermuda. The story as told is as follows. On that particular day *Illustrious* was at anchor, but there was a stiff wind across the flight deck and the decision was made that it was sufficient to carry out a full flying training programme and Swordfish and Skuas took off without any difficulty from the stationary vessel. The training programme was duly carried out, but, during the period of their absence, the wind dropped. Now a dilemma of the nicest balance presented itself. For the *Illustrious* to raise sufficient steam to get underway so that there would be enough wind over her deck for the aircraft to land safely, required at least an hour, but, having exercised fully,

none of the aircraft had sufficient fuel remaining to stay airborne that
long! Apparently, any suitable airfields were out of range and there were
no flat places or suitable lengths of tarmac road for an emergency landing
to be made.

The final hope was to land back aboard and trust to luck. The flying
barriers were duly lowered, the arrester wires raised and the attempt was
begun. The Swordfish, with their low landing speed, were brought down
first. Even so, as they 'took' the wire, their arrester hooks were pulled out
to the fullest extent. The Skua, heavier with its higher landing speed:

> ... demonstrated to the unfortunate 'someone', two immutable laws
> – firstly, Murphy's and secondly that kinetic energy increases as the
> square of velocity. As each Skua hooked a wire, and pulled it out to
> its full extent, it kept going, tearing the arrestor hook out of every
> aircraft.[7]

It was stated that some of the Skuas managed to stop by cold-bloodedly
nosing into the ship's island; others went into the sea over the front of the
flight deck, a long drop. One Skua, it was alleged, and one only, managed
to stop, 'teetering on the brink', to the cheers of many of the ship's company, who were crowding every vantage point to watch this spectacular
retrieval. Another Skua, which touched down at a good rate of knots, had
the hook torn off, but had sufficient momentum to get airborne again for
a second attempt. This was done on the local golf course, shedding both
wings in the process, which cannot have pleased the millionaire oldest
members or the committee too much!

Apparently, this was the Royal Navy record for deck landing accidents,
the writing off of an entire squadron in 20 minutes. Remarkably, there
was no loss of life, but a considerable loss of face!

A great yarn indeed, but true? Maybe partially so. John Brandon told
the author[8] that the story was 'not entirely accurate'. He learnt that the
Illustrious, far from being at anchor, was actually under way when the
landings were made, and, although some aircraft might have been lost, it
was not the whole squadron. One thing was confirmed and that was that
one Skua landed on Bermuda golf course. The pilot was Lieutenant
Commander Nichols. Far from becoming a pariah for churning up the
sacred turf, when he eventually revisited the club in the 1980s, 'he was
given a tremendous reception'.

For the true account of what occurred, we again have the reliable Sub-
Lieutenant Hogg's journal:

> At the end of a week we were more or less saturated in the delights
> of Bermuda and commenced to do some flying with the carrier
> anchored just outside the dockyard. This flying off a stationary
> carrier was responsible for Black Sunday.

Five Skuas and two Fulmars took off to carry out interception exercises; the Skuas were to dive-bomb the harbour and the Fulmars were to try and stop them with mock fighter attacks. When we set off there was a fairly good wind speed but it died away while we were in the air, leaving no wind speed over the deck. The result was that when landing, the relative speed of approach was higher, putting greater strain on the aircraft deck-landing hooks.

Finishing the exercise, I prepared to land and, coming up astern, noticed an aircraft hanging over the side from the starboard crane. This was not entirely unusual and I paid no attention, pulling off a fast but uneventful landing. I went down to the hangar with my Fulmar, but arrived on deck again in time to see Eric land. He touched down, travelling at a terrific speed, caught a wire and tore his hook off; unhindered, the aircraft rolled down the flight deck and slowly trickled over the bows. There was a concerted rush and I got there just as Eric climbed out of his still floating Skua.

The deck was made ready again for Nick to land and the ship's company lined the side to watch the fun. He also landed successfully but tore his hook out; taking no chances, he opened his throttle and took off – minus a hook.

It was now impossible for him to land on the ship so he flew off to have a look at the prospects of landing on the golf course, as there was no land aerodrome on Bermuda at that time. He flew, low, along one of the airways to make sure that there were no bunkers and was so intent on his task that he flew straight into a wood and crashed. He and his observer climbed out, badly shaken, and set off to the club-house. On the way there they were waylaid by an American who asked, in a nasal twang, if they were 'naval aviators'.

The Skua I had seen hanging from the crane was the CO's. His hook had also broken off, the aircraft had swung towards the side and the undercarriage was sliced off by a small obstruction. He and V. J. sat there for a minute until, suddenly, the same thought struck them simultaneously – Fire. They shot out of their cockpits like startled rabbits.

Robert, new to the Squadron, had had a narrow escape, his aircraft finishing its landing with the tail hanging over the port side. Both Fulmars landed safely due to the fact that their hooks were new and strong.

We did not fly in harbour again unless half a gale was blowing!

So there it is, there were two Fulmars and five Skuas of No. 806 Squadron involved on that day, out of a total complement of three Fulmars and nine Skuas. Despite the subsequent embellishments down the years, as befits a 'golfing' yarn, not least by Hogg's father ('They landed on the 16th fairway, Mid Ocean Club! The engine finished on the 17th Green') *all* the aircraft were recovered and taken back aboard *Illustrious* again. That same worthy was also responsible for the conspiracy theory that it was all a plan to get rid of the old aircraft and the only way to get new ones. However, if that was so it backfired, for none were total write-offs, even the one that Sub-Lieutenant O. J. R. Nicholls landed on the green itself (L2904), finished her days quietly with No. 770 Squadron at far-away Crail in April 1943.

But of course the entire Skua complement aboard *Illustrious* could not have been wiped out as described, for when the squadron re-equipped with the Fairey Fulmar at Eastleigh on 15 July, there were just not enough of the new fighters available. The *Illustrious* sailed to the Mediterranean with at least six Skuas on No. 806 Squadron's strength and these were not disposed of until after the carrier reached Alexandria. Those of her Skua complement that survived, ended up at various locations in the Eastern Mediterranean, including at least two that carried out deck landings and take-offs aboard the carrier *Eagle*.

It is still a great story, but it should probably enter the record books as a particularly good 'line-shoot', rather than as yet another slur on the Skua.

That is not to say that No. 806 Squadron did not lose Skuas on this voyage. On 11 June, Sub-Lieutenant (A) L. F. Lowe, with Naval Airman P. R. L, Douet, had flown from Worthy Down in L2965, but had to force-land in the sea. Both men were rescued safely and the aircraft was salvaged. However, on the way back to England they did lose one, totally without trace. On 17 July, Skua L2941 went into the Atlantic with the loss of both her aircrew, Lieutenant Peter N. Dean, RN and Naval Airman K. L. Jones. Sub-Lieutenant Hogg witnessed the whole tragedy:[9]

> Peter was a fairly new arrival who had replaced Jack when that worthy went to hospital after his crash. He was flying round the ship when he saw a Swordfish below him and decided to do a dummy attack on it; it was fairly low on the water and Peter went right up behind, until he must have hit the slipstream, stalled and span into the sea. A destroyer raced to the rescue and found nothing.
>
> As I stood watching from the flight deck I happened to look down, to see a shark stalking us. Poor Peter.

Nor were coincidences hard to find, as Hogg himself testified:

> ... we arrived safely off the West coast of Scotland and the Squadron flew off to Donisbristle, landing at Prestwick for lunch. I sat next to an engineer who was marvelling at a Skua that he had received for repair.
>
> 'I have never seen anything like it. The damned thing's riddled through and through – how the pilot escaped, I don't know. The back

cockpit is drenched in blood and the front one surrounded by bullet holes.'

At this I pricked up my ears and asked its number. He told me – it was my Channel machine!

Pilot error

There have been several descriptions of how the Skua flew by very famous pilots. These range from Squadron Leader D. H. Clarke's, 'one of the six best aircraft I have flown'[10] to Captain Eric Brown's 'stately',[11] but even the most staid aircraft could be lethal in uncertain hands. The example below can suffice to illustrate this point.

On 12 November 1939, Sub-Lieutenant E. S. Woodford of No. 774 Squadron was flown from Eastleigh to collect Skua L3036 from No. 5 Maintenance Unit at Kemble. Woodford's task was to ferry this almost brand-new aircraft[12] to Worthy Down, which appeared simple enough. The young Sub-Lieutenant had been taught to fly at Sywell in June 1938, and had mustered 54 hours dual and 181 hours solo flying, but was comparatively inexperienced on the Skua, with only 8 hours' flying time on the type.

At 1245 hours, before Woodford took off, a weather report and route forecast covering his journey was obtained from Abingdon Meteorological Office. This report was pretty grim and ran:

Weather overcast, occasional rain. Visibility 2,000/4,000 yards. Clouds 8–10/10 at 1,000/2,000 feet, lowering to 600 feet and covering high ground in rain. Surface wind S.S.W. 15/20 mph at 2,000 feet. 230° 30–40 mph. Freezing level 8,000 feet.[13]

After some thought, the officer in command of the Testing Flight at Kemble considered that it was safe to go ahead. However, a proviso attached to this authorisation was that Woodford strictly followed a track from Kemble to Harwell, then Harwell to Reading and finally Reading to Worthy Down. Such a route would enable the pilot to follow the railway line the whole way and would avoid all the intervening high ground. This safe route was duly entered into the Authorisation Book, and Woodford read it and signed as having understood. To make absolutely certain that he was 'on message', the station commander took him aside again just before his departure and reiterated just how poor conditions would be over high ground and that he should keep to the agreed track. Woodford stated that he understood and took the weather report with him when he finally took off at 1320 hours.

The pilot did a quick circuit of the airfield to satisfy himself that the Skua was airworthy and then took his departure and was lost to view. For some reason, which will never be known, Woodward ignored all the

advice and instead selected almost a straight-line course from Kemble to
Worthy Down, which meant flying across the high ground he had been
warned to avoid.

Some 27 miles out from Kemble, L3036 was next seen at 1345 hours by
many witnesses. They stated the Skua was flying 'dangerously low and
partly enshrouded in mist and low cloud', just above the tops of the trees
of Savernake Forest. Reaching the south-western corner of the forest, still
flying in mist and cloud, it was seen to make two steeply banked left-hand
circuits. On completion of the second circuit and when still very steeply
banked, and with the engine running at full power, the aircraft dived into
open ground some 30 yards from the edge of the forest. Woodford was
killed instantly.

The Accidents Investigations Branch (AIB) was notified by RAF
Upavon at 2145 hours the same evening, and was at the scene of the crash
the next morning. The AIB quickly confirmed what the eyewitnesses had
already reported, that the Skua had dived into the earth at a steep angle
with the engine still running 'at considerable power'. The wreckage was
sifted through carefully. The crash occurred at a height of 636 feet above
sea level. The undercarriage and flaps were both fully up and no defects
could be found in the aircraft's structure or controls, which could not be
attributed to the impact. The cockpit instruments were also examined in
detail, and the Sperry gyro horizon was judged to have been functioning
normally right up to the moment of impact.

The summary of the AIB Inspector was brutally frank:

> Uncertain of his position when flying in mist at a dangerously low
> altitude over high country, this comparatively inexperienced pilot
> lost control of his aeroplane at too low a height to effect recovery.

He added:

> The pilot disregarded the route given him by the officer i/c Testing
> Flight, Kemble and instead of flying so as to avoid all high ground
> attempted to fly directly from Kemble to Worthy Down across the
> highest ground in the district.[14]

It was a needless tragedy.

Some you walk away from – and some you don't

You could smash a Skua up and walk away intact because she was
capable of withstanding all manner of indignities. One pilot who proved
this fact was Lieutenant John William Lucas, RN, of No. 778 Squadron,
the Service Trials Unit, which moved from Lee-on-Solent to Abroath that
month. On 27 July 1940, Lucas clambered aboard Skua L2944, which had
been standing out in the rain, and Leading Airman Alan Dudley Rosser,

his TAG, climbed into the back ready for take-off. Lucas was no tyro, but had never flown a Skua before, although 2 months previously he had taken a Roc up for 40 minutes. His Skua debut was to prove of even shorter duration, however.

Lucas started the engine, conducted the pre-take-off checks, and then was away. The Skua lifted a little, then almost immediately, with the flaps and undercarriage still fully down, made a steep turn, stalled and fell into the ground, injuring both men. Once the mess and men had been cleared away a full Board of Inquiry was convened on 8 August.

Engine failure was the reason put forward for this incident and the Board considered two options. Rosser postulated that the heavy shower some 25 minutes prior to take-off might have been the cause. Just before the crash Rosser saw a puff of black smoke from the engine, which indicated to him some sort of temporary partial failure in the ignition system from the rainwater. No such indications were found by the examination of the Skua's engine later, but by that time the sun was out and the water, if there was any, would have evaporated, removing the evidence.

The Board dismissed this notion, stating that there was not sufficient evidence to conclude that engine failure was a contributory factor. The Board came to a very different conclusion. They thought that Lucas might have throttled back, when in fine pitch, to about half throttle in the cruising range, in order to reduce rpm. Having operated the pitch change lever, he might have got the impression that his engine was failing within a few seconds, due to the immediate reduction in engine noise and rpm combined with the lack of power when the airscrew moved into coarse pitch at so small a throttle opening. They therefore concluded that the accident was due to, 'an error of judgement on the part of the pilot'.[15]

Whether the Pegasus was really to blame for Lucas's severe injuries can never be proved, but it undoubtedly led to the death of 20-year-old Sub-Lieutenant A. J. Newton and his TAG more than 2 years later. They belonged to No. 776 Squadron, based at Woodvale, and were ferrying Skua L2892 from that base to Speke, near Liverpool, on 2 February 1943, when the engine stopped in the vicinity of Bolton, Lancashire. Newton apparently attempted to make a glide landing, with the undercarriage still retracted, but had little time to be choosy about where to set down. What the young pilot desperately searched for was any bit of flattish land in this predominantly hilly area. In the event, the aircraft descended at high speed in a rain-soaked and sodden field near Dunscar, Bolton, sliding along on impact with the propeller 'feathered'. Unfortunately, the Skua failed to tip up on her nose, as she normally did, so the momentum was maintained and she quickly ran out of grass. The aircraft continued on her belly toward the edge of a disused quarry, then fell into it. Although full of water, this failed to cushion the impact sufficiently to prevent L2892 exploding as she hit, killing both the aircrew instantly. The wreck sank immediately, taking both bodies down with her to a depth of some 60 feet.

The next day a considerable recovery operation was set in motion by No. 75 Maintenance Unit, RAF. The area around the rim of the quarry was like a quagmire, ruling out use of the unit's mobile crane, and improvised sheer-legs had to be erected. Between 4 and 6 February, using this with an arrangement of pulleys and cables, and with the help of naval divers, the wreck was finally lifted and the bodies recovered. But the pulverised mass of the engine had settled deep in the bottom mud and proved intractable, so was left *in situ.*[16]

The guilty party, that fickle Perseus, lay undisturbed in its watery grave for another 30 years, but, in 1974 members of the Bolton Sub-Aqua Club finally located it and recovered it. It was conveyed to the nearby Institute of Technology who cleaned it up as an exercise, before gifting it to the RAF Museum. The museum had no space for it, so it was placed in store at Cardington airfield near Bedford. The quarry that had been hidden for so long, also passed away, being filled in and turned into a park and a children's playground. It was a happy final outcome to a miserable accident that had cost the lives of two young men, not much older than those who play there today.

'Throw the machine about'

Although inexperienced pilots might come to grief from time to time, even veterans could pay the price if vigilance was not maintained. Sub-Lieutenant (A) G. R. Cruickshank of No. 801 Squadron was a young pilot, but he had clocked up an impressive 77 hours on the Skua, and was hardly a novice. On the afternoon of 15 May 1941, he was detailed to conduct a 2-hour flight of Skua L2887, which had just had an adjustment to the airscrew supply line. According to the official report Cruickshank received no definite instructions, but the understanding seemed to be that he would 'throw the machine about'. Conditions were good; it was a typical spring afternoon, with an 8 to 12 mph wind from the NNE, 7/10th stratus cloud at 2,000 to 3,000 feet and 6-mile visibility. Taking Sub-Lieutenant (A) R. C. Brownie as his rear-seat man for what promised to be a pleasant jaunt, acrobatics with official blessing, Cruickshank took off at around 1400 hours.

An hour later, an observer on the ground near Itchen Abbas, about 3 miles due east of Winchester, was startled to see an aircraft spinning or spiralling down to the right, from a height when first seen of about 1,000 feet. The aircraft's tail plane broke away at low altitude and the machine dived straight into the ground, bursting into flames on impact. It was L2887 and neither Cruickshank nor Brownie were seen to make the slightest attempt to bale out. Both men were killed instantly.

The AIB at Gloucester were alerted by a telephone call from Lee-on-Solent and the team made its way to the crash site. What they found made sobering reading. The Skua's tail plane was located some 30 yards away from the main wreckage. It had fallen vertically into a wood from low altitude and suffered only minor damage. The tail plane of the Skua, as we have noted, was attached to the fuselage at three points. The front attachment comprised eight high-tensile $3/16$ inch bolts through the web of the tail plane front spar and the bulkhead of the detachable tail unit. These bolts were screwed into anchor nuts riveted to the front face of the bulkhead. The second attachment was at the rear spar and the third at the false spar. 'Built like a Battleship', was supposed to be Blackburn's trademark. However, tough old bird as the Skua undoubtedly was, she had an Achilles' heel.

A close examination found that the tail plane had broken away in a direction port tip upwards and backwards. The front attachment showed clear evidence of 'chatter' at the points of contact between the face of the front tail plane spar and the fuselage bulkhead along the line of the bottom row of bolt holes. The final failure of the bolts was upward. The holes they passed through were also elongated downward, showing that the tail plane spar was moving in both directions. To the experienced team it was obvious that the bolts here had been loose for some time and that there had been partial failure long before the fatal last manoeuvre. Pulling the aircraft out of a dive into a climbing turn only increased the tension on these already loose bolts and concentrated the load on the secure bolts, which then failed in turn as they had insufficient strength to withstand the pressures of further aerobatics. As the angle of incidence increased, the Skua was thus locked in an unrecoverable spiral dive.

The history of the airframe was checked. L2887 was first delivered by Blackburn on 24 January 1939, but had not been allocated to No. 801 Squadron until 15 December 1940, when it already had 324 hours 'on the clock'. This machine had already undergone Modification No. 121, strengthening the tail-wheel strut attachment, on 11 September, which had entailed the removal of the tail plane. Since then, the Skua had flown another 46 hours, during which the bolts, which had been replaced, had not been checked by removing the inspection covers located for that purpose near the leading edge. The daily inspection did not specifically call for this to be done only to 'Examine the fin and tail plane attachments for security'. The inspection conducted on the morning of the accident, therefore, merely involved flexing the tail plane unit, when no looseness was detected.

This type of accident had occurred before, a similar incident taking place on 14 June 1940. Again four of the attachment bolts were found to have sheered and the remaining holes had elongated and, again, the Skua concerned had flown about 46 hours since the last inspection. Four other

Skuas from No. 801 Squadron, all of which had been grounded, were examined. In each case the bottom row of bolts was found to be loose, with, in two cases, the bolts being unscrewed for $^1/_4$ and $^3/_8$ inch respectively. In another Skua the top pair of holes and the outer holes in the fuselage bulkhead were elongated in and up and down direction, with the signs of chatter closely resembling those on L2887. In every case the bolts could be finger turned, despite the fact that the threaded portion projected through the fibre of the locknut.

The report concluded that the existing anchor nut was ineffective as a means of locking bolts that were subject to vibration and 'Inadequate maintenance inspection must be considered a contributory factor'.[17] Chief Inspector, Group Captain Vernon Brown, noted: 'Action has already been taken to carry out an immediate inspection on all Roc and Skua aircraft. It has also been decided to introduce immediately a modification to strengthen the front tail plane attachment.'[18]

Even then, no chances were taken. Captain Eric Brown, RN, that most distinguished of naval airman, wrote that when he test-flew the Roc and Skua, he found that: 'Aerobatics were prohibited below 5,000 feet (1,525 metres) and deliberate spinning was prohibited under any circumstances, although I was never quite sure why.'[19] Cruickshank's unfortunate demise was why!

And so the Skua passed into history. The very last Skua in FAA service was L3034, which served with No. 776 Squadron until March 1945. Almost totally unknown to the British public in general, scorned and derided by aviation buffs, except in the fading memories of a few navy flyers the Skua seemed destined to fade into oblivion as the decades passed.

The Skua had surprised people before, and she was destined to do so yet again. Operation *Skua* was about to take place. But that, as they say, is *another* story!

NOTES

1. *Ships of the Royal Navy, A Historical Index, Vol. 1 – Major Ships.*
2. See Correspondence from W. H. C. Blake to Lieutenant Commander (A) L. A. Cox, dated 30 December 1978. (Held in Archives, Fleet Air Arm Museum, RNAS Yeovilton.)
3. John D. R. Rawlings, *Pictorial History of the Fleet Air Arm*, Ian Allan, Shepperton, 1973.
4. Squadron Leader D. H. Clarke, DFC, AFC, *The Shunned Skua*, article in *RAF Flying Review*, December 1961.
5. *Ibid.*
6. *Ibid.*
7. See John Brandon, *Seafires and Superchargers, Part 2 – How you really shouldn't do it!* In *Australian Ultralights* magazine. See also the similar version in Charles Lamb, *War in a Stringbag*, Cassell, 1977.
8. John Brandon to the author, Thursday, 12 January 2006.

9. Hogg manuscript, *op cit.*
10. Clarke, D. H. Blackburn, *B-24 Skua. What were they like to Fly*, Ian Allan, Shepperton, 1964.
11. Brown, Capt. Eric *Wings of the Navy: Flying Allied Carrier Aircraft of World War Two.* Edited by William Green, Airlife Publishing Ltd, Shrewsbury, 1987.
12. L3036 had been delivered to Kemble from Brough on 6 October 1939 and had just 2 hours 15 minutes 'time in air' when Woodford took off.
13. Patrick G. Tweedie, Inspector, Service Accident Report W-708. 23rd November 1939. RN (contained in National Archives AVIA 5-19).
14. *Ibid.*
15. Report of the Board of Inquiry in the accident to aircraft No. L2944, RN Air Station, Lee-on-Solent, dated 9 August 1940 (contained in National Archives AVIA 5/20).
16. Operational Record Book of No. 7 MU, RAF. See Ray Sturtivent, *Fleet Air Arm Aircraft 1939–1945, op cit.* and Lancashire Aircraft Investigation Team 8 October 2003.
17. Special Accident Report W-1023A – Flight Lieutenant R. Wilson, AIB, 6 June 1941. (National Archives, London, AVIA 5/20).
18. *Ibid* – Group Captain Vernon Brown, Chief Inspector.
19. Captain Eric Brown, CBE, DSC, AFC, RN, *Wings of the Navy: Flying Allied Carrier Aircraft of World War Two*, Airlife Publishing Ltd, Shrewsbury, 1987.

Appendix 1

SKUA 'FIRSTS'

The Blackburn Skua was notable for a Royal Navy aircraft for the large number of 'firsts' she notched up in such a short career:

First – monoplane in Royal Naval service;

First – all-metal aircraft in Royal Naval service;

First – British aircraft to shoot down a Confirmed German aircraft in the Second World War;

First – aircraft in the world to sink a major warship by dive-bombing;

First – British aircraft to have a bomb-ejector fork for bomb to clear propeller in dive;

First – British aircraft with sleeve-valve engine;

First – British aircraft to feature Koffman starter gun for engine;

First – British aircraft to mount four Browning guns clear of prop. No CC gear;

First – British aircraft to feature two-speed propeller (two pitch positions);

First – and only aircraft to be fitted with anti-spin tail parachute;

First – British aircraft equipped with radio-homing beacon on new VHF;

First – British aircraft to have front gun reflector sight;

First – British aircraft fitted with oxygen bottles and supply lines.

Appendix 2

SKUA COMBAT UNITS – COMMANDING OFFICERS

No. 800 Squadron

Lieutenant Commander G. N. Torry, RN (Flight Lieutenant RAF) – November 1938 to April 1940.
Captain R. T. Partridge, RM – April 1940 to May 1940.
Lieutenant E. G. D. Finch-Noyes, RN (Temp) – May 1940 to June 1940
Lieutenant R. D. Smeeton, RN – June 1940 to May 1941.

No. 801 Squadron

Lieutenant Commander H. P. Bramwell, RN – January 1940 to April 1940.
Lieutenant C. P. Campbell-Horsfall, RN – April 1940 to June 1940.
Lieutenant I. R. Sarel, RN – June 1940 to May 1941.

No. 803 Squadron

Lieutenant Commander D. R. F. Campbell, RN – March 1939 to February 1940.
Lieutenant W. P. Lucy, RN – February 1940 to May 1940.
Lieutenant Commander J. Casson, RN – May 1940 to June 1940.
Lieutenant J. M. Bruen, RN – June 1940 to October 1940.

No. 806 Squadron

Lieutenant Commander G. L. G. Evans, DSC, RN – February 1940 to June 1941.

Appendix 3

FAA SQUADRONS WITH SKUA COMPLEMENT

No. 755	No. 767	No. 774	No. 782	No. 792
No. 757	No. 769	No. 776	No. 787	No. 794
No. 758	No. 770	No. 778	No. 788	No. 797
No. 759	No. 771	No. 779	No. 789	
No. 760	No. 772	No. 780	No. 791	

Appendix 4

LOSSES IN NORWAY 1940

The dedicated Norwegian staffs at the Bodø Norsk Luftfartmuseum are continuing Operation *Skua*, and are active every year hunting for wrecks. Many have been located and hopes are high of reassembling another Skua in full for display. In June 2006 I was privileged to be their guest and was given much insight into the work they are conducting.

Date	Serial	Marking	Unit	Aircrew	Location
12 April	L3037	A7Q	803	Petty Officer J. A. Gardner Naval Airman A. Todd	Marikaved, Askey
25 April	L2903		803	Lieutenant H. E. R. Torin R. F. Ronald Hurford	Stokksund, Roan
25 April	L2918	8A	803	Lieutenant A. B. Fraser-Harris Leading Airman G. S. Russell	Rissa, Husbysjøen
25 April	L39048	A8	803	Lieutenant G. R. Collingham Naval Airman D. Prime	Namsos, Spillumstranda
26 April	L2940	A6A	800	Captain R. T. Partridge, RM Lieutenant R. Bostock	Tafjord, Breiddalsvatnet
26 April	L2991	8Q	803	Lieutenant Cecil H. Filmer Petty Officer K. G. Baldwin	Ålesund, Ålesund havn
8 May	L2916	8M	803	Sub-Lieutenant Philip N. Charlton Naval Airman F. Curriford	Astafjorden, Tovika
9 May	L3055	6H	800	Midshipman C. Treen Naval Airman A. E. Goble	Narvik, Grøndalsuannlt
13 May	L3001	6K	800	Lieutenant J. A. Rooper Petty Officer W. Crawford	Harstad, Slakstad
14 May	L2918	8G	803	Lieutenant T. E. Gray Leading Airman Clayton	Coast above Ramsa
16 May	L2910	8K	803	Lieutenant L. A. Harris Lieutenant J. H. R. Vereker	Narvik, Sør av Øyord
21 May	L3010	8B	803	Sub-Lieutenant I. Easton Naval Airman A. J. Hayman	Harstad, Sandsøya
13 June	L2963	7F	803	Lieutenant C. H. Filmer Midshipman T. A. McKee	Orkanger, Frøsetskjaeret
13 June	L2992	7L	803	Sub-Lieutenant J. A. Harris Naval Airman S. R. D. Stevenson	Orkanger, Tømmeråsen
13 June	L3000	6F	800	Lieutenant G. E. D. Finch-Noyes Petty Officer H. G. Cunningham	Trondheim, Møllebakken
13 June	L2992	7A	803	Lieutenant Commander John Casson Lieutenant P. E. Fanshawe	Orkanger, Utenfor Langvika

Date	Serial	Marking	Unit	Aircrew	Location
13 June	L3047	6H	800	Midshipman D. T. R. Martin Leading Airman W. J. Tremeer	Trondheim
13 June	L2955	7Q	803	Sub-Lieutenant R. E. Bartlett Naval Airman L. G. Richards	Rennebu, Vagnillgrenda
13 June	L2995	6A	800	Captain R. T. Partridge Lieutenant R. S. Bostock	Rissa, V/Bessholmen
13 June	L3028	6G	800	Midshipman L. H. Gallagher Petty Officer W. Crawford	Rissa, Templet
13 Sept.	L2912		801	Petty Officer Edward G. H. Harwin Naval Airman John R. Maunder	Svartedalen, Andvik
22 Sept.	L2942		801	Sub-Lieutenant B. F. Wigginton Ken. R. King	Ramsele
16 Oct.	L2902		801	Lieutenant E. G. Savage/ Lieutenant H. S. Hayes	Vassare Trask, Gallivarre

Appendix 5

DIAGRAMS

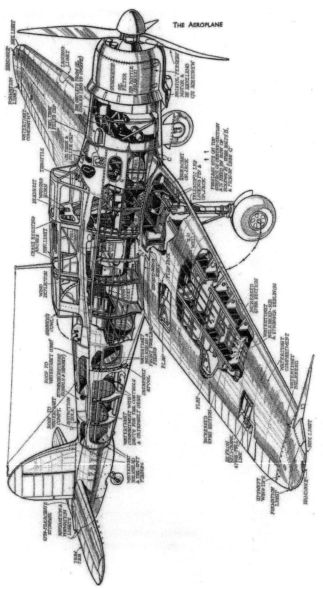

A cut-away illustration of the Skua

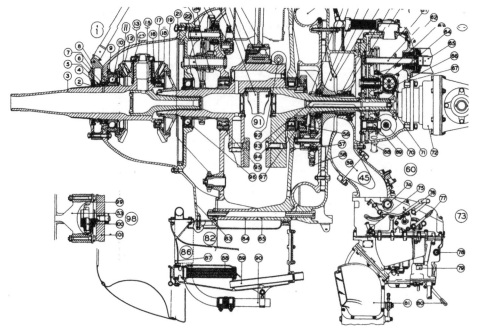

The general arrangement of the Perseus engine

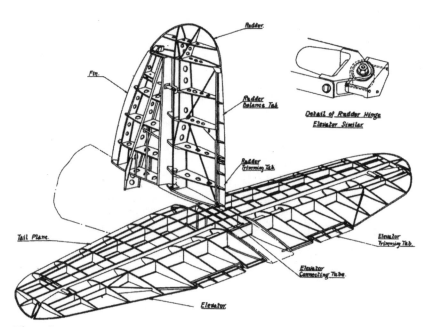

The tail unit

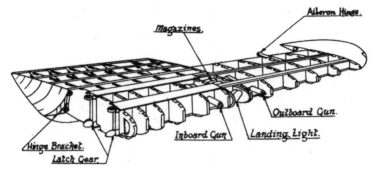

The mainplane

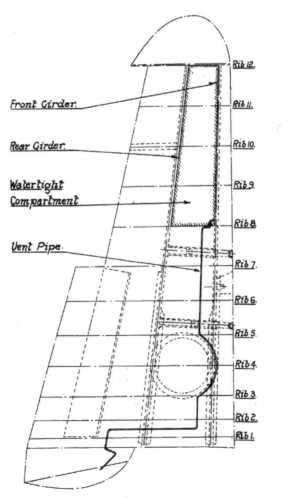

Watertight compartments in the mainplane

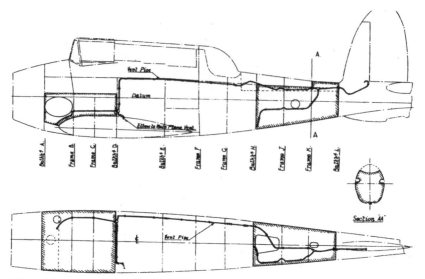

Watertight compartments in the fuselage

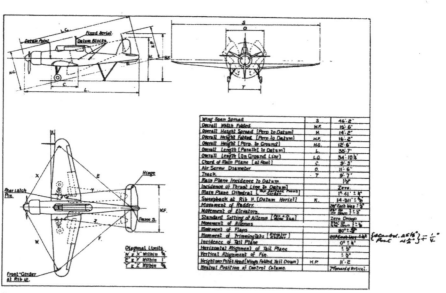

Rigging

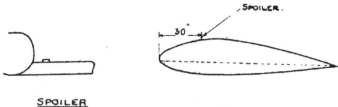

SPOILER
3" CHORD, 8" SPAN, 8" FROM WING ROOT.

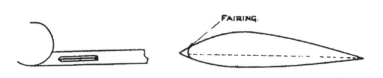

POINTED FAIRINGS ON LEADING EDGE
4" CHORD, 40" SPAN, 8" FROM ROOT.

Spoiler and wing leading edge

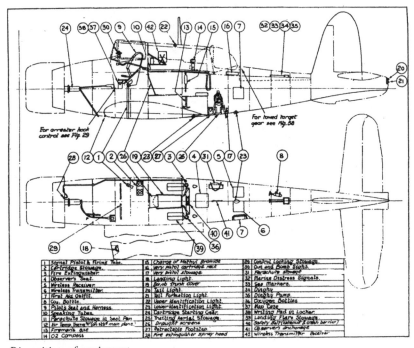

Disposition of equipment

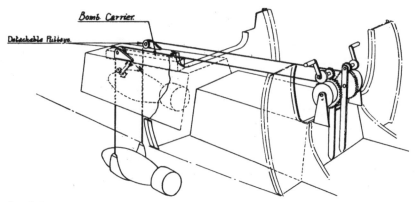

Bomb hoist gear

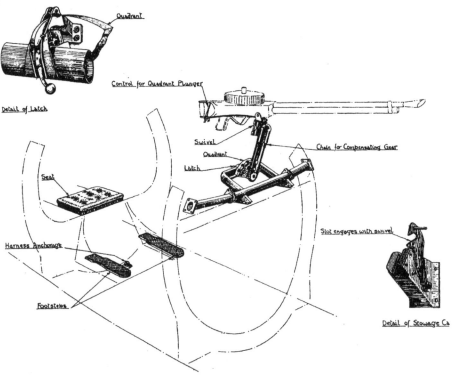

Rear gun mounting

Lining up target vessel with electronic ring and bead sight. Gunsight used for dive bombing.

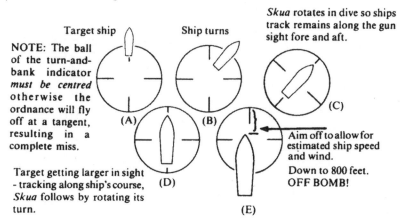

NOTE: The ball of the turn-and-bank indicator *must be centred* otherwise the ordnance will fly off at a tangent, resulting in a complete miss.

Target ship   Ship turns

Skua rotates in dive so ships track remains along the gun sight fore and aft.

(A)   (B)   (C)

Target getting larger in sight - tracking along ship's course, *Skua* follows by rotating its turn.

(D)

Aim off to allow for estimated ship speed and wind.
Down to 800 feet.
OFF BOMB!

(E)

Electronic ring and bead gun-sight used for dive-bombing (Based on information from Skua pilots)

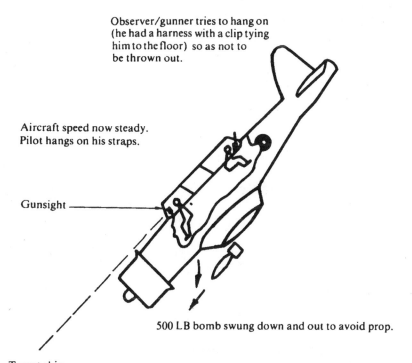

Observer/gunner tries to hang on (he had a harness with a clip tying him to the floor) so as not to be thrown out.

Aircraft speed now steady. Pilot hangs on his straps.

Gunsight

500 LB bomb swung down and out to avoid prop.

Target ship

Skua final attack dive

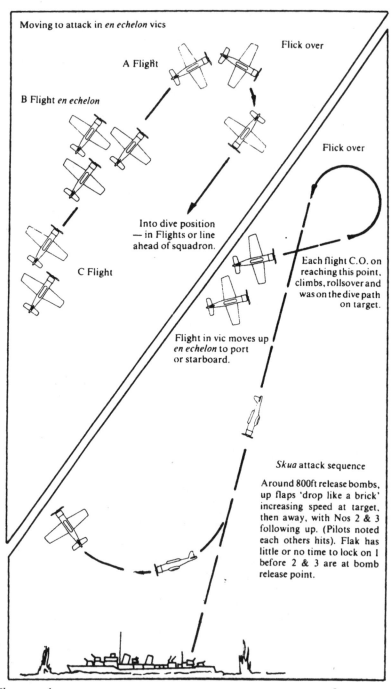

Moving to attack in *en echelon* vics

A Flight

Flick over

B Flight *en echelon*

Flick over

Into dive position
— in Flights or line
ahead of squadron.

Each flight C.O. on
reaching this point,
climbs, rollsover and
was on the dive path
on target.

C Flight

Flight in vic moves up
en echelon to port
or starboard.

Skua attack sequence

Around 800ft release bombs,
up flaps 'drop like a brick'
increasing speed at target,
then away, with Nos 2 & 3
following up. (Pilots noted
each others hits). Flak has
little or no time to lock on 1
before 2 & 3 are at bomb
release point.

Skua attack sequence

The rough position of the bombs during the *Königsberg*'attack 10 April 1940.

N.B. The single hit forward penetrated through her fo'c'sle. The combination of the hit amidships and a near miss closely adjacent probably put her under.

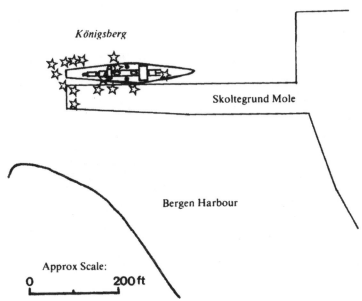

Bomb placement in the attack on the Königsberg *at Bergen on 10 April 1940*

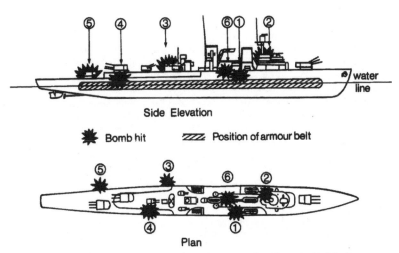

Bomb hits on the Königsberg *(Based on the report by Captain Ruhfus)*

BIBLIOGRAPHY

Original documents

Admiralty: Squadron Diaries and Standing Orders 1939–1957 (National Archives ADM 207).

Admiralty: Various Combat Reports (contained National Archives ADM 199/479 and 480; AIR50, AIR 207 and AIR27/2387).

Admiralty: London, BR 1736 (6). *Naval Staff History Second World War – Selected Operations (Mediterranean), 1940. No. 9. Action off Cape Spartivento, Sardinia.* Historical Section, Admiralty, London, 1957, p 68.

Admiralty: Report of Proceedings, Operation *Menace* by Admiral Sir John D. Cunningham (contained in National Archives ADM 199/906/907).

Admiralty: Smeeton, Lieutenant, *Confidential Report on Dive Bombing Attack on ships in Dakar Harbour by six aircraft of No. 800 Squadron on 24th September 1940.* ADM199/907.

Admiralty: Combat report extracts for No. 803 Squadron, *Mers-el-Kebir Action*, dated 6 July 1940 (contained in National Archives ADM/166).

Admiralty: Admiral Sir James Somerville, *Report of Proceedings* (contained in National Archives ADM 199/392).

Admiralty: No. 801 Squadron, *Operational Record Book*, 31 May 1940 (contained in National Archives AIR 27/2387).

Admiralty: *FAA Official History, Vol. 1* (contained in National Archives ADM/234/383).

Admiralty: Commanding Officer, No. 801 Squadron, RAF Station Detling, Maidstone, Monthly Letter of Proceedings, dated 13 June 1940 (B/G 18/3 contained in National Archives ADM 199/115).

Admiralty: No. 801 Squadron, *Operational Record Book*, 31 May 1940 (contained in National Archives AIR 27/2387).

Admiralty: Commanding-in-Chief, Home Fleet, HMS *Rodney*, Memorandum – *Dive Bombing attack by Skuas of 800 and 803 Squadrons on enemy warships at Trondheim on Thursday, 13th June, 1940*, dated 27 June 1940 (1118/H.F. 1359 contained in National Archives ADM 199/480).

Admiralty: Lieutenant Commander Charles Evans, RN, *Operations of No. 806 Squadron while working in conjunction with the RAF Coastal Command from 27 May to 3 June, 1940, dated 11 June 1940. (1712/155 contained in National Archives ADM 199/115).*

Admiralty: No. 801 Squadron, *Operational Record Book*, 31 May 1940 (contained in National Archives AIR 27/2387).

Admiralty: *Notes by Director of Naval Air Division on Report on sinking of* Königsberg, dated 25 April 1940 (X/L04326 contained in National Archives ADM 199/478).

Admiralty: Report No. 11, *Attack on enemy warships in Trondheim Harbour*, dated 13 June 1940 (CAFO 3572/39 contained in National Archives ADM 199/480).

Admiralty: Lieutenant C. H. Filmer, RN, *Report of attack on three Junkers 88s and subsequent forced-landing of Skua L2991 in Aalesund Harbour*, copy in author's collection.

Admiralty: Operation *Paul* (contained in National Archives document, ADM 199/1930).

Admiralty: *Notes by Director of Naval Air Division on Report on sinking of Königsberg*, dated 25 April 1940 (X/L04326 contained in National Archives ADM 199/478).

Admiralty: Lieutenant Commander Campbell, *Roc and Skua Aircraft – Squadron Establishment*; Memo dated 30 January 1940, Ref: O 7 (contained in National Archives ADM 1/10749).

Admiralty: *The Blackburn Skua I* (in National Archives R.T.P. 4618/291).

Admiralty: *Memorandum on Naval Air Policy, Vol. 1.* DNAD Naval Staff, dated 13 March 1936 (contained in National Archives ADM 116/4030).

Admiralty: Vice-Admiral S. J. Meyrick, CB, RN, *FAA Tactics and Equipment – Observations on Draft Memorandum*, dated 24 February 1937 (M05506/36 contained in National Archives ADM 116/4030).

Admiralty Handbook, *Aircraft Attack and Defence* (National Archives ADM 186/96).

Admiralty: Admiral Sir Roger Backhouse, 7 May 1937 (contained in National Archives ADM 116/4030).

Air Ministry: Patrick G. Tweedie, Inspector, Service Accident Report W-708, 23 November 1939 RN (contained in National Archives AVIA 5-19).

Air Ministry: Air Publication 1570A, Vol. 1, 1st Edition, October 1938. Skua I Aeroplane (Perseus XII Engine) A. W. Street. Reprinted December 1939 (FAA Museum, Yeovilton).

Air Ministry: Air Publication 1589C, Vol. 1. November 1939. Perseus XII Aero-Engine.

Air Ministry: Special Accident Report W-1023A –Flight Lieutenant R. Wilson, AIB, 6 June 1941 (National Archives, London, AVIA 5/20).

Air Ministry: Air Marshal Sir E R Ludlow-Hewitt, DCAS, during the *12th Meeting of the Advisory Committee on aircraft for Fleet Air Arm, held at the Air Ministry*, 15 November 1934 (contained in National Archives AIR 2/607/359533/34).

Air Ministry: *Minutes of the 2nd Meeting of the Dive-Bomb-Sight sub-committee of the Bombing Committee, held at the Air Ministry on Wednesday, December 2nd, 1936.* Secret. S 38156/AC. 16602 (contained in National Archives AIR 20/4155).

Air Ministry: *Minutes of the 3rd Meeting of the Dive-Bomb-Sight sub-committee of the Bombing Committee, held at the Air Ministry on Monday, December 18th, 1937.* Secret. S 38156/AC 16602 (contained in National Archives AIR 20/4155).

Air Ministry Pamphlet AP 1589C, Vol. I (M24019/18. January 1940. C&P) (copy in author's collection).

Air Ministry: *Minutes of the 1st Meeting of the Dive-Bomb-Sight sub-committee of the Bombing Committee, held at the Air Ministry on Monday, May 11th, 1936.* Secret. S 38156/AC 16602 (contained in National Archives AIR 20/4155).

Air Ministry: Johnston and Smith; *Note on wind tunnel tests on the longitudinal stability of the Blackburn O.27/34 (Skua)*, RAE Report No. BA 1453 (3395), December 1937.

Air Ministry: Francis, *Safety devices for full scale spinning trials.* RAE Report No. BA 1195 (1779) April 1935.

Air Ministry: Finn and Stephens, *Model spinning tests of the Blackburn O.27/34*, RAE Report BA 1306, June 1936.

Air Ministry: Finn and Stephens, *Model spinning tests of the Blackburn O.27/34*, RAE Report BA 1306, June 1936 DGRD/ACAS *Liaison Meetings. 3rd Meeting. Conclusion 10, 23.3.39. Skua* (contained in National Archives AVIA 46/144).

Blackburn B-24 Skua. Specification No. O.27/34/Dive Bomber Fighter (R016084, RAF Museum, Hendon, London).

Blackburn B-24 Skua. AP 1570. Vol. 3, Pt 1. Schedule of spare parts for Skua 1. 1. Ed. September 1938 (012823) 2. Ed. June 1940 (012824) RAF Museum, Hendon, London).

Blackburn B-24 Skua. AP 1746. Performance Tables of British Service Aircraft. * Amended to AL Nr. 1, December 1940 (011266, RAF Museum, Hendon, London).

Blackburn B-24 Skua. Air Transport Auxiliaries. Ferry Pilots Notes. (R017394) AL No. 1–4 20 April 1941 & No. 5 3 May 1941 (R014106).

Amended to AL Nr. 26, 1 August 1941 (RO 14194).

Amended to AL No. 32 (RO1803) (RAF Museum, Hendon, London).

Blackburn B-24 Skua. AP 1570 Vol. 2 Part 1. General Orders and Modifications for Skua-I. Leaflets A.2W – 2.23 W (inclusive). 1939–41. (RO16493. RAF Museum, Hendon, London).

Blackburn B-24 Skua. AP 1570A, Vol. 2, Part 2. Maintenance Schedule Skua I. 1st Edition 1938. (020140. RAF Museum, Hendon, London).

Blackburn B-24 Skua. AP 1570A Vol. 2 Part 3. Instructions for Repair of Skua I. November 1939. (R020141).

AL Nrs 1 & 3 October 1940. and September 1941. (R016404 RAF Museum, Hendon, London).

Blackburn B-24 Skua. AD 1173. Camouflage scheme for single-engine monoplane 1939 (C5 RAF Museum, Hendon, London).

Blackburn B-24 Skua. AP 1384. Vol. II, Part II (Skua). Unit Equipment Tables for Armament 1938 (M020520 RAF Museum, Hendon, London).

Blackburn B-24 Skua. AP 1538, Vol. I Adjustable and variable pitch airscrews. * Attached to AL No. 23, January 1941. (010966 RAF Museum, Hendon, London)

Blackburn B-24 Skua. 1/72nd Scale Drawing (AI.111.495. RAF Museum, Hendon, London).

Blackburn B-24 Skua. 1/72nd Scale Drawing (ARP.I.12 (P02164) RAF Museum, Hendon, London).

Blackburn B-24 Skua. 1/72nd Scale Drawing (AN.VII.16 RAF Museum, Hendon, London).

Churchill College Archives, Cambridge. The Somerville Papers (SMVL 7/1-15 Series – relating to Force 'H').

Fleet Air Arm Museum: Fact Sheet, *800 Naval Air Squadron – A History Nunquam Non Paratus 1933–1972* (Fleet Air Arm Museum Archives, RNAS Yeovilton, Somerset).

Griffith, RN, Diary of Midshipman, No. 803 Squadron, handwritten copy in author's collection.

W. J. Griffiths, Diary No. 803 Squadron, 1 July 1940 to 23 December 1940. FAA Museum Acq. No. 90/197. BKs: 7/59.

Hogg, Sub-Lieutenant (A) Graham Angus, DSC*, RNVR. *The Camouflaged Coward*, edited by D. I. Hogg, 1965 (Fleet Air Arm Museum, Yeovilton).

Pilot's Flying Log Book of A. B. Fraser-Harris (Fleet Air Arm Museum, Yeovilton).

Pilot's Flying Log Book of Sir Donald Gibson (Fleet Air Arm Museum, Yeovilton).

Pilot's Flying Log Book of Group Captain D. E. Gillam. 15.5.41 to 15.10.50 (M10,523. RAF Museum, Hendon, London).

Pilot's Flying Log Book of A. H. St G. Gore-Langton (Fleet Air Arm Museum, Yeovilton).

Pilot's Flying Log Book of Lieutenant Commander T. E. Gray (Fleet Air Arm Museum, Yeovilton).

Pilot's Flying Log of Squadron Leader N. R. Lecher 27.10.41 to 6.1.45 (M10,570. RAF Museum, Hendon, London).

Pilot's Flying Log Book of Lieutenant Commander (A) I. L. F. Lowe (Fleet Air Arm Museum, Yeovilton).

Pilot's Flying Log Book of Mr L. W. Miles (TAG) (Fleet Air Arm Museum, Yeovilton).

Pilot's Flying Log Book of Petty Officer (A) G. S. Russell (TAG) (Fleet Air Arm Museum, Yeovilton).

Pilot's Flying Log Book of Lieutenant Commander A. W. Sabey (Fleet Air Arm Museum, Yeovilton).

Pilot's Flying Log Book of Commander J. H. Stenning, RN 9.36 to 20.1.56 (MF 10003/1. RAF Museum, Hendon, London).

Pilot's Flying Log Book of Mr L. Stevens (TAG) (Fleet Air Arm Museum, Yeovilton).

Pilot's Flying Log Book of C. F. Unwins, 17.4.36 to 20.8.42 (B1030. RAF Museum, Hendon, London).

Pilot's Flying Log Book of Flying Officer L. M. S. Whetham 15.3.33 to 9.9.40 (MF 10050/8. RAF Museum, Hendon, London).

Pilot's Flying Log Book of Lieutenant Commander R. H. Williams, MBE (Fleet Air Arm Museum, Yeovilton).

Pilot's Flying Log Book of Sub-Lieutenant T. Winstanley, RN 2.50.39 to June 1940 (B1425)

20.7.40 to 6.6.45 (B1426) (RAF Museum, Hendon, London).

Pilot's Log Book of Squadron Leader F. W. M. Jensen 2.7.39 to 15.3.50 (MF1001/7. RAF Museum, Hendon, London).

Pilot's Log Book of Wing Commander John Alexander Kent, DFC, AFC, MV, 2.4.35 to 20.10.66 (M10,044. RAF Museum, Hendon, London).

Pilot's Flying Log Book of Flying Officer E. G. Libby 30.8.38 to 17.4.41 (41304) RAF Museum, Hendon, London).

Pilot's Flying Log Book of Lieutenant David Michael Bay, FAA, 21.3.41 to 16.9.57 (M10.159. RAF Museum, Hendon, London).

Pilot's Flying Log Book of Squadron Leader J. G. Butt-Reed 15.9.39 to 24.2.44 (B2121. RAF Museum, Hendon, London).

Pilot's Flying Log Book of Lieutenant Commander H. St. J. Fancourt 14.1.30 to 22.5.41 (MF 10006/11. RAF Museum, Hendon, London).

Pilot's Flying Log Book of Wing Commander M. B. Hamilton 6.10.36 to 10.11.47 (B1219. RAF Museum, Hendon, London).

RAE Farnborough, Secret, RAE Departmental Note No. H.240, *Note on the tests of the RAE Dive Bombsight Experimental Type A*, Inst/S.953/29, September 1937 (contained in National Archives).

RAE: Report No. B.A. 1458, March, 1938, Royal Aircraft Establishment, Farnborough, R.H. Francis, M.Sc and G.E. Pringle, PhD, *Note on flight tests of the Blackburn Skua prototype* (A.M. Reference 409111/35/R.D.A.2; RAE Reference BA/633/R/47; Item No. 12K/1/38 (contained in National Archives DSTR 23/6787; 3536 Src.945. DSTR 2116787).

RAE: Johnston and Smith; *Note on wind tunnel tests on the longitudinal stability of the Blackburn O.27/34 (Skua)*, RAE Report No. B.A. 1453 (3395), December 1937.

RAE Francis, *Safety devices for full scale spinning trials.* RAE Report No. B.A. 1195 (1779) April 1935.

RAE, Royal Aircraft Establishment, Farnborough, *Dive Bombing as practiced by the German Air Force and a Comparison with proposed British system*, London, 1940.

Ruhfus, Captain, *Über den Einsatz des Kreuzers 'Königsberg' bei der Besetzung Bergens am 9. April und den Untergang des Schiffes an 10. April 1940.* (Official Report on the damage to the cruiser *Königsberg* on 9 April and the sinking of the ship on 10 April 1940), 1.Abt. Std. 307683 (copy in author's collection).

Published books

Admiralty, *Fleet Air Arm*, Ministry of Information Pamphlet, HMSO, London, 1943.

Air Ministry, *Coastal Command – The Air Ministry account of the part played by Coastal Command in the Battle of the Seas 1939–1942*, Ministry of Information Booklet 70-411, HMSO, London, 1943.

Anon. *The Blackburn Story 1909–1959*, Blackburn Aircraft Limited, Brough, 1960.

Berenotti, Admiral G., Official Narrative, *The War at Sea*, Ministry of Marine, Rome.

Brown, Capt. Eric, *Wings of the Navy: Flying Allied Carrier Aircraft of World War Two*, Edited by William Green, Airlife Publishing Ltd, Shrewsbury, 1987.

Chesneau, Roger (Editor), *Conway's All the World's Fighting Ships, 1933–1946*, German section by Erwin Sieche.

Clarke, D. H., *Blackburn B-24 Skua. What were they like to Fly*, Ian Allan, Shepperton, 1964.

Evans, David C. Evans and Peattie, Mark R., *Kaigun: Strategy, Tactics, and Technology in the Imperial Japanese Navy 1887–1941*, Naval Institute Press, Annapolis, 1997.

Franks, Norman, *Air Battle Dunkirk 6 May – 3 June 1940*, Grub Street, London, 2000.

Gibson, Vice-Admiral Sir Donald, *Haul Taut and Belay*, Spellmount, Tunbridge Wells, 1992.

Grenfell, Captain Russell, *Main Fleet to Singapore*, Faber & Faber, London, 1951.

Jackson, A. J., *Blackburn Aircraft since 1909*, Putnam, London, (Revised Edition) 1989.

Jameson, William, *Ark Royal 1939–1941*, Hart Davis, London, 1957.

Jenkins, C. A., *HMS Furious/Aircraft Carrier 1917–1948*, Profile Publications, Windsor, 1972.

King, H. F., *Blackburn B-24 Skua, The World's Strike Aircraft*, The Bodley Head, London, 1973.

Lamb, Charles, *War in a Stringbag*, Cassell, 1977.

Macintyre, Donald, *Fighting Admiral: the Life of Admiral of the Fleet Sir James Somerville, GCB, GBE, DSO*, Evans, London, 1961.

Madden, B. J. G., *A History of the 6th Battalion, The Black Watch, 1939–45*, D. Leslie, Perth, 1947.

Marder, Arthur J., *Operation Menace*, OUP, London, 1976.

Partridge, Richard Thomas, *Operation Skua*, Picton Publishing, London, 1983.

Rawlings, John D. R., *Pictorial History of the Fleet Air Arm*, Ian Allan, Shepperton, 1973.

Richards, Denis, *Royal Air Force 1939–1945, Volume 1, Collapse in the West*, HMSO, London, 1953.

Rotherham, G. A. 'Hank', *It's Really Quite Safe*, Sunflower University Press, Manhattan, Kansas, 1985.

Roskill, Captain Stephen, RN, *Naval Policy Between the Wars, Vol 2. The period of reluctant rearmament*.

Roskill, Captain Stephen, RN, *The War at Sea. Vol: The Defensive 1939–1941*. HMSO, London, 1954.

Roskill, Captain Stephen, RN, *Churchill and the Admirals*, Collins, London, 1977.

Roskill, Captain Stephen, *Naval Policy Between the Wars, 2 Vols*, Collins, London 1968 & 1976.

Simpson, M. (Editor), *The Somerville Papers*, The Navy Records Society, London, 1975

Smith, Peter C., *Dive Bomber! An illustrated history*, Moorland Publishing, Ashbourne, 1982.

Smith, Peter C., *Impact! The dive bomber pilots speak*, William Kimber, London, 1982.

Smith, Peter C., *Fist from the Sky*, Crécy Publishing, Manchester, 2006.

Smith, Peter C., *Straight Down*! Crécy Publishing, Manchester, 2000.

Smith, Peter C., *Petlyakov Pe-2 Peshka*, Crowood Press, Ramsbury, 2003.

Smith, Peter C., *Destroyer Leader: HMS Faulknor 1935–1946*, Crécy Publishing, Manchester, 2004.

Smith, Peter C., *Action Imminent*, William Kimber, London, 1980.

Smith, Peter C., *Into the Assault*, John Murray, London, 1985.

Sturtivant, Ray, *The Squadrons of the Fleet Air Arm,* Air-Britain, 1984.

Sturtivant, Ray, I.S.O. with Burrow, Mick, *Fleet Air Arm Aircraft 1939 to 1945*, Air-Britain Publication Tunbridge Wells, Kent, 1995. pps 31–7.

Till, Geoffrey, *Air Power and the Royal Navy 1914–1945, an Historical Survey*, Jane's Publishing, London, 1979.

Ufficio Storico, Roma. *La Marina Guerra Mondiale, Vol. II, La Guerra Nel Mediterrano Le Azione Navali Dal 1 Giugno 1940 all' 31 Marzo 1941. G. Fioravanzo, Ufficio Storico Della Marina Militare, Roma*, 1960.

Wegmann, Rolph & Widfleldt Bo, *Making for Sweden. Part One – The Royal Air Force*, Air Research Publications, Walton-on-Thames, 1997.

Wilkenson, Erik, *Dive Bombing: A Theoretical Study*, Norrkopings Tidningars Aktiebolag, Sweden, 1947.

Articles

Brandon, John, 'Seafires and Superchargers, Part 2 – How you really shouldn't do it!'. In *Australian Ultralights* magazine.

Clarke, Squadron Leader D. H., DFC, AFC, 'The Shunned Skua', article in *RAF Flying Review*, December 1961.

Clarke, Squadron Leader D. H., DFC, AFC, 'The Decision Is Always the Pilot's', article in *RAF Flying Review*, October 1961.

Clarke, Squadron Leader D. H., DFC, AFC, 'Ghost Fighters – over Dunkirk', article in *RAF Flying Review*, April 1959.

Goble, A. E. T., 'Oh Calamity!!!', presented to the author by the late A. E. T. 'Doc' Goble. (First printed in *TAGS*, the Fleet Air Arm Telegraphist Air Gunners Association Magazine.)

Rolph, R. S., BEM, 'The *Königsberg* Story', draft article for *TAG Magazine* (presented to the author prior to publication).

Rolph, R. S, BEM, *The Society of Friends of the Fleet Air Arm Museum, Newsletter*, No. 49, January 1997, p 13 (copy presented to the author).

Rolph, R. S, BEM, Dickie, in *The Society of Friends of the Fleet Air Arm Museum Newsletter*, No. 40, January 1997.

Smith, Peter C., 'Sitting Duck: A Harsh Lesson Imparted', article in *Army & Defence Quarterly Journal*, Volume 119, No. 4, Tavistock, October 1989.

Films

Partridge, Captain R. T. *Operation Skua 1974*, Charterhall Films Ltd.

Operation Skua 30th Anniversary, 2004. Skred Film.

Joyce, Alexander, *Comrade*, with Horst Schopis (in preparation).

INDEX